*Hymn Tune
Names*

Hymn Tune

Names

THEIR SOURCES AND SIGNIFICANCE

Robert Guy McCutchan

Abingdon Press

NEW YORK   NASHVILLE

HYMN TUNE NAMES

Copyright © MCMLVII by Abingdon Press

Library of Congress Catalog Card Number: 57-6756

SET UP, PRINTED, AND BOUND BY THE
PARTHENON PRESS, AT NASHVILLE,
TENNESSEE, UNITED STATES OF AMERICA

To Helen

WITHOUT WHOSE SYMPATHY, UNDERSTANDING,
AND MORE OR LESS GENTLE THOUGH PERSISTENT PRODDING,
THIS PROJECT MIGHT NOT HAVE BEEN COMPLETED

Preface

If you bee curious to know who hath undergone these paines for your benefits, I profess myself a Welwiller of Musick, who in love and paines for advancement thereof will yield to few, though in qualification to many: I have spent too much tyme, travell, and expense on that facultie, if my skill come short of this present task: *sed exitus acta probet*. The motives moving mee hereunto are chiefly God's glorie, the advancement of this Art, the saving of paines to teachers thereof; the inclination of others to greater acts of this kind, the earnest desire of some well affected, the imployment of my poor talent; . . . and the Church Music made more plausible by publishing this book.

This quotation admirably expresses my thought in undertaking this work. It is part of an "Address" to the "Good and Gentle Reader" in that version of the Scottish *Psalter* printed in Edinburgh in 1635 by the Heirs of Andrew Hart.

I distinctly remember—although I was not yet four years of age at the time—hearing my elder brother say one morning at family worship, "Let's sing 'Avison.' " The word "Avison" intrigued my boyish fancy, and when my father told me the tune we had just sung was known by the name of its composer, an interest was born which remains to this day. For the greater part of my life I have been wondering how hymn tunes got their names.

There was scarcely a moment during the waking hours of the McCutchan family that there was not some tune being sounded about the home. It was a daily custom to sing hymns—at family worship as well as at odd moments. Always the tunes were designated by name; only the gospel hymns, of which we sang but a few, were known by title or by their first lines. Thus, through the years there has continued for me the desire to know more about hymn tunes, why they were given the names they bear, and to discover any interesting incidents connected with their christening.

There is almost no literature on the subject. Occasional references which have appeared in *The Musical Times* (London) and *Notes and Queries* from time to time have in nearly every instance been authoritative and of real value in the search which has been made. A chapter in

James T. Lightwood's *Hymn Tunes and Their Story,* another in Carl F. Price's *The Music and Hymnody of the Methodist Hymnal* (of 1905), two articles by Charles N. Boyd in *The Etude* some years ago, a few paragraphs contributed to *The Choir* (London) by H. J. Staples, and occasional references in different publications by various writers, including recent handbooks of denominational hymnals, have appeared. I know of nothing else of a scholarly nature which has been published.

As this is a pioneer work, no bibliography is given. There is none, as such. It would be an almost if not quite impossible task to list all the sources of information which have been gleaned through the years from scores of hymn and tune books, encyclopedias, dictionaries, gazetteers, histories, biographies, odd volumes about odd things, newspaper and other clippings from a wide variety of publications, and so on, almost without limit.

That there are many who are interested in the subject has been abundantly evidenced to me through my several decades spent in following clues. In practically all parts of the country where I have lectured on the general subject of hymnology it has been a frequent experience to have someone ask about the word which appears as a heading to each tune, why it was there and what it means.

There is a reason. I have endeavored to discover it and to state it in such manner as to make it interesting and informative to the layman as well as to the initiated. Having spent many years in the study of all aspects of hymnology, I have found the matter of tune names to be one of its most intriguing phases. The wide variety of names given the tunes, where they came from, why they were chosen, what significance they have, has offered a challenge which has entailed wide and painstaking research. It has led into many fields and to the gathering of much material. The search for further information still goes on, for it is far from complete. And as new tunes will be composed as long as new hymns are written, or as changes of musical settings for the older texts may be desired, there will never be a point at which one may be able to say there is nothing more to be discovered about them.

The whole subject of names makes a romantic, fascinating study; many scholars have devoted years of their lives to various phases of it. The number of books which have been written about it, were they all gathered together with works on closely allied subjects, would comprise a very respectable library, if the number of volumes may be considered a criterion of its respectability. We have books on the place names of various countries and states, on surnames of persons, their given names, names for babies, names of plants, of minerals, and so on *ad infinitum.*

Preface

In its issue of July 31, 1948, *The Saturday Evening Post* carried a serious article on the giving of names to race horses!

Names may be, and often are, quite significant. Plato advised men to be careful "in giving far and happy names," as the Pythagoreans affirmed "the minds, actions, and successes of men" to be "according to their Facts, Genius, and Name." We know that among Orientals the appellations given as names always have meaning.

The first imposition of names was grounded upon as many occasions as were hard to be specified, but the most common in most antient nations, as well as Hebrews, was upon future good hope conceived by parents of their children, in which you might see their first and principal wishes toward them.[1]

Lewis the Eighth, King of France, sent two of his ambassadors to Alphonso, King of Spain, to solicit one of his daughters in marriage. When the young ladies, whose names were Urraca and Blanche, were presented to the ambassadors, they made choice of Blanche, though far less beautiful than her sister, assigning a reason that her name would be better received in France, as Blanche signifies fair and beautiful. So the proverb *Bonum nomen bonum omen* ("A good name is a good omen").[2]

The French law, it may be said in passing, recognizes no name not borne by a saint or a historical personage. While this may seem arbitrary, it does have some merit, for it prevents such perversions of names as have been, and are, evident in this country and especially in England. The curiosities and infelicities through marriage might easily fill a large volume; they are of no concern here.

"To find out the true origin of surnames," said Camden, "is full of difficulties, so it is not easy to search all the causes of alterations of surnames." A surname is a family name so called because it was originally written *over* the given name instead of after it; from the French *surnom* or the Latin *super nomen*, "above the name."

As research scholars have had difficulty in tracing the origin of surnames and the changing of them, I have found comparable difficulty in a like search for the names of hymn tunes, for hymn-tune names and surnames have much in common. Which brings us to the study with which this book is concerned—the source or origin of the names given our hymn tunes originally, the reason these names were given, and the subsequent changing of many of them.

According to the survey made in 1948 by the American Music Conference, it was discovered that the church is the most important factor other than the home in stimulating an interest in music, and that 59.5

[1] W. Camden, *Remains Concerning Britain* (Brittania), 1764 reprint.
[2] William Arthur, *Etymological Dictionary of Family and Christian Names*, 1857.

9

per cent of the American people like hymns and other types of church music better than any other kind. They enjoy the hymns because of their tunes; no hymn has ever received general acceptance that did not have an attractive and fitting tune. Each tune has been given a name. Why, for instance, did John Bacchus Dykes give the name NICAEA to the tune he wrote for Reginald Heber's hymn beginning, "Holy, holy, holy! Lord God Almighty"? Why St. CHRISTOPHER, by Frederick C. Maker, for "Beneath the cross of Jesus"? Why DUKE STREET, OLD HUNDREDTH, and many others, almost without end?

As is frequently the case, what begins as mere curiosity becomes a sort of hobby and then develops into a major undertaking. No other research projects, however difficult and trying, which have interested me have been so elusive as this. The search developed into an undertaking of no mean proportions; the result will be found in the following pages.

To Agnes Holmes, whose dependable knowledge of hymn tunes aided materially in her typing of the manuscript, I wish to express real appreciation.

There are doubtless some who will wonder about this book, as did the "some" at Bethany, "Why is this waste of ointment made?" Perhaps a fitting reply would be by way of paraphrasing the last of Mark 14: "This also that he hath done shall be spoken of as a memorial to him."

ROBERT GUY MCCUTCHAN

Contents

———————◆———————

WHY THIS BOOK?

Why Names for Hymn Tunes?

———————◆———————

I

Although the Lutheran Reformation initiated a great era of congregational singing, there had been earlier leaders who also believed in the spiritual efficacy of hymn singing: Huss, Wycliffe, certain early and medieval Church Fathers, and long before that, the Hebrews.

In the days of the psalmists the melodies which were selected by the Levites as settings for the psalms and sung by them in the tabernacle services were designated by names.

Several of these names are recorded in the superscriptions to individual psalms. The meanings of some of them are still a mystery, but those which seem certain are translated in the Revised Standard Version. Here we find that Psalm 22 was sung to "The Hind of the Dawn," 45 and 69 to "Lilies," 56 to "The Dove on Far-off Terebinths," and 57, 58, 59, and 75 to "Do Not Destroy." In "Lilies" and "Do Not Destroy" we have the earliest known examples of the use of "common" tunes. These are tunes written in such metrical form as to allow them to be accommodated to any text in the same meter. Centuries later, as Christian song developed, certain tunes (plain song) were appointed to be sung to certain canticles. In many instances these associations still obtain. *Dies Irae* is an example. These plain-song melodies were "proper" tunes, those which established the custom to have only one musical setting to a fixed text. (Meters and metrical markings are discussed in Section III of this chapter.)

Robertson Smith, in *The Old Testament in the Jewish Church*, tells us some interesting things about early titles given to the tunes to which the Psalms were sung:

Four (lvii-lix, lxxv) have the title, "Al-tash-cheth," *Destroy Not*, possibly the vintage song to which there is an allusion in Is. lxv. 8, "When the new wine is found in the cluster," says the Prophet, "men say, 'Destroy it not, for a blessing is in it.'" These words in the Hebrew have a distinct rhythm. They are the first line of one of the vintage songs so often referred to in Scripture. And so we learn that the early melody of Israel had a popular origin, and was closely connected with the old joyous life of the nation.

The practice of appropriating an already existing popular secular melody for use as a hymn tune was adopted by our early Church Fathers centuries later. One of them, *Puella Turbata,* "The Troubled Maiden," or "The Distressed Damsel," may be found in its original form and under that name in the Historical Edition of *Hymns Ancient and Modern.*

In the Roman Church the Gradual, which is a respond between the Epistle and the Gospel, is followed immediately by the Alleluia, which is sung by the people. It was the custom to prolong the last syllable of the Alleluia in order to allow the officiant sufficient time to change stations. In the eighth and ninth centuries this developed into an extreme type of florid song so difficult that it could be sung only by a choir of trained voices. One name given it was *Jubilus.* In order to satisfy the people's need for participation in the service, a second *Jubilus,* usually a familiar folklike tune, frequently from Byzantine sources, was added. The *Puella Turbata* was one of them.

It was not until the ninth century that melodies, though previously known through having been passed on from musical father to musical son, were incorporated into choir books, and then it was in connection with their use as settings for Sequences. Not every Sequence had its own melody; often several were written to go with a common one. The Sequence (or Prose, because it was not written in any metrical pattern) was a hymn which was introduced into the Mass on certain days such as festival occasions. Its name derives from its being sung after the Epistle and the Gradual. Although an enormous number of Sequences were written during the Middle Ages, only five are now sanctioned by the Roman Church—namely, *Victimae Paschali, Veni Creator Spiritus, Lauda Sion, Stabat Mater,* and *Dies Irae.* Of the five all but *Lauda Sion* have found their way, to a greater or lesser extent, into modern Protestant hymnody.

Obviously it was desirable to identify the Sequence melody with a distinctive word, that chosen being called its *title.* Although some three hundred such titles have been found in the old manuscripts, it should not be inferred there were only that many used, for numbers having no title have come down to us.

As was natural, many of the titles were taken from the first word of the original Sequences and the melodies used with texts of later composition. These melodies furnished the pattern for such texts much as the manner in which well-known and favorite hymn tunes often suggest the metrical patterns used by modern hymn writers. Some of the earliest examples of melody titles are: ALMIPHONA, CREATOR POLI, DIGNA CULTU, EXSULTET ELEGANTIS, FULGENS PRAE-CLARA, and so forth.

As the earliest Sequences were written to fit the melodies sung to the final syllable of the Alleluias (*Alleluia-jubilus*), the titles of such melodies were quite appropriately taken from the Alleluia-verse. Hence we have such titles as OSTENDE, LAETATUS SUM, VENI DOMINE, DOMINUS REGNAVIT, DIES SANCTIFI-CATUS, MULTIFARIS.

The difference increased between the Alleluia-verse and the Sequence proper. As the latter developed, additional tunes were composed for the new texts, and more titles were needed. Whether for novelty or for some other reason, the practice arose of choosing important words from the body of the Sequence text for use as titles. For example:

Sequence: *"Quid tu virgo mater ploras."*
Title: VIRGO PLORANS.

14

Sequence: *"Hanc concordi famulatu."*
Title: CONCORDIA.

Apparently some titles were chosen, or formed, on the principle of analogy. Such Sequence beginnings as *"Lyra pulchra regen"* and *"Nostra tuba nunc tua"* give LYRA and NOSTRA TUBA. These are especially interesting, as they seem to indicate that instruments had been introduced into the choral service. In this category, also, are CITHARA, ORGANA, TYMPANUM, TUBA, and others.

Some titles suggest the places of origin of the tunes: GRAECA, ROMANA, OCCIDENTANA; or they may have been merely casually selected geographical names. As with modern hymn-tune names, others are inexplicable: CIGNAE, FRIGDOLA, DUO TRES, VITELLIA.

Choosing titles from the *Incipit* ("here begins") of the Alleluia-verse or the Sequence was customary in France, but at St. Gall and throughout Germany titles were never chosen from this source, the result being that many of the latter, some quite unusual, have little or no meaning or significance. This seems strange in the light of the later fact that titles of the chorales (German) are, almost without exception, taken from the first words of the first stanza of each text. There are certain exceptions to which attention will be called at the proper time and place. In nearly all cases, however, the tunes were "proper." Precedent for the naming of "common" tunes had been set long before the practice began in England.

II

Returning from Geneva to England, the Marian exiles brought with them the psalm tunes they had learned at that center of Calvinism. Reasons why the German chorale did not appeal to the English need not be gone into here; suffice it to say that efforts to transplant it in England did not succeed, just as the Ainsworth *Psalter* brought to America by the Pilgrims failed to take root among those who settled New England. Those psalm tunes which first appeared in the *Strassburg Psalter* (1539) and succeeding ones up to and including that of 1562 were those which became the basis for our later hymn tunes.

These psalm tunes were "proper" tunes set to individual psalms and known by the number of the psalm, as, for example, Ps. 100. Later, when other tunes were written for, or adapted to, Psalm 100 and others, the Genevan tunes were distinguished and characterized by the prefix "Old." Thus we have OLD 100TH, OLD 84TH, OLD 134TH, and so on.

Thomas Est (Este, East) in his *Psalter* (1592) established in England the principle, now common, of individualizing tunes by giving them names. Somewhat timid about it, he named only three: GLASSENBURIE TUNE (to Psalm 88), KENTISH TUNE (to Psalm 92), and CHESHIRE TUNE (to Psalm 146), but by naming these he suggested the feasibility of the use of place or locality names, a custom still prevalent.

Twenty-nine years later Thomas Ravenscroft extended the practice by giving names to all the tunes in his book, which had the imposing title *The Whole Book of Psalmes, with the hymnes evangelicall and songs spirituall composed into four parts by sundry composers, to such severall tunes as have beene and are usually sung in England, Scotland, Wales, Germany, Italy, France, and the Netherlands. By Thomas Ravenscroft, Bachelor of Musicke, 1621.* Commenting on this, John Hawkins in his *History of Music*, Vol. I (1776), says:

Here we have the origin of a practice respecting the names of our common church tunes, that prevails among us to this day, namely, the distinguishing them by the name or adjunct of a particular city, as Canterbury, York, Rochester, and many others. It was much about the time of the publication of this book that King Charles I was prevailed on by the clergy to attempt the establishment of the liturgy in Scotland; and perhaps it was with a view to humor the people of that kingdom that some of the new-composed tunes were called Dumferling, Dundee, and Glasgow.

He says further, in a footnote:

It is in this collection of Ravenscroft that we first meet with the tunes to which the Psalms are now most commonly sung in the parish churches of the Kingdom, for excepting those of the eighty-first, hundredth, and hundred and nineteenth psalms, the ancient melodies have given place to others of a newer and much inferior composition. The names of these new tunes, to give them in alphabetical order, are: Bath and Wells or Glastonbury, Gloucester, Hereford, Lincoln, Litchfield and Coventry, London, Norwich, Oxford, Peterborough, Rochester, Salisbury, Winchester, Windsor or Eaton, Worcester, Walverhampton; and, to give what are styled northern tunes, in the same order, they are Carlisle, Chester, Durham, Manchester, Southwell, and York. The Scottish tunes are Abbey-tune, Duke's, Dumferling, Dundee, Glasgow, King's, and Martyrs; and the Welch, St. Asaph, Bangor, St. David's, Landaff, and Ludlow: so that the antiquity of these may be traced to the year 1621.

YORK was one of the very few tunes sung by our New England forefathers and was in quite common use until recently. We still use WINDSOR, WINCHESTER (OLD), DUNDEE generally and BANGOR occasionally. These five tunes may be found in *The Hymnal 1940* (Protestant Episcopal).

Ravenscroft also classified his tunes according to the districts or countries from which they came, or from which he thought they came—i.e., English tunes (as noted above), tweny-two; Northern tunes and Scottish tunes, each six; "Welch" tunes, five; "French tones," and, representative of the earlier psalters, "English tunes, imitating the High Dutch, Italian, French, and Netherlandish tunes."

F. L. Ritter, in *Music in England* (1883), says:

That particular manner of distinguishing hymn-tunes by names, such as "St. Anne's," "Dundee," etc., used in English and Scotch "tune-books," seems to have originated with Este; Hawkins and Burney, and many other writers, have erroneously attributed the custom to Ravenscroft.

Which is both true and untrue; perhaps "half-truth" would be a better word to use. Ritter, an exceedingly dogmatic as well as egotistical German musician who found the United States a much more profitable field in which to labor than his own country, was prone to belittle anything musical in both America and England. He was especially sarcastic whenever he found occasion to mention hymn tunes, hymn-tune books, and singing-school teachers. Nor was he a dependable historian. While Este was the first to use place names for tunes, his names suggested that the three he named were well known in certain localities. Ravenscroft really set the pattern for naming all tunes used in a given book.

Forty years after Ravenscroft's book appeared, John Playford, in his *Psalms and Hymns in Solemn Musick in Foure Parts on the Common Tunes to the Psalms in Meter* (1761), used a number of tunes from Ravenscroft, but he gave different names to several of them, thus becoming the first compiler of hymn and tune books to needlessly confuse hymn-tune nomenclature.

It is in this Playford book that hymns for the first time are given a place of their own together with the psalms, on the title page as well as in the book itself. Seemingly Playford worked independently of Ravenscroft even though he used tunes which had been brought out by the latter. Because this book of 1761 was of too high quality for the time, only six years later he published his *Whole Book of Psalms,* which was recognized for the next hundred years or more as the standard of what like books should be. At frequent intervals reprints of it continued to appear until well into the last century. He did not use the Welsh or Scottish tunes of the Ravenscroft book, saying they were "outlandish," with the exception of ST. MARY, which was known to the American Puritans as HACKNEY, and which, according to Louis C. Elson, *American Music,* was one of the five tunes they sang as settings to their psalms. The use of ST. MARY marks the beginning of the custom of naming tunes after saints, or after churches named for saints. ST. DAVID'S, used by Ravenscroft, was a place name, and it is possible ST. MARY might have been also. But in Playford's book we also find a ST. PETER'S.

III

As the number of tunes put forth by their writers increased, especially after Isaac Watts (1674-1748) began paraphrasing the Psalms and writing original hymns, the composers, or compilers and/or editors of tune books were sorely put to it to find names enough to go around. Because Watts wrote his versions of the Psalms in the commonest metrical forms, there was created a demand for a great number of "common" tunes. Most of Watts's renditions were in Long Meter, Common Meter, Short Meter, and 8s 7s, together with their "doubles."

Here is as good a place as any to discuss the various meters and their markings. Meter has to do with the arrangement of language in successive movements in such rhythmic patterns as may readily appeal to the ear; it is verse as opposed to prose. As hymns are a type of religious poetry having a varying number of stanzas to be sung to but one tune, it is necessary that a common rhythmic pattern prevail. Thus:

Long Meter (L. M.) is a four-line stanza, each line having eight syllables.

Common Meter (C. M.) contains four lines, the first and third having eight syllables, the second and fourth six each.

Short Meter (S. M.) contains four lines, the first, second, and fourth with six syllables, the third with eight.

If a "D" is added (L. M. D., C. M. D., S. M. D., etc.), it simply means the verse pattern has been doubled, making each an eight-line hymn. Seldom are there more than four, six, or eight lines to a stanza.

Where the pattern differs from the above, it is customary to indicate the number of syllables in each line by Arabic numerals. Examples: 8 7 8 7 (8s 7s), the first and third lines eight, second and fourth seven; 10 10 10 10 10 10, each line with ten; 7 7 6 D, a six-line stanza, the first, second, fourth, and fifth lines with seven, the third and sixth with six each, etc. "Irr." means "irregular"—i.e., the comparable lines of the different stanzas do not always conform as to the number of syllables. Note values in the melody may be adjusted to make this possible. The marking "P. M." (Particular, or Peculiar, Meter) will be found only in the older hymnals; it is no longer used.

IV

With the coming of the hymns of Charles Wesley (1707-88), with their wide assortment of metrical designs, a new element entered the picture. It has been said that Charles Wesley wrote his hymns in a greater variety of meters than any other poet used in any and all poetic forms. Horace is his nearest competitor.

The Wesleys, both John and Charles, with their followers, while never withdrawing from the Anglican Church, were looked upon by uncompromising churchmen as heretics, or deserters from the church. Leading musicians of the time who were at all interested in writing for the church were connected with the Established Church and had little or no sympathy with, or for, the Dissenters, whatever their hue; if they wrote hymn tunes at all, they continued writing them in the long-established metrical patterns. One of them, William Shrubsole (1760-1806), composer of the long-familiar and deservedly popular MILE's LANE, was sympathetically disposed toward the Dissenters and their views although he was the organist at Bangor Cathedral. Because of Shrubsole's "having given great offence to the Dean and Chapter" (at Bangor) by associating with "one Abbot" and "by his frequenting conventicles," the Dean was "impowered to discharge the said William Shrubsole from his place as organist" if he associated further with "said Abbot" or was "found to frequent any conventicle or religious assembly, where anything is taught which is contrary to the Doctrines or Discipline of the Church of England." Two months after this action was taken (in November, 1793), Shrubsole was given notice of his dismissal, whereupon he returned to London and began his duties at Spa Fields Chapel, one of Lady Huntingdon's communion, where he remained until his death. Church musicians who cared to retain their positions in the Church of England did not attend conventicles, associate with Dissenters, or write tunes for their hymns.

This situation gave opportunities and encouragement for amateur musicians to exercise what talent they had, and as a result some astonishingly good tunes were produced. The amateurs seemingly took pride in naming their products, and we note names of obscure places creeping in, as well as names of persons, names suggested by the sentiment of the hymns, street names, church names, and so on. From this time on, we find considerable variety. In addition to those mentioned there are the given names of persons, names of saints, geographical names, single words from a text or from the Bible (especially the Old Testament), Latin and Greek titles, and a goodly number of names especially manufactured for the purpose—"made names." It was said that frequently it was easier to write a new tune than it was to find a suitable name for it when it was written.

Why Such a Variety of Names?

I

As suggested in the preceding chapter, in the many years before Isaac Watts and Charles Wesley began writing hymns, composers found little difficulty in selecting names for their tunes. There was a natural desire on their part to give distinction and individuality to their product, so the quest for significant variety in nomenclature became a matter of real concern when the new tunes greatly increased in number during and following the Wesleyan Revival. Other than those already mentioned, titles which were suggested by, or referred to, all sorts and manners of things began to be used; even the names of pagan philosophers were chosen.

Denominational leanings have produced some interesting examples of tune names. In a United Presbyterian Psalter of the late nineteenth century the names of various mission stations supported by that denomination were used. The Lutherans have shown a preference for choosing names of places with which Johann Sebastian Bach had some association. Methodists have chosen many place names associated with John and Charles Wesley and their travels: Gwennap, a pit in Cornwall which had an attraction for John and where he held some successful meetings; Moorfields, great London preaching center; Aldersgate Street, where John Wesley's heart was "strangely warmed"; Fetter Lane, where there was a Moravian chapel filled with memories of the Wesleys, Whitefield, and Zinzendorf—all have been used as names for tunes.

Among other names, some noted by Carl F. Price, were those suggested by acts of worship, such as PRAISE, BAPTISM; by Christian virtues, FORTITUDE; heaven, PARADISE, HOMELAND; time of day, MORNING HYMN, NIGHTFALL; authors of hymns, KEBLE, ALFORD; composers, EWING, HAYDN; original works, CREATION, SAMSON; names of certain persons, FREDERICK, RUTHERFORD, OXNAM; saints, ST. AGNES, ST. ANSELM; churches, ST. ANNE, REGENT SQUARE; native towns of composers, ROTTERDAM, RACINE; countries, AUSTRIAN HYMN, FINLANDIA; mountains and hills, MT. CALVARY, ARTHUR'S SEAT; dwellings, HOLLINGSIDE; colleges, HOLYOKE, BELOIT, DePAUW; made names, MERRIAL, SHIRLYN.

A great many are biblical place names, and we find a goodly number of names of places prominent in religious history, among the latter such as NICAEA, WORMS, HERRNHUT. From personal names may be selected those of friends, relatives, biblical characters. This device is frequently used by editors for tunes submitted without titles.

Apparently hymn-tune writers of an earlier day were more literal Bible students and theologians than those of the present day, for we do not find such names as WRESTLING JACOB, DYING STEPHEN, or JUSTIFICATION, ATONEMENT,

19

used now. The custom of using biblical names has been more prevalent in England than in the United States.

The geographically minded choose place names. Names popular at the moment are often used: one tune is said to have been named for the wife of Jefferson Davis and another for Theodore Roosevelt. There was a tune named ELBA which appeared in a book published soon after Napoleon's exile to that island, and NARAVINO came soon after the battle, in 1854, that inspired the writing of "The Charge of the Light Brigade." Environment, too, has been a convenient source of names: Edward J. Hopkins, it is said, liked to vacation in Devonshire, England; hence some of his tunes carry names found in that part of the country. John B. Dykes's career, we have been told by James T. Lightwood, may be traced by way of tunes named after places and incidents in his life.

Folk tunes, or those of this type, when adapted as hymn tunes—a custom which has become quite prevalent in the twentieth century—when first used are frequently identified by names taken from the original text, only to lose them when taken over and put to new or different texts—i.e., when used in new books. ST. HUGH, in the *English Hymnal,* became DOVEDALE when it was later included in the British *Methodist Hymn-Book.* Many of the English traditional melodies which have recently found their way into our modern hymnals have been given the name of the place, or vicinity, where they were noted by the folk-song enthusiasts who discovered them. The early American custom was to be frank and use the exact title: FEMALE CONVICT and CAPTAIN KIDD were quite popular along the American frontier a century or more ago.

Names and tunes, especially new ones, which appear in a compilation and are pertinent to it may not outlive the book in which they appear. In his essay on the names of the new tunes which came out in the 1905 *Methodist Hymnal,* Carl F. Price made mention of forty; only four were continued in the next succeeding edition, in 1935.

II

Our dictionaries are constantly being enlarged by the introduction of "made names." The following are examples of the interesting way some of them came into being: Constable of Police became "Cop"; original World War II army specifications calling for a *general purpose* vehicle, which was shortened to "GP" to speed paper work, resulted in the new word "jeep." When a manufacturing company in Illinois wanted a name for a new steam engine, they made one from the name of the founders of the company, A. L. Ide and Sons; so we have the "Ideal" engines. "Radar" comes from "RA" (radio), "D" (distance), and "A" "R" (range).

In the 1880's the eight original settlers of a community on the northern peninsula of Michigan wanted a post office in order that the delivery of their mail might be facilitated. They chose the initial letters of the surnames of those interested, Grant, Edge, Robinson, Mead, French, Ackley, Sheppard (or Shepherd), and Knaggs (or Keinag) and got "Germfask," which is located in Schoolcraft County of that state.

In somewhat similar fashion LeMars, Iowa, secured its name. John Insley Blair, organizer of the railroad which became the Chicago and Northwestern, once took an excursion party which included a number of women to the western-most end of construction of the Sioux City Railroad, now a part of the Illinois Central system. Having decided to locate a new town at that point, he offered to let the ladies choose the name it should bear. Not being satisfied with those suggested, one lady proposed that a name be coined from the initials of each one's Christian name. Both "Selmar" and "LeMars" were possibilities; "LeMars" received the most votes, and Blair abided by their choice.

Dr. Neil Ross, noted Celtic scholar, in discussing "made names" used by James Macpherson, in his *Poems of Ossian*, said: "Macpherson, like Dickens, had a faculty for coining new names. . . . His fine-sounding names were popular. It is not surprising that even psalm-tunes composed in that period [*ca.* 1775] should be called by such lovely, mystical, but mythical names. They are poetic merely." MORVEN and SELMA are two used as tune names.

Thus the coining of names for hymn tunes is not at all new. MERRIAL, to which most of the Christian world sings Baring-Gould's "Now the day is over," comes from a young lady's name, Mary L. Robinson. The interesting story of the evolution of this name is told at length in the Alphabetical List of Tunes.

An unusual example of a "made" tune name is that of ELLAH, a tune which won a prize from the Hymn Society of New York (now the Hymn Society of America) for a setting for a prize hymn for airmen. Lily Rendle, English composer, wrote the tune, combined the initial letters of her name, "L" and "R," for its name, and arrived at ELLAH.

Other names for hymn tunes, while not "made" ones, have been selected for equally interesting reasons. It is not unusual for a hymn tune to be named for a town or city, but when we learn that just the reverse has been the case, we give it more than passing notice. The well-known cities of Bangor, Maine, and Bethlehem, Pennsylvania, are examples. Another is that of a town in Indiana. About the late 1830's a group of settlers in Stuben County, at a loss to find a mutually satisfactory name for their proposed post office, agreed to give their new town that name which would appear on the upper half of the left-hand page when the singing-school book they were then using was opened at random. There is some question as to the title of the long, end-fold book used, but there is none concerning the name of the tune found; it was ORLAND, by an unknown composer. Reference to any good road map of Indiana will reveal that there is a small town in Stuben County called Orland.

III

Saints' names were for a long time popular ones for tunes, but they now seem to be passing out of favor; at least not so many names of saints as such are found in our latest hymnals as in the older ones, but those of churches named for saints still find favor. A study made in 1955 shows that there is now an average of about thirty-seven saints' names per book, whereas there were nearly eighty per book a generation ago.

It is worth noting that those denominations which prefer formality in worship services have, in their hymnals, more tunes named for saints than their less formal brethren; their ratio to diminishing interest in formality is noticeable. Taking the latest editions of hymnals (from 1930 to 1940) used by six of our leading Protestant groups, we find *The Hymnal 1940* (Protestant Episcopal) has sixty-three; *The Hymnal* (Presbyterian), forty-five; *The Pilgrim Hymnal* (Congregational), forty-one; *The Methodist Hymnal,* thirty-five; and *Christian Worship* (Disciples and American Convention Baptist), twenty-nine. This, of course, does not tell the whole story, for there are a good many instances of the use of "common" tunes to more than one hymn.

Charles Wheatly, in *On the Common Prayer,* has this comment on the naming of churches after saints:

Though all churches were dedicated to none but God, as appears by the grammatical construction of the word *church,* which signifies nothing else but the Lord's house; yet at their consecration they were generally distinguished by the name of some angel or saint; chiefly that the people, by frequently mentioning them, might be excited to imitate the virtues for which they had been eminent: and also that those holy saints themselves might by that means be kept in remembrance.

H. J. Staples' statement that we may assume saints' names used for hymn tunes are after churches is not altogether true. There are those named after various chapels, after the saints themselves, and for persons who have been especially "canonized" for hymn-tune-name purposes, such as ST. GERTRUDE, ST. BARBARA, and others. One cannot assume that saints' names derive from any one source.

IV

With the increasing use of fine Welsh tunes in our hymnals, a word about their names should be in order. The Welsh people love their hymn tunes, are justifiably proud of them, and their composers seemingly give more than passing thought to their christening. The names intrigue us; Americans have little or no idea as to how they should be pronounced. While it seems impossible to indicate, on paper, some of their letter sounds, perhaps the following, taken from Welsh dictionaries, may give some clues to their proper pronunciation:

A as in *palm, pat*
C as in *cat*
Ch as in Scottish *loch*
Dd as *th* in *this*
E as in *there, then*
F as *v*
Ff as *f*
G as in *gig*
I as in *marine, pin*
Ll has no English equivalent; approximately a soft *thl*
Ng as in *sing*
O as in *more, not*
Ph as in *physic*
Rh has no English equivalent; approximately *r* with breathing
Th as in *thick*
U (in South Wales) almost as Welsh *I*—i.e,, *meet, pin;*
 (in North Wales) almost as French *u* or German *ü*
W as English *oo* in *cool, cook*
Y has two sounds: 1) as *u* in *curve, cut;* 2) as Welsh *u* in
 final syllables (with many exceptions)
Au final very nearly sounds *ay*
Aw sounds *ow*

Other letters are pronounced as in English. Welsh words are generally accented on the penultima, with exceptions, of course.

The Welsh have always been a devout people, and the church has had a large say in Welsh nomenclature. There are about 150 churches (Llanfair, etc.) called after the Virgin Mary alone. By far the commonest prefix is *llan*, a church. Crookford's *Classical Dictionary* lists 465, but his list does not include Lamphrey, formerly Llandyfli, and some others. In addition there are many *capels*, or chapels, such as Capel Garmon, and *bettws*, prayer houses, as in *Bettws y Coed*, "prayer house, or church, in the woods."

There should be made mention also of the villages named by the Baptists, Methodists, and other Protestant groups, such as Bethesda, Hebron, Pisgah, and the like.

V

While C. Est began, timidly, to give names to hymn tunes in England, and T. Ravenscroft a few years later went the whole way in giving place names to all his tunes, John Playford began scrambling them; and this process has been continued ever since. The former Dean Peter C. Lutkin, of the School of Music of Northwestern University, an able maker of hymnals yet himself an offender in this respect, has complained that this multiplication of names causes the hymn-tune researcher much concern. He says hymnbook compilers, as a rule, will invent names of their own rather than go to any trouble in the matter if the authentic name of a tune is not readily at hand.

When anti-British feeling was running high in the Colonies and proposals were being made that American names be substituted for those stemming from British sources, Thomas Jefferson remarked that "a name when given should be deemed a sacred property." As will be seen later in this chapter, the results of changing names are sometimes ridiculous, or worse.

The interchange of tunes has also produced some effects which, to say the least, are puzzling to the layman. It can be a violation of good taste, as was the case of the dual use of NICAEA in a certain hymnal in 1931. NICAEA was written by John B. Dykes especially for Reginald Heber's great hymn to the Trinity, "Holy, holy, holy!" and given its name because the doctrine of the Trinity was definitely fixed at the Council of Nicaea in the year 325. It not only was not good taste, it was a blunder, to give this tune, which had become so firmly wedded to Heber's hymn, to one by William C. Gannett beginning, "Bring, O morn, thy music," which is one of those included in the section entitled "God the Father"—anything but a Trinitarian hymn. Other examples, but less flagrant, will be referred to in the Alphabetical List of Tunes.

Another instance making for "confusion worse confounded" is that of different composers' giving the same name to more than one of their tunes. A casual examination of a number of books has shown that the name REST has been assigned to tunes by twenty-one, two of them using it twice each. In *The Methodist Hymnal* (1905), of which Dean Lutkin and Karl P. Harrington were the musical editors, John Stainer's tune PASTOR BONUS was given the new name ST. HILL. Doubtless the reason was that Alfred J. Caldicott's tune, also called PASTOR BONUS, was used in the same book with the hymn numbered 300 while that with the setting of Stainer was 683. Having used the Caldicott tune first, the editors renamed that of Stainer, a better and more favorably known one, by giving it the second given name of the author of the hymn, W. St. Hill Bourne. The title PASTOR BONUS would have fitted both hymns equally well. It would have been a much simpler device, as well as one more satisfying, had the titles PASTOR BONUS (CALDICOTT) and PASTOR BONUS (STAINER) been used. The use of names of composers in conjunction with the tune name proper as a means of identifying them is common and justifiable; which would be the reasonable thing to do, not only in this case but in similar ones such as that of REST.

The movement in the direction of bringing about some sort of union of our Christian churches should result, as it gains headway, in the issuing of an ecumenical hymnal. In such a book a precedent fixing names for tunes should be set which could be followed by future compilers and editors of books of sacred songs. Why should YORKSHIRE have at least thirteen different names? TALLIS' CANON twelve? TRINITY ten? In all probability each of these tunes has other names. A very large number of inexcusable duplications may be noted in the long list given in this book. But I should not be too critical of what others have done in this respect lest the reaction, which is sure to come, give my complacency too much of a jolt; I have been a co-culprit in the changing of some names. My only excuse is that I thought I might be helping to better some things—if I thought about it at all.

VI

This part of this book should contain a few instances of the use of curious names given tunes by certain compilers and editors of a century or more ago. Usually suggested by the sense of the text, they are not, it is needless to say, now included in any of our more sedate hymnals. The *Missouri Harmony* (1837), a popular book of the period, is a source of many of them, such as LEPROUS JEW (from the first line of the hymn beginning "Behold, the leprous Jew"), EVENING SHADE, and MASONIC ODE (a sort of defense against the anti-Masonic agitation of the time). Other curious tune names are found in *Southern Harmony, Mercer's Cluster, Plymouth Hymnal* (Henry Ward Beecher's book), and many other books of various dates and places of publication. Among these names are:

AN ADDRESS FOR ALL, C. M., set to William Walker's:

> I sing a song which doth belong
> To all the human race,
> Concerning death, which steals the breath,
> And blasts the comely face.

CAPTAIN KIDD, 6 6 6 3 6 6 6 6 6 3, from *Mercer's Cluster*. This tune was sung to a 25-stanza ballad, a sort of dying speech and testament, popular about 1701, the year Captain Kidd and his nine associates were hanged in Execution Dock, and later. As was usual with ballads of similar type, it contained advice against wrongdoing. This queer form of stanza was imitated in several other folk-spiritual songs and continued to be imitated for a long time after the original had lost its popularity.

FEMALE CONVICT, 12 11 12 11 D (somewhat irregular), was very popular in the early 19th century. The full title is self-explanatory: "A Female Convict, After receiving pardon in the sight of God, thus addressed her Infant. Set to music by R. Boyd."

24

Why This Book?

OCEAN GRAVE, C. M., by Charles Beecher, brother of Henry Ward Beecher. It appeared in the *Plymouth Hymnal* (1855) to:

> Not in the church-yard shall he sleep
> Amid the silent gloom,
> His home was on the mighty deep,
> And there shall be his tomb.

SURPRISE, C. M., anonymous, to:

> Our life contains a thousand strings
> And dies if one be gone;
> Strange that a harp of thousand strings
> Should keep in tune so long.

WAR DEPARTMENT, 11 11 11 11, text from *Mercer's Cluster:*

> No more shall the war-whoop be heard,
> The tomahawk buried, shall rest in the ground,
> The ambush and slaughter no longer be fear'd
> And peace and good-will to the nations abound.

RALEIGH, a now unfamiliar tune, was given this name because the business of its composer, David Grant, of Aberdeen, Scotland, was that of a tobacco merchant. (It was Sir Walter Raleigh who introduced the tobacco weed into the British Isles.)

AHIRA is a curious example of random, careless choosing of names. This name was given to a tune, first called LEIGHTON (which see), that was used with Horatius Bonar's hymn, the second and third stanzas of which are:

> O Everlasting Light,
> Shine graciously within;
> Brightest of all on earth that's bright,
> Come, shine away my sin.

> O Everlasting Truth,
> Truest of all that's true;
> Sure Guide of erring age and youth,
> Lead me, and teach me too.

At the time this change in name was made, in the latter part of the last century, Ahira was said to mean "Brother of evil." [3] However, in the light of modern scholarship it is concluded to be a half-Egyptian name meaning "Ra (or Re—i.e., the Egyptian sun god) is a brother or protector." [4]

Why include such names as these? Few tunes are dull or weak enough not to have some defenders; custom dulls the edge of the critical faculty, and judgment tends to be very lenient with the faults of tunes endeared by early association.

---

[3] Robert Young, *Analytical Concordance to the Bible,* 1889.
[4] See *The Interpreter's Bible* (New York and Nashville: Abingdon Press) , II, 144.

Why Did Composers Give Their Tunes the Names They Bear?

"Hymn tunes are often christened in an arbitrary manner. Their designation gives no clue to their origins."—*Musical Times* (London: October, 1904).

Why did composers give their tunes the names they bear? In a very few instances those who did so have told us why, some have followed a general plan, others have taken it for granted the name was chosen for an obvious reason, while still others have left the task for someone else to perform.

In *Hymns of the Church* (1912) the editors were thoughtful and considerate in indicating by an asterisk in the Index of Tunes those tunes for which they had provided a name, but they did not tell why the names were given. In similar indexes the asterisk usually means that the tunes so marked have been composed or arranged by the editor or compiler; sometimes it indicates the tune is copyright and used by permission of the owner.

Some of the composers who gave reasons for naming their tunes or who followed a definite pattern are:

Orlando Gibbons (1585-1625) simply numbered the tunes he wrote for George Wither's *The Hymnes and Songs of the Church* (1623) thus: THE FIRST SONG, SONG 2, SONG 3, and so on.

Richard Redhead (1820-1901) also numbered his tunes: REDHEAD No. 1, REDHEAD No 2, continuing in numerical order. In recent books, however, some of the better-known ones have been given names; PETRA, or GETHSEMANE, sung to James Montgomery's touching "Go to dark Gethsemane," is REDHEAD No. 76.

Olinthus Barnicott (1844-1908) likewise used the same simple scheme except that he called his tunes WARRENNE No. 1, WARRENNE No. 2; the use of "Warrenne" is a mystery.

Joseph Barnby (1838-96), a prolific writer of hymn tunes, seemed to have little or no imagination when he came to christening them; he gave names in but few instances. In 1871 Barnby issued *Hymns and Tunes,* numbering 81, and twelve years later *Hymns and Tunes, Volume II,* with 91, neither giving any titles. The year after his death, 1897, the material found in these two books, with a number of his other tunes, was included in a third volume called *Hymn Tunes* and published by Novello and Company, London. Here we find names given to 105 of the 246 tunes in the book; some of these names were chosen, probably, by some member or employee of the publishing firm. In 1872 *The Hymnary* was compiled and edited by Barnby. It was an excellent book, but none of the tunes was named, no Index of Tunes included, and no reason given for the omissions. In the light of all this it is strange that later editors did not take

26

more liberties with the naming of the Barnby tunes; those first given them have been quite generally retained.

Thomas Commuck, a Narraganset Indian, issued *Indian Melodies* in 1845; the tunes were harmonized by Thomas Hastings. Commuck left no doubt as to why his tunes received the names they bear. At the close of the Preface to his book he wrote:

> As the tunes in this book are the work of an Indian it has been thought proper by the author to have it all of a piece. The tunes therefore will be found to assume the names of noted Indian chiefs, Indian females, Indian names of places, etc. This has been done merely as a tribute to the memory of some tribes that are now nearly if not quite extinct; also as a mark of courtesy to some tribes with whom the author is acquainted. Manchester, Wisconsin Ter., March 7, 1845.

Some of the names: PEQUOT, MUNPONSET, KISKARRAH, POCAHONTAS, OSCEOLA, TECUMSEH, POQUYANTUP, SEMINOLE, CAYUGA, KUSICK, MASSASOIT.

Frances Ridley Havergal (1836-79) issued *Havergal's Psalmody* in 1871. It contained something over two hundred musical settings by her father, W. H. Havergal (1798-1870), with some few by herself. Possibly instigated by the indifference to hymn-tune nomenclature of Barnby, a contemporary, Miss Havergal is explicit in telling how the naming of the tunes in this book was planned:

> The tunes are systematically named from the *Natural Geography* of the Bible. Mountains, hills, vallies, rivers, plains, and other geographical objects, often replete with poetry, are thus used for musical nomenclature. As a *system,* this method of deriving names for psalm tunes does not seem to have been previously adopted. Happily,—just enough of a sufficiently euphonious character have been found for the present volume.

And in "Supplementary Remarks" appended to the Preface from which the above quotation was taken, Miss Havergal says further:

> The nomenclature of *Havergal's Psalmody* is systematic. The *name* of each tune at once supplies information as to its origin. Old English, Scotch or German tunes, bear respectively English, Scotch or German names; those by the Rev. W. H. Havergal are named (with few exceptions) from the natural geography of the Bible; the added tunes are named from "the friends of St. Paul." No departure has been made without some necessitating reason.

"The friends of St. Paul" were AQUILA, ARISTARCHUS, CARPUS, and DAMARIS. Among the "natural geography" names were EPHESUS, SMYRNA, PERGAMOS, SARDIS, LAODICEA, ZAANIAM, ZOHELETH. ZAANIAM, meaning "a double migratory tent," and the name of a place near Kedesh, is set to a hymn beginning:

> Glory, glory everlasting
> Be to Him who bore the cross

and is quite evidently an arbitrary selection. ZOHELETH, meaning "a serpent," and the name given to a stone near En-rogel, southeast of Jerusalem, is set to:

> The Lord of might, from Sinai's brow,
> Gave forth His voice of thunder;

And Israel lay on earth below,
Out-stretched in fear and wonder.
Beneath His feet was pitchy night,
And at His left hand and His right,
The rocks were rent asunder.

The relation between tune name and hymn text, if any, is difficult to determine.

"The nomenclature of *Havergal's Psalmody* may have been "systematic" and "of a sufficiently euphonius character," but that did not prevent the making of some unhappy choices. FIELD OF ZOAN (ZOAN in *The Hymnal 1940*), an excellent tune, was used by Havergal with Reginald Heber's "From Greenland's icy mountains." Now Zoan, on the east bank of the Tanitic arm of the Nile, was the seat of a dynasty and capital of Egypt in the days of Psammetichos, but it had little in common with "Greenland's icy mountains." ZOAN was nothing other than another chance selection.

The difference between such random selections from the Old Testament made by Havergal, and earlier by Lowell Mason, and the meticulous care exercised by John Stainer in his selections is striking and will be evidenced later.

F. L. Ritter, sometime teacher of music at Vassar College, "selected and arranged" the music for *Laudamus, A Hymnal for Women's Colleges and Schools* (1887). In the Preface to this book he says:

The well-known favorites, re-arranged by me in the accompanying collection, will be at once recognized by their familiar names. I have also retained the names of a few tunes well known in England; but in the naming of those melodies which have never before appeared in an English collection, I have respected the especial intention of this hymnal, and given the tunes in question (which comprise more than half of the entire list) feminine names, and names having more or less reference to women's interests, education, or association. In this baptism I gratefully acknowledge the able assistance of two ladies, deeply interested in the hymnal.

He did not give the names of the two ladies.

Thomas Campbell, in a small book called *The Bouquet*, published in 1825, used botanical names for twenty-three of the tunes, one being SAGINA, a genus of the pink family. *Pearlwort* is a general name for the species. SAGINA is a Latin word which means "to stuff, or to cram; to fatten." The plant grew luxuriantly on the thin, rocky soil of the Roman Campagna and furnished abundant spring food for the large numbers of sheep which pastured there.

John S. B. Hodges (1830-1915), onetime rector of St. Paul's Parish, Baltimore, in his privately printed *Hymn Tunes* containing only tunes composed by him, named but one out of a total of seventy-six.

Arthur H. Mann (1850-1929) wrote many hymn tunes and gave them a wide variety of names. Among them we find EUCLID, after the famous mathematician, and LASUS, Greek poet and musician; both were pagan philosophers.

John B. Dykes (1823-76), an able as well as a voluminous composer, perhaps as well and favorably known as any writer of hymn tunes, displayed a warm-hearted simplicity in choosing their names. Although many of them have Latin titles, they are always significant; for instance LUX BENIGNA to "Lead, kindly Light." He wrote four Processional tunes, giving each a Latin title suggested by its hymn text:

28

EXSURGE, to "Awake! Awake! put on thy strength," anonymous.

AMOR FIDELIS, to "Faithful in Thy love" by S. Childs Clarke.

ECCE SIGNUM, to "Forward! be our watchword" by Henry Alford.

IN NOMINE DOMINI, to "Onward in God's Name we wend" by R. F. Littledale.

Of 259 tunes in Dr. Dykes's *Hymn Tunes*, 82 have Latin titles. His long association with Durham Cathedral is reflected in his tune names: he named three of them ST. OSWALD, and there are also ST. HELEN and ST. CUTHBERT. The name of the cottage home, Hollingside, to which he brought his bride is used, and there are many associative place names, numerous names of saints, those suggested by the sentiment of the words of the hymn texts, and at least one playful one, SEKYD, his surname spelled backwards.

Arthur S. Sullivan (1842-1900) followed no plan in making his choices but, on occasion, could be whimsical. He "canonized" the given name of his hostess over a week end in the country for one tune he wrote while there and used the name of her estate for another. These are ST. GERTRUDE and HANFORD, respectively.

John Stainer (1840-1901), scholarly musician and able though somewhat pedantic composer, was, perhaps, as painstaking in his choice of names for his hymn tunes as any writer we have had or are likely to have for he took his hymn-tune writing very seriously. Almost without exception his titles are meaningful because they were suggested by the sense of the text. In most cases this meaning has been lost when his tunes have been divorced from their original words. During his lifetime he refused to give permission to use his tunes to texts other than those for which they had been originally composed. He wrote: "A hymn-tune is, or ought to be, essentially a vehicle of the spirit of the words; it is unfair, therefore, to judge of its worth when divorced from them." The tune names CROSS OF JESUS, ALL FOR JESUS, and ADORATION, settings for the texts beginning, respectively, "Cross of Jesus, Cross of sorrow," "All for Jesus, All for Jesus," and "I adore Thee, I adore Thee," taken from his Good Friday cantata, *The Crucifixion*, are meaningless when associated with other hymn stanzas. The mood of the tune CROSS OF JESUS does not suit that of the texts beginning, "God is love; His mercy brightens" or "There's a wideness in God's mercy," to which it has been used. And it helps little, if any, to change the name of the tune; it doesn't fit those hymns.

Knowing Stainer's meticulosity, James T. Lightwood, in *Hymn Tunes and Their Stories*, wonders why he called one of his tunes JAAZANIAH and what connection there might be when this tune is used with Horatius Bonar's "When the weary, seeking rest." This is the hymn better known a generation ago than now, to our loss, which has the refrain:

> Hear then, in love, O Lord, the cry,
> In heaven, Thy dwelling place on high.

Now, *Jaazaniah*, a Hebrew word, means "Jah is hearing," according to Young's *Concordance;* or, as a later authority has it, "whom God always hears." This is not a bad choice at all, even though Lightwood says:

It is to be hoped that Stainer was not always responsible for naming his compositions, for whoever selected "Jaazaniah" certainly hit on a most unmelodious name for a most melodious tune; and, further, its difficult for a layman to discover any connection between this somewhat obscure Old Testament hero and Bonar's hymn.

Had Lightwood thought to consult a good concordance, he probably wouldn't have written that. What could be a better name for a musical setting for a hymn bearing the refrain, "Hear then, in love, O Lord," than a word meaning "God always hears"?

Sometimes Stainer's selection of a name is quite simple and homely, as was his choice of WHERE BRETHREN MEET for his tune to Henry F. Lyte's:

> Sweet is the solemn voice that calls
>   The Christian to the house of prayer;
> I love to stand within its walls
>   For Thou, O Lord, are present there.

Unlike others who published books of their tunes, music only, Stainer used the texts also in order to "show the general character of the thoughts which suggested their musical setting."

This is from the Preface to his *Hymn Tunes* (1900):

Bearing in mind the small portion of tunes which survive any particular period, I cannot hope that many [of his own] are destined to enjoy a long existence; but I can honestly say, that if any single one of my tunes should for a few centuries float along the ever-gathering stream of sacred song, even unlabelled with my name, I shall not have lived in vain.

Peter C. Lutkin (1840-1931) showed a fondness for family names and places. Ralph Vaughan Williams (1872-   ), eminent English composer and diligent collector of little-known traditional melodies, has shown preference for Latin names for his original compostions but gives to his arrangements of the English traditional melodies the names of the localities in which he discovered them.

Lowell Mason (1792-1872) gave no reasons for his choice of names but, in some of his books, did follow a pattern, such as it was. He is discussed last in this group because, undoubtedly, he had to find names for more hymn tunes than any other compiler confronted with a similar task. His grandson, Henry L. Mason, in *Hymn-Tunes of Lowell Mason* (1944), gives the names of 1126 "Original Hymn-Tunes" and 497 "Hymn-Tune Arrangements," a total of 1623 for which his grandfather was responsible.

Where did Lowell Mason get tune names for all these? Of this large number but sixty-two are "hymn-tunes bearing associative names," which suggests he gave but little consideration to their selection. The grandson says his grandfather did not give the names of saints to his original tunes; those which have saints' names are adaptations of tunes written by others than himself. Only rarely does he use a personal one; occasionally the name is suggested by the words; many come from towns, villages, and cities of his native New England and from Old England, which he visited.

By far the greater number has been taken, apparently at random, from the Old Testament. He chose thirty-five names from the fifteenth chapter of Joshua, alone. This is the chapter which deals with the "borders of the lot of Judah" with "Caleb's portion" (the boundaries of the land of the tribes of

Judah drawn by lot) and which gives the names of the cities of Judah. The names are a curious lot, and no good case could be made for any of them as being a purposeful choice. Here, with corrections in spelling are the names:

AIN	KARHAA (Karkaa)
ANAH (Anak)	KEDESH
APEKAH	KEILAH
ARBA	KENAZ
ASHNAH	KINAH
AZEKAH	KIRJAH JEARIM (Kirjath-jearim)
AZEM	LACHISH
AZMON	LEBAOTH
BEER-SHEBA	LIBNAH
BETHZUR	MAKKEDAH
CABBON	MISPAH (Mizpah)
EGLON	NAAMAH
EKROM (Ekron)	NIBSHAN
GILGAL	SEIR
HEBRON	TAPPNAH (Tappuah)
HORMAH	TIMNAH
JARMUTH	ZIPH
KADESH	

These names do not run consecutively in the book, perhaps for the reason they are set to tunes in different keys.

Parenthetically, it may be of interest to readers to learn it was the custom, in making up the old singing-school books in which we find most of Mason's tunes, to arrange in groups the tunes of equal difficulty and common key. There would be so many easy-to-sing tunes in the key of C, followed by others of the same type in the keys of G, D, A, and E, consecutively, they in turn being followed by the "flat keys" of F, B♭, E♭, A♭, and occasionally D♭. The same pattern of grouping would then follow with tunes of greater difficulty. There would sometimes be three sections before the tunes were used indiscriminately. This, of course, was a phase of the then general style of teaching.

Jocose references have been made to Havergal's having used such Hebrew words as *Zaaniam* and *Zoheleth* as names for tunes. Those selections of Havergal compare favorably with many of those of Mason, for in the latter's *Modern Psalmist* (Boston, 1839) he has given us, in his "Table of Tunes," as rare and uncommon a list of names as can be found anywhere. Out of a total of fifty-six tune names beginning with the letter "a," forty are Old Testament names. And we find that all the names beginning with the letters "k" (seventeen) and "z" (nineteen) are ancient Hebrew ones, some however being corruptions.

In using these many names from the Old Testament, Maosn followed tactics similar to those of DeWitt Clinton, as told in Halleck and Drake's *Coker Papers* (1819), when he was called upon to find names for new post offices to be opened in western New York state. He chose them at random from Lemprière's *Bibliotheca Classica* ... (1839) ; we find such names as Sempronius and Lysander. In similar manner Surveyor-General Simeon DeWitt, in the late eighteenth century, "shook his pepper-pot" of names over other sections of New York, giving many of its little villages such names as Carthage, Ilion, Marcellus, Ovid, Pompey, Syracuse, Utica, and those of other cities and men of classical antiquity. It is more than conceivable that Mason, too, was familiar with Lemprière's dictionary.

It is only occasionally one finds a name that has even the appearance of appropriateness. ADDISON, to 'The spacious firmament on high," is all right, for Joseph Addison wrote the hymn; and so is SEASONS for the same author's "Thy Goodness, Lord, doth crown the year"; but such suitable choices are rare.

One of Lowell Mason's worst infelicities was the giving of the name ZEPHON, which means "dark, wintry," to this text by Isaac Watts:

> Stand up, my soul; shake off thy fears,
>   And gird the gospel armor on;
> March to the gates of endless joy,
>   Where Jesus, thy great Captain's gone.
>
> . . . .
>
> There shall I wear a starry crown,
>   And triumph in almighty grace;
> While all the armies of the skies
>   Join in my glorious Leader's praise.

Another, which may have had connotations for the ancient Israelites that it does not have for members of this twentieth-century generation was ZERAH, meaning "sprout," to a tune for another of Watts's hymns, beginning:

> To us a child of hope is born,
> To us a son is given.

It may be because of Mason's unhappy choices that English compilers of hymn and tune books almost invariably give other than their original names to his tunes when they use them.

However much may have been said to the contrary, composers are merely people. Some, of course, will question whether or not writers of hymn tunes may rightly be called composers. This will be true of many a writer of a sonata or a symphony who looks with disdain on a simple, singable, eight- or sixteen-measure harmonized melody, yet whose symphony will never be heard by more than a handful of listeners if ever by any. Dean Lutkin, who was a composer of much more than ordinary ability, has said it is often much more difficult to write an acceptable hymn tune than to produce a work in larger forms. The hymn tunes of many a composer known for little else will be heard long after his more ambitious attempts have been forgotten.

As for myselfe, I acknowledge that I cannot satisfie neither them, nor myselfe in all particularities: and well therefore I do like him that said, *He doth not teach well which teacheth all; leaving nothing to subtill wits to sift out.*—Camden.

And so I do bequeath to more "subtill wits" the joy of sifting out puzzles raised by the work herein begun.

ALPHABETICAL LIST OF TUNES

Fifty or more years ago John Julian, of *Dictionary of Hymnology* fame, said that more than 400,000 Christian hymns had been written up to that time; the number has materially increased in the last half century. Inasmuch as each of these hymns has sometime, somewhere, been sung to some tune, it will at once be recognized how impossible it would be to give a complete list of the names of all the tunes used. Some 2,000 will be found in the following lists.

If the name of a tune does not appear or if any alternative name is not discussed, it is because the author has no information concerning its source.

German chorale titles are not listed except in the few instances where there has been some comment made on the tune or its associations. Almost without exception, the chorales are known by the first words of the texts for which they were written.

So that the reader may be able to identify the melody of the tunes in this alphabetical list without the aid of any musical instrument, the following simplified notation has been provided.

The initial letters of the syllables used in singing the major diatonic scale are used—d r m f s l t, indicating *do re mi fa so la ti*. If the melody extends below the basic scale, capital letters are used. The higher notes above the basic scale are indicated by italic letters. For example:

S L T d r m f s l t *d* *r* *m*

The time is indicated by the number of counts (beats, pulses) in the measure: 2, 4, 3, 6, 9, shown respectively in (a), (b), (c), (d), (e), below. It is not necessary to specify the value of the notes, because if there are four counts to a measure, for instance, it makes no difference whether they be eighth, quarter, half, or whole notes. The measures are marked by diagonal lines.

2: *d*   s s / m   s / *d*

a) SILVER STREET

4: m m f s / s f m r /

b) Hymn to Joy

3: d d d / d T d / r m r / d /

c) Hursley

6: d / L F r T S d / m m r d /

d) Joanna

9: m r d / s — — s — f s l / s — — — — —

e) Blessed Assurance

No key signature is necessary, as all intervals in the scale are relative whether the key be (a) major or (b) minor.

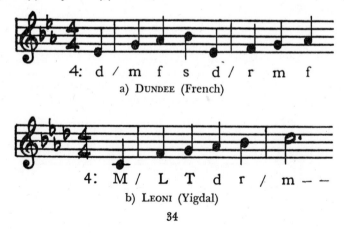

4: d / m f s d / r m f

a) Dundee (French)

4: M / L T d r / m — —

b) Leoni (Yigdal)

When a note is held more than one count, the extended time is shown by one or more hyphens.

4: d — m f / s — l t / d — t l / s ———/

DUKE STREET

The note following a dot (separated from it by a thin space) has half the time value of the note preceding the dot.

4: m — r. d / d. L L—/

BETHANY

Where more than one note occurs on one count either (a) tied or (b) grouped, the letters have no space between them.

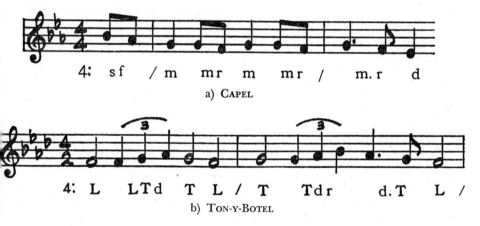

4: s f / m mr m mr / m. r d

a) **CAPEL**

4: L LTd T L / T Tdr d.T L /

b) **TON-Y-BOTEL**

Accidentals are indicated by the usual signs: ♯, ♭, or ♮. These occur in both (a) major and (b) minor tunes.

4: m / m. m ♯r m / s s ♯f

a) **REST (Elton)**

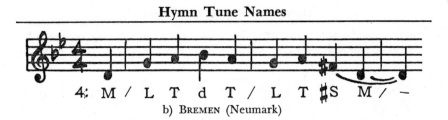

4: M / L T d T / L T ♯S M / −

b) BREMEN (Neumark)

A

A CHRISTMAS CAROL. See ST. SYLVESTER.

ABENDS [L. M. (3: S d T / L - L / f - m / r -); Herbert S. Oakeley, 1873]. The word is a German adverb meaning "at evening." The tune was written for the evening hymn "Sun of my soul" by John Keble.

ABERGELE [C. M. (3: S L T / d - d / m - r / d -); John A. Lloyd, 1873]. A town near the Irish Sea in North Wales not far from Mold, Wales, the birthplace of the composer. The word (Welsh) is pronounced "a-ber"-gay'-ly" and signifies "at the mouth of the River Gele": *aber*, "river"; and *gele*, "a leech." Formerly leeches were common there. Abergele is the seat of transactions of great historical interest. It has been justly said that on no spot in the principality of Wales have there been more sanguinary conflicts than in the defile of Levn Ogo, near Abergele.—From Lewis.

ABERYSTWYTH [7 7 7 7 D (4: L LT dr m / d T L -); Joseph Parry, 1879]. Pronounced "a-bur"-ust'-with" (commonly "a-brust'-with"). So named because written at the town of Aberystwyth, a seaside resort and the foremost university town in Wales. It was the home of the composer, a leading Welsh musician and professor of music at the University College of Wales. The town is located at the mouth of the River Ystwyth: *aber*, "river mouth"; *Ystwyth (Ystwich, Ustwith)*, "flexible, pliant."

————— [S. M. (4: m / r d T T / L -); Frederick A. G. Ouseley, 1860].

This appeared in the original edition of *Hymns Ancient and Modern*, the most representative collection of the hymnody of the Church of England which has appeared to this date. First published in 1861 and at various dates since, it has had a greater sale than any other hymnal ever published.

ABRIDGE [C. M. (3: d / s - d / d t l / s f m / m r); Isaac Smith, *ca.* 1770]. This well-known tune probably received its name from the village of Abridge near Theydon Bois, in Essex, not far from Epping Forest, England. The town name comes from "Aeffa's bridge," or possibly "at the bridge." The composer spent most of his life in London but may have visited Abridge.

Also called ST. STEPHEN.

ABSENCE. See GREENVILLE.

ADDISON'S 19TH PSALM. See DUKE STREET.

ADESTE FIDELES [Irr., with Refrain (4: d / d - S d / r - S -); 1751; source unknown]. Literally, "Be present (or near), ye faithful." From the first words of the Latin hymn:

> *Adeste, fideles,*
> *Laeti triumphantes:*
> *Venite, venite in Bethlehem.*
> *Natum videte,*
> *Regem angelorum:*
> *Venite, adoremus Dominum.*

So far as is known, the tune was first printed in a small book, *An Essay on the Plain Chant* (London, 1782), some time after it was discovered in manuscript form in a volume dated 1751 at Stonyhurst College, Lancashire, England. It was the work of

John F. Wade, who seems to have employed himself writing, or copying, music for Roman Catholic institutions and families. Whether or not it is an original work by him has not been discovered.

Also called OPORTO, PORTUGAL NEW, PORTUGUESE HYMN, TORBAY.

The account of the popular name, PORTUGUESE HYMN, is given by Vincent Novello in a note in connection with this tune in *Home Music, the Congregational and Chorister's Psalm Book, &c.* (London, 1843):

This piece obtained its name of "The Portuguese Hymn" from the accidental circumstance of the Duke of Leeds, who was a director of the Concert of Ancient Music, many years since (about the year 1785), having heard the hymn first performed at the Portuguese Chapel, and who, supposing it to be peculiar to the service in Portugal, introduced the melody at the Ancient Concerts, giving it the title of "The Portuguese Hymn," by which appellation this very favorite and popular tune has ever since been distinguished; but it is by no means confined to the choir of the Portuguese Chapel, being the regular Christmas hymn, "Adeste Fideles," that is sung in every Catholic chapel throughout England.

OPORTO may be accounted for from the fact that Marcus Antonio da Foncesca, a Portuguese composer and director of operas, known in Italy as Il Portogollo, was for long thought by some to have composed this famous tune. Oporto, a city in Portugal, may be the source of this name, or it may have been coined from the first two syllables of "Portogollo." This appellation is no longer used.

ADRIAN   [11 10 11 10 (4: d - d d / d - - r / d T L T / r - d -); Thomas F. Rinehart, 1901]. For the city, in Lewanee County, Michigan, where the composer lived for forty years or more, acting as organist at the Plym-outh Methodist Protestant Church, and, for a time, as Director of Music at Adrian College. The name is a variant of Hadrian, made famous by the Roman emperor who built a wall across northern England.

————   [8 7 8 7 D (4: s . m r d / m d L S); Robert P. Stewart, *ca.* 1890]. Probably a personal name. Used in some English books as a setting for "Once to every man and nation" by James Russell Lowell.

ADVENT   [8 7 8 7 D (4: s m r d / s m m r); Berthold Tours, 1881]. Literally, "approach"; commonly applied to the coming of Christ. The tune usually used with Cecil F. Alexander's Epiphany hymn beginning, "Saw you never, in the twilight." It is strange that the tune for an Epiphany hymn is called ADVENT.

Also called, much more appropriately, THE WISE MEN.

————   [8 8 6 D (6: m / m - r d r m / s - s s - -); a "Western melody," early 19th century; source unknown]. This tune was widely used during the early camp-meeting days to a variety of texts and was given a variety of names. Usually these names were suggested by the sense of the text; for that beginning, "When Thou, my righteous Judge, shalt come," names such as ANTICIPATION and SOLEMN INQUIRY were given.

ADWINKLE. See CHESTERFIELD.

AGAPÉ   [8 7 8 7 (3: S L T / d - m / m r L / d - T); Charles J. Dickinson, 1861]. Literally, "love" (Greek). Presumably from the character of the hymn "For the bread which Thou hast broken," with which it is used. The terms "Agapé," "Lord's Supper," "Eucharist," and "Communion" have, loosely and mistakenly, come to have a somewhat common meaning. The Agapé was the love feast of the primitive Christians when all members of the congregation, rich and poor, master and slave, met at a common meal, following which they celebrated the Eucharist as brothers and sisters of the same family.

Under Christianity the history of the Agapé coincides with that of the Eucharist until the end of the second century.

Also called (originally) SANCTUARY.

AGATHA. See JEWETT.

AHIRA. See LEIGHTON.

AILEEN. See ST. ANDREW by Barnby.

AJALON. See GETHSEMANE by Redhead.

ALBANY. See ANCIENT OF DAYS.

ALDERSGATE STREET [8 8 8 8 8 8 (4: m / r m f l / s r m); Egbert F. Horner, 1904]. Because used with William Boyd Carpenter's hymn beginning:

Before Thy throne, O God, we kneel;
Give us a conscience quick to feel,
A ready mind to understand
The meaning of Thy chastening hand,

and other hymns suggesting John Wesley's experience at Aldersgate Street when he was converted and his "heart was strangely warmed."

ALETTA [7 7 7 7 (3: m s d / r - r / r d r / m - -); William B. Bradbury, 1860]. Written for a stanza from Augustus M. Toplady's hymn beginning:

Weary sinners, keep thine eyes
On the atoning sacrifice.

——— [7 7 7 7 5 D (4: m r d T / dr m L -); John Stainer, late 19th century]. "Aletta" was the name of the mother of St. Bernard. Her last words were, "By Thy cross and passion, Good Lord, deliver us." Her son heard these words, and it has been thought this hymn was inspired by his memory of the scene; it was a prayer for his last hours. Written for St. Bernard's hymn beginning, "Hail, Thou Head! so bruised and torn," translated by Elizabeth Charles and Godfrey Thring.

ALFORD [7 6 8 6 D (4: m / f.f d r / m d -); John B. Dykes, 1875]. Written for the hymn beginning, "Ten thousand times ten thousand," by Henry Alford, onetime Dean of Canterbury. Dykes gave various tunes he composed the names of persons with whom he had been closely associated.

——— [8 8 8 6 (4: L.L L L / d T L ♯S); Josiah Booth, 1909(?)]. Written as a setting for Dean Alford's hymn beginning, "Lo! the storms of life are breaking."

Also called ASHTON.

ALIDA [C. M. D. (6: S / d - d m r d / L - L d T -); early American melody]. "Alida" (or "Aledo"), a feminine name, is from "Alida," a city in Asia Minor where "splendid garments were manufactured." It might be translated "the richly clad." "Alida" is the name popularly given to a heroine of the War of 1812. In 1840 there was published a book which became very popular entitled *Alida, or Miscellaneous Sketches, or Incidents During the Late American War. Founded on Fact with Poems by the unknown Author of the former editions. Mrs. Amelia Stratton Camfeld.* This tune was well known before the War Between the States. It is quite possible there is some connection between the name of this unknown heroine and that of this tune.

ALIFF STREET. See HANOVER.

ALL SAINTS [S. M. (4: L / M L d T / L - -)]. See ST. BRIDE'S.

——— [C. M. (3: S / d - L / S - dr / m - r / d -)]. See MARTYRDOM.

——— [C. M. D. (4: S / M.F S d / d. T T)]. See ALL SAINTS, NEW.

——— [L. M. (3: d / d T L / S - d / r d T / d -)]. See WAREHAM.

——— [7 7 7 7 (4: m.f / s d t l / s -)]. See INNOCENTS.

——— [8 7 8 7 7 7 (4: d s l l / s. f m d)]. See ALL SAINTS, NEW.

——— [10 10 10 10, with Alleluias

(4: s - m f / s - s - / 1 1 1 1 / 1 - s -)].
See SARUM.

ALL SAINTS, NEW [C. M. D. (4: S / M. F S d / d. T T) ; Henry S. Cutler, 1872]. Written for Bishop Heber's hymn for St. Stephen's Day beginning, "The Son of God goes forth to war," which refers not only to "the martyr first," but to "a glorious band" and to the "noble army, men and boys, the matron and the maid" who "climbed the steep ascent to heaven," the name ALL SAINTS is even more appropriate than the others by which the tune is known—CUTLER, for its composer, and EMULATION, from the sentiment of the hymn. The "New" is simply to identify this particular tune; there were earlier ones called ALL SAINTS.

The power of canonization assumed by the Popes toward the end of the 10th century, increased the number of saints, till the frequency of Church holydays became most inconvenient. These celebrations were removed from the reformed offices; but *All Saints' Day* was retained in commemoration of all the known and unknown departed Christian worthies, and of the communion of the Church triumphant with the Church as yet militant on earth.—Procter, *History of the Book of Common Prayer.*

ALL THE WORLD [10 4 6 6 6 6 10 4 (4: s / d. t 1 s / fm rm f) ; Robert G. McCutchan ("John Porter"), 1930]. From the first line of George Herbert's hymn beginning, "Let all the world in every corner sing."

ALLA TRINITA. See ALTA TRINITA BEATA.

ALLA TRINITA BEATA. See ALTA TRINITA BEATA.

ALLELUIA [8 7 8 7 D (4: d d T d / L S L T) ; Samuel S. Wesley, 1868]. The source of this name is obvious; the tune was composed for "Alleluia, sing to Jesus," first line of the well-known hymn by William C. Dix. The

"Alleluia" is "the war cry of the Church Militant aspiring to become the Church Triumphant."—Anonymous.

This word is Hebrew and means "God hath appeared; praise ye Him and glorify Him;" for *Al* stands for God who hath outwardly come, while *El* means God. And since this expression signifies the coming of God the Word, the Church ordained that it be chanted between the reading of the Epistle and the Gospels, as well as on days of jubilation, as in the Antiphonaries of the Dominical Feasts, when we say, "Save us . . . that we may sing unto Thee, Alleluia." And this is sung in all churches in the original Hebrew because John in his revelation thus heard it from the beautiful angels.—*Nature of Hymns in Orthodox Churches* (Catholic) (New York: Bradshaw Press, 1838) .

To sing praises, that is, "Alleluia," is a song of the Hebrews. . . . The apostle St. John in the "Apocalypse" relates that, by a revelation of the Holy Spirit, he saw and heard the celestial host of angels saying "Alleluia" with a voice as formidable as thunder. No one should then doubt that when this mystery of praise is celebrated with fitting faith and devotion, the angels join in it. "Alleluia," like "Amen," is never translated from the Hebrew into the Latin tongue; not that they are wholly untranslatable, but as the learned say, because their antiquity is respected on account of their holy authority.—*Anonymous.*

It has been said the word *Hallelujah* was introduced into Christian worship about the year 390 by Jerome. It is, simply, "Alleluia" with the Greek "rough breathing" mark, '. Only in Revelation 19: 1, 3, 4, 6, is the word used in the New Testament. The original Hebrew word appears often in the Psalms, where it is translated, "Praise the Lord."

ALLELUIA DULCE CARMEN. See ORIEL and TANTUM ERGO.

ALLELUIA PERENNE [10 10 7 (4: s - / m. m m f / s d l d / s - -); William H. Monk, 1868]. *Alleluia Perenne:* "endless Alleluia." Set to John Ellerton's translation:

Sing Alleluia forth in duteous praise,
Ye citizens of heav'n; O sweetly raise
An endless Alleluia!

———— [10 10 7 (4: s / d t d s / l sf m ♯f / s - -); B. Luard Selby 1909]. From the sentiment of its hymn.

Also called CIVES COELI, meaning "citizens of heaven."

ALMA. See CONSOLATION by Webbe.

ALMA REDEMPTORIS. See above.

ALMSGIVING [8 8 8 4 (3: m m r / d - S / d - r / m -); John B. Dykes, 1865]. From sentiment of Christopher Wordsworth's offertory prayer beginning, "O Lord of heaven and earth and sea": all except one of the stanzas closing with, "Who givest all." This hymn appeared in Wordsworth's *Holy Year* (1863), third edition, "Charitable Collection."

Also called ELLIOTT, because it has been used with Charlotte Elliott's hymn beginning, "My God, is any hour so sweet."

ALNWICK. See FIAT LUX.

ALTA TRINITA BEATA [8 7 8 7 D (4: d dr m rd / f mr m m); arr. in 1782 by John Burney from a 14th-century Italian melody]. *Alta Trinita beata:* Italian for "To the blessed Trinity." When John Burney, English musical historian, discovered the manuscript of this tune in the Biblioteca Nazionale Centrale, Florence, Italy, in 1770, he misread the first word of the hymn to which it was set, making it *"alla"* instead of *"alta"* His error has been quite consistently followed by hymnbook editors with but few exceptions. The error seems to have been discovered first by the Reverend W. H. Frere, who wrote the Introduction to *Hymns Ancient and Modern,* Historical Edition (1909).

Also called FLORENCE, ST. CHRYSOSTOM'S, TRINITY. FLORENCE: doubtless because of *Laudisti,* a Religious Confraternity instituted at Florence in 1310. There was compiled for their use a series of collections of devotional music known as *Laudi Spirituali.* TRINITY: obvious.

ALTORF. See LUTHER.

ALVERSTOKE [11 10 11 10 (4: m - ♯r m / s - - T / T d r m / m - L -); Joseph Barnby, 1883]. Its composer identified it by using the first line of the hymn for which it was written, Harriett B. Stowe's "Still, still with Thee." Some later editor of hymnals named it ALVERSTOKE. Alverstoke is a watering place in southern England.

According to an ancient chronicle, Henry de Blois, Bishop of Winchester, and brother of King Stephen, on his return from Normandy, being overtaken by a storm in the bay, between the Isle of Wight and Alverstoke, made a solemn vow to build a church on the spot where he should first land in safety; and, having landed at this place [Alverstoke], is said to have erected the parish church, about the year 1130.—Lewis.

Also called ALVERSTROKE, a misspelling of Alverstoke.

AMAZING GRACE [C. M. (3: S / d - md / m - r / d - L / S -); early American melody]. From the first words of John Newton's hymn, the first stanza of which is:

Amazing grace! how sweet the sound,
That saved a wretch like me!
I once was lost, but now am found,
Was blind, but now I see.

Also called HARMONY GROVE, NEW BRITAIN, REDEMPTION, SOLON, SYMPHONY.

REDEMPTION: from sentiment of the hymn; the other names have no significance.

AMBROSE [7 7 7 5 (4: S L d d / d r d -); Henry J. Gauntlett, *ca.* 1850]. An arrangement from an old Gregorian Tone, which may account for the name.

Also called ST. ANTHONY.

——— [Irr. (4: s ss s s / s - - -)]. See DULCE DOMUM.

AMEN, JESU HAN SKAL RAADE [8 7 8 7 7 7 (4: s - m - / r r m f / f - m); Anton P. Berggreen, 1849]. From the first line of a Scandinavian hymn with which it is used. Translated, it reads, "Amen, Jesus, He shall reign." "Amen" at the end of a prayer is "so be it"; at the close of a creed it signifies "so it is." The word, Hebrew, equivalent to "yea" or "truly," is used extensively.

AMERICA [6 6 4 6 6 6 4 (3: d d r / T. d r]; Henry Carey(?), 1774]. So called only in the United States because of its association with our National Hymn, "My country, 'tis of thee."

Also called CREATION, NATIONAL HYMN, STAMFORD, WHITEFIELD'S TUNE.

NATIONAL ANTHEM: the title used throughout the British Commonwealth, as it is sung to "God save the King!" WHITEFIELD'S TUNE: the name given it in James Lyon's *Urania* (1761), one of the earliest songbooks printed in America. It is quite possible that the famous preacher Whitefield first popularized it in this country, and Lyon may have thought it was Whitefield's composition.

AMSTERDAM [7 6 7 6 D (4: d S d r / m r mf s); from *The Foundery Collection*, 1742]. Since nothing is known as to the source of this tune, any reason assigned for giving it this name would be mere speculation. This famous tune has been published in American books at least since Andrew Law used it in his *Select Harmony* in 1779.

——— [7 6 7 6 D (4: mf / s d t l / s - m)]. See TOURS.

AN ANCIENT LITANY. See INNOCENTS.

ANCIENT OF DAYS [11 10 11 10 (4: s sss s.l / sd tm l s); J. Albert Jeffery, 1886]. From the first words of the hymn for which it was written, beginning, "Ancient of Days, who sittest throned in glory." ALBANY is the name given it by its composer, who was living at Albany, New York, when he wrote it.

ANGEL VOICES [8 5 8 5 8 4 3 (6: m - m m f m / r - ♯d r - S); Arthur S. Sullivan, 1872]. From the first words of Francis Potts's joyful hymn beginning, "Angel voices, ever singing," for which it was written.

——— [8 5 8 5 8 4 3 (4: m s l s / d l s m); E. G. Monk, 1861)]. See above.

ANGELIC VOICES. See TIDINGS.

ANGELS [L. M. (4: d - d d / r - m - / f r s -); Orlando Gibbons, 1623]. Written for one of George Wither's hymns, the first stanza of which is:

> The angels sung, and thus sing we:
> To God on high all glory be;
> Let Him on earth His peace bestow
> And unto men His favor show.

Also called ANGEL'S SONG, ANGELS' SONG, SONG 34.

ANGEL'S SONG, or ANGELS' SONG. See ANGELS.

ANGEL'S STORY [7 6 7 6 D (:4: m / m. m r d / d - T); Arthur H. Mann, 1881]. The composer named it from the sentiment of Emily H. Miller's children's hymn beginning:

> I love to hear the story
> Which angel-voices tell.

Also called CRUX CHRISTI, RIVERMOUTH, WATERMOUTH. Watermouth is a picturesque little harbor on Bristol Channel, England.

ANGELUS [L. M. (3: d d r / m ♯f s / s - ♯f / s -); Georg Josephi, 1847].

Georg Josephi, German court musician of the seventeenth century, composed tunes for a number of hymns by Johann Scheffler (1624-77), who adopted the name Angelus Silesius. Lochner says Scheffler probably adopted the name after a sixteenth-century mystic, John ab Angelis, when the latter was received into the Roman Catholic Church on June 12, 1653. Later he added Silesius, "the Silesian," because he was born at Breslau, Silesia, and wanted to be distinguished from Johann Angelus, of Darmstadt.

Also called WHITSUN HYMN.

ANGLIA. See EASTER HYMN.

ANNE'S. See ST. ANNE.

ANNUNCIATION [Irr. (4: S / S d d rm / fm rd T) ; traditional Dutch melody]. Named by David McK. Williams, who harmonized the melody for *The Hymnal 1940* (Protestant Episcopal), as the setting for the hymn beginning, "A message came to a maiden young."

ANTIOCH   [C. M., with Repeats (4: *d* - t. l / s - - f / m - r - / d - -); said to have been arr. from George F. Handel, 1836]. "Antioch" is derived from a Greek word the meaning of which is uncertain; therefore one conjectures whether or not the text may have had some bearing on the naming of a tune to be used with "Joy to the world, the Lord is come." It may well have. Lowell Mason took Bible names at random, usually from the Old Testament. The fact that he used few from the New Testament gives encouragement to the thought that this is a significant name. There is a very old tradition, preserved by Socrates the historian, that Ignatius, martyred in A.D. 107, was led by a vision, or dream, of angels singing hymns antiphonally to the Holy Trinity, to introduce antiphonal singing of hymns into the church at Antioch. From this the custom quickly spread to other churches. If Mason knew this, it might have given further point to its selection. Antioch, the ancient Syrian city, lies not far west of the more modern Aleppo. Founded about 300 B.C., it became a city of great extent and remarkable beauty. After suffering pillage from successive conquerors and destruction from numerous earthquakes through the years, it is now greatly reduced in size, and its beauty has departed. It was at Antioch that the disciples were first called Christians. No city, after Jerusalem, is so intimately connected with the apostolic church.

Also called COMFORT, HOLY TRIUMPH, JERUSALEM, MEDIA, MESSIAH.

COMFORT is the name by which this tune is known in England. HOLY TRIUMPH: from the sentiment of the hymn. MESSIAH: because it is said to have been made up of portions of Handel's oratorio by that name.

ARCHANGEL. See VESPER HYMN by Bortniansky.

ARGYLE. See EWING.

AR-HYD-Y-NOS   [8 4 8 4 8 8 8 4 (4: d. T L d / r. d T S) ; Welsh traditional melody, 1784]. Pronounced "Arr-heed'-i-naws"; word-for-word translation, "on length of night." "All through the night" is the beginning of the text with which this lovely melody has long been associated. Lowell Mason called it WELCH AIR when he used it to "When the spark of life is waning," in *The Choir* (1832).

ARIEL [8 8 6 D (3: s / s m m / m d d / d T dm / m r) ; arr. by Lowell Mason, *ca.* 1830]. See page 30 for comment on Lowell Mason's use of Old Testament names. The word "Ariel" appears several times in the Old Testament: (1) as the name of a person whom Ezra sent along with others to Iddo at Casiphia, 457 B.C., and (2) as a symbolic name for Jerusalem. It is of uncertain meaning;

perhaps "God's altar hearth," given to Jerusalem by Isaiah (29:1, 2, 7), or according to some philologists, "light," or "Lion of God." Its secular associations connote "lightness, sprightliness." In mythology and fiction it is used freely and variously: in the demonology of the Cabala "Ariel" is a water spirit; in medieval folklore a light, graceful spirit of the air; Shakespeare, in *The Tempest,* has him an airy, tricky spirit able to change his shape at will to serve his master, Prospero; Milton, in *Paradise Lost,* has him one of the rebel angels overthrown by Abdiel; Pope, in *Rape of the Lock,* makes him a sylph, the special guardian of Belinda.

ARLEY. See ORIENTIS PARTIBUS.

ARLINGTON [C. M. (3: d- / m. m m- r- / d. d d-); Thomas A. Arne, 1762]. A note in the *National Psalmist* (1849) is interesting in the light of the common use of ARLINGTON today:

This has long been a popular tune. With care on the part of the choir not to hurry the time, it may be sung congregationally; but when so sung, the first two notes in the first, second, fifth, and sixth measures should be of about equal length.

Also called ARTIXERXES, PRINCE'S STREET (a variant), TRIUMPH. There is no apparent reason for calling this tune either ARLINGTON or PRINCE'S STREET. TRIUMPH: from the sentiment of the hymn "O for a faith that will not shrink," with which it is so frequently used. ARTIXERXES: because the original melody which suggested this first appeared in the composer's opera of that name.

ARMAGEDDON [6 5 6 5 D (4: S S m r / d - S -); adapted from John Goss, 1872]. "Armageddon" is a symbolic name for the scene of some great spiritual contest. It is derived from Rev. 16:16, and is a Greek word which means "the plain of Megiddo." Theodore Roosevelt gave currency to the word when he used the phrase, "We stand at Armageddon and battle for the Lord," at the close of his speech which launched the "Bull Moose" political party in 1912. The tune is universally used with Frances R. Havergal's "Who is on the Lord's side?"

ARMES [L. M. (3: s m r / d - d / 1 - 1 / s -); Philip Armes, 1875]. Named after the composer. Called GALILEE in England, it was written as a setting for "Jesus shall reign where'er the sun" for *Hymns Ancient and Modern,* Revised Edition (1875).
Also called ST. JUDE.

ARMS OF JESUS. See IN SINE JESU.

ARNSTADT. See SEELENBRÄUTIGAM.

ARTHUR'S SEAT [6 6 6 6 8 8 (4: S / d. d T L / S -); arr. from John Goss, 1874]. A famous hill overlooking Edinburgh from the East.

Arthur's Seat, terminating in a rocky point, 700 feet from the base, abounding in spars, ores, and rocky plants, is supposed to take its name from Arthur the British prince, who defeated the Saxons in the neighborhood.—Gough.

ARTIXERXES. See ARLINGTON.

ASCALON. See CRUSADERS' HYMN.

ASCENSION [S. M. D. (4: S / S d d m / s - -)]. See OLIVET by Dykes.

——— [7 7 7 7, with Alleluias (4: m s d d / r f m -); William H. Monk, 1861]. From the sentiment of the hymn, Charles Wesley's "Hail the day that sees Him rise."

——— [7 7 7 7, with Alleluias (4: d. d r m / f l s -); John B. Dykes, 1857]. See above.

ASCHAM. See CARTER.

ASHTON. See ALFORD.

ASMON. See AZMON.

ASSISI [8 8 7 8 8 (free: d d d / r d T T / L); Alfred M. Smith, 1940]. Written for Howard Chandler Robbins' translation of St. Francis of Assisi's Song of the Creatures ("The Canticle of the Sun"), the Umbrian dialect form beginning, *Altissimu omnipotente bon signore,* which the Saint is said to have composed "when he fell into an ecstacy."

Ass's SEQUENCE. See ORIENTIS PARTIBUS.

ASSURANCE [9 10 9 9, with Refrain (9: m r d / s - - s - - f s l / s - -); Mrs. Joseph F. Knapp, 1873]. From the second word of the text and the predominating sentiment of Fanny Crosby's gospel hymn, "Blessed assurance, Jesus is mine." Mrs. Knapp composed this tune with no special text in mind. Taking it to her friend, Fanny Crosby, and playing it over for her, she asked, "What does it say, Fanny?" With almost no hesitation Mrs. Crosby replied, "Blessed assurance."

—— [8 7 8 7 D (4: L LTd T L / T Tdr d. T L)]. See TON-Y-BOTEL.

ATHENS. See SWEET STORY.

ATTITUDE. See GRATITUDE by Bost.

ATTWOOD [8 8 8 8 8 8 (3: s / s d tl / s - m / d - r / m -); Thomas Attwood, 1831]. For the composer, who was organist at St. Paul's Cathedral, London. It is taken from his anthem "Come, Holy Ghost." Written in haste at the request of his bishop, it proved so satisfactory it was sung at Trinity Sunday service, 1833.

AUGHTON. See HE LEADETH ME.

AUGSBURG [11 10 11 10 (4: m - r. d / s f -)]. See CONSOLATION by Mendelssohn-Bartholdy.

—— [11 10 11 10 (4: s - m d / l. s s -)]. See CONSOLATION by Webbe.

—— [Irr. (4: M / L T d T / L T *S M)]. See BREMEN by Neumark.

AUGUSTINE [8 7 8 7 (4: d T d. r / m sf m r)]. See SARDIS.

AULD LANG SYNE [C. M. D. (4: S / d. d d m / r. d r); Scottish melody, *ca.* 1782]. This Scottish song title means "days gone by," especially happy ones.

Also called GRATEFUL MEMORY, PLENARY.

AURELIA [7 6 7 6 D (4: m / m m f m / m - r); Samuel S. Wesley, 1864]. *Aurelia:* "brilliant, glorious" (feminine of *Aurelius*). The composer wrote this tune for "The voice that breathed o'er Eden," John Keble's wedding hymn; but before it was published in that connection, he used it as the setting for John M. Neale's translation of three cantos taken from St. Bernard's long Latin hymn, *Hora novissima:* (a) "Brief life is here our portion," (b) "For thee, O dear, dear country," and (c) "Jerusalem, the golden" (this name having been suggested by the last word, the Latin *aurum,* "gold").

AUS DER TIEFE. See HEINLEIN.

AUSTRIA. See below.

AUSTRIAN HYMN [8 7 8 7 D (4: d. r m r / f m rT d); Francis J. Haydn, 1797]. Because written in honor of an Austrian emperor's birthday and first performed in Vienna. It was set to the hymn *"Gott erhalte Franz den Kaiser"* by the poet Hauschka.

Also called AUSTRIA, BETHLEHEM, CHEADLE, EMPEROR'S HYMN, HAYDN, HAYDN'S, HAYDN'S HYMN, ROHRAU, VIENNA, WESTBOROUGH. AUSTRIA, EMPEROR'S HYMN, HAYDN, HAYDN'S, HAYDN'S HYMN, and VIENNA should be obvious with the above in mind.

ROHRAU: birthplace of the composer.

VIENNA: home of the composer.

AUTUMN [8 7 8 7 D (3: dr / m. r dL / S M); arr. from François H. Barthélémon, *ca.* 1796]. Also called CONSTANCY, ERITH, JANES, JAYNES, MADRID, MANT, SABBATH, SARDIUS. Some of these names may indicate some connection between the sentiment of a text or, perhaps, an author; but I have not seen anywhere any comment on any of the names used.

AVENTINE. See HAMBURG.

AVISON [11 11 12 11, with Refrain (3:

44

s. l s / l s *d* / r m f / mr mf sl);
Charles Avison, *ca.* 1766]. The name
of the composer; usually sung to
"Shout the glad tidings, exultingly
sing" by William A. Muhlenberg.
From Robert Browning's *Parleyings
with Certain People; with Charles
Avison,* the reference being to Avison's "Grand-March":

—bang the drums,
Blow the trumpets, Avison! March-mo-
tive? that's
Truth which endures resetting. Sharps
and flats,
Lavish at need, shall dance athwart thy
score
When ophicleide and bombardon's up-
roar
Mate the approaching trample, even now
Big in the distance—or my ears de-
ceive—
Of federated England, fitly weave
March-music for the Future!

Also called MIRIAM, because set to
Thomas Moore's hymn beginning,
"Sound the loud timbrel o'er Egypt's
dark sea."

AVON. See MARTYRDOM.

AZMON [C. M. (3: S / dd r r / mr d);
Carl G. Gläzer, *ca.* 1839]. *Azmon:*
"fortress" (Hebrew). Named by
Lowell Mason. A place on the south
of Canaan near the torrent of Egypt,
Wady-el-arish. It is mentioned three
times in the Old Testament: Numbers 34 (twice) and Joshua 15. A
"torrent" may be dry most of the
time but carry a raging stream when
it is in flood. *Wady* means "river."
Also called ASMON, DEERFIELD, GAS-
TON.

B

BABYLON'S STREAMS [L. M. (free: L /
d r m - m / r d T); Thomas Cam-
pian]. Because set, in Campian's
First Book of Ayres (1601), to a
metrical rendition of Psalm 137, beginning:

As by the streams of Babilon
Farre from our native soyle we sat.

Campian (or Campion) was a "doctor in physic," not a doctor in music.
In a book on "A new way of making
foure parts in Counterpoint . . ."
(second edition, 1660), which he
dedicated to "Charles, Prince of
Great Britaine," he "apologizes for
his offering 'a worke of musicke to
his Highness by the example of
Galen,' who, he says, became an ex-
pert musician and would needes ap-
ply all the proportions of music to
the uncertaine motions of the pulse."
—Hawkins.

BALERMA [C. M. (3: d / m - r / d - L /
S - L / d -); adapted from a melody
by François H. Barthélémon by
Robert Simpson, 1833]. Also spelled
"Ballerma." See the account of the
tune AUTUMN in my book *Our
Hymnody,* in which reference is made
to the naming of this tune.
Also called SPANISH AIR.

BALFOUR [C. M. (free: *d* / s s d m /
r l s -); 18th-century hymn melody
arr. by Geoffrey Shaw, 1919]. Named
for Arthur James Balfour, first Earl
of Balfour, whose influence was at
its height at the time this arrangement was made. It was Lord Balfour,
as foreign secretary of Great Britain,
in November, 1917, who gave the
promise of the British government to
provide a "national home" in Palestine for the Jews at the conclusion of
World War I.

BALLINA. See GOD BE WITH YOU.

BANGOR [C. M. (4: m / d T L m /
l sf m); William Tans'ur, 1724]. A
very famous old tune, used by Ravenscroft (see p. 16). Named for the
ancient city in Wales, and for generations used with the lugubrius
hymn text beginning, "Hark! from
the tombs a doleful sound." When occasionally used now, it is set to texts
of quite different sentiment.

Bangor, derived from "ban gor" or the "great circle," a generic British word for a "religious congregation" or "fraternity."—*Old England.*

Bangor, Wales, a rectory dedicated to St. Dinoth, Abbot of Bancornaburg, or Bangor, in the days of St. Augustine. It is "celebrated as being the site of the most ancient British monastery" (rather seminary) which contained two thousand four hundred monks.—Pennant.

Earliest authentic accounts of Bangor are that a college "for the instruction of youth" was established here in 525 by a son of the Abbot of Bangor Iscoed (the adjunct to distinguish it from the city of Bangor) which was the most ancient monastery founded in Britain. Its history is rich in interesting incidents. Bangor, Maine, was named after this tune. The inhabitants of the small Maine village called Sunbury delegated their minister, the Reverend Seth Noble, to ride to Boston and make application for a post office. While waiting to be served at the proper office, the reverend gentleman kept humming this tune to himself. After Noble stated his case, the clerk, somewhat abruptly, said, "What name?" "Bangor," was the immediate reply. So little Sunbury became Bangor.

BANNOCKBURN. See CALEDONIA.

BARBY TUNE. See ST. ANDREW.

BARMOUTH [7 7 7 7 7 7 (4: d r / m. m m f / s -) ; Walter Macfarren, ca. 1875]. This tune was written for William H. Monk for use in the Revised Edition of *Hymns Ancient and Modern.* Monk called it BARMOUTH because he and Macfarren were lost for a day and a night in the Welsh mountains while on a vacation at Barmouth.

Barmouth is an Anglicism of the original *Aber Maw,* denoting its location at the mouth of the River Maw. The

change was made in 1768 at a meeting of ships' masters who decided, in the light of a marked increase in shipping from the port, it would be better to have an English than a Welsh name inscribed on their vessels' sterns.—Lewis.

BARONY. See COURAGE, BROTHER.

BARRE. See WINCHESTER, NEW.

BARTHELEMON. See MORNING HYMN.

BARTHOLDY. See MUNICH.

BASIL. See CASWALL.

BEACON HILL [Irr., with Refrain (4: SS / S M d. T / T L) ; Harry S. Mason, 1925]. Earl Marlatt, who wrote his hymn "Are ye able?" to go with this tune, has written:

He [the composer] wrote the tune, "Beacon Hill," in the spring of 1925 while he was doing work in Boston University School of Religious Education, and living at The Hermitage, 9 Willow St., Boston; hence the name, "Beacon Hill."

Beacon Hill, north of Boston Common,

derived its name from the fact that in the ancient colonial days permanent arrangements were made for beacon-fires to be kindled here to alarm the country in case of danger or attack."—Osgood.

BEALOTH [S. M. D. (4: m mm m r / d - -) ; from *Mason's Sacred Harp,* 1843]. BEALOTH (Hebrew): "citizens." A city in the southeast of Judah, near Salem; now called Kurnub, Southern District of Palestine. BEALOTH first appeared in a book by Lowell and Timothy B. Mason, which may explain why such an odd name was given it. This tune, used with "I love Thy kingdom, Lord," is a great favorite among the Disciples of Christ, who always call it PHILLPUT. Inquiries made of many members of that denomination have failed to elicit any information concerning it.

BEATI. See REST (ELTON) by Maker.

BEATITUDO [C. M. (3: d r m / s - m / d - f / m -) ; John B. Dykes, 1875].
Beatitudo, a word coined by Cicero, means "the condition of blessedness." Written for Isaac Watts's hymn beginning, "How bright those glorious spirits shine," which has to do with the joy and bliss of the saints in heaven. It is a commonly used tune.

BECK. See ELLERS.

BEDFORD [C. M. (4: s / m d l s / f m r) ; William Wheall, early 18th century]. From *Musical Times*, September 1, 1897, and March 1, 1908: Wheall (or Wheal, Wheale, Wale), died 1727 (not 1745), was organist at St. Paul's Church, Bedford. The tune is found in the scarce Matthew Wilkins' *Book of Psalmody*, but its first appearance is not known. Wilkins was jointly butcher and psalmodist in Great Milton, an out-of-the-way village "where some of the Havergal family can trace their ancestors." The tune was first named BEDFORD in *The Divine Music Scholars' Guide* (*ca.* 1715), but it gained prominence through being included in John Wesley's *Foundery Collection* (1742). It is Wheall's only known tune. There are several other tunes called BEDFORD, but they are little known and are by slightly known composers.

Bedford, "called . . . by the Saxons *Bedanford* or *Bedicanford* (which terms are expressive of its character as a place of public accommodation at the passage of a river)," is about fifty miles Northwest of London.—Lewis.

It was at Bedford that John Bunyan was imprisoned for 12½ years.
Also called LIVERPOOL.

BEECHER. See LOVE DIVINE by Zundel.

BEETHOVEN. See GERMANY.

BELIEF. See CAMPMEETING.

BELLEVUE. See FOUNDATION.

BELLINA. See GOD BE WITH YOU.

BELMONT [C. M. (3: S / m - r / d - T / T L d / S -) ; from *Sacred Melodies* by William Gardiner, 1854]. Lewis says that Beau-Manor was anciently the residence of the Beaumont (Belle-mont) family, and that it is in the county of Leicester, England. The home of William Gardiner, compiler of *Sacred Melodies* (1815), which contains the tune from which this one was arranged, was in Leicester. There may be some connection even though the tune had no name in the Gardiner book.
Also called BERNARD, ENTREATY, VIGILS.

BELOIT [L. M. (3: S / S L T / d r m / m f ♯d / r -) ; Carl G. Reissiger, early 19th century]. *Beloit* is a coined word, selected "by a committee, to whom it was suggested by the name *Detroit.*" Possibly the tune was named for the Beloit College, Wisconsin, which takes its name from the city in which it is located.

BELOVED [11 8 11 8 (4: d / d . r m f / s . l s f / m - r r / d - -) ; Freeman Lewis, 1813]. Evidently taken from a much older tune called DAVIS, which may be found in *The Sacred Melodian.*
Also called BETHEL, DELIGHT, DULCIMER, MEDITATION, MY BELOVED, THE BELOVED OF ZION, VOICE OF MY BELOVED. These names have all been suggested by the sentiment of Joseph Swain's hymn beginning, "O Thou, in whose presence my soul takes delight," with which the tune definitely seems to be wedded.

BEMBERG. See PASSION CHORALE.

BEMERTON. See CASWALL.

BENEDICTION [L. M. (4: s / s f m r / d l s)]. See MELCOMBE.

—— [8 7 8 7 8 7 (4: d r m f / s f m r)]. See TANTUM ERGO.

—— [10 10 10 10 (4: S - S L /

S - d - / d T d r / m - - -)]. See ELLERS.

BENTICK. See TRINITY.

BERA [L. M. (4: m - m r / d - s - / s r m f / m -) ; John E. Gould, 1849]. *Bera* (Hebrew) : "gift."

Otherwise *excellence,* but more probably for *son of evil.* King of Sodom at the time of the invasion of the five kings under Chedorlaomer, which was repulsed by Abraham.—McClintock and Strong.

A random Old Testament selection by Gould.

BERLIN. See MENDELSSOHN.

BERNARD [C. M. (3: S / m - r / d - T / T L d / S -)]. See BELMONT.

—— [7 6 7 6 D (4: d / r d f m / r - d)]. See EWING.

BERRIEN. See MAITLAND.

BERTHOLD. See TOURS.

BERWICK. See TALLIS' CANON.

BETHANY [6 4 6 4 6 6 6 4 (4: m - r. d / d. LL -) ; Lowell Mason, 1859]. The word means "house of the dates, or figs." The town, so well known through Jesus' having spent so much time there, is a village at the Mount of Olives, about two miles east of Jerusalem. Mason used this name for various tunes he composed; therefore it probably has no significance in its use with "Nearer, my God, to Thee."

—— [8 7 8 7 D (4: m l / s m d. r / d T) ; Henry Smart, 1867]. See above. Henry Smart called his tune BETHANY, but it has been given the name CRUCIFER by later editors because of its association with the hymn beginning, "Jesus, I my cross have taken," for which it was written.

BETHEL [L. M. (4: d / d T d d / r r m)]. See TALLIS' CANON.

—— [11 8 11 8 (4: d / d. r m f / s. l s f / m - r r / d - -)]. See BELOVED.

—— [7 7 7 7, with Alleluias (4: d d m m / s fm r -)]. See LLANFAIR.

—— [6 4 6 4 6 6 4 (4: m - m m / m. r r -)]. See KEDRON.

BETHLEHEM [C. M. D. (4: S / d d T L / S. L S) ; Gottfried W. Fink, 1841]. The name is derived from the Syrian *beit el lerhm,* "house of bread," alluding to the productive region about the town. The tune was so named because used with "While shepherds watched their flocks." Sir Arthur Sullivan, however, who first used it as a hymn tune in 1874, called it OLD CAROL. Many other composers than those here mentioned have used the name BETHLEHEM, usually associated with Christmas texts. Among them: J. Barnby, H. P. Main, J. Wainwright, C. E. Willing, R. H. Woodman.

Also called EVANGEL, OLD CAROL, SERAPH.

—— [7 7 7 7 7 7 (4: d Td r d / f f m -)]. See DIX.

—— [7 7 7 7 D, with Refrain (4: S d d. T / d m m r)]. See MENDELSSOHN.

—— [8 7 8 7 D (4: d. r m r / f m rT d)]. See AUSTRIAN HYMN.

BEULAH. See ST. MICHEL'S.

BIRMINGHAM [10 10 10 10 (4: d - m d / s - - m / l s l t / d -) ; from Cunningham's *A Selection of Psalm Tunes,* 2nd ed., 1834]. In a letter dated June 14, 1943, John R. Van Pelt wrote me:

. . . recently taken over from *Songs of Praise* [an English publication] by H. Augustine Smith under the name Birmingham. I may remark that the tune appeared in various American collections *before* 1834 (the date of the Birmingham collection) but always under the name Brewer. It was always given without a composer's name, but several times said to be "English." The place of publication of the Cunningham *Collection* gives the name to the tune.

Also called BREWER. The BREWER referred to is a Long Meter tune, the same as the above.

———— [Irr. (4: d dr / m ll s f / m -) ; Felix Mendelssohn-Bartholdy, 1846]. Set to "Cast thy burden on the Lord," it is from the oratorio *Elijah*. Perhaps this name has been used because *Elijah* was first performed at Birmingham, England, August 26, 1846.

———— [C. M. (4: S / d r T S / d r m)]. See ST. MAGNUS.

———— [C. M. (4: m / s s d *d* / t l s)]. See WESTMINSTER.

BIRR. See WENTWORTH by Handel.

BISHOP. See ROCKINGHAM by Miller.

BISHOPGARTH [8 7 8 7 D (4: S / m m m m / f. m r) ; Authur S. Sullivan, 1897]. For the bishop's house at Wakefield, England, *garth* meaning "a garden," "a yard," or "a close." The evolution of the English word "bishop" and its French equivalent, *évêque*, both stemming from the Latin *episcopus*, and neither having a single letter belonging to the other, is interesting. The gradations: English: episcopus, episcop, piscop, biscop, bishop. French: *episcopus, episc, epesc, evesc, evesque, évêque.*

BLAENHAFREN [8 7 8 7 D (2: L L / SF M / dT L / TL ²S) ; traditional Welsh melody]. *Blaen Hafren,* pronounced "blen-hav'-ren," is the name of a farm or homestead.

BLAIRGOWRIE [13 13 13 13 (4: m / r m f l / s - m m / s. m d r / m - -) ; John B. Dykes, 1872]. The word *"Blairgowrie"* is Gaelic, *"blar'-ghobhar,"* signifying "plain of the wild goats." This tune name is usually given with the identifying name of the composer, thus: BLAIRGOWRIE (DYKES), to distinguish it from that of the same title by Robert G. Thomson. Blairgowrie is a small inland town northwest of Dundee, Scotland, or, as officially designated, "Police burgh, Perthshire, Scotland." Lying in a beautiful part of Scotland, the town is of little interest historically and seems to be best known as the center of a prosperous raspberry-growing area.

Also called UNION SQUARE.

———— [8 8 8 6 4 6 (4: m / s. f m s / m r d) ; Robert G. Thompson, 1933]. See BLAIRGOWRIE by Dykes.

BLANFORD TUNE. See WAREHAM.

BLENCATHRA [6 5 6 5 D, with Refrain (6: S L d rm f r) ; Arthur Somerville, 1925]. Named for a mountain in Cumberland County, England, better known as "Saddleback."

BLOOMSBURY [12 11 12 11 (3: d / d s l / l s f / m r d / s -)]. See MONTGOMERY.

———— [Irr. (3: s / d s l / s s f / m r d / s s)]. See MAGDALEN by Jarvis.

BOLTON. See WINDSOR.

BONN [L. M. (3: S d T / d - r / S L T / d - -)]. See GERMANY.

———— [8 3 3 6 D (free: d - r - / m - - r m s / l - s -)]. See EBELING.

BORTNIANSKY. See ST. PETERSBURG.

BOSTAL. See MARTYRDOM.

BOSTON [L. M. (4: d - d r / m - r m / f - m r / m - - -)]. This is the name used in English books for Lowell Mason's tune HAMBURG (which see).

It is named for the English city of Boston. Boston [Lincolnshire, England] derived its name from St. Botolph, a Saxon, who founded a monastery at St. Botolph's Town about 650. The present name is a contraction. In the reign of Edw. I, Boston was said to have been so rich that upon the occasion of its burning by Robert Chamberloyne and his associates, "veins of melted gold and silver" ran "in one common current" down the streets.—Lewis.

BOYCE (SHARON) [7 7 7 7 (4: m d s d / r f m -) ; William Boyce, 1765]. From the name of the composer; the qualifying "Sharon" unknown.

Also called HALTON HOLGATE, SHARON.

BOYLSTON [S. M. (3: s / mf s l / s -) ; Lowell Mason, 1832]. A town and village in Massachusetts as well as a well-known street in Boston. Philo A. Otis says the tune was named after the street; Frank J. Metcalf says it was after the town. It is quite likely one of them is correct in his statement, even though Henry L. Mason says it is not an "associative name."

Also called MASON, for the composer.

BRADBURY [8 7 8 7 D (4: m m mr mf / s *d* s m) ; William B. Bradbury, 1859]. For the composer of this and many other tunes, most of them for common use. This, however, definitely seems to be wedded to the text "Saviour, like a Shepherd lead us," ascribed to Dorothy Ann Thrupp.

Also called SHEPHERD, from the first line of the text.

BRADFORD. See MESSIAH.

BREAD OF LIFE [6 4 6 4 D (4: m - d m / s l s -) ; William F. Sherwin, 1877]. From the first line of the text of Mary A. Lathbury's scripture hymn beginning, "Break Thou the bread of life."

BREMEN [Irr. (4: M / L T d T / L T ♯S M) ; Georg Neumark, 1657]. Also called AUGSBURG, NEUMARK. BREMEN and AUGSBURG are geographical names given by editors. NEUMARK: for both author and composer, for Georg Neumark wrote both text and tune. The hymn, as translated by Catherine Winkworth, begins, "If thou but suffer God to guide thee."

—— [7 6 7 6 (4: d / m r m f / s - m) ; Melchior Vulpius, 1662]. Also called HEIDELBERG, LINCOLN, MEIN LEBEN, VULPIUS. BREMEN and HEIDELBERG are merely geographical names which may or may not have some association with the composer or use of the tune. VULPIUS: for the composer. MEIN LEBEN: from the first line of the Old German *"Christus, der ist mein Leben,"* which melody Bach used in his *chorale* cantata by the same name. LINCOLN is the name given this tune in the *Pilgrim Hymnal* (1931), after it had been called

VULPIUS at an earlier number in the same book.

—— [8 8 6 8 8 6 (6: S / d - d m r d / r - r f) ; Thomas Hastings, *ca.* 1830]. A geographical name. The first few notes are the same as those in ALIDA, which see.

BRENTWOOD. See TALLIS' CANON.

BREWER. See BIRMINGHAM from F. Cunningham's *Selection.*

BRIDGET. See ST. BRIDE'S.

BRIDGET'S. See ST. BRIDE'S.

BROADMEAD. See DAVID'S HARP by Daniel.

BROCKLESBURY [8 7 8 7 (4: m r d S / T L L S) ; Charlotte A. Barnard ("Claribel"), 1868]. Brocklesbury, England, is near Dover, where the composer died. There may be some connection.

BROMLEY [L. M. (3: d / m - fr / d m s) ; Jeremiah Clarke, 1700]. From Bromley, a small town in England. So called from its broom fields.

BROMSWICK. See HANOVER.

BROOKFIELD [L. M. (3: S / m - m / m r L / T d r / d) ; Thomas B. Southgate, 1887]. A place name.

Also called GIDEON.

BRUCE'S ADDRESS [7 7 7 6 D (6: S - S S - M / S - L d - -)]. See CALEDONIA.

BRUCE'S ADDRESS SPIRITUALIZED. See above.

BRUNSWICK. See WENTWORTH by Handel.

BRYANT. See HOLBORN HILL.

BUCER. See SCHUMANN.

BULLINGER [8 5 8 3 (3: S L S / d - m / r L T / L - S) ; Ethelbert W. Bullinger, 1874]. Named for its composer.

BUNHILL. See REQUIESCAT.

BURFORD [C. M. (3: L / L - T / d - r / m r d / T) ; attributed to Henry Purcell, 1718].

Also called NORWICH, UXBRIDGE, WALTON, YORK. This is not to be confused with either Lowell Mason's

UXBRIDGE or the older C. M. tune called YORK, or THE STILT.

BURLEIGH [10 10 10 10 (4: *d* - s m / r - d -) ; Joseph Barnby, 1872]. For William H. Burleigh, the author of the hymn beginning, "Lead us, O Father, in the paths of peace," for which it was written and with which it seems to be quite definitely wedded. Barnby did not give it a name. Also called DIRIGE, VERITAS. *Dirige* (Latin) : "lead us"; from the first word of each stanza. *Veritas* (Latin) : "truth"; from the last word of the first line of the second stanza, as well as from the general sentiment of the hymn.

——— [11 10 11 6 (4: m - s *d* / t - - l / s m d r / r - m -)]. See DIADEMA.

BURLINGTON [C. M. (4: dr / m fm r l / s d r) ; John F. Burrowes, 1830]. A town name which has no special significance.

BURTON [12 11 12 11 (3: *d* / d s l / l s f / m r d / s -)]. See MONTGOMERY by Stanley.

——— [Irr. (3: s / d s l / s s f / m r d / s s)]. See MAGDALEN by Jarvis.

BYRD [C. M. (4: s / *d d d d* / t l s); Rob Roy Peery, 1929]. The composer wrote me August 4, 1936, that the tune which he wrote for Henry Webb Farrington's "Airmen's Hymn" "was named for the distinguished aviator, Richard Byrd, of Virginia."

C

CAITHNESS [C. M. (4: d - / m f s d / T d r) ; melody from *Scottish Psalter,* 1635]. Caithness is the extreme northeasterly county of Scotland.

CALCUTTA. See PATNA.

CALEDONIA [7 7 7 6 D (6: S - S S - M / S - L d - -) ; traditional Scottish melody]. CALEDONIA is the old, common bagpipe air which "roused" Robert Burns's "rhyming mania" (his own words) , resulting in "Scots wha hae

wi' Wallace bled," the famous poem entitled "Bannockburn," commonly called "Wallace's Address," or "Bruce's Address." Known as "Hey tuttie taitie" when it came to Scotland after it first appeared in print, around 1500, this tune has for more than four centuries been one of the best beloved of the many beautiful Scottish melodies. The word "Caledonia" (Greek *Kaladonia,* "the province of the ancient Britons"; Latin *Caledonia,* "the highlands of the northern part of Scotland") is now used as a poetical designation of Scotland. These words doubtless evolved from the Celtic *celyddon,* meaning "a dweller in woods and forests." The word *celt,* itself a contraction of the same word, *celyd,* has the same meaning. The poet Lucan, *circa* A.D. 60, was the first to name the "Caledonii."

Also called BANNOCKBURN, BRUCE'S ADDRESS, BRUCE'S ADDRESS SPIRITUALIZED, FRIENDS OF FREEDOM, WALLACE. All these names, while song names, were also used as hymn-tune names.

CALKIN. See WALTHAM.

CAMDEN. See WALTHAM.

CAMPIAN [7 7 7 7; Thomas Campian, *ca.* 1600]. Named for the composer. See BABYLON'S STREAMS.

CAMPMEETING [C. M. (3: d / Tr r r / dm m) ; early American melody]. Because the tune was a popular one in the old camp-meeting days.

Also called BELIEF, because used with the familiar revival refrain beginning, "I do believe . . ." and to John Newton's hymn beginning:

How sweet the name of Jesus sounds
In a believer's ears.

CANA. See VULPIUS.

CANDLER. [L. M. D. (6: S / d - d r d r / m s m r d r) ; Scottish traditional melody. This is "Bonnie Doon," the melody which Bishop Warren A. Candler, long-time leader in the former Methodist Episcopal Church, South, loved to sing to Charles Wesley's great poem known as "Wrestling Jacob." As the canto from this hymn was inserted largely for historic reasons and as Bishop Candler was a greatly loved member of the commission which compiled *The Methodist Hymnal* (1935), it was decided to use the tune and to honor the Bishop by giving it his name.

Also called STAR OF BETHLEHEM when used, as it has been, to the Christmas hymn beginning, "When marshalled on the nightly plain."

CANNON TUNE. See TALLIS' CANON.

CANNONS [L. M. (4: 1 / m. ♯s l t / d. r t) ; George F. Handel, *ca.* 1750]. A. H. Mann, in *The Church of England Hymnal*, says, "The name has been given by modern editors."

CANON. See TALLIS' CANON.

CANON TUNE. See TALLIS' CANON.

CANONBURY [L. M. (4: S / m m m fm / r dr m) ; Robert Schumann, 1839]. Probably received its name from some association with the street or square having this name in Islington, London. The manor of Canonbury, given to the Priory of St. Bartholomew by Ralph de Berners before the time of Henry III, doubtless obtained its name when the first residence of a canon, or prior, was built on the square. "Bury," or "burg," meant "dwelling." Near the square stands the old Canonbury Tower, sixty-six feet high, where, late in the eighteenth century, certain literary lights, among them Oliver Goldsmith, took lodging for reasons of economy and because of "the purity of the air." Ephraim Chambers, of encyclopedia fame, lived and died there. Close by the Tower is Canonbury House, where Queen Elizabeth I is said to have stayed from the time of her accession to the English throne until her coronation.

Also called ZADOK.

CANTATE DOMINO. .See JORDAN by Barnby.

CANTERBURY [7 7 7 7 (4: m f s l / r r m -)]. See GIBBONS by Gibbons.

———— [L. M. (4: L / ♯S L T d / rd TL ♯S -) ; anon., 1718]. Canterbury, origin not definitely known, was a place where the early Britons celebrated their religious rites prior to the Christian Era. The Christian religion had been partially promulgated during the occupation of the city by the Romans, and two churches had been built in the second century, one of which, on the arrival of Bertha, wife of Ethelbert (whom he married in France, where she had been taught the principles of Christianity), was consecrated by the bishop of Soissons and dedicated to St. Martin. Canterbury has been the seat of the metropolitan see for more than fourteen centuries and has had an uninterrupted succession of bishops during that time.—From Lewis.

Also called CRUCIFIXION, NEWBERRY.

CANTICUM REFECTIONS [10 10 10 10 (4: d - / s l s m / f m r r / m -) ; David McK. Williams, 1941]. Name quite obvious; composed as the setting for Horatius Bonar's Communion hymn beginning, "This is the hour of banquet and song."

CAPEL [C. M. (4: sf / m mr m mr / m. r d) ; traditional English melody]. A village near Horsham, England, where Miss Lucy Broadwood, authority on English traditional melodies, heard three gypsies named Goby sing this tune to an old ballad, "King Pharim." There is an old carol known as "King Pharim [Pharaoh] and the cock" which tells the story of two of the miracles performed in Egypt by the infant Jesus. It may have some connection with the apocryphal *Gospel of the Infancy*. (See *The Catholic Encyclopedia*.)

CAREY [8 8 8 8 8 8 (3: s / m - l / T - d / f m r / m -); Henry Carey, 1723]. Named for the composer; first set in hymn form to Addison's rendition of the Twenty-third Psalm, "The Lord my pasture shall prepare." John Hawkins says Carey was "slenderly accomplished in his art" and, as a musician, "seems to have been the first of the lowest rank."

CARLISLE [S. M. (4: d / s d mr dT / d - -); Charles Lockhart, 1792]. First called INVOCATION, the tune was later given the name CARLISLE, after the former Carlisle Chapel, now Holy Trinity Church, W., London.
Also called EWELL, HAMPTON.
——— [C. M. (4: d / d L r T / m d r); Thomas Ravenscroft]. This is from Ravenscroft's *Whole Booke of Psalmes*, 1621; there called a "Northern Tune." (See p. 16.)
Also called NORTHERN TUNE.
——— [C. M. (4: d / d T d m / r r d)]. See ST. FLAVIAN.

CAROL [C. M. D. (6: S / m - r r d L / S - L S -); Richard S. Willis, 1850]. Because of its carol-like character and that of the hymn to which it is always sung, "It came upon the midnight clear," by Edmund H. Sears. Pointing back to pagan times, the derived meaning of the word "carol" may be said to be "a dance with song," once meaning "to dance in a ring." By way of the Old French *caroler*, the Latin *choraula*, and the Greek *choraulus*, it goes back to the older Greek word, *choros* ("circle dance"), used in reference to the Attic drama. Percy Dearmer says the word, although retaining its dancing connections, changed its meaning and became "respectable" by the fourteenth century, doubtless through its use in the medieval plays.
Also called NORTHERN TUNE.

CARROLL. See ST. MAGNUS.

CARTER [8 7 8 7 (4: S S S dT / L L L r); Edmund S. Carter, 1865]. For the composer.
Also called ASCHAM, DAY BY DAY, SLINGSBY, WREFORD. DAY BY DAY: because written for John Ellerton's "A Morning Hymn for Children." The first stanza:

Day by day we magnify Thee,
 When, as each new day is born,
On our knees at home, we bless Thee
 For the mercies of the morn.

SLINGSBY: because it was composed at Slingsby, East Yorkshire, England.

CASSEL. See OLD 113TH.

CASWALL [6 5 6 5 (4: m m r r / d - T -); Friedrich Filitz, 1847]. From Edward Caswall, translator of the Latin Passion hymn, "Glory be to Jesus."
Also called BASIL, BEMERTON, FILITZ, NEANDER, WEM IN LEIDENSTAGEN. FILITZ: from the composer. WEM IN LEIDENSTAGEN: because used with Siegmund H. Oswald's hymn beginning with these words.

CATON. See ROCKINGHAM by Miller.

CECILIA. See DOMINUS REGIT ME.

CELESTIAL VOICES [8 3 8 3 (4: m. m r m / f m L T / d - r - / m - -); Richard F. Floyd, 1922 (?)]. Because written for Marie Corelli's prayer and Communion hymn beginning:

In our hearts celestial voices
 Softly say . . .

CHALVEY. See LEOMINSTER.

CHAMPLAIN. See PENTECOST.

CHAPEL ROYAL. See PURCELL.

CHARITY [7 7 7 5 (4: d f m r / d r S -); John Stainer, 1868]. Name suggested by the text of Christopher Wordsworth's hymn beginning, "Gracious Spirit, Holy Ghost," the sixth stanza of which is:

Faith and hope and love we see,
Joining hand in hand, agree;

But the greatest of the three,
And the best, is love.

CHARTERHOUSE [7 7 7 7 7 7 (4: m l s m / r mf m) ; Alexander S. Cooper, *ca.* 1875]. "Charterhouse" is an English corruption of the French *maison chartreux,* a peculiarly arranged Carthusian monastery. The name is found in various localities in England but is most familiarly applied to the one in London. In 1611 one Thomas Sutton, who had made a fortune in coal, endowed a hospital and school with sufficient funds to support eighty pensioners ("decayed gentlemen") and to educate forty-two boys. Many boys who attained high places in their later lives received their preparatory training at the Charterhouse in London. Among them were John Wesley and Joseph Addison.—From Lewis.

――――― [11 10 11 10 (4: S d r / m - - d / f m r m / d - L -)]. See CHARTERHOUSE by Cooper.

CHATHAM. See SEYMOUR.

CHAUTAUQUA [7 7 7 7 4, with Refrain (6: d - d d - L / S - #F S - -) ; William F. Sherwin, 1877]. From the place, Chautauqua, New York, where it was written. *Chautauqua* is an Indian name, variously interpreted to mean: "a foggy place," "place where a child was washed away," "place of easy death," "bag tied in the middle," "where the fish was taken out." Variety enough to satisfy almost any taste!

Also called EVENING PRAISE, because it is the setting for the evening hymn beginning, "Day is dying in the west."

CHEADLE. See AUSTRIAN HYMN.

CHENIES [7 6 7 6 D (4: S / S m m r / d - S) ; Timothy R. Matthews, 1855]. The composer was for a time tutor in the family of the Reverend Lord Wriothesley Russell, canon of Wind-

sor and rector of Chenies; hence the name.

CHERTSEY. See EISENACH.

CHESHIRE TUNE [C. M. (4: L / L T d d / T T L) ; from Thomas Este's Psalter, 1592]. Formerly spelled "Chesshire," it is now generally known as CHESHIRE. This is one of the three names given tunes in the 1592 *Psalter* of Thomas Este. It was in this book that hymn tunes were first given names. The two others were GLASSENBURIE TUNE and KENTISH TUNE.

Also called GLASSENBURIE, KENTISH.

CHESTER [8 7 8 7 (4: S S S LT / d T T L) ; William S. Chester, 1897]. Written as a setting for "Jesus calls us, o'er the tumult," it was first called WILLS after the first president of the Brotherhood of St. Andrew in New York City, but later was given the name of its composer.

CHESTERFIELD [C. M. (3: S d m / s - f / m f r / d -) ; Thomas Haweis, 1792]. After Lord Chesterfield, statesman and author, who frequently visited Selina, Countess of Huntingdon, while the composer was chaplain to her. It was originally set to Haweis' "O Thou from whom all goodness flows."

Also called ADWINKLE, MT. CALVARY, HAWEIS, MARINERS, RICHMOND, SPA FIELDS CHAPEL. There is a slight difference in the last line between CHESTERFIELD and RICHMOND (Haweis), the former being an adaptation of Haweis' tune by Samuel Webbe the Younger. Some books use both tunes, but the alternative name is usually given when but one (either) is used. See RICHMOND by Everett, as well as RICHMOND by Haweis.

CHILDHOOD [8 8 8 6 (4: dm / s. l sf mr / d d d) ; from *A Students' Hymnal,* 1923]. From the sentiment of the hymn beginning, "It fell upon a summer's day"; its character seemingly calls for this title.

CHRIST CHURCH. See ST. PETER.

CHRIST IS MY LIFE. See VULPIUS.

CHRISTI MUTTER [8 8 7 (3: s - s / 1 - s / f - m / s - - / m - -); from Corner's *Gesangbuch*, 1625]. *Christi Mutter:* "Mother of Christ." From the German translation of the first words of the Latin hymn, beginning, *"Christi mutter stund vor schmergen."* Also called CORNER.

CHRISTMAS [C. M., with Repeat (4: m.f / s d t l / s d.r m̃); arr. from George F. Handel, 1815]. From the sentiment of the hymn with which it is generally used, "While shepherds watched their flocks by night" by Nahum Tate. The melody comes from Handel's opera *Siroe*, first performed in 1728. For many years this **tune was a great** favorite in Scottish churches. Other tunes of lesser merit also have the name CHRISTMAS. The word "Christmas" is derived from the Middle Lower German, *Kerstesmisse*, "Christ's Mass" or Holy Day. The festival of the Christian church which is observed annually, properly begins with Christmas Eve, December 24, and continues through Epiphany, January 6, the whole period being known as Christmastide. It is more particularly observed on December 25, Christmas Day. Also called HARLEIGH, LUNENBURG, SAXONY.

CHRISTMAS HYMN. See YORKSHIRE.

CHRISTMAS SONG [6 6 6 6 12 12 (3: SL / S d L / T -); Karl P. Harrington, 1904]. Named from the sentiment of the hymn beginning, "There's a song in the air," one of the most popular Christmas songs in America.

CHRISTUS DER IST. See VULPIUS.

CHRISTUS REX [8 8 8 8 8 8 (4: d - m s / d. t l s / l l s -); David McK. Williams, 1941]. A setting for George K.

A. Bell's hymn beginning, "Christ is the King!"

CHURCH MILITANT. See ST. GERTRUDE.

CITY OF LIGHT [7 6 7 6 7 4 (4: S / M S d r / m - m); Arthur V. Coster, 1909]. The last line of the first stanza of the hymn for cities, "King of the City Splendid" by George F. Coster, the father of the composer, is "Cities of Light." The whole hymn, for which this tune was written, is a plea for cities to be motivated by Christian principles.

CIVES COELI. See ALLELUIA PERENNE by Selby.

CIVITAS DEI. See MATERNA.

CLAIRVAUX [C. M. (3: m r d / s - m / f. m r / m -); Herman A. Polack, 1912]. The composer has said he named his tune for Bernard of Clairvaux, author of *Jesu, dulcis memoria*, familiarly known in Caswall's translation, "Jesus, the very thought of Thee."

CLAUDIUS. See WIR PFLÜGEN.

CLEANSING FOUNTAIN [C. M. D., with Repeat (4: dm / s.l s d / d.l s); arr. from Lowell Mason, early 19th century]. Early known as a "Western melody," the reason for its selection as the tune's name is obvious, as the tune was written for William Cowper's:

There is a fountain filled with blood
  Drawn from Immanuel's veins;
And sinners, plunged beneath that flood,
  Lose all their guilty stains.

CLÔD. See FFIGYSBREN.

COELITIS PLAUDANT [11 11 11 5 (4: d - s l / s. f m); Rouen Church melody, 17the century]. *Coelitis:* literally, "those who dwell in heaven"; *plaudant:* also literally, "applaud." *Coelitis* is an alternative spelling for *caelitis*, the latter being the classical form. The source of the tune is unknown; undoubtedly the name given it comes from the sentiment of the hymn with which it is used, "Honor and glory, power and salvation." The name may be translated, "the inhabitants of heaven applauding," or, more poetically, "angels praising."

COLCHESTER [C. M. (3: *d* / *d*. t l / s - f / m. r d / s -) ; William Tans'ur, 1770]. CROFT'S 148TH (6 6 6 6 8 8) and HUDDERSFIELD (S. M.) are also called COLCHESTER. HUDDERSFIELD, also known as DURHAM HAMPTON, comes from Aaron Williams' *Psalmody*, and is probably by Williams, although sometimes credited to Henry Purcell (1685). Colchester, England, on the river Colne, a municipal borough in Essex, is the ancient Roman town, Camulodunum, founded by Claudius as a municipality for discharged soldiers. COLCHESTER seems to have been in favor as a name for a hymn tune among English composers for many generations of them, but why is a question. Constantine the Great is traditionally said to have been born in Colchester. —From Lewis.

———— [8 8 8 8 8 8 (4: m / s d f r / d T d). Samuel S. Wesley, 1872]. See COLCHESTER by Tans'ur.

———— [6 6 6 6 8 8 (4: s / *d* t *d* s / l - -)]. See CROFT by Croft and COLCHESTER by Tans'ur.

COLESHILL. See WINDSOR.

COLUMBIA. See OLD 113TH.

COMBE MARTIN [S. M. (4: m - / r s dT d / T -) ; Basil Harwood, 1908]. Combe Martin is a "long village" on Bristol Channel, England. "Combe Martin derives its name from its location in a deep valley, *combe*, and from its proprietor, Martin, at the time of the Conquest." —From Lewis.

COMFORT. See ANTIOCH.

COMMUNION [L. M. (3: d / m f r / d - m / s - l / s -)]. See ROCKINGHAM by Miller.

———— [8 7 8 7 8 7 (4: m mr d d / r r mr d)]. See GREENVILLE.

CONDOLENCE. See PLEYEL'S HYMN.

CONFLICT. See LABAN.

CONQUEROR. See VICTORY.

CONQUEST [8 6 8 6 8 8 (3: s *d* l / s - m / d - r / m - -) ; Donald S. Barrows. 1941]. From the sentiment of William C. Bryant's text beginning, "O North, with all thy vales of green!"

CONSECRATION [8 8 8 8 6 (free: d / d - r / f m r d / r - -) ; Anne J. Morse, 1941]. Because written for George Matheson's "O Love that wilt not let me go."

———— [L. M. D. (3: d / m - f / s - s / l - t / *d* -)]. See SWEET HOUR.

———— [7 7 7 7 7 (4: d d dS dm / s f m -)]. See HENDON.

CONSENT. See ST. NICHOLAS.

CONSOLATION [11 10 11 10 (4: s - m d / l. s s -) ; arr. from Samuel Webbe, 1792]. From the thought expressed in Thomas Moore's poem beginning, "Come, ye disconsolate," with which it is commonly used. Also called ALMA, ALMA REDEMPTORIS, CONSOLATOR, CONSOLER, OLIVIA. ALMA and ALMA REDEMPTORIS: because first used with the Latin hymn beginning, *Alma redemptoris.* Variants on ALMA REDEMPTORIS are called AUGSBURG, COME, YE DISCONSOLATE, CONSOLATOR, and CONSOLER.

———— [11 10 11 10 (4: m - r. d / s f -) ; arr. from Felix Mendelssohn-Bartholdy, 1833]. The tune is from one of Mendelssohn's "Songs Without Words." The name, given by Mendelssohn, was doubtless chosen because of the character of the melody. This is a common name; other composers using it are W. B. Bradbury, L. M. Lindeman, and J. H. Maunder. Also called AUGSBURG, EPIPHANY HYMN, FELIX, REYNOLDS. EPIPHANY HYMN: when used with "Brightest and best of the sons of the morning," Reginald Heber's deservedly popular Epiphany hymn. FELIX: the given name of the composer. AUGSBURG: It is strange that this same name should have been given to Webbe's CONSOLATION. Even though the two are in the same meter, they are entirely different in character.

———— [L. M. D. (3: d / m - f / s - s / l - t / d -)]. See SWEET HOUR.

CONSOLATOR. See CONSOLATION by Webbe.

CONSOLER. See CONSOLATION by Webbe.

CONSTANCY. See AUTUMN.

CONTRAST [L. M. D. (6: d - - / d S d m d m / s - -); early American melody]. From the theme of the hymn beginning, "How tedious and tasteless the hours," by John Newton. Also called DE FLEURY, GREENFIELD, GREEN FIELDS, NEWTON. DE FLEURY: because the tune has been attributed to Maria de Fleury. GREENFIELD and GREEN FIELDS: because this tune was undoubtedly taken from the melody of a secular song, "Farewell, ye Green Fields and Sweet Groves." NEWTON: from the author of the hymn to which it is commonly sung.

CONVENTION. See FOUNDATION.

CONVERSE [8 7 8 7 D (4: s. s ls md / d - L -); Charles C. Converse, 1870]. From its composer.

Also called ERIE, FRIEND, WHAT A FRIEND. Erie was the home of Converse. The first known inhabitants of the region in northwest Pennsylvania, where the city of Erie is located, were Indians of the Eriez Nation, from which both Lake Erie and the city received their names. FRIEND and WHAT A FRIEND: because written for "What a Friend we have in Jesus."

COPELAND [L. M. (4: S / d r m. m / s f m); Karl P. Harrington, 1905]. For Benjamin Copeland, author of "Christ's life our code," for which it was written.

CORINTH [8 7 8 7 8 7 (4: d r m f / s f m r)]. See TANTUM ERGO.

———— [8 7 8 7 8 7 D (4: d d d d / r m f m)]. See ORIEL.

CORMAC [Irr. (4: SS / d md r T / d. T S); Irish traditional melody]. *Cor-mac:* "son of a chariot." The name first given to a prince of Leinster (Ireland), it is said, who happened to be born in a chariot while his mother was making a journey This description of Cormac is from the *Book of Ballymote,* written around the end of the fourteenth century:

Beautiful was the appearance of Cormac. Flowing and slightly curling was his golden hair. And buckler, with stars and animals of gold and fastenings of silver upon him. A crimson cloak in wide descending folds around him, fastened at his neck with precious stones. A rich torque of gold around his neck. A white shirt with a full collar and intertwined with red gold thread upon him. A girdle of gold inlaid with precious stones around him. Two wonderful shoes of gold with golden loops upon his feet. Two spears with golden sockets in his hands with many rivets of red bronze. And he was himself besides symmetrical and beautiful of form without blemish or reproach.

CORNER. See CHRISTI MUTTER.

CORONAE [8 7 8 7 4 7 (4: m m s s / d d m m); William H. Monk, 1871]. Set to Thomas Kelly's "Look, ye saints, the sight is glorious," the fifth line of each stanza being, "Crown Him! Crown Him!"

CORONATION [C. M., with Repeat (4: S / d d m m / r d r); Oliver Holden, 1793]. From the theme, "Crown Him Lord of all," of the hymn beginning, "All hail the power of Jesus' name," for which it was written. Other tunes of lesser merit have the same name.

CORTON. See ORIENTIS PARTIBUS.

COVERT. See ST. BERNARD.

CORWIN [8 6 8 6 6 D (4: S / d S m d / s. m d); J. W. Lerman, *ca.* 1908]. "Corwin" doubless derived from the Latin *corbin,* raven. The raven, anciently the badge of a warrior, was not considered a bird of ill repute; quite the contrary. "Corwin" is probably the name of some person, and there probably should be no significance in the above sense attached to its selection as a tune name, but when used with Samuel Longfellow's hymn beginning:

God's trumpet wakes the slumbering world,
Now each man to his post!

it seems quite a fitting title.

COURAGE, BROTHER [8 7 8 7 D, with Repeat (4: S S d d / dT LT d S); Arthur S. Sullivan, 1872]. From the first words of Norman Macleod's hymn beginning, "Courage, brother, do not stumble."
Also called BARONY.

COVENANT [6 6 8 4 D (4: S / d m r d / s - -); John Stainer, 1889]. From the sentiment of Thomas Oliver's great hymn beginning, "The God of Abraham praise," for which it was written.

COWPER [C. M. (3: mf / sl s m / dl s); Lowell Mason, early 19th century]. Written for William Cowper's hymn beginning, "There is a fountain filled with blood."

CRAMER. See GREENVILLE.

CRANHAM [Irr. (4: m. f s m / r - d -); Gustav Holst, 1906]. Probably from Cranham Woods, birthplace of the composer, one of the beauty spots near Cheltenham, England.

CRASSELIUS. See WINCHESTER, NEW.

CREATION [L. M. D. (4: S / d - - d / r - - r / m d L r / d - T); arr. from Francis J. Haydn, 1798]. Named after the oratorio by Francis J. Haydn from which it is taken; an adaptation of the first part of the famous chorus, "The heavens are telling." It is appropriately named to go with Joseph Addison's hymn beginning, "The spacious firmament on high."

Also called NEW CREATION.
—— [6 6 4 6 6 6 4 (3: d d r / T. d r)]. See AMERICA.

CRETE. See ST. ANDREW OF CRETE.

CROFT [6 6 6 6 8 8 (4: s / d t d s / l - -); William Croft]. This is called both CROFT'S 136TH and CROFT'S 148TH. Probably the first is correct, as it comes from Playford's *The Divine Companion: or David's Harp New Tun'd* (1709), where it is the setting for Psalm 136.
See COLCHESTER by Tans'ur.

CROFT'S 136TH. See CROFT.

CROFT'S 148TH. See COLCHESTER by Tans'ur, and CROFT.

CROSS AND CROWN. See MAITLAND.

CROSS OF JESUS [8 7 8 7 (4: m d S S / S d d T); John Stainer, 1887]. From the first words of the chorale under this title used in the composer's *Crucifixion*, a cantata for Good Friday.

CROSSING THE BAR [Irr. (4: m mm s. s / d - -); Joseph Barnby, 1892]. The name of Lord Tennyson's poem for which this was written.

CRUCIFER. See BETHANY.

CRUCIFIXION [C. M. (3: S / m - m / s - d / m - r / d -)]. See SPOHR.
—— [L. M. (4: L / ♯S L T d / rd TL ♯S -)]. See CANTERBURY.

CRUSADER [C. M. D. (4: S / d. S LT dr / m - -); Samuel B. Whitney, 1889]. Because written for Reginald Heber's hymn beginning, "The Son of God goes forth to war."

CRUSADERS' HYMN [5 6 8 5 5 8 (4: d - d d / r T d -); from *Schlesische Volkslieder*, 1842]. CRUSADERS' HYMN because it was believed to have been sung by the Crusaders. See *Our Hymnody* for a complete statement concerning this tune.
Also called ASCALON, ST. ELIZABETH. ST. ELIZABETH: because in 1862 Franz Liszt wrote a cantata entitled *The Legend of St. Elizabeth,* in which he used this tune. St. Elizabeth was the mother of John the Baptist.

CRUX CHRISTI. See ANGEL'S STORY.

CULFORD [7 7 7 7 D (4: m m s s / d d s -) ; Edward J. Hopkins, 1867]. There is a parish in Suffolk County, England, by that name. Culford Hall, situated in a spacious park, was the birthplace of Lord Cornwallis, of American Revolutionary War fame.

CUTHBERT. See ST. CUTHBERT.

CUTLER. See ALL SAINTS, NEW, by Cutler.

CWMDU [8 3 3 6 (4: m r d. d / f m m r) ; David C. Evans, 1927]. Pronounced "koom-dü'." *Cwm*, "valley"; *dü*, "black"; the "black vale." It is the name of a township in the county of Glamorgan, South Wales.

CWM RHONDDA [8 7 8 7 8 7 (4: S L S. d / dT dr m r) ; John Hughes, 1905]. Pronounced "koom rrhawn'-tha" (*th* as in *this*.). Originally called RHONDDA; the *Cwm* was added to distinguish it from another tune of the same name. *Cwm* means "valley"; Rhondda is the name of a river in Wales. The valley of the Rhondda is the heart of the coal-mining industry in that part of the country.

D

DALEHURST [C. M. (4: m / r d f m / m. r d) ; Arthur Cottman, 1874]. From the name of a homestead or estate.

DAN. See DENNIS.

DANE. See SARDIS.

DARMSTADT. See SEELENBRÄUTIGAM.

DARWALL [6 6 6 6 8 8 (4: d / m d s m / d - -) ; John Darwall]. Named for its composer. A new organ was opened in Walsall Parish Church (England) during the week of Whitsunday, 1773; at the close of the service this tune by the new vicar, John Darwall, was sung.
Also called DARWELL, DARWALL'S 148TH, ZION. DARWELL: Darwall's name misspelled. DARWALL'S 148TH: because originally used with Psalm 148.

DARWALL'S 148TH. See DARWALL.

DARWELL. See DARWALL.

DAVID [L. M. D. (3: d / m r d / s f m / r -) ; arr. from George F. Handel, *ca.* 1784]. This has been arranged by someone unknown, probably Samuel Arnold (English), from an anthem, "Lord, remember David," which had been in turn adapted from the air *Rendi il sereno al ciglio*, from Handel's opera *Sosarme*. THATCHER is the name by which this tune is known in America.

——— [6 5 6 5 D (4: m S m r / d - L -) ; Thomas Morley, *ca.* 1865].

DAVID'S HARP [8 8 8 8 8 8 (4: m rd T d / r mf m) ; Robert King]. Set to Myles Smith's metrical version of Psalm 101 in *The Divine Companion, or, David's Harp New Tun'd* (1709). Name given by a later editor.

——— [L. M. (3: m / s - dT / d - l / r - s / m - -) ; John Daniel, 1842]. From the sentiment of the hymn with which it was used at the time it was named.
Also called BROADMEAD. The composer is supposed to have had "some connection" with Broadmead, a district in Bristol, England.

DAWN [6 4 6 4 6 6 6 4 (3: m r d / r. m r / d L S / L - -) ; T. H. Ingham, 1931]. Suggested by the last line, "Day has begun," of John Struther's text for which it was written.

DAY. See ST. FLAVIAN.

DAY BY DAY. See CARTER.

DAY OF REST [7 6 7 6 D (4: d / m s l s⁜f / s - m) ; James W. Elliott, 1874]. Because written for Christopher Wordsworth's "O day of rest and gladness."

DEDHAM. See PETITION.

DEDICATION [7 5 7 5 D (4: s m f s / l. l l -) ; George A. Macfarren, 1889]. Written for Laurence Tuttiett's New Year's hymn:

> Father, let me dedicate
> All this year to Thee.

——— [S. M. (3: d / d - m / r d T / d -)]. See St. Edmund.

DEEPER LIFE [11 10 11 10 (4: m - m f / s - s - / l t d r / d - t -) ; Lindsay B. Longacre, 1928]. Katharine Lee Bates entitled one of her poems, beginning, "Dear God, our Father, at Thy knee confessing," *For Deeper Life.* This was the name its composer gave his tune written especially for Miss Bates's lines. When asked permission to shorten the tune name to DEEPER LIFE, Dr. Longacre gave his consent.

DEERFIELD. See AZMON.

DEERHURST [8 7 8 7 D (4: m s m d / T d r m) ; James Langran]. Originally set to "Lord, dismiss us with Thy blessing." From an article about the composer in *Musical Times,* February 1, 1907:

His tunes may be found in the *Mitre Hymnal,* socalled from the mitre embossed on the front cover. 6 tunes: Mt. Olive, Miriam, Deerhurst, Evensong (now St. Agnes), and Highnam. . . . "They were named," he says, "by Mr. Hall, then my vicar and proprietor of the book. . . . The latter's father, same name, had issued (1836) word edition. He had been curate at Hasfeld, Gloucestershire, (from 1853 to 1860) and this accounts for Deerhurst and Highnam, while Miriam was named after one of his sisters." Deerhurst, by the way, is near Tewksbury and its Priory Church is one of the oldest ecclesiastical buildings of any importance that yet remains in England.

Also called HIGHNAM, HOLY VOICES, MIRIAM, MT. OLIVE, ST. AGNES. HOLY VOICES: because set to Christopher Wordsworth's hymn beginning, "Hark! the sound of Holy Voices."

DE FLEURY. See CONTRAST.

DEIRDRE [C. M. (3: d.L / d- S- L.r / d- d-) ; Irish traditional melody]. This is an old Irish air arranged by Sir Charles Stanford to be sung to the "Hymn of St. Bernard," *Jesu, dulcis memoria,* but commonly used as a setting to the last part of the

Lorica, or "St. Patrick's Breastplate." (See St. Patrick.) *Deirdre* (dar-dre) is the name of the heroine of an Irish story told by Yeats and others.

DELIGHT. See BELOVED.

DENNIS [S. M. (3: m / m d m / r T r / d -) ; arr. from Hans G. Nägeli, 1845]. A village in Massachusetts. First used with the hymn beginning, "How gentle God's commands," with which it has long been definitely associated.

Also called DAN, PRAYER, RIPON.

DEPAUW [L. M. (4: s - m. r / d - - d / m - s - / d - - -) ; Robert G. McCutchan, 1928]. After DePauw University, Greencastle, Indiana, where I was dean of its School of Music when I wrote the tune.

DERBY [12 11 12 11 (3: d / d s l / l s f / m r d / s -)]. See MONTGOMERY.

——— [Irr. (3: s / d s l / s s f / m r d / s s)]. See MAGDALEN.

DERRY. See ST. NICHOLAS.

DERWENT. See MAGDALEN.

DESSAU (LIEBSTER JESU) [7 8 7 8 8 8 (4: m rd r s / m d r -) ; Johann R. Ahle, 1664]. The name DESSAU was given to distinguish this tune from LIEBSTER JESU, WIR SIND HIER (which see), of which it is another form. Dessau is a town about seventy miles southwest of Berlin, Germany. Dessau's importance began late in the sixteenth century as a consequence of the Lutheran movement and of the religious emancipation of the Jews.

Also called NUREMBERG, because of some association with the city of that name.

DEVA [6 5 6 5 D, with Refrain (4: m r m f / s - s -) ; Edward J. Hopkins, 1887]. H. J. Staples, English organist, in an article in *The Choir,* says: "The late E. J. Hopkins when editing the 1887 Congregational Book evidently had a pleasant holiday down in Devon, for he has bequeathed us 'Hortland,' 'Isca,' 'Bideford,' and 'Deva.'" Hortland and Bideford are in Devonshire, and Exeter, the present county town of Devonshire, was the Roman-British county town of *Isca-Damnoniorum.* But numerous gazetteers consulted give no Deva in that county. The *Encyclopaedia Britannica,* mentioning but one Deva, that being the ancient name of Chester, England, says it was for more than two centuries the station of the twentieth Roman Legion.

DEVONSHIRE [7 6 7 6 (3: d / mm m. m / mr d -) ; Old English melody]. From "The Unquiet Grave," a North Devonshire folk song.

———— [L. M. (4: s / m T d l / s f m)]. See WILTON.

DIADEM [C. M., with Repeats (3: S / d - r / mf s d / r d T / d -) ; James Ellor, 1838]. From the line "Bring forth the royal diadem," in the hymn beginning, "All hail the power of Jesus' name."

DIADEMA [11 10 11 6 (4: m - s d / t - - l / s m d r / r - m -); Joseph Barnby, 1883]. Named for the last line of the last stanza, "Our crown beyond the cross," of "Still will we trust," for which it was written. In *Sursum Corda* (1898) it was named BURLEIGH. This was the book in which a very great many of the familiar names by which tunes had become known were changed, apparently for no good reason. So many changes were made that the editors needed to add an unusual index, "Variations in Tune Names." In this "variations" index this tune is called LESTER.

DIADEMATA [S. M. D. (4: d dd m m / l - -) ; George J. Elvey, 1868]. The word, meaning "crowns," was selected because the tune was written for the hymn beginning, "Crown Him with many crowns."

DIES IRAE [8 8 8 (free: f m f r m d r r -) ; Old Latin;

plain-song sequence of the 13th century]. This is the name given by many composers to their settings of the old sequence which begins with these words; and all have used it for the same reason.

DIJON [8 7 8 7 (4: d - - d / d d T d / m - r -) ; Old German melody]. Dijon, a town of prominence in eastern France which was the Roman *divis* or *Divonense Castrum,* has had a long and honorable history. During the thirteenth century it was one of the great intellectual centers of France. Also called GERMAN EVENING HYMN.

DILIGENCE. See WORK SONG.

DIRIGE. See BURLEIGH by Barnby.

DISCIPLE. See ELLESDIE.

DISMISSAL. See SICILIAN MARINERS.

DIX [7 7 7 7 7 7 (4: d Td r d / f f m -) ; Conrad Kocher, 1838]. For William C. Dix, the author of the first English hymn with which it was used, beginning, "As with gladness men of old."
Also called BETHLEHEM, ORISONS. BETHLEHEM: because of its association with the hymn mentioned above.

DOANE. See WALTHAM.

DOLCE DOMUM. See DULCE DOMUM.

DOLOMITE CHANT [6 6 6 6 (2: m / m m / f m / r); Old Austrian melody]. This melody acquired its title as a result of its popularity in the Dolomites, a district in the South Tyrolese Alps formed of dolomite, a magnesian limestone. It is a district quite well known to tourists.

DOMINICA [S. M. (4: S SS d r / m - -) ; Herbert S. Oakeley, 1875]. Because written for John Ellerton's Sunday hymn beginning, "This is the day of light." Dominica, one of the Lesser Antilles, a British possession, is from the Spanish *Domingo,* "Sunday." Columbus, on his second voyage, named the island thus because he sighted it on a Sunday.

DOMINUS REGIT ME [8 7 8 7 (4: m /

s f m m / r r d); John B. Dykes, 1868]. This Latin title of Psalm 23, "The Lord rules me," is an instance of Dr. Dykes's happy use of Latin titles for his hymn tunes. He wrote this for Henry W. Baker's beautiful rendering of the beloved psalm which begins, "The King of Love my Shepherd is."
Also called CECILIA.

DORCHESTER. See YORKSHIRE.

DORRANCE. See below.

DORRNANCE [8 7 8 7 (3: mm / m d rr / m m); Isaac B. Woodbury, 1845]. Probably this comes from Dorrance Township, Luzerne County, Pennsylvania. Inasmuch as there are other town names in that vicinity which Woodbury used, it may be assumed that this is simply a misspelling of Dorrance. Dorrance Township was named after early German settlers.

DORT [6 6 4 6 6 6 4 (3: d m d / s. l s); Lowell Mason, 1832]. Probably after Dort, or Dordrecht, town and riverport in southwest Netherlands, although Henry L. Mason says it is not an associative name. Pierre van Paassen refers to Dort in his *Days of Our Years,* saying that Dort, as the citadel of Calvinism, was referred to in the same manner as was Rome.

The Provincial Synod of Dort (1574) directed all ministers to use the same forms of public prayer. These were, however, never employed exclusively, and gradually fell into disuse, while the Forms for the administration of Baptism and the Lord's Supper and those for the ordination of Elders and Deacons have continued to be used to the present time.—From the Introductory Note to *The Liturgy of the Reformed Church in America.*

DOVEDALE. See ST. HUGH, OLD ENGLISH.

DOWN AMPNEY [6 6 11 D (4: d - r m / s - 1 - / s - - -); Ralph Vaughan Williams, 1906]. From the birthplace, in the county of Gloucester, England, of the composer.

DRESDEN [L. M. (3: d T d / S - d / T - d / r - -)]. See MENDON.

——— [7 6 7 6 D, with Refrain (4: S / d d S S / m - d)]. See WIR PFLÜGEN.

DRUMCLOG. See MARTYRDOM.

DUANE SRTEET [L. M. D. (4: S / d m m d / r f f); George Coles, 1835]. After Duane Street Church, New York City, where, in 1839, during the centennial celebration of the establishing of that church, the Reverend George C. Coles preached his famous sermon on "The History and Character of Methodism."

DUBLIN [C. M. (3: d / d - S / d r m / f m r / m -)]. See IRISH.

——— [8 7 8 7 D (3: dr m r / m - d / d - f / mr d -)]. See PURCELL.

DUBLIN TUNE. See PURCELL.

DUKE STREET [L. M. (4: d - m f / s - l t / d - t l / s - - -); John Hatton]. The composer lived in a house on Duke Street, in St. Helen's, Windle, Lancaster, England, which, along with his own name, accounts for four of these names.
Also called ADDISON'S 19TH PSALM, HATTON, HORITON, NEWRY, ST. HELEN'S, WINDLE. ADDISON'S 19TH PSALM was the first name given it when it appeared anonymously in 1793.

DULCE CARMEN. See ORIEL.

DULCE DOMUM [Irr. (4: s ss s s / s - - -); Robert S. Ambrose, *ca.* 1903]. *Dulce domum:* Latin for "sweet home." The tune was written for Phoebe Cary's poem beginning, "Nearer home," which emphasizes the thought that she is "nearer home today" than ever before. There is a holiday song of Winchester School (England) by the title *"Dulce Domum."* It is said to have been written by a boy of St. Mary's College, Winchester, who during the Whitsuntide holidays was confined for misconduct and, as legend has it, "tied to a pillar." On the evening preceding this holiday "the master, scholars, and choristers of the above college walk in procession around the 'pillar' chanting the six stanzas of the song." In the March, 1796, *Gentlemen's Magazine*, there appeared a translation of the song, signed "J. R." (for John Reading, who wrote it). The chorus of the song is:

> *Domum, domum, dulce domum!*
> *Domum, domum, dulce domum!*
> *Dulce, dulce, dulce domum;*
> *Dulce domum resonemus!*

These lines, translated, are:

> Home, home, joyous home!
> Home, home, joyous home!
> Joyous, joyous, joyous home;
> Hurrah for joyous home!

Also called AMBROSE, for the composer; and DOLCE DOMUM, simply a misspelling of the first word, probably by confusion with the Italian musical term.

DULCIMER. See BELOVED.

DULCINA [8 7 8 7 (4: m. f / s s f m / r d) ; Old English melody]. "Dulcina" is the folk spelling of "Dulcinea," a ladylove. Name taken from the first line of the old song "As at noon Dulcina rested."

DUMFERLING. See DUNFERMLINE.

DUNDEE [C. M. (4: d / m f s d / r m f) ; from *The Scottish Psalter*, 1615]. From the *National Psalmist* (1849) : "The name of this tune in the old books is French. The Dundee of Scotland is the same as Windsor, or Coleshill in most English and American books of psalmody."

Doubtless named for the town of Dundee, which bore such a prominent part in propagating the doctrines of the Reformation that it was styled "the Scottish Geneva." The town's name was likely derived from the Gaelic *Dun Taw*, "the fort of the

Tay," because of its location near the mouth of the Firth of Tay. David, Earl of Huntingdon, younger bother of William the Lion, designated it as "Dunde" in a deed of gift, *circa* 1200, its first authentic mention. It has been known variously as Donde, Dondie, Dondei, Dunde, Dundee. Dundee is now a commercial city having little attraction for visitors. Also called DUNDY, FRENCH, NORWICH. Seems to have been known first as FRENCH TUNE. Ravenscroft renamed it DUNDY in his *Whole Book of Psalms* (1621), where in his Index it is classed as a "Scottish Tune." (See p. 16.)

DUNFERMLINE [C. M. (4: d / d r m f / s s m) ; from *The Scottish Psalter*, 1615]. Dunfermline, Fifeshire, Scotland, for which the tune is named, has been a royal burgh since early in the twelfth century. The word is Gaelic and means "the town, or fort, of the crooked line." "Dumferling" is an old spelling. The burgh was for some time the capital of Scotland, and few places can vie with it in historical interest. Coal was mined at Dunfermline as early as 1291, the earliest record in Scotland. The tune was listed in Ravenscroft's book as a "Scottish Tune" and was given the name DUMFERLING. It was said to have been composed by one Dean John Angus, who had some connection with the "Abbacie of Dunfermling" at the time of the Reformation. It was at this place that Charles II signed the National League and Covenant. Dunfermline was the early home of Andrew Carnegie, who gave the place bonds worth more than $2,500,000 per year for the support of his many benefactions.

Also called SOUTHAM. Ravenscroft says it is "wrongly" called by this name but does not comment further.

DUNDY. See DUNDEE.

DUNSTAN. See ST. DUNSTAN'S.

DURHAM [C. M. (4: d - / s m l s / m d r -) ; from Ravenscroft's *Psalter,* 1621]. One of the tunes "styled northern tunes" by Ravenscroft. Durham, in the English shire of that name, is an ancient city, the seat of the famous Cathedral. The Saxons called it *Dunholme (dun,* "hill"; *holme,* "a river island")* ; the Normans made it *Duresme,* and it is from the Norman name that the present "Durham" more immediately derived.

The earliest account of this place is in 995, when the monks of Lindisfarne, afterwards called Holy Island, who had removed to Chester-le-Street, and afterwards to Ripon, for sanctuary from the violence of Danish aggression, were returning to their church at Chester-le-Street, after an absence of four months, with the disinterred body of St. Cuthbert, which had been buried at Lindisfarne, in 687. According to the superstitious legend, on their arrival at the spot where Durham now stands, a miraculous interposition rendered the carriage which conveyed the body and other relics, immovable; and this incident they construed into a divine prohibition against the return of the saint's remains to their former resting place. They likewise interpreted some other circumstances into an intimation that *Dunholme* was destined to receive the sacred relics; and there are still some emblematic devices . . . designed to commemorate this occurrence. They forthwith proceeded to construct a sort of ark, or tabernacle, or wicker-work, wherein they deposited the saint's body; they subsequently erected a more appropriate edifice, called the White Church, and three years after their arrival, a stone church was built by Bishop Aldun, and dedicated to St. Cuthbert, whose remains were removed and enshrined in it. Determined on permanent residence, the strangers cleared away the trees which skirted the hill, and began to build substantial houses; and thus arose the Saxon town of *Dunholme,* about the commencement of the eleventh century, the increase of which, both in buildings and population, was so rapid, that in 1040, being then partially fortified, Duncan of Scotland besieged it, but his forces were totally vanquished, and the heads of the Scottish leaders, who were slain or captured, were fixed on poles around the market-place.—Lewis.

Durham underwent various and extreme vicissitudes for the next half century, during which time St. Cuthbert's bones were transferred again to Landisfarne. It was not until 1093 they were finally brought to the new church which had been erected at Durham. See ST. CUTHBERT.
———— [7 7 7 7 (4: m. f / s d l / s -)]. See INNOCENTS, from *The Parish Choir.*
DURHAM HAMPTON. See COLCHESTER.

E

EASTER ALLELUIA. See LASST UNS ERFREUEN.
EASTER HYMN [7 7 7 7, with Alleluias (4: d m s d / f l l s); from *Lyra Davidica,* 1708]. Also called ANGLIA, EASTER MORN, MORGAN, SALISBURY, THE RESURRECTION, WORGAN, EASTER HYMN, EASTER MORN, and THE RESURRECTION: because of its use with the Easter hymns beginning, "Jesus Christ is risen today," and "Christ the Lord is risen today." Perhaps THE RESURRECTION is the most appropriate of the three. SALISBURY is the name John Wesley gave it when he used it in his *Foundery Tune Book,* possibly because of his visits to Salisbury to see his mother. WORGAN: because, among others, Dr. J. Worgan has been credited with its writing. MORGAN is probably "Worgan" misspelled.
EASTER MORN. See EASTER HYMN.
EBELING [8 3 3 6 D (free: d - r / m - - r m s / l - s -) ; from Johann G. Ebeling, 1666]. From the composer from whose work it was taken. It was used as a setting for the German hymn beginning, *"Warum sellt ich*

64

mich denn graemen?" by which first line the tune is sometimes listed. Also called BONN.

EBENEZER. See TON-Y-BOTEL.

EDNA. See HAYDN.

EDYFIELD. See SAVANNAH.

EIN' FESTE BURG [8 7 8 7 6 6 6 6 7 (4: *d* / *d d* sl t / *dt* l s) ; Martin Luther, 1529 (?)]. From the first words of Luther's famous hymn. There has been no general acceptance of any one of the scores of translations made of the first line of Luther's hymn, *"Ein' feste Burg ist unser Gott";* by the close of the first decade of this century more than eighty had appeared in over fifty languages. Perhaps the most commonly known one is "A mighty fortress is our God." The first one, which appeared within ten years after the hymn was first published, was made by Miles Coverdale (1488-1568), the first to translate the whole Bible into English. It was "Oure God is a defence and towre." Also called LUTHER, WORMS. LUTHER: for the author and composer. WORMS: because of Luther's close connection with that place.

EISENACH [8 7 8 7 8 8 (free: d / m - m s - s / f m r -.), or (4: dr / m f s s / f m r); Johann H. Schein, 1628]. By omitting the repeat of the first two lines of music, this is sometimes used as a Long Meter tune. One of the few German chorales with a specific name, it first appeared in the second edition of *Cantionale,* or *Gesangbuch Augsburgischer Confession* (Hymnbook for the Brethren Church). The fact that Luther stayed with the Cotta family in Eisenach in 1498 and that the famous castle of the Landgraves of Thuringia (the Wartburg, made famous by Wagner in his *Tannhauser*), where Luther remained hidden after his return from the Diet at Worms, translating the Bible meanwhile, may have something to do with the selection of this name. H. J. Staples, however, says it was called EISENACH because that city was the birthplace of Johann Sebastian Bach, who was very fond of this tune.

Also called CHERTSEY, LEIPSIC, MACHS MIT MIR, SCHEIN. LEIPSIC: perhaps because of Bach's association with that town. MACHS MIT MIR: the first words of the German text for which it was written. SCHEIN: for its composer.

ELIM. See HESPERUS.

ELIZABETH. See STOCKTON.

ELLACOMBE [7 6 7 6 D (4: s / *d* tls *d* / m f s) ; from *Gesangbuch der Herzogel, Wirtemburgischen Katholischen Hofkapelle,* 1784]. Evidently an English name given by an English editor; a place, or locality, name. "Combe," or "Coom," a popular term in southern and southeastern England, signifies a small coastal feature (though it may be an island), or a side of a "down," treeless chalk uplands. Its etymology is not clear. The Welsh *"cwm,"* in place names (see CWM RHONDDA), means "valley," or "hollow." There is also a French dialect word, *"combe,"* meaning valley. "Combe" often appears as a prefix (Combemartin), or as a suffix (Infracombe). In this case is it "Ellacombe"? There have been many combinations of "Ella" with other words, such as "Ellamay," "Elladine," and others. *Ella* (Anglo-Saxon) is from "elfin," an elf. Elves were supposed to influence or advise persons; hence they were believed to be supernatural beings.

ELLAH [10 10 10 10 (4: m mm r l / s. f m r / m - -) ; Lily Rendle, 1930]. Miss Rendle wrote me in January, 1936:

The title, "Ellah," was given to it entirely without my knowledge. I used the word (invented from my own initials, L. R.) purely as a synonym on the, otherwise, blank envelope containing the hymn-tune for competition and it was copyrighted before I knew anything about it. I think I should have suggested "Eastbourne" for the name of the tune.

Eastbourne, England, is the home of the composer. The competition referred to was a hymn-tune contest conducted by the Hymn Society of New York (now the Hymn Society of America).

ELLERS [10 10 10 10 (4: S - S L / S - d - / d T d r / m - - -) ; Edward J. Hopkins, 1869]. It has been suggested that the name ELLERS was coined from the first part of the name of John Ellerton, the author of the evening hymn beginning, "Saviour, again to Thy dear name we raise," to which it is definitely wedded.

Also called BECK, BENEDICTION, ELLERTON, IRENE. BENEDICTION: because it was written for the benediction hymn above noted. ELLERTON: from the author of the hymn.

ELLERTON. See above.

ELLESDIE [8 7 8 7 D (4: d. d d d / m. r rd d) ; arr. from Mozart, 1831]. ELLESDIE is said to be a "made name" —from the initial letters "L. S. D." of some person unknown.

Also called DISCIPLE, OCEAN, THE CROSS, VIOLET, VONDEVENTER. DISCIPLE: from the sentiment of the hymn, "Jesus, I my cross have taken," by Henry F. Lyte. OCEAN: The first line of the second stanza of Daniel March's hymn beginning, "Hark, the voice of Jesus calling," is, "If you cannot cross the ocean." Some editor of a hymnal issued the latter part of the last century seized on the last word of the line and used it for the tune name. THE CROSS: from the sentiment of Lyte's hymn.

ELLIOTT. See ALMSGIVING.

ELLON [7 6 7 6 D (4: S / d d d d / m. r d) ; George F. Root, ca. 1871].

Possibly a "made name" from the initials "L. N." of some person unknown.

ELTON [8 6 8 8 6 (4: m / m. m ♯r m / s s ♯f ♮f / m. d d r / r - -) ; Frederick C. Maker, 1887]. Elton is a very common English local name. Formerly written *Eald-ton,* it means "ancient town."

Also called PENZANCE, REST, WHITTIER. REST: because used with John G. Whittier's hymn beginning:

Dear Lord and Father of mankind,
Forgive our foolish ways.

(See REST by Maker for comment on tunes with this name.) WHITTIER: the name of the author of the hymn to which it is commonly sung.

—— [7 6 7 6 D; J. E. Henry, date unknown]. See above.

ELY. See ST. CATHERINE.

EMELAR. See MERRIAL.

EMMELAR. See MERRIAL.

EMPEROR'S HYMN. See AUSTRIAN HYMN.

EMULATION. See ALL SAINTS, NEW, by Cutler.

ENERGY. See ST. ETHELWALD.

ENGLAND. See TRINITY.

ENGLAND'S LANE [7 7 7 7 7 7 (4: d mr / d s m d / s -) ; traditional English melody, 1919]. Adapted from the old English song "England's Lane," by Goeffrey Shaw.

ENSIGN. See WALTAM.

ENTREATY. See BELMONT.

EPHESUS. See NEANDER.

EPHRATA. See VENI IMMANUEL.

EPIPHANY HYMN. See CONSOLATION by Webbe.

ERFURT [L. M. (4: d / t l t s / l t d) ; Martin Luther, 1539]. This is a place name given to the tune originally composed for *"Vom Himmel Hoch,"* a well-known German chorale. It is one of the few tunes perhaps as well known by this name as by the first words of Luther's hymn, *"Vom himmel hoch da kom ich her."* Erfurt was the seat of the monastery where Luther lived as a friar.

Also called VOM HIMMEL HOCH.

—— [8 6 8 6 8 8 (4: S / L T d r / m r d) ; Herman A. Ilse, 1910]. See above. Because of its Lutheran associations. The composer was a member of the Committee which compiled *The Lutheran Hymn-Book* (1938), in which the tune appeared. This committee naturally used many names of interest to the Lutherans.

ERIE. See CONVERSE.

ERIN. See ST. COLUMBA.

ERITH. See AUTUMN.

ERNAN [L. M. (4: s mf s *d* / dt lt *d* -) ; Lowell Mason, 1850]. This word appears several times in the Old Testament. See p. 30 for Mason's use of Old Testament names. There was a priest of this name who was an uncle of St. Columba (see KILMARNOCK), but it is doubtful that Mason knew anything about him.

ES IST KEIN TAG. See MEYER.

ETERNAL LIGHT [8 6 8 8 6 (free: d / d - T / L - m f l / #s - -) ; Kenneth E. Runkel, 1941]. Set to Thomas Binney's hymn beginning, "Eternal Light, Eternal Light!"

ETON [C. M. (4: L - L T / d - T - / L L #S -) ; from Este's *Psalter*, 1592, by G. Kirby]. One of the earliest of English Common Meter tunes, it was given the name WINDSOR or EATON by Ravenscroft; see p. 16. In late editions of Este it was called SUFFOLK TUNE and in Scotland, DUNDEE. It should not be confused with other tunes bearing any of these names.

EUCHARIST [L. M. (4: m - m m / s - - s / l s f s / m - -) ; Isaac B. Woodbury, 1856]. First called OLIVET by its composer, the change in name was made to avoid confusing it with Lowell Mason's better-known hymn tune by the same name. The hymn with which this tune is always used, "When I survey the wondrous cross," is one of those quite generally used in Communion services; hence the name of its tune. "Eucharist" refers to the sacrament of the Lord's Supper, yet the original Greek, *eucharistia*, properly signifies "gratitude," derivatively "a givng of thanks": from "the hymns and thanksgivings which accompanied the holy service in the primitive church." Its literal meaning is "thank offering."

After we have exercised our charity, repentance, and faith, the next part of the office (holy communion) is thanksgiving, which is so considerable a part of our present duty, that it hath given name to the whole, and caused it to be called *Eucharist*, or *Sacrifice of Praise.—* Wheatly, *On the Common Prayer.*

EUCHARISTIC HYMN [9 8 9 8 (3: s s f / m - s / f m r / mf s -) ; John S. B. Hodges]. See EUCHARIST. Because it is used with the Communion hymn "Bread of the world, in mercy broken," by Bishop Heber. It was given the name it now bears by the editor of *The Hymnal* of 1869 (Protestant Episcopal), in which it first appeared. In the composer's *Hymn Tunes* (1891), an edition of musical settings for hymns, he gave no names to them, each being designated, after the German custom, by the first few words of the text for which it was written.

Also called PANIS (Latin, meaning "bread, a loaf").

EUDOXIA [6 5 6 5 (4: m m f f / s - m -) ; S. Baring-Gould, 1868]. *Eudoxia,* accurately spelled *Eudocia,* is a Greek word meaning "esteemed," "honored," "of good report." Eudoxia was an Eastern Roman empress, wife of Arcadius, who supported Chrysostom and helped him organize the nightly processions with hymn singing, wax candles, silver crosses, and other trappings of ceremonial pomp at the time of his controversy with the Arians. Her daughter, also named Eudoxia, married the Roman Emperor Maximus and invited Genseric the Vandal into Italy. (See Lampiere's *Classical Dictionary*.) Baring-Gould probably had the former Eudoxia in mind when he named his tune. This is the tune Baring-Gould wrote to be used with his evening hymn beginning, "Now the day is over." A queer name to be given a tune used as a setting for a children's hymn!

EVAN [C. M. (3: S / Sd m r / dL S); William H. Havergal, 1847]. This interesting tune, deservedly popular among Presbyterians generally, was made by Lowell Mason from a longer one by W. H. Havergal. When Mason first used it in his *New Carmina Sacra* (copyright July 18, 1850), he called it EVA. Less than a month later, when he included it in his *Cantica Laudis* (copyright August 10), he gave it the name EVAN, which it now bears. In March, 1870, Mr. Havergal, on a copy of this tune given to a friend in response to a request for his autograph, wrote, in part: "The tune 'Evan' comprises only a part of the original melody. . . . The American arrangement was a sad estrangement. . . . Why it was called 'Evan' I know not. . . . Still I do not approve the tune." In 1872 Mrs. Havergal wrote to a Mr. J. O. Anderson, of Edinburgh, giving her opinion as to the origin of the name EVAN:

In visiting Scotland last year, I for the first time saw the little stream Evan, and *I* have a fancy that Dr. Lowell Mason took the nomenclature from that, as he in the very year in which he first had this piece ("O Thou dread Pow'r") and sent it out to America as a hymn tune, had visited that part of Scotland— Moffatt—where the stream is. I have written to ask the question of him, though when asked by my dear husband he could not remember *why* he had given the name. My reminding him of this stream may recall it to his memory.

Dr. Mason did not reply to Mrs. Havergal's inquiry, as he was ill and died but a few weeks after receiving it. "Mrs. Havergal's surmise, however, hardly coincides with the following facts," says James Love in his *Scottish Church Music:*

1st, That Dr. Mason originally named the tune "Eva"; 2d, That it was first published by him in 1850; 3d, That he did not visit Scotland till 1852, and that in his journal no mention is made of having visited Moffatt; 4th, That the existence of such an insignificant stream is hardly likely to have been known to Dr. Mason.

Also called MONA.

EVANGEL. See BETHLEHEM.

EVANGELIST. [C. M. (3: S / d - T / L - S / f - m / r ·); from Felix Mendelssohn-Bartholdy, 1836]. "Evangelist" is from the Greek word meaning "one who announces good tidings." Suggested by the text of the chorus from the composer's oratorio *St. Paul,* "How lovely are the messengers that preach us the gospel of peace. To all nations is gone forth the sound of their words; throughout all the world their good tidings" (Romans 10:15, 18).

EVANSTON [C. M. (4: m mr d r / m s s); Karl P. Harrington, 1905]. For one of the cities in which the commission met which prepared *The Methodist Hymnal* of 1905. Finding some new tunes were without names, the musical editors, Peter C. Lutkin and the composer of this tune, decided to christen some of them with the names of cities where the commission had held meetings. Other tunes, which have not appeared in any other books, were called WASHINGTON and NEW YORK.

EVENING. See MERRIAL.

EVENING HYMN. See TALLIS' CANON.

EVENING PRAISE. See CHAUTAUQUA.

EVENING PRAYER [8 7 8 7 (2: S L / L. S / S d / d T); George C. Stebbins, 1876]. The composer's name for the tune which he wrote for "Saviour, breathe an evening blessing."

———— [8 7 8 7 (4: s s s f / m m m r); John Stainer, 1898]. This was written for Mary L. Duncan's "Jesus, tender Shepherd, hear us," an evening prayer hymn for children. This title has no significance when used with the benediction hymn "May the grace of Christ our Saviour."

EVENSONG. See LANGRAN.

EVENTIDE [10 10 10 10 (4: m - m r / d - s - / l s s f / m - -); William H. Monk, 1861]. Named by its composer when he wrote it for Henry F. Lyte's hymn "Abide with me: fast falls the eventide." This title has been responsible for many editors of hymn and tune books listing this hymn among those for use at evening services of worship. Lyte did not write it for that purpose; the hymn deals with the evening of life, not merely that of day.

EVERETT. See RICHMOND by Everett.

EVERSLEY. See GRÄFENBERG.

EVERYLAND No 1 [C. M. D. (4: S / d - r - / m - - d / m f s l / s f m r / m -); Lily Rendle, 1933]. From the last line of Henry Hallam Tweedy's hymn beginning, "Eternal God, whose power upholds": "And every land is Thine." The suffix "No. 1" distinguishes this from another setting for this hymn, EVERYLAND No. 2, by Miss Rendle.

EWELL. See CARLISLE by Lockhart.

EWING [7 6 7 6 D (4: d / r d f m / r - d); Alexander Ewing, 1853]. From the name of the composer. Also called ARGYLE, BERNARD, JENNER, JERUSALEM, ST. BEDE'S. BERNARD: because written for Bernard's (of Cluny) hymn beginning, "Jerusalem the golden." JENNER: because wrongly attributed to H. J. Jenner. JERUSALEM: the first word of Bernard's hymn. ST. BEDE was the name given it in its original form (3-time) which is not now used.

EXETER. See LONDON NEW.

F

FABEN [8 7 8 7 D (3: ss / s. m rm / d s); John H. Willcox, 1849].

FABER [8 8 8 8 8 8 (3: S d m / s - - / m r m / d - -); Arthur H. Mann, ca. 1875]. For Frederick W. Faber, writer of many hymns.

FAIRFORD. See TRINITY.

FALCON, or FALCON STREET. See SILVER STREET.

FAREWELL. See GOD BE WITH YOU.

FARRANT [C. M. (4: d / d. r m r / d f r); Richard Farrant, 1847]. This tune was adapted from an anthem, "Lord, for Thy tender mercies' sake," generally attributed to Farrant (hence the name); however, Groves says it was by one John Hilton, while Canon Dearmer says it is by William Mundy.

FATHERLAND. See ST. EDMUND by Sullivan.

FEDERAL STREET [L. M. (4: m - m m / f - m s / s - f - / m - - -); Henry K. Oliver, 1836]. Lowell Mason asked the composer for this tune to use in his forthcoming *Boston Academy's Collection of Church Music* (1836) and received permission to do so. Oliver wanted to name the tune for his wife, Sally (Cook), but, thinking the name not euphonious enough and failing in his attempts to poetize it,

he decided to call the name of the tune after the name of the street in Salem [Massachusetts] in a house in which she was reared, wooed, won, and married, and from which, to the music of the same tune, she was many years afterward buried.—Brooke.

Frank J. Metcalf says, also, that it was the street where Oliver lived in his late years, and that it was the name of a street in Boston where there stood a church which he had attended as a child.

FELIX. See CONSOLATION by Webbe.

FENWICK. See MARTYRDOM.

FERTILE PLAIN. See SAUL.

FESTAL SONG [S. M. (4: S / d S M S / L - -) ; William H. Walter, 1874]. From the sentiment of the hymn for which it was written, beginning "Awake, and sing the song," by William Hammond.

FFIGYSBREN [10 10 10 10 (2: d mm / m s / fm rr / m -) ; Welsh hymn melody, 1840]. Approximate English pronunciation, "fi'-gus-bren." The word means "fig tree." It is evidently the name of some farm or homestead. Also called CLÔD, which is the Welsh word for "praise." The tune is known by this name in Wales.

FIAT LUX [6 6 4 6 6 6 4 (3: S d r / m. r d) ; John B. Dykes, 1875]. John Marriott's hymn beginning, "Thou, whose Almighty Word," has as the last line of each stanza a perfect translation of this hymn-tune name— "Let there be light."
Also called ALNWICK.

FIELD [10 10 10 10 (4: S - d r / m - s - / f m r m / d - - -) ; Calvin W. Laufer, 1919]. Named after and dedicated to a friend of the composer, the Reverend Herbert H. Field, pastor of the Flatbush Presbyterian Church, Brooklyn.

FIFE. See O PERFECT LOVE.

FILITZ. See CASWALL.

FILLMORE [8 8 8 8 8 8 (3: d / m.r d / r - m / r - d / r -) ; Jeremiah Ingalls, late 18th century]. Probably for Millard Fillmore, onetime president of the United States.

FINGAL [6 6 6 6 D (3: m m m / m d r / m -) ; traditional Irish melody]. From an old song about the legendary "Fingal"; from *Finn mac Cumhail*,

"Finn, the son of Cumhail." *Fingal* is the title of the famous poem by James MacPherson in six books, ascribed to the Gaelic bard Ossian. See MORVEN and SELMA.

FINLANDIA [10 10 10 10 10 10 (4: m r m / f - - m / r m d.r / r m - -) ; Jean Sibelius, arr. 1932]. From the composer's tone poem by this name, from which it was taken.

FLEMMING [8 8 8 6 (4: d - d d / r - r - / m d d r / d - T) Friedrich F. Flemming, 1811]. After the composer, a German physician, whose name, it is frankly stated, is listed in *Grove's Dictionary of Music and Musicians* solely because he wrote this tune.
Also called INTEGER VITAE, NACHTLIED, ST. THERESA. INTEGER VITAE: the opening words of the Latin poem for which it was written (for male voices).

FLORENCE [6 6 4 6 6 6 4 (3: s m d / r d T / d - -)] See TRINITY.

—— [8 7 8 7 D (4: d dr m rd / f mr m m)]. See ALTA TRINITA BEATA.

FOR ALL THE SAINTS. See SARUM.

FORD COTTAGE [8 6 8 6 8 6 (4: d / m. s d d / r mf m) ; Frederick C. Maker, 1909]. Undoubtedly a homestead or residence name. This composer showed a preference for such names.

FOREST GREEN [C. M. D. (4: S / d d d r / mr mf s) ; traditional English melody]. Because the air was noted by Ralph Vaughan Williams at Forest Green, Surrey, England, in 1903, while he was searching for source material in his studies of the English folk song. This melody was used with the old narrative ballad "The Ploughboy's Dream."

FORTITUDE [2 10 10 10, with Repeat (4: m / m.r r d / f m r d / 1 - s f / m - -) ; David S. Smith, 1904]. Suggested by the thought of the hymn for which it was written, beginning,

"Be strong! We are not here to play," by Maltbie D. Babcock.

———— [5 5 5 5 6 5 6 5 (4: S. L S - / m - d - / L - T d / S - M -); William C. Filby, 1874]. The setting for "Breast the wave, Christian," opening line of a hymn by Joseph Stammers.

FORTUNE [5 4 5 4 D (4: L - L. T / d - - T / L m r d / T - - -); traditional English melody]. This tune for "Fortune my foe" was popular in the sixteenth and seventeenth centuries in England; many ballads were written to be sung to it.

FOUNDATION [11 11 11 11 (2: SL / d Ld / S dd / m dm / S); Early American melody]. From a word in the first line of the popular anonymous hymn "How firm a foundation," as well as from its general sentiment.

Also called BELLEVUE, CONVENTION.

FOUNT. See GREENVILLE.

FOWLER [8 4 8 4 8 4 (6: m m m s - d / T d r d -); Robert G. McCutchan]. In 1929, with Carl Fowler Price, I was compiling a hymn and tune book. In response to Mr. Price's request that I try my hand at writing a tune which might more comfortably comply with the somewhat irregular accents in Adelaide A. Procter's hymn beginning, "My God, I thank Thee, who hast made," I wrote this tune. I gave the tune the name "Price" but was informed that another tune by another composer had so honored Mr. Price. I then named it "Carl" but soon discovered another one that had been christened after William C. Carl, the well-known New York organist. I then tried, successfully, Mr. Price's middle name, "Fowler," which name had been given the distinguished authority on hymns and their tunes after Bishop Charles H. Fowler. Thus the hymn tune bears the name of two churchmen at one and the same time—a great ecclesiastic and an honored layman.

FRAMINGHAM. See HURSLEY.

FRANCONIA [S. M. (4: d / r m f s / m - -); adapted by W. H. Havergal, 1847]. The tune is said to be founded on a melody by J. B. Koenig (1738). Koenig was director of music in some churches in Frankfurt-am-Main, in old Franconia.

———— [7 6 7 6 D (4: S / d. d m d / d - L)]. See WEBB.

FRANKFORT [8 8 7 8 8 7 8 4 8 4 (4: d / s m d s / l l s); Philip Nicolai]. During a severe visitation of the plague while he was serving as minister at Unna, Westphalia, Nicolai was moved to write *Wie schön leuchtet der Morgenstern* and this tune, both of which appeared in *Freuden-Spiegel des ewigen Lebens*, which he published in Frankfort in 1599.

———— [L. M. (4: S / d S L L / S F M)]. See WINCHESTER, NEW.

FREDERICK [11 11 11 11 (3: S / d d r / m l sm / r. d r / m -); George Kingsley, *ca.* 1873] This is said to be named for the Reverend Frederick T. Gray, friend of the composer.

FRENCH. See DUNDEE.

FRIEND [8 7 8 7 D (3: S / Sm m f / mr r); George C. Stebbins, 1878]. Suggested by the words from the gospel song "I've found a Friend, O such a Friend."

———— [8 7 8 7 D (4: s. s ls md / d - L -)]. See CONVERSE.

FRIENDS OF FREEDOM. See CALEDONIA.

FULDA. See GERMANY.

G

GAINSBOROUGH. See ST. MARTIN'S by Tans'ur.

GALILEE [8 7 8 7 (3: mS / r r rS / d d); William H. Jude, 1874]. The second stanza of the hymn for St. Andrew's Day beginning, "Jesus calls us, o'er the tumult," by Mrs. Cecil F. Alexander, reads:

As of old, St. Andrew heard it
  By the Galilean lake,
Turned from home, and toil, and kindred,
  Leaving all for His dear sake.

The word "Galilee," referring to the lake of this name in Palestine, means "circuit." It is the Greek form of the Semitic word *g'lil,* "circle," and was used by the Jews who walked around the section so called because it was partly inhabited by Gentiles.

Also called ST. JUDE, the name of the composer "canonized" by some editor.

—— [L. M. (3: s m r / d - d / 1 - 1 / s -)]. See ARMES, and ST. JUDE by Jude.

GARDEN CITY [S. M. (4: S / L d m r / d - -); Horatio W. Parker, 1890]. Composed for the dedication of a new church building and for his Cathedral Choir at Garden City, Long Island, where the composer was a teacher before going to Trinity Church, Boston, and Trinity Church, New York.

GARDINER. See GERMANY.

GARTON [6 7 6 7 (4: d. r m l / s - s -); traditional Irish melody]. This is a misspelling of "Gartan" which occurs in many books. It is a favorite tune in County Donegal, Ireland, and takes its name from *Lough Gartan,* a small lake in that county.

GASTON. See AZMON.

GEIBEL [7 6 7 6 D, with Refrain (4: S / m m m m / m - m); Adam Geibel, *ca.* 1900]. From its composer, who was a well-known blind musician of Philadelphia.

GENTLE JESUS [7 7 7 7 (3: mf s m / fm r -); Martin Shaw, 1915]. From the first words of Charles Wesley's single acceptable hymn for children beginning, "Gentle Jesus, meek and mild."

GERALD [C. M. D. (6: s / s - f m - d / t - 1 1 -); Louis Spohr, 1834]. Here is an instance of the inexplicability of an occasional tune name unless one has firsthand knowledge of the reason for its choice. GERALD was the name selected for this tune by the editorial committee preparing *The Methodist Hymnal* of 1935. The tune had been used in earlier editions under the name SPOHR, that tune generally called SPOHR by others having the misnomer SIMPSON. In order to accord with common custom, the name SPOHR was given to the better-known tune. At the last meeting of the committee it was discovered that no name had been selected for this tune. In the preceding edition (1905) there was a tune named PARKER, after Dr. Fitzgerald Sale Parker, a greatly loved member of the commission which compiled it. He was now the secretary of the later commission. Since the tune called PARKER had not been retained for use in the new book, a suggestion was made that, in order to retain the name, this tune should be given that title. Dr. Parker demurred, and made the countersuggestion to recognize the assistance of Miss Geraldine Reid Sherrill, secretary to the editor, who had been in attendance at many of the meetings. A compromise was suggested: "Gerald" being the last part of Dr. Parker's first given name as well as the first part of Miss Sherrill's, it was selected for use; both were fittingly honored.

Also called ILLA, SPOHR.

GERMAN AIR. See MENDON.

GERMAN EVENING HYMN. See DIJON.

GERMAN HYMN. See PLEYEL's HYMN.

GERMANY [L. M. (3: S d T / d - r / S L T / d - -); from *Sacred Melodies,* William Gardiner, 1815]. Called GERMANY because Beethoven, whom Gardiner asserted wrote it, was a German. In the Preface to *Boston Academy's Collection of Church Music* (1836) Lowell Mason comments on certain tunes, among them GERMANY:

These [German] melodies are often delicate, chaste, and beautiful in the highest degree; but as they require a finished and tasteful style of performance, they cannot be very extensively used as common church tunes.

Were he living today, Mason would be surprised at the popularity of GERMANY and the heartiness with which it is sung by congregations throughout the Protestant churches. Also called BEETHOVEN, BONN, FULDA, GARDINER, MELCHISADEC, WALTON. BEETHOVEN: because Gardiner said, "It is somewhere in the works of Beethoven, but where I cannot now point out." Nor has anyone else been able to do so. BONN: the birthplace of Beethoven, where a monument was erected to his memory. GARDINER: who compiled the book from which the tune has been taken.

GERONIMO [8 8 8 8 8 6 (4: s / d t d s / f m s -); Charles Stanford, 1909]. Named not after the savage North American Indian, chief of the Chiricahua band of the Apaches, who was finally captured by General Nelson A. Miles after making things very uncomfortable for the early settlers of Arizona, but after St. Geronimo (Spanish for "Jerome"), who translated the Bible from Greek into Latin.

[He] made the great Eastern book, the Bible, legible to the West; he was the first great teacher of the nobility of ascetic scholarship and courtesy as opposed to ascetic savageness; the founder properly of the ordered cell and tended garden, where before was but the desert and the wildwood.—Ruskin.

GERONTIUS [C. M. (3: m m r / d - S / d - m / s - -); John B. Dykes, 1868]. Originally composed for "Praise to the Holiest in the height," taken from *The Dream of Gerontius* by John Henry Newman. See NEWMAN.

GERTRUDE. See ST. GERTRUDE.

GETHSEMANE [7 7 7 7 7 7 (4: d d r m / f. f m -); Richard Redhead, 1853]. Redhead was one composer who did not name his tunes, rather numbering them in sequence as he wrote them. This is, properly, REDHEAD No. 76. Called GETHSEMANE because of its use with James Montgomery's hymn beginning, "Go to dark Gethsemane." This name is equally appropriate when the tune is used, as it is, with Robert Grant's "Saviour, when in dust to Thee."

Also called AJALON, HAZEN, PETRA.

—— [7 7 7 7 7 7 (4: L L L L / L. L L -); Frederick A. G. Ouseley, 1869]. This is the tune found in *Book of Common Praise* (1908), of the Church of England in Canada, used with John Ellerton's hymn beginning, "Throned upon the awful tree."

—— [7 7 7 7 7 7 (4: m f s d / r f m -); John B. Dykes, 1872]. Originally set to "Rock of Ages."

—— [7 7 7 7 7 7 (4: m m m l / l ♯s l -); William H. Monk. Used with "Go to dark Gethsemane." This tune is an adaptation of a tune from Christopher Tye's twelfth chapter in his *Acts of the Apostles* (1553).

—— [7 7 7 8 (4: s s s m / d d t -); Philip P. Bliss, 1891]. This is the gospel song known as "Hallelujah! What a Saviour!" The first stanza is:

Man of Sorrows! What a name
For the Son of God, who came
Ruined sinners to reclaim!
Hallelujah! What a Saviour!

GIARDINI's. See TRINITY.

GIBBONS [7 7 7 7 (4: m f s l / r r m -); Orlando Gibbons, 1623]. Named for the composer. It is one of the tunes for George Wither's *Hymns and Songs of the Church* (1623), set to Song XIII.

Also called CANTERBURY, NORWICH, ST. IRENAEUS, SIMPLICITY, SONG 13.

——— [7 6 7 6 D (4: d / d d r m / f r m -); Edmund Sedding, 1861]. In *Hymns Ancient and Modern*, where it appears, it is said to be "founded on Orlando Gibbons." It was written for "Jerusalem the golden."

GIDEON. See BROOKFIELD.

GLADNESS [10 10 10 10, with Refrain (6: S S S S S S / S d r m - -); Philip P. Bliss, 1870]. From the gospel hymn "I am so glad that our Father in heaven"; both words and music by Bliss.

——— [7 6 7 6 D (4: s / s m r m / r - d)]. See ST. ANSELM.

GLASSENBURIE. See CHESHIRE TUNE.

GLOAMING [8 4 8 4 D (4: m / f r m m / f r m -); John Stainer, 1898]. To Robert Wamsley's:

> The sun declines; o'er land and sea
> Creeps on the night. . . .

GLORIA [8 7 8 7, with Refrain (4: m m m m ms / s. f m d); old French carol]. From the words of the refrain used with the hymn-carol beginning, "Hearken all! what holy singing." The refrain is, "Gloria in excelsis Deo," repeated.

GLORIA PATRI. See TANTUM ERGO.

GLORIFICATION [7 5 7 5 D (4: d S d d / r r m -); Johann H. Tscherlitzky, 1832]. Used as a setting for Lawrence Tuttiett's New Year's hymn beginning, "Father, let me dedicate," and has "Glorify Thy name" as the last line of each stanza.

GOD BE WITH YOU [9 8 8 9, with Refrain (4: m. m mm mm / s r m -); William G. Tomer, 1882]. From the first words of Jeremah E. Rankin's familiar gospel song.

Also called BALLINA, FAREWELL.

GODESBERG. See WALTHAM.

GODWIN [L. M. (3: m f m / r - - / s r f / f m -); William G. Blanchard, 1934].

From the maiden name of the composer's mother, Hattie Godwin Blanchard.

GOODWIN. See WEBB.

GOPSAL [6 6 6 6 8 8 (4: s / l s m. ⁴f / s - -); George F. Handel, 1750]. This is one of three tunes written by Handel for hymns by Charles Wesley. Arthur H. Mann, editor of the *Church of England Hymnal*, says, in a footnote: "The name 'Gopsal' has been given by modern editors."

GORDON [11 11 11 11 (4: d / m - f f / m. r d m / r - T T / d - -); Adoniram J. Gordon, 1864]. named for its composer.

GOSHEN. See ST. MICHEL'S.

GOSPEL BANNER. See MISSIONARY HYMN.

GOSSNER. See HURSLEY.

GOTTSCHALK. See MERCY.

GRÄFENBERG [C. M. (2: d LS / d r / mm r); Johann Crüger, 1653]. From a town, a water-cure place, the first of its kind (hydropathy), in Silesia, Austria. Founded by a farmer, Vincent Priessurtz, who became famous in the 1820's for his cures. In the *Church of the Brethren Hymnal* (1925) a 4/4 arrangement of the tune is called KAZBEEL and credited to Johann G. C. Störl, 1744.

Also called EVERSLEY, NUN DANKET ALL, ST. MARY MAGDALENE.

GRANTON. See MELCOMBE.

GRATEFUL MEMORY. See AULD LANG SYNE.

GRATITUDE [L. M. (3: s / s d m / m s m / r f T / d -); Paul A. I. D. Bost, 1837]. The name doubtless derives from its former and general use with Isaac Watts's hymn beginning, "My God, how endless is Thy love," but it is equally appropriate when used with Frances R. Havergal's "Lord, speak to me."

Also called ATTITUDE.

——— [6 6 6 6 8 8 (4: s / d r T d / r - -); George W. Martin, 1862]. From the sentiment of Bishop Heber's hymn beginning, "On wings of living light," with the refrain-like lines:

Your voices raise with one accord
To bless and praise your risen Lord.

—— [6 7 6 7 6 6 6 6 (4: s / s s l l / s - -)]. See NUN DANKET.

GREEK AIR [Irr., or 7 6 7 6 D, or 11 8 11 9 11 8 12 9 (4: dr / m mm mr mf / l ss s)]. The same tune with different meter markings. See SWEET STORY.

GREEK HYMN [6 5 6 5 D (4: d. T L d / r d - -) ; Joseph P. Holbrook, 1870]. Because it was written for John M. Neale's translation of a Greek hymn by St. Andrew of Crete.

GREEN FIELDS. See CONTRAST.

GREEN HILL [C. M. (4: m / m. m r d / f. f m) ; Albert L. Peace, 1885]. Written for Cecil F. Alexander's hymn beginning, "There is a green hill far away." Also used with stanzas from "The Eternal Goodness" by Whittier; not a satisfactory name for a tune used with these stanzas.

GREENFIELD. See CONTRAST.

GREENLAND [7 6 7 6 D (4: m / s s s s / d - m) ; from the *Lausanne Psalter*, 1790]. Called GREENLAND from its use with Bishop Heber's hymn beginning, "From Greenland's icy mountains." Eric the Red, using the tactics of the modern realtor, named the island "Greenland," having in mind the lure of an attractive place name. He wrote: "Much people will go thither if the land has a pleasant name."
Also called HEBER, LAUSANNE, MILLENIUM, MISSIONARY, NEWBERRY. HEBER: from the author of the hymn with which it was formerly quite commonly used. LAUSANNE: because taken from the *Lausanne Psalter*. MILLENIUM: because of its use with Edward H. Bickersteth's hymn beginning, "O God, the Rock of Ages." MISSIONARY: because of the thought expressed in Bishop Heber's hymn.

—— [7 6 7 6 D (4: s / s m f l / s - m)]. See LANCASHIRE.

GREENOCK. See ST. MAGNUS.

GREENSLEEVES [8 7 8 7, with Refrain (6: L / d - r m f m / r - T S L T); Old English melody]. This tune is a setting for a New Year's carol, even though it is found in *New Christmas Carols* (1642) "to the tune of Greensleeves." It had earlier secular associations; both ballad and tune are mentioned by Shakespeare (*Merry Wives of Windsor,* Act II, scene 1) . The ballad, entitled "A new Northerne dittye of the Lady Green Sleeves," was entered in the Stationers' Register (England) in September, 1580, but the tune, known also as "The Blacksmith" or "The Brewer," is claimed to be as old as the time of Henry VIII. It is the tune to "Though laws are made for every degree" in the *Beggar's Opera.* Hawkins, in his *History of Music* (1776) , quotes a popular poem written in honor of one John Est, a barber, who became a famous player on the cittern, a part of which is:

In former time 't hath been upbraided thus,
That barber's music was most barberous,
For that the cittern was confin'd unto
The Ladies Fall, or John come kiss me now,
Green Sleeves, with Nell's delight,
Winning of Bolloigne, Essex' last good night.

In old England the profession of music had some connection with the trade of barber, and the cittern was a part of the furnishing of a barber shop, much as are the newspaper and magazine today.

GREENVILLE [8 7 8 7 8 7 (4: m mr d d / r r mr d) ; Jean J. Rousseau, 1825]. GREENVILLE is a common place name. Also called ABSENCE, COMMUNION, CRAMER, FOUNT, ROUSSEAU, ROUSSEAU'S DREAM. COMMUNION: doubtless because of its onetime association with a hymn for Communion. FOUNT: from a word in the first line of William Cowper's familiar "Come, Thou Fount of every blessing." ROUSSEAU: the name of the composer. ROUSSEAU'S DREAM: Tradition has it that the composer, while sleeping one day, dreamed he was in heaven, where he saw angels standing about the throne of God singing this tune.

GREENWOOD [S. M. (3: m r d / S - L / S - -); Joseph E. Sweetser, 1849]. A town, village, and county name, common to many states in the United States.

GREGORIAN CHANT. See HAMBURG.

GROSSER GOTT. See HURSLEY.

GWALCHMAI [7 7 7 7, with Alleluias (2: m- s- / d- rm / f- m- / r-); Joseph D. Jones, 1868]. Gwalchmai was a Welsh bard who flourished 1150-90 and who has left on record his *Gorhoffedd* ("Boasting"), a spring song similar to much that was produced at the time. It is also the name of a town in Angelsey.

—— [7 4 7 4 D; Welsh hymn melody]. This is the same as the above tune but with a different meter marking.

GWALIA [8 7 8 8 7 7 7 7 (3: m - f / sf m r / d - r / mr m -); sometimes as 8 7 8 7 D, called LOVE DIVINE; Welsh hymn melody, 1769]. "Gwalia" is a poetic name for Wales coined during the Middle Ages. It may be related etymologically to the Latin *Gallia*. The name "Wales" is English rather than native Welsh, being derived from an old Anglo-Saxon word meaning "foreign." "Cymru" is the name the Welsh use when referring to their country.

GWYNETH [8 8 8 6 (4: d - T L / d - T L / T - L - / L - ⁸S); John Price, late 19th century]. "Gwyneth" is the English form of the Welsh *Gwynedd*, and is pronounced as spelled, with a strong accent on the first syllable. It is a place name in Northwest Wales. *Gwyn* means "white"; *eth* is a case ending. Gwynedd in Saxon times was a principality including what is now Angelsea, Carmarthen, and Marioneth counties. The poetry which flourished under the princes of Gwynedd, whose court was at Aberffraw, in Angelsea, represented the original Celtic tradition in literature.

H

HAARLEM. See SEELENBRÄUTIGAM.

HACKNEY. See ST. MARY.

HALIFAX [C. M. D. (4: S / L L L T / dr m m); from *Harmonia Sacra*, 1753]. This air is from Handel's little-known oratorio, *Susanna*. After the first presentation of the opera the tune became immensely popular, being used with all sorts of words and adapted for every variety of instrument. It was made into a hymn tune and included in Thomas Butts's *Harmonia Sacra*, which was widely used by early Wesleyans even though John Wesley did not wholly approve of the book. How this very popular tune of two hundred years ago got this name is a mystery. Halifax, in the West Riding of Yorkshire, England, was originally called Horton. It is said by some authorities to have derived its name from the Anglo-Saxon words *hālig*, "holy," and *feax*, "hair," because in early days many pilgrims visited the isolated spot to view "the head of a virgin, the victim of a rejected suitor's revenge, and which, after decapitation, was affixed to a yew-tree, and preserved as a holy relic." Others interpret the name as signifying a "holy face," from a relic called the Face of St. John, said to have been preserved in a lonely hermitage which occupied the site of the present church.—From Lewis.

HALL [10 10 10 10 (4: s - m r /

d. r m - / f - s l / s - - -) ; Calvin W. Laufer, 1918]. Named for Dr. William Ralph Hall, of the Board of Education of the Presbyterian Church, a friend of the composer.

HALLE [L. M. (3: d d d / d T d / r m r / d - -)]. See HURSLEY.

———— [8 4 7 8 4 7 (3: m - fr / m f s / l - rt / d s)]. See HAYDN (ca. 1794).

HALLELUJAH. See NETTLETON.

HALTON HOLGATE. See SHARON by Boyce.

HAMBURG [L. M. (4: d - d r / m - r m / f - m r / m - - -) ; Lowell Mason, 1824]. A common town name. Gannett says a town in Erie County, New York, one in Aiken County, South Carolina, and "twenty other places" are named for the city in Germany. Henry L. Mason says this tune name is not an associative name. Also called AVENTINE, BOSTON, GREGORIAN CHANT.

HAMPTON. See CARLISLE by Lockhart.

HANFORD [8 8 8 4 (4: s ss s. s / f m r -) ; Arthur S. Sullivan, 1871]. A place name in Dorsetshire, England, the home of Mrs. Gertrude Clay-Ker-Seymour, in whose home the composer was a guest when this tune and ST. GERTRUDE (which see) were written.

HANKEY [7 6 7 6 D, with Refrain (4: S / d. S S d / m. r d) ; William G. Fischer, ca. 1872]. For Katherine Hankey, who wrote the stanzas of the fine gospel hymn "I love to tell the story." The refrain was added by the composer.

HANNA [7 7 7 5 (4: m s / r d f f / m -) ; Calvin W. Laufer, 1917]. According to the 1935 Handbook of the Hymnal (Presbyterian), this was named for two women of that name who were taken into membership in the First Presbyterian Church of Union City, Pennsylvania, when the composer was serving a pastorate there.

HANOVER [10 10 11 11 (3: S / d d r / m - s / d r T / d -) ; William Croft, 1708]. This famous tune became HANOVER when George III, of the house of Hanover, ascended the British throne. John Wesley called it BROMSWICK (for the then reigning house of Brunswick?) in his Foundery Tune Book (1742), later changing its name to TALLY's, probably thinking it had been composed by Thomas Tallis. Its original title in the sixth edition of the New Version of the Psalms (Tate and Brady), when it first appeared, was "A New Tune to the 149th Psalm of the New Version, and the 104th of the Old." Also called ALIFF STREET, LOUTH, 104TH PSALM, PSALM 149, ST. GEORGE'S TUNE, ST. MICHAEL'S, TALLE'S, TALLY'S. TAILE'S: a misspelling of "Tallis'." ST. GEORGE'S TUNE: perhaps from George III.

HAPPINESS. See RAPTURE.

HAPPY DAY [L. M., with Refrain (3: -S dr / m. S dr / m -) ; adapted from Edward F. Rimbault, 1854]. Philip Doddridge's hymn beginning, "O happy day, that fixed my choice," with the added refrain, "Happy day, happy day . . . , repeats the words "Happy day" twenty-one times; sufficient reason for giving its tune the name it bears. It is taken from Rimbault's century-old popular song:

Happy land! Happy land!
 Whate'er my fate in life may be.

HAPPY LAND. See INDIANA.

HARBOROUGH. See MILES' LANE.

HARLAN. See OLIVET by Mason.

HARLEIGH. See CHRISTMAS.

HARMON. See TRINITY.

HARMONY GROVE. See AMAZING GRACE.

HARWELL [8 7 8 7 7, with Alleluias (3: SS / d. S dm / r r) ; Lowell Mason, 1841]. An English residence, or homestead, name. Perhaps a place name also. Henry L. Mason says it is not an associative name.

HASLEMERE [5 5 5 5 (4: d d m m / r - - -) ; old German air, harmonized by Martin Shaw, 1931]. This child's song was named after a market town in Surrey, England. In or near Haslemere, past and present, have lived such distinguished persons as George Eliot, Lord Tennyson, John Tyndall, Grant Allen, G. Bernard Shaw, and A. Conan Doyle.

HATTON. See DUKE STREET.

HAWEIS. See CHESTERFIELD.

HAYDN [8 4 7 8 4 7 (3: m - fr / m f s / l - rt / d s); arr. from Francis J. Haydn, ca. 1794]. Named after the composer of the symphony from which the tune is taken. Also called EDNA, HALLE, LUX PRIMA. HALLE: because of the composer's association with that Austrian city. LUX PRIMA (Latin): literally "first light"; because of its association with Henry J. Buckold's translation of Friedrich R. L. von Canitz' hymn:

Come, my soul, thou must be waking;
Now is breaking
O'er the earth another day.

—— [7 6 7 6 D (3: S / m. r dT / TL S)]. See PETITION.

—— [8 7 8 7 D (4: d. r m r / f m rT d)]. See AUSTRIAN HYMN.

HAYDN'S or HAYDN'S HYMN. See AUSTRIAN HYMN.

HAZEN, See GETHSEMANE by Redhead.

HE LEADETH ME [L. M., with Refrain (4: s / m. r d s / l f f); William B. Bradbury, 1864]. From the many times the words "leadeth me" are used in John H. Gilmore's well- and favorably-known gospel hymn. Also called AUGHTON.

HEATH. See SCHUMANN.

HEBER [C. M. (3: mf / ss s m / ll l) ; George Kingsley, ca. 1873]. Because set to Reginald Heber's hymn beginning, "By cool Siloam's shady rill."

—— [8 7 8 7 4 7 (4: d d r m / r r m f); Edward J. Hopkins, 1868]. This was written for Dorothy A. Thrupp's "Saviour, like a Shepherd lead us." The Hebrew word *Heber*, which means "companion," is an excellent choice as a name for such a hymn.

—— [7 6 7 6 D (4: dr / m m m m / m - d)]. See PATNA.

—— [7 6 7 6 D (4: d - / m s s l / s - m)]. See MISSIONARY HYMN.

—— [7 6 7 6 D (4: m / s s s s / d - m)]. See GREENLAND.

HEBRON [7 7 7 7 8 8 (4: m d L T / d. T L -); Joseph Barnby, 1874]. Named by its composer; a setting for John Ellerton's hymn beginning, "Now the laborer's task is o'er." The name may have some significance, for *Hebron* is a combination of two Hebrew words, one meaning "ford," the other "company." The first stanza of the hymn is:

Now the laborer's task is o'er;
Now the battle day is past;
Now upon the farther shore
Lands the voyager at last.
Father, in Thy gracious keeping
Leave we now Thy servant sleeping.

—— [L. M. (3: S / MS L S / LT d); Lowell Mason, 1830]. One of Mason's Old Testament names; not associative.

HEIDLEBERG. See BREMEN by Vulpius.

HEINLEIN [7 7 7 7 (4: m m L T / d r m -); anon., 1676]. Because attributed to Paul Heinlein (or Hainlein), 1626-86, German composer of Nuremberg. But it is also attributed to one Martin Herbst. Also called AUS DER TIEFE.

HELLESPONT. See MORECAMBE.

HENDON [7 7 7 7 (4: d d dS dm / s f m -); H. A. César Malan, 1827]. A village, or rural district, in Middlesex, England, on the river Brent, only a few miles northwest of St. Paul's Cathedral, London. Its name

—probably from *Hean-dune*, "the high hill," for it is situated on an eminence—is found in the *Book of Domesday* as "Handone." César Malan, the tune's composer, spent some time in England, and there may be some incidence between town and tune name.

Also called CONSECRATION.

HENLEY [11 10 11 10 (4: s - m m / m - r - / d d r r / m - d -); Lowell Mason, 1854]. One Reverend P. Henley contributed to *Warren's Psalmody*, an English publication, which undoubtedly influenced Mason. There may be some connection, but the tune name is not listed as an associative name by Henry L. Mason.

HERALD ANGELS. See MENDELSSOHN.

HEREFORD [Irr. (4: SS / d dd dT d / s - m -); Francis D. Heins, 1930]. The composer has written that he named his tune after his birthplace, an episcopal city of ancient origin, in Herefordshire, England. The name implies a "military ford," from its having been a pass over the River Wye, on the bank of which it is situated. The triennial meetings of the Three Choirs (Hereford, Worcester, and Gloucester), established in 1724 or earlier, are held in Hereford during three days in September. The establishment of the Three Choirs' Festival, although first held in Gloucester, was mainly promoted by the Reverend Thomas Bisse of Hereford.

HERMAS [6 5 6 5 D, with Refrain (4: m. m m r / d - L -); Frances R. Havergal, 1871]. *Hermas* (Greek): "interpreter." First set to the anonymous hymn beginning, "Earth below is teeming," this tune was named for one of "the friends of St. Paul." (See p. 27.) This friend was Hermas, an early Roman writer to whom Paul sends greetings in his Epistle to the Romans (16:14). This Hermas should not be confused with another author of the same name.

HERRNHUT. See SAVANNAH.

HERZLICH. See PASSION CHORALE.

HESPERUS [L. M. (3: m m m / s - d / r - r / m - - / s s s / f - r / m - f / r - -); Henry Baker, 1866]. First called WHITBURN, perhaps from the small town on the North Sea a few miles north of Sunderland, England; the changing of the name to HESPERUS was quite justified when the tune was used with:

Sun of my soul, Thou Saviour dear,
  It is not night if Thou be near:
O may no earthborn cloud arise
  To hide Thee from Thy servant's eyes,

for *Hesperus* is "the evening star." But other names for the tune, ELIM, QUEBEC, and VENN, are not so easily explained. *Elim* is a Hebrew word meaning "palm trees." *Quebec*, the name of a Canadian city, was derived either from *Quel bec!* ("What a break!"), which the Norman sailors shouted on first seeing the lofty precipice on which the city now stands, or else from *Quebeio*, an Algonquin word meaning "strait" (various other Indian meanings: "being shut," "narrow," "fearful rocky cliff"). "Venn" is probably a family name.

————. See SCHUMANN.

HEZEKIAH [10 10 10 10 (4: s - s m / l - s - / s f m s / r - - -); Orlando Gibbons]. Called HEZEKIAH because it was originally set to a paraphrase of Hezekiah's prayer (Isaiah 37) in George Wither's *Hymns and Songs of the Church* (1623).

Also called SONG No. 22. See p. 156.

HIGHNAM. See DEERHURST.

HIGH ROAD [10 4 6 6 6 6 10 4 (6: s / d - d d - r / d t l s - l / t -); Martin Shaw, 1915]. Set to George Herbert's "Let all the world in every corner sing."

HILDA. See ST. HILDA by Knecht.

HINTON. See ST. MICHEL'S.

HIPPOLYTUS. See MORNING HYMN.

HODNET [7 7 7 5 (4: d r m l / s. f m -);
John B. Dykes, 1870]. Lightwood says
this tune was written for Bishop
Heber's hymn beginning, "Brightest
and best of the sons of the morning,"
and was named HODNET because
Heber was born there and was for
fifteen years rector of the Hodnet
parish. This must be an error so far
as the hymn mentioned is concerned,
for Dykes's tune was written for a
7 7 7 5 text by Heber beginning,
"Lord of mercy and of light."
———— [7 6 7 6 D (3: m / m. m fr /
m m); Sigismund Thalberg]. Not
now in use; formerly the setting for
"All glory, laud, and honor" in
Edwin F. Hatfield's *Church Hymn
Book* (1875).
———— [13 11 13 11 (4: mf /
s ld t ls / m rm r d); Battison
Haynes, 1898]. Used in Scotland to
Bishop Heber's hymn beginning,
"Thou art gone to the grave."

HOLBORN. See ZION by Morley and
by Hastings.

HOLBORN HILL [L. M. (3: m m m /
f - m / m - r / d - -); from *St.
Alban's Tune Book*, 1866]. This tune
first appeared in the *Appendix to the
Hymnal Noted,* commonly called *St.
Alban's Tune Book* because of its
use at St. Alban's Church, Holborn,
located on Holborn Hill, London.
St. Alban was highly revered in pre-
Reformation times, having been the
first English saint and martyr.
Also called BRYANT, PENITENCE, and,
from the name of the church, ST.
ALBAN.

HOLINESS [6 5 6 5 D (6: m - - m r m /
f - - m - -); George C. Stebbins, 1890].
From the sentiment of W. D. Long-
staff's touching gospel hymn, "Take
time to be holy."

HOLLEY [7 7 7 7 (4: m - *r m /
d - m - / r m f s / m - - -); George
Hews, 1835]. Probably from a village

in Orleans County, New York, which
in turn was named for Byron Holley,
one of the first canal commissioners
of that state. The tune name sometimes appears spelled "Holly."

HOLLINGSIDE [7 7 7 7 D (4: m s l s /
s. f m -); John B. Dykes, 1861]. "Hollingside" was the cottage home of
Dykes while he served as precentor
and minor canon at Durham Cathedral. "If he took the name from the
cottage, the cottage took *its* name
from the beautiful wood adjoining,
which perhaps ought to be considered the source of both."—*Musical
Times,* Vol. 45.

HOLSTEIN. See SEYMOUR.

HOLY CHURCH [7 6 7 6 D (4: d /
m r d S / L - S); Arthur H. Brown,
1862]. Written to be sung to "Jerusalem the golden," a part of Bernard
of Cluny's *De Contemptu Mundi,* in
its greater part "a savage satire on
the vices and follies of the church"
of his time. Even though this portion
of the poem has to do with the de-
lights of the Celestial City, HOLY
CHURCH seems an inappropriate
name for its tune.

HOLY CROSS [C. M. (3: S / m - r /
d - S / T - L / S -); adapted by
James C. Wade]. Probably for the
"Gild of the Holy Cross," an association partly religious and partly charitable, of Birmingham, England, in
which city the arranger of the tune
lived for a time. In the parish church
the "Gild" maintained a "chantry"—
that is, a chapel—in which minor
services for singing, prayer, Sunday-
school gatherings, and the like were
held. It is possible that the tune was
used with a hymn for Holy Cross
Day, September 14, in the Roman
calendar, which would account for
the name. In *Musical Times,* September 1, 1906, there is an account of
"the Abbey Church of Waltham Holy
Cross," which questions whether or
not Wade was ever at Waltham.

Near Waltham Abbey, some two miles from the west margin of Epping Forest, is Waltham Cross. Edward I erected crosses wherever the body of his queen, Eleanor, rested on its way from Nottinghamshire, where she died, to London, where she was buried in Westminster Abbey. Waltham Cross is one of these spots. Charing Cross, London, received its name because it was the location where the last stop of the journey was made. From Wheatly:

The fourteenth of this month [September] is called *Holy-cross-day*, a festival deriving its beginning about the year 615, on this occasion: Cosroes king of Persia having plundered Jerusalem, (after having made great ravages in other parts of the Christian world,) took away from thence a great piece of the cross, which Helena had left there: and, at the times of his mirth, made sport with that and the Holy Trinity. Heraclius the emperor giving him battle, defeated the enemy, and recovered the cross: but bringing it back with triumph to Jerusalem, he found the gates shut against him, and heard a voice from heaven, which told him, that the King of kings did not enter into that city in so stately a manner, but *meek and lowly, and riding upon an ass*. With that the emperor dismounted from his horse, and went into the city not only afoot, but bare-footed, and carrying the wood of the cross himself. Which honor done to the cross gave rise to this festival.

And this, also from Wheatly:

The third of this month [May] is celebrated as a festival by the Church of Rome, in memory of the *Invention of the Cross*, which is said to be owing to this occasion. Helena, the mother of Constantine the Great, being admonished in a dream to search for the cross of Christ at Jerusalem, took a journey thither with that intent: and having employed labourers to dig at Golgatha, after opening the ground very deep, (for heaps of rubbish had purposely been thrown there by the spiteful Jews or heathens,) she found three crosses, which she presently concluded were the crosses of our Saviour and the two thieves who were crucified with him. Being at a loss to know which was the cross of Christ, she ordered them all three to be applied to a dead person. Two of them, the story goes, had no effect; but the third raised the carcass to life, which was an evident sign to Helena, that that was the cross she looked for. As soon as this was known, every one was for getting a piece of the cross; inasmuch that in Paulinus's time (who being a scholar of St. Ambrose, and bishop of Nola, flourished about the year 420) there was much more of the relics of the cross, than there was of the original wood. Whereupon that father says, "it was miraculously increased; it very kindly afforded wood to men's importunate desires, without any loss of its substance."

Also called REMEMBER ME.

HOLY INNOCENTS   [C. M. (4: dr / m m r dT / LT dr T); D. Vincent Gray, 1941]. Written for the Holy Innocents' Day hymn beginning, "When Christ was born in Bethlehem," by Laurence Housman. For comment on Holy Innocents' Day see INNOCENTS, 7 7 7 7.

HOLY NIGHT. See STILLE NACHT.

HOLY OFFERINGS [7 7 7 7 8 8 8 8 (6: m - r f - m / m - r d - -); Richard Redhead]. To John S. B. Monsell's "Holy offerings, rich and rare," written for the Offertory at the opening, in 1867, of St. Mary Magdalen Church, Paddington, England, where the composer was organist at the time.

HOLY ROOD [S. M. (4: S / d r m f / s - -); Arthur H. Brown, 1863]. For use with a hymn for Holy Cross Day, September 14, in the Roman calendar.

Holy Cross Day, or *Exaltatio Crucis*, in commemoration of the erecting of our Saviour's Cross, which had been recovered from the Persians, on Mt. Calvary, by the Emp. Heraclius, A.D. 629. Cross in Saxon is called Rood, and therefor this is vulgarly called Holy Rood Day.—Bates.

Frequently spelled "Holyrood."
HOLYROOD [S. M. (4: d / m s s l / s - -) ; James Watson, 1867]. Written for "Not by Thy mighty hand" by James R. Woodford.
———— [7 8 7 8 7 7 (4: m f / s l t d / s -) ; Robert P. Stewart, 1873]. For use on Holy Cross Day.
HOLY SEPULCHRE   [8 8 8 (4: d / d. d d m / s r m) ; Edward H. Thorne, 1863]. From the third stanza of "By Jesus' grave on either hand" by Isaac G. Smith:

Deep in the rock's sepulchral shade
The Lord, by whom the worlds were made,
The Saviour of mankind, was laid.

Also called ST. SEPULCHRE, SEPULCHRE.
HOLY TRINITY [C. M. (4: d / t l s ⅟f / l. l s) ; Joseph Barnby, 1861]. Name suggested by the first two lines of the last stanza of the hymn beginning, "As now the sun's declining rays":

To God the Father, God the Son,
And God the Holy Ghost.

This hymn is a translation, by J. Chandler, of C. Coffin's Latin hymn "Labente jam solis rota." The tune was not named by Barnby in his Hymns with Tunes (1869) ; it was given this name in the posthumous edition of his Hymn Tunes (1897).
HOLY TRIUMPH. See ANTIOCH.
HOLY VOICES. See DEERHURST.
HOLYWELL [C. M. (4: s / d tl s. f / m r d) ; William Joy, ca. 1850]. From the inspirational character of John Keble's hymn beginning, "There is a book, who runs may read." Holy wells

were objects of pilgrimage, of voture offering, and of prayer . . . of which some 500 have been enumerated in England, and round London no fewer than sixteen. The origin of Holy Wells is a subject that belongs to archaeology and scholarship. . . . Streams, rivers, fountains, springs, have all been accounted holy, and possessed each its nymph, or its god, who demanded sacrifice. Wells were dressed with flowers; they were used for divination; long before Christianity newly-born children were passed through water; coins have been found by the hundred in wells where they were thrown in order to read an oracle from the troubling of the waters; there were superstitions about the springs; there were superstitions about water drawn on certain nights; there were wishing wells; there were wakes of the well; it was in some places held necessary that converts should be baptized in clear running water. Wells cured different diseases; one was good for the eye, and one for the ear, and so on.—G. C. Home and Edward Foord, Mediaeval London (London: Ernest Benn, Ltd., 1927). Used by permission of the publishers.

John Hawkins, in his History of Music, Vol. II (1776), tells of a pamphlet which was published in London in 1694 with the title A true and exact account of Sadler's Wells lately found at Islington, treating of its nature and vertues; together with an enumeration of the chief diseases which it is good for, and against which it may be used, and the manner and order of taking it, published for the good of the publick by T. G., Doctor in Physick.

The author says the water of this well was before the reformation very much famed for several extraordinary cures performed thereby, and was thereupon accounted sacred, and called Holywell. The priests belonging to the priory of Clerkenwell using to attend there, made the people believe the virtues of the water proceeded from the efficacy of their prayers. But upon the reformation the well was stopped up, upon a supposition that the frequenting of it was altogether superstitious; and so by degrees it grew out of remembrance, and was wholly lost, until found out by the labourers which Mr. Sadler, . . . being surveyor of the highway, had employed to dig gravel in his garden, in the midst whereof they found it stopped up, and covered with a carved arch of stone, in the year 1683. It is here also said to be of a ferruginous taste, somewhat like that of Tunbridge, but not so strong of the steel. It is recommended for opening all obstructions, and also for purging and sweetening of the blood, &c. And Dr. Morton had that summer advised several of his patients to drink it, as the owner also was to brew his beer with it.

Mr. Sadler's garden was converted into a theatre in 1765.—From E. C. Brewer.

HOLYWOOD. See ST. THOMAS, from Wade.

HOME [C. M., with Repeat (3: -s dr / m- s- dr / m- -); Van Denman Thompson, 1935]. From the sentiment of the poem beginning, "Bless the four corners of this house," which Arthur Guiterman, its author, called "House Blessing." It has been taken over for use as a hymn for the dedication of a new home.

HOMELAND [7 6 7 6 D (4: d / m m 11 / s - s); Arthur S. Sullivan, 1867]. From this repeated word and the theme of Hugh R. Haweis' hymn beginning, "The Homeland, O the Homeland."
Also called O BONA PATRIA (Latin), meaning "O good fatherland."

HORBURY [6 4 6 4 6 6 4 (3: d r m / s. f m); John B. Dykes, 1861]. The composer wrote this setting for "Nearer, my God to Thee" while on a visit to the Reverend John Sharp, at Horbury, near Wakefield, England, where Dykes preached and made his first confession.

HOREB. See NIGHTFALL.

HORITON. See DUKE STREET.

HORSHAM [7 7 7 7 (4: m m f s / m - r - / d - - -); traditional English melody]. From the small town by this name in West Sussex, England, distinguished by a grammar school founded in 1532, where the melody was heard and noted.

HOSANNA [L. M., with Refrain (3: sl / d s mr / ms s); Arthur H. Mann, ca. 1876]. See HOSANNA by Elliott.

—————— [8 8 8 8 4 7 (4: s / d s m. f / s r m); Joseph Barnby, 1872]. See HOSANNA by Elliott.

—————— [8 8 8 8 11 (3: S / d. d dT / TL L); Alan Gray, ca. 1900]. See HOSANNA by Elliott.

—————— [L. M., with Refrain (4: d / s f m m / r r d -); John B. Dykes, 1865]. See below.

—————— [8 8 8 8 7 (4: d / s m f r / d T d); James W. Elliott, 1875]. This and each of the above entitled HOSANNA was written for Bishop Heber's:

> Hosanna to the Living Lord!
> Hosanna to the Incarnate Word!
> To Christ, Creator, Saviour, King—
> Let earth, let heaven, Hosanna sing!
> Hosanna, Lord!
> Hosanna in the highest!

Hosanna, a Hebrew exclamation, or prayer, used by Jesus on the day of the Feast of the Tabernacles: literally, "save now," implying, "we beseech Thee."

—————— [7 6 7 6 D, with Refrain (6: S / d m s T r f / m - - d - -); anon., date unknown]. To J. King's "When His salvation bringing," to which the refrain, "Hosanna to Jesus we'll sing," has been added.

—————— [5 5 5 11 D (3: m / m r l / s -); Henry J. Gauntlett, ca. 1850]. To Gerard Moultrie's "Our voices we raise," a harvest hymn.

HOTHAM [7 7 7 7 D (4: s d r l / s f f m); Martin Madan, 1769]. Written for "Jesus, Lover of my soul," it was named for Sir Charles Hotham, a friend of the Wesley family.

HOYTE [13 13 13 14 (4: d / m s d s / 1 - s s / d t d r / m - -) ; W. Stevenson Hoyte, *ca.* 1875]. Named for the composer.

Also called ST. COLUMBA.

HUDDERSFIELD. See COLCHESTER by Tans'ur.

HUNGARIAN MELODY. See HURSLEY.

HURSLEY [L. M. (3: d d d / d T d / r m r / d - -) ; adapted from *Katholisches Gesangbuch,* late 18th century]. Hursley is the name of a parish in England where the Reverend John Keble, author of the hymn beginning, "Sun of my soul, Thou Saviour dear," with which this tune is so definitely associated, was vicar for thirty years. He was buried in the churchyard at Hursley. The present church there was rebuilt from the profits from his *Christian Year.*

Also called FRAMINGHAM, GOSSNER, GROSSER GOTT, HALLE, HUNGARIAN MELODY, LAUDAMUS, PARIS, PASCHAL, STILLORGAN, TE DEUM.

HYFRYDOL [8 7 8 7 D (3: d - r / d . r m / f - m / r d r) ; Rowland H. Pritchard, 1855]. The word means "good cheer," and is pronounced "hu'-fru-dul." It is one of the "common" tunes from Wales.

HYMN OF JOY. See HYMN TO JOY.

HYMN OF NATIONS [6 6 4 6 6 6 4 (4: d - m s / 1. #f s -) ; Leonard B. Mc-Whood, 1933]. Given by its composer as a fitting title for a hymn and tune he wrote. The hymn which begins, "All people of the earth," is a plea for all nations to live together "in a spirit of goodwill and understanding."

HYMN TO JOY [8 7 8 7 D (4: m m f s / s f m r) ; Ludwig van Beethoven, 1824]. Taken from the Finale of Beethoven's *Ninth Symphony* (the "Choral"), with which the composer used the text of Schiller's *Ode to Joy.* The name seems to have been hap-

pily chosen. Especially is this true when it is used with Henry van Dyke's exuberant hymn beginning, "Joyful, joyful we adore Thee."

Also called HYMN OF JOY, LAETITIA.

HYMN TO THE TRINITY. See TRINITY.

I

ILLA. See GERALD.

ILLSLEY TUNE. See JAM LUCIS, plainsong melody.

ILONA [11 10 11 10 (4: -d rm / f. m mr sm / r - d -) ; J. W. Lerman, 1908]. A feminine personal name (Hungarian), meaning "light."

INCARNATION [7 6 7 6 D (4: S / d T d m / m - r) ; Alfred Wooler, *ca.* 1920]. Suggested by the words of the text of Dean Wilbur F. Tillett's hymn beginning, "O Son of God incarnate." It was named by the author of the hymn.

INDIANA [6 4 6 4 6 7 6 4 (2: m mr / ms s) ; old Hindu air]. According to Hoosiers, this name, meaning "land of plenty," is not an unhappy selection of a name for the old, old "There is a happy land."

Also called HAPPY LAND.

IN DULCI JUBILO [6 6 7 7 7 8 5 5 (6: d / d - d m - f / s - 1 s -) ; Old German melody]. From the first line of the fourteenth-century macaronic hymn, a free translation of which is "In sweet shouting" (or jubilation).

INNOCENTS [7 7 7 7 (4: m. f / s d t 1 / s -) ; from *The Parish Choir*]. Because appointed to be sung to an Innocents' Day hymn when first published in its present form in a magazine, *The Parish Choir,* Vol. III (London, 1850). "Innocents" was the

name given, from early times, to the infants whom Herod massacred at Bethlehem. They were termed in Latin *innocentes,* from *in,* not, and *nocere,* to hurt. These harmless ones were revered by the Church from the first, and honored, on the third day after Christmas, as martyrs; and with them were connected many strange observances, such as the festival of the boy-bishop, and in opposition to this, the whipping children out of their beds on that morning. In the modern Church the feast of the Holy Innocents is celebrated as a special holiday by the young, and many curious and sportive customs connected with it prevail in Catholic countries.—Wheeler.

L'Estrange, in *Alliance of Divine Offices* (1690), gives as the reason for the order of the day: St. Stephen first, as being the first martyr for Christianity; St. John second, as being the disciple which Jesus loved; the Innocents third, because their slaughter was the first considerable consequence of our Saviour's birth: "that martyrdom, love, and innocence are first to be magnified, as wherein Christ is most honored."

REDHEAD No. 45, also called ARLEY, is but a very slight variant of IN-NOCENTS, about the only difference being that it is in 4/4 time.

Also called AN ANCIENT LITANY, ALL SAINTS, DURHAM, MONTGOMERY, OLD FRENCH MELODY.

——— [8 8 8 8 8 8 (free: d - / d r m d m f / s -)]. See OLD 113TH.

INNSBRUCK [7 7 6 7 7 8 (4: m / d r mf s / f - m) ; Old German melody]. *Innsbruck,* which means "bridge over the Inn River," is frequently spelled "Innspruck," which means nothing. The tune was originally a German folk song sung in the fifteenth century to the words, "Innsbruck, I must leave thee." It was used by Bach in his *Passion According to St. Matthew.*

Also called NUN RUHEN ALLE WÄL-DER, from the first line of Paul Gerhardt's hymn.

INNSPRUCK. *See* INNSBRUCK.

IN SINE JESU [7 6 7 6 D, with Refrain (4: m rd S d / m. f m -) ; William H. Doane, late 19th century]. The

setting for the well-known funeral gospel hymn "Safe in the arms of Jesus."

Also called ARMS OF JESUS, REFUGE, SAFE IN THE ARMS, THE HEART'S REFUGE.

INTEGER VITAE. See FLEMMING.

INTERCESSION [7 5 7 5 D, with Refrain (4: S. m m r / d d d -) ; William H. Callcott, 1865]. Name suggested by the theme of "When the weary, seeking rest" by Horatius Bonar, the refrain being two lines taken from Mendelssohn's *Elijah:*

Open the heavens and send us relief,
Help, help Thy servant, now, O God.

——— [L. M. (3: S d m / m - r / d - T / d - -) ; Archbishop Maclagan, *ca.* 1875]. Set to "Lord, speak to me, that I may speak" by Frances R. Havergal.

——— [L. M. (3: d / m r d / f m r / d r T / d -) ; From *Easy Music for Church Choirs,* Part III, 1853]. *The Hymnal 1940* gives credit to John B. Dykes (1853) as arranger of this tune. The tune appeared in the Appendix to the Original Edition (1861) of *Hymns Ancient and Modern.* The unusually meticulous Historical Edition (1875) of this great work does not credit Dykes with the arrangement of the tune.

Also called ST. LUKE.

INTERCESSOR [11 10 11 10 (free: l s f / m m f l d d / t - l) ; C. Hubert H. Parry, 1904]. From the first line of the last stanza of Ada R. Greenaway's hymn beginning, "O word of pity, for our pardon pleading," which is, "O Intercessor, who art ever living."

INVERNESS. See MARTYRDOM.

INVITATION [6 6 6 6 D (4: m - m m / m. r r) ; Frederick C. Maker, 1881]. Named by its composer because of the sentiment expressed in John M. Wigner's invitation hymn beginning, "Come to the Saviour now."

—— [9 9 9 6, with Refrain (4: S LS M S / d rd L -); George F. Root]. Because of its use with Root's text beginning, "Come to the Saviour, make no delay," a gospel song very popular in the late nineteenth century.

—— [L. M. (4: s / m T d l / s f m)]. See WILTON.

INVOCATION. See CARLISLE by Lockhart.

IOWA [S. M. (3: S / d - Ld / r - dL / S -); a "Western melody," anon.]. One of the states' names given to various anonymous tunes from the American frontier in Henry Ward Beecher's famous *Plymouth Hymnal* (1855).

IPSWICH. See KEBLE.

IRBY [8 7 8 7 7 7 (4: S T / d. d dT dr / r d); Henry J. Gauntlett, 1858]. The tune, originally published as a Christmas carol, had as its name the first line of Cecil Francis Alexander's hymn for children beginning, "Once in royal David's city," for which it was written. From the *Musical Times,* London, December 1, 1902:

The tune . . . called "Irby," probably after one of the villages in Lincolnshire, so named. The early Vikings, after carrying on raids in Ireland, were known in England as the "Irishmen," and gave their name "to certain Irbys, Irebys, and Iretons."

IRENE [7 7 7 5 (4: S S L S / d d T -); Clement C. Scholefield, 1874]. "Irene" means "peace." Written for John Ellerton's evening hymn beginning, "When the day of toil is done."

—— [7 7 7 7 (4: s sf m r / dr m r -)]. See SAVANNAH.

—— [10 10 10 10 (4: S - S L / S - d - / d T d r / m - - -)]. See ELLERS.

IRISH [C. M. (3: d / d - S / d r m / f m r / m -); melody from *A Collection of Hymns and Sacred Poems,* 1749]. Caleb Ashworth called it IRISH

TUNE in his *Collection of Tunes,* the few which were included in the back of his *Collection of Hymns and Sacred Poems* published at Dublin, Ireland, about 1760. The only known copy of this book is in the Warrington Library, Western Theological Seminary, Pittsburgh, Pennsylvania. Also called DUBLIN, from the place of publication of the book.

ISLEWORTH [8 8 8 6 (4: m / l m f r / d T L); Samuel Howard, 1765]. A place name.

ISTE CONFESSOR [11 11 11 5 (free: sls m f s s - l f l *d* tl s -); medieval plain song, mode VIII].

—— [11 11 11 5 (4: S - d T / L - S - / d. T d r / m - m -); Angers Church melody, 16th or 17th century].

—— [11 11 11 5 (4: L - m d / r - m - / L. T d r / d T L -); Rouen Church melody, 17th century]. This is an unmeasured melody; such are not included, as a policy, but in this case there might be some confusion with the other tunes by this name. The name comes from the first words of a very early Latin hymn, *"Iste Confessor Domine sacratus (colentes)*," an eighth-century office hymn.

ITALIAN HYMN. See TRINITY.

J

JAM LUCIS [L. M. (free: d d d d d r d d -); plain-song melody]. From the first words of the Latin hymn for which it was written, *"Jam lucis orto sidere,"* roughly translated, "Now the heavenly light appears"; more poetically, "Now that the daylight fills the skies."

—— [L. M. (4: d / d S dr m / fm r d); John Bishop, early 18th century]. See above.

Also called ST. BARTHOLOMEW, ILLSLEY TUNE.

JANES. See AUTUMN.

JAYNES. See AUTUMN.

JEHOVAH NISSI [8 8 6 8 8 6 (4: m /

s f m m / m. r d) ; Edward P. Crawford, 1907]. *Jehovah nissi* (Hebrew) :
"Jehovah is my banner." Exod. 17:15:
"And Moses built an altar, and
called the name of it Jehovah-nissi."
This was to commemorate the defeat
of the Amalekites. The tune was
written as the setting for Elizabeth
Wordsworth's hymn beginning, "O
Lord our Banner, God of might,"
which she wrote while the war in the
Sudan was being carried on during
the winter of 1884-85. Headed "Jehovah-Nissi, a Hymn for Our Soldiers," the hymn also appeared as a
leaflet during the war in South
Africa. Miss Wordsworth, a daughter
of Bishop Wordsworth, gave this information to James Edmund Jones
as stated in his Annotated Edition
of the *Book of Common Praise*
(1909) .

JENNER. See EWING.

JERUSALEM   [L. M. D. (6: d m s /
1 - - *d* l sf / s - -) ; C. Hubert H.
Parry, 1916]. The word "Jerusalem,"
meaning "foundation of peace," is
derived from two Hebrew words:
Yarah, "foundation," and *shalaim*
(or *shalem*) , "peace, perfect, whole."
Parry's tune of this name is the
setting for William Blake's hymn
which Canon Dearmer has said was
"almost a second national anthem in
England":

And did those feet in ancient time
  Walk upon England's mountains green
. . . .
And was Jerusalem builded here
  Among those dark satanic mills?
. . . .
I will not cease from mental fight
  Nor shall my sword sleep in my hand
Till we have built Jerusalem
  In England's green and pleasant land.

———— [C. M. (4: S / m. m f m /
r m d) ; T. Worlsley Staniforth, 1866].
This quite common tune is used with
a part of "Jerusalem my happy
home."

———— [C. M. (3: d / d. r m / f. s l /
s - m / s -) ; C. F. Roper, 1872]. Setting for "O Mother dear, Jerusalem."

———— [7 6 7 6 D (4: s / d t l t /
d - s) ; John Stainer, late 19th cen-
tury]. Written for "Awake, awake,
O Zion" by Benjamin Gough, date
unknown.

———— [C. M. (3: S / d - d / r - S /
m f m / m r) ; Simeon Grosvenor, *ca.*
1850].

———— [7 6 7 6 (4: s / f m r mf /
r - d) ; John B. Dykes, 1862].

———— [7 6 7 6 D (4: m / r m d r /
m - m) ; Jacob Arcadelt, 16th cen-
tury]. This and the above tunes entitled JERUSALEM are used with hymns
having Jerusalem, the heavenly
home, as their theme.

———— [C. M. (3: S / m - m / s - d /
m - r / d -)]. See SPOHR.

———— [C. M., with Repeats (4:
d - t. l / s - - f / m - r - / d -)]. See
ANTIOCH.

———— [6 6 8 4 D (4: M / L T d r /
m - -)]. see LEONI.

———— [7 6 7 6 D (4: d / r d f m /
r - d)]. See EWING.

JERVAULX ABBEY [8 8 8 8 8 8 (4: d - /
s f m r / d - r - / m -) ; *French Psalter*
melody, 1562]. Jervaulx Abbey, Yorkshire, England, was built by Cistercians in 1156. Only ruins remain.
The "Cistercians," the gray, or white,
monks (from the color of the habit
they wore) , were the great farmers
of the Middle Ages and contributed
much to the advancement of the
civilization of the time. Organized in
France, they passed over to England
and assisted in that country's commercial development through the ex-
port of wool. The Reformation and,
later, the French Revolution almost
wholly destroyed the Order, but
since the middle of the nineteenth
century there has been made a considerable recovery. Extreme austerity
has always been observed by them.
Also called PSALM 84.

JESU REDEMPTOR. See MENDELSSOHN.

JEWETT [6 6 6 6 D (4: s - m dm / r.fm r -) ; from Carl M. von Weber, 1820]. It is not known who gave the tune the family name which means "the little Jew; the son of a Jew." Also called AGATHA, WEBER. AGATHA: E. M. Oakeley, writing a *Memoir* of Herbert S. Oakeley in *Musical Times*, Vol. 44 (London) , refers to this tune as AGATHA and comments briefly but unfavorably on it. WEBER: from the composer.

JOANNA [11 11 11 11 (6: d / L F r T S d / m m r d -) ; Welsh melody, 1839]. *Joan, Johanna, Joanna* (Greek feminine form used by Luke) are Hebrew words meaning "the Lord is gracious." Joanna was the wife of Chuza, Herod's steward, who, having been called by our Saviour, followed him and ministered unto him.
Also called ST. DENIO, the Latin form of "St. Dennis."

JORDAN [L. M. D. (4: m / s l s mr / d r m) ; Joseph Barnby, 1872]. An arbitrary name given by one other than the composer; used commonly. Also called CANTATE DOMINO, because used with "Sing to the Lord a joyful song."
——— [C. M. (3: d / s - f / m - d / r m r / d -) ; old Psalm tune]. Written as a setting for Isaac Watts's paraphrase of the last part of Revelation 7, beginning, "How bright these glorious spirits shine."

JOURNEY'S END [11 10 11 6 (4: s - s s / s - s - / s s l s / s - #s -) ; William K. Anderson, 1930]. Because written for John G. Whittier's poem "At Last," which begins, "When on my day of life the night is falling." For the full story of the writing of this tune, see *Our Hymnody*, p. 501.

JUBILATE [6 6 6 6 8 8 (4: s / d. s m d / 1 - -) ; Horatio Parker, 1894]. *Jubilate:* Latin for "rejoice." Set to Charles Wesley's "Rejoice, the Lord is King."

——— [7 6 7 6 D (4: d / m d s m / 1 -) ; C. Hubert H. Parry, *ca.* 1900]. Used with a variety of joyful texts.

JUDEA. See LEONI.

JUDGMENT HYMN. See LUTHER.

JUDSON. See LUX EOI.

K

KAZBEEL. See GRÄFENBERG.

KEBLE [L. M. (4: S SL L S / d r m) ; John B. Dykes, 1875]. For John Keble, author of the hymn beginning, "Sun of my soul," for which it was written.
Also called IPSWICH, SHIRLEY.

KEDRON [6 4 6 4 6 6 4 (4: m - m m / m. r r -) ; Ann B. Spratt, 1866]. From the sentiment of the text beginning, "No, not despairingly"; this seems to warrant the selection of this Hebrew word which literally means "dark." *Kedron*, or Kidron (called "Cedron" in John 18:1, in the King James Version) , the stream into which the reformer King Josiah threw all the paraphernalia connected with the worship of Baal, runs through the valley between Jerusalem and the Mount of Olives, emptying into the Dead Sea. Beyond this "black torrent" was the Garden of Gethsemane. It is now known as *Wady Nar*.
Also call BETHEL (Hebrew) , meaning "House of God."
——— [L. M. (3: dT / LL m - m - / rd T -) ; from *Southern Harmony*, 1835]. Set to "Thou Man of Griefs, remember me." In *Southern Harmony* it is credited to "Dare." When used, as it is in *The Hymnal 1940* (Protestant Episcopal) , to Howard Chandler Robbins' translation, beginning, "Sunset to sunrise changes now," of St. Clement of Alexandria's hymn, the name has no significance.

KENDAL. See REST.

KENDALL. Another spelling of "Kendal." See REST.

KENT. See WILTON by Lampe.

KENTISH. See CHESHIRE TUNE.

KERR [10 10 10 6 (4: m - T d / f - m - / r L T d / T - -); Calvin W. Laufer, 1932]. Named for Hugh T. Kerr, of Pittsburgh, Pennsylvania, who was chairman of the committee which compiled the Presbyterian *Hymnal* of 1933.

KERSALL. See ST. BRIDE'S.

KEVIN. See ST. KEVIN.

KILMARNOCK [C. M. (4: d / m s l sm / m r d); Neil Dougall, 1831]. The composer wrote tunes on scraps of paper which he kept in a desk drawer. A caller one day asked him if he had anything new—"no scraps to divert us?" Upon being handed some and humming over one, he commented, "A very pretty melody; and what do you call it?" Being told it had not yet been christened, the visitor asked for a copy of "your nameless tune." "With pleasure," said the composer, "and we'll christen 't 'Kilmarnock.'" "Kilmarnock," formerly "Kilmernoke," is derived from the Church of St. Marnoc, *ma Ernanoc*, "my dear little Ernan." Marnoc, for whom the church was named, was an uncle of St. Columba. The town is about twenty miles from Greenock, the home of the composer, and is of interest because of its associations with Robert Burns. The first edition of Burns's poems was published there in 1786.

KING'S LYNN [7 6 7 6 D (4: m / r m L T / d r s); traditional English melody]. Ralph Vaughan Williams, who arranged this melody for use as a hymn tune, in his searches for traditional melodies of England named them from the places where he discovered them. King's Lynn (*Lynn Regis*) is a seaport in Norfolk, England, about a hundred miles northeast of London.

KINGS OF ORIENT [8 8 8 6, with Refrain (3: m - r / d - L / T d T / L - -); John H. Hopkins, 1862]. From the first line of the composer's hymn which begins, "We three Kings of Orient are." Three kings of the Orient, Kaspar (or Gaspar, or Jasper), Melchior, and Balthazar, according to tradition, came to offer gifts to the Infant Jesus. Bede (seventh century) not only gives a particular description of the three kings but also describes their dresses and tells which king offered which gift: Melchior, the gold; Gaspar (or Jasper), the frankincense; and Balthazar, the myrrh.

KING'S WESTON [6 5 6 5 D (3: LT d T / L - S); Ralph Vaughan Williams, 1925]. A country house on the River Avon, near Bristol, England, noted for its beautiful park.

KINGSFOLD [C. M. D. (4: dT / L L L S / d d r); traditional English melody, arr. 1906]. Ralph Vaughan Williams noted a version of this melody at Kingsfold, Surrey, England; hence the name.

KINGSTON. See MAGDALEN COLLEGE.

KINGTON [8 6 8 4 (4: m / d r m s / 1 sm s); F. Llewellyn Edwards, *ca.* 1900]. From the composer's birthplace, Kington, Magna, Dorset County, England. In his late years the composer became rector of the church of the village of his birth.

KIRBY BEDON [6 6 4 6 6 6 4 (4: m mm r d / f - - -); Edward Bunnett, 1887]. The name signifies "the church near Bedon." There are two hamlets by this name comprising the parishes of St. Andrew and St. Mary about three miles southeast from Norwich, County of Norfolk, England. "Kirby" is but a form of *Kirkby*, "church place." In the Canadian *Book of Common Praise* this tune is called KIRKBY BEDON, which is probably the correct form.

KREMSER [Irr. (3: s / s.l s / m f s / f.m r / m d); Netherlands folk song]. Named for the arranger of the tune, Edward Kremser, noted Vienna chorus master.

KRONSTADT. See ST. THEODOLPH.

L

LABAN [S. M. (4: m. f / s s s *d* / s -); Lowell Mason, 1830]. An Old Testament name used by Mason; a Hebrew word meaning "white, glorious." Laban was the father of Rachel and Leah. This is not an associative name.

Also called CONFLICT, a more fitting name for the tune when it is used with "My soul, be on thy guard," as seems to be always the case.

LABOR [8 8 8 4 (4: L / d r m m / f r m); Alfred M. Smith, 1941]. From sentiment of John Oxenham's hymn beginning, "All labor gained new dignity," for which it was written.

LAETITIA. See HYMN TO JOY.

LAKE ENON [S. M. (4: S / S m m r / d - -); Isaac B. Woodbury, 1854]. It is a place name which probably has no significance in this connection. Gannett says there is an Enon, a village in Clark County, Ohio, which was named for a river in Palestine. Enon is a scriptural name meaning "an abundance of water." William Warren Sweet tells of an early Methodist circuit in Lawrence County, Indiana, in the lower Whitewater country that was named "Enon" because a preacher in making his rounds had to cross so many creeks.

Also called MERCERSBURG, because used with "Jesus, I live to Thee," Henry Harbaugh's "Mercersburg Hymn."

—— [S. M. D. (4: S / S S m. r / d - -)]. See MONTGOMERY by Sullivan. Also, for the name, see above.

LAMBETH [7 7 7 7 (3: m - f / s d t / r *d* l / s - -); anon., date unknown]. The district of Lambeth, in London, which was reclaimed from marshy land in very early days, lies directly south of the Thames. The parish of Lambeth was taken into the city in 1636, being included in the Bills of Mortality. A Bill of Mortality, in England, was a weekly return issued under the supervision of the parish clerks showing the number of deaths in a parish. King Charles I used it as a scheme to assume greater control over the suburban areas of London. In 1728, when the ages of the deceased were included in these reports, the statistics thus gained served as the basis of the science of life insurance.

—— [C. M. (3: m m m / f - T / L - T / d - -); William A. F. Schulthes, *ca.* 1871].

—— [8 8 8 8 8 8 (4: d / m m mf s / sl s#f s -); S. Akeroyde in the *Divine Companion,* 1701].

—— [6 6 6 6 8 8 (2: *d* / s ls / f m / r); Charles Lockhart, late 18th century]. See LAMBETH, anon.

LANCASHIRE [7 6 7 6 D (4: s / s m f l / s - m); Henry Smart, 1836]. From the county in England in which is located Blackburn, the place where the composer was located as organist when he wrote this tune for Heber's "From Greenland's icy mountains," for the tercentenary of the Reformation.

Also called GREENLAND, because used with "From Greenland's icy mountains" by Reginald Heber.

LANGDALE. See ST. BEDE by Dykes.

LANGFORD. See ST. MAGNUS.

LANGRAN [10 10 10 10 (4: m - d r / m - s - / f m m r / d - - -); James Langran, 1861].

Also called EVENSONG, ST. AGNES. EVENSONG: because written for "Abide with me." See also DEERHURST. ST. AGNES: as an appropriate name for an evening song. See reference to St. Agnes' Eve, as well as to the saint, under ST. AGNES by Dykes.

LANHERNE [11 10 11 10 (4: m - m f / s - s - / s d t l / s - m -); Henry

Hayman, date unknown]. See LLAN-
HERNE concerning name.

LANIER [Irr. (6: m. m m m r d /
r - L L - -) ; Peter C. Lutkin, 1905].
For Sidney Lanier, author of the text
beginning, "Into the woods my Master went," for which Dean Lutkin
wrote this tune.

LASST UNS ERFREUEN [8 8 4 4 8 8, with
Alleluias (3: d / dr md mf / s -) ;
melody from *Geistliche Kirchenge-
säng*, 1623]. From the first line of the
German Easter hymn, *"Lasst uns
erfreuen herzlich sehr."*
Also called EASTER ALLELUIA, ST.
FRANCIS, VIGILES ET SANCTI, VIGILI.
EASTER ALLELUIA: a favorite at
Easter time. ST. FRANCIS: because of
its association with the famous "Sun
Song," or "Song about Creatures,"
by Francis of Assisi. VIGILES ET
SANCTI: from the first words of the
hymn beginning, "Ye watchers and
ye holy ones."

LAST HOPE. See MERCY.

LASUS [L. M. (4: S - L T / d - d - /
r - m f / m - - -) ; Arthur H. Mann,
ca. 1900]. For the Greek lyric poet
and musician, Lasus. Mann named
some of his tunes for old pagan
philosophers.
Also called NORWICH, for the birthplace of the composer.

LAUDAMUS. See HURSLEY.

LAUDES DOMINI [6 6 6 6 6 6 (4: m /
f s l *d* / t - l) ; Joseph Barnby, 1868].
The title, translated, is "Praises of
the Lord." Especially appropriate as
the setting for "When morning gilds
the skies," translated from the German by Robert Bridges.

LAUDSBERG. See LUTHER.

LAUFER [7 6 7 6 D (4: m / m f s d /
d - T) ; Emily S. Perkins, 1925].
Named by the composer for her
friend the Reverend Dr. Calvin W.
Laufer, one of the editors of *The
Hymnal* (Presbyterian), 1933.

LAUSANNE. See GREENLAND.

LEAMINGTON. See YORKSHIRE.

LEBANON. See TANTUM ERGO.

LEBBAEUS [7 7 7 6 (4: m. m m r /
d d S -) ; from *St. Alban's Tune
Book*, 1866]. A Bible name meaning
"man of heart." Lebbaeus was an
apostle surnamed Thaddeus; supposed to be the same as Jude the
brother of James.

LEEDS. See ST. ANNE.

LEIGHTON [S. M. (3: m / m. r dr /
m -) ; Henry W. Greatorex, 1849].
Perhaps a family name.
Also called AHIRA, which has already
been mentioned (p. 25) as being
an inappropriate name for a hymn
tune. The second stanza of Horatius
Bonar's hymn "O everlasting Light,"
with which this tune is sometimes
used, is:

> O Everlasting Truth,
>   Truest of all that's true,
> Sure guide of erring age and youth,
>   Lead me, and teach me, too.

LEIPSIC. See EISENACH.

LENOX [6 6 6 6 8 8 (4: d - / d d S L /
S - -) ; Lewis Edson, 1782 or '83]. A
village in western Massachusetts, a
few miles south of Pittsfield, in the
heart of the Berkshire Hills. Henry
Ward Beecher used to spend sum-
mers there. At that time Lenox was
a favorite resort, and it was there
that he wrote his *Star Papers*, published in 1855. A quotation is interesting:

Lenox, known for the singular purity
and exhilarating effects of its air, and
for the beauty of its mountain scenery.
If one spends July or October in Lenox,
he will hardly seek another home for the
summer. The church stands upon the
highest point in the village, and if, in
summer, one stands in the door and
gazes upon the vast panorama, he might,
without half the Psalmist's devotion,
prefer to stand in the door of the Lord's
house to a dwelling in tent, tabernacle,
or mansion.

Fanny Kemble (Butler) owned a cottage at Lenox and spent many months there. Her difficulties there are interestingly told by Margaret Armstrong (in *Fanny Kemble*), who also reports that in pre–Civil War days Lenox was so attractive to literary leaders that it was called "a jungle of literary lions." Mrs. Kemble said she wished to be buried in the Lenox graveyard: "I will not rise to trouble anyone if they will let me sleep here. I will only ask to be permitted once in a while, to raise my head and look out upon this glorious scene."

Beecher, commenting, wrote: "May she behold One so much fairer that this scenic beauty shall fade to a shadow."

Also called TRUMPET, because written in the "Trumpet" meter used by Charles Wesley in the hymn beginning, "Blow ye the trumpet, blow!" F. Luke Wiseman, in *Charles Wesley,* says:

The Trumpet Meter (6.6.6.6.8.8.) is so called, I believe, because it is the meter of "Blow ye the trumpet, blow," with its trumpet refrain:
  The year of jubilee is come!
  Return, ye ransomed sinners, home.

According to the law of the ancient Hebrews, the Year of Jubilee (each fiftieth year—Leviticus 25) was that in which all land that had passed out of the hands of its original owner was restored to him or his heirs, all who had sold themselves into slavery were restored their freedom, and, according to the unsupported testimony of Josephus, all debts were canceled. Whether or not the law was enforced is a question. The opening of the year, on the Day of Atonement, was announced throughout the land by the blowing of the *yobel,* a kind of trumpetlike horn. In modern times the "Year of Jubilee,"

in general, means the completion of fifty years of continuous activity, the celebration of it, or an occasion of special festivity. The Diamond Jubilee of Queen Victoria, celebrating the fiftieth year of her reign (1897), is an example.

LEOMINSTER [S. M. D. (4: m / m m m m / f - -) ; George W. Martin, 1862]. From the town in Herefordshire, England, the name of which is supposed to have been derived from *Leof-minister,* "the church of Leofic," the Mercian earl who was the husband of the celebrated Lady Godiva. Merewald, King of Mercia, is said to have founded a religious house there in 660.

Also called CHALVEY, ST. BASIL, THE PILGRIM SONG. PILGRIM SONG: because the tune was originally a part song called "The Pilgrim Song."

LEONARD. See ST. LEONARD by Hiles.

LEONI [6 6 8 4 D (4: M / L T d r / m - -) ; ancient Hebrew melody]. Sometime in the year 1770 Thomas Olivers heard Meyer Lyon, or Meier Leon (i.e., *Leon Chazzan,* "singer" or "precentor") , known by the Italianized form, "Leoni," sing the *Yigdal* at the Great Synagogue, Duke's Place, London. Shortly after this occurrence he showed the hymn "The God of Abraham praise" to a friend, telling him that he had

rendered it from the Hebrew, giving it as far as I could a Christian character, and I have called on Leoni the Jew who has given me a Synagogue Melody to suit it. Here is the tune, and it is to be called *Leoni.*

Through Olivers this tune was brought to the attention of Christians generally. The *Yigdal* is a Hebrew doxology, a sort of Confession of Faith. The lines from which it takes its name, with the *Adon Alam,* share the place of honor at the opening of the morning and the close of the evening services. The *Adon Álam* is one of the most familiar and beloved of all Jewish traditional hymns. Employed in the various rituals in use all over the world, it is not always used at the same period of the service nor on the same occasions. Traditional tunes for it are very few; only four or five deserve to be placed in this category. *Yigdal* has a much greater number of tunes than *Adon Álam; The Jewish Encyclopaedia* lists seven. Francis L. Cohen, Sydney, Australia, an authority, says for two centuries a tradition of tunes, varying as to occasion, has been assigned to the hymn. All are antiphonal between *hazzan* ("overseer," or "director: communal officer") and congregation. *Yigdal*, the most popular, is used on Friday evening. Cohen says the melody may date from the seventeenth century, or perhaps earlier. Also called JERUSALEM, JUDEA, THE GOD OF ABRAHAM, YIGDAL; but in most Anglican and Nonconformist Protestant churches the tune is known as LEONI.

LESTER. See DIADEMA.

LIEBSTER JESU. See DESSAU.

LIGHT [7 6 7 6 D (4: L - / M L S S / d. T L); from *The Christian Lyre*, 1832]. Because written for William Cowper's hymn beginning, "Sometimes a light surprises the Christian while he sings."

LINCOLN [C. M. (4: d / r m r d / d T d); from Ravenscroft's *Psalter*, 1621]. Was one of the so-called "English" tunes; set to Psalms 7 and 56. See p. 16. Lincoln, founded by ancient Britons, has been distinguished as a city of importance from the most remote period of English history.

——— [7 6 7 6 (4: d / m r m f / s - m)]. See BREMEN by Vulpius.

LITANY [7 7 7 6 (4: S L T d / d L T -); Frederick A. J. Hervey,

1875]. Because written in the metrical pattern of a litany—viz., a short prayer, or series of them (usually, when sung, three lines), followed by a supplication such as, "We beseech Thee, hear us," or the like. Strictly, it should be sung antiphonally between officiant and people. A litany has a certain psychological value in that it tends to produce a cumulative emotional effect. There are many tunes of this name, usually in this meter (7 7 7 6), nearly always identified by the name of the composer, thus: LITANY (HERVEY).

Also called LONDON.

LITTLE CORNARD [6 6 6 6 8 8 (free: L dr m m l -); Martin Shaw, 1915]. A village in Suffolk, England, where the composer spent his honeymoon.

LIVERPOOL [L. M. (4: d - d m / r - l - / s - f - / f - m -); Richard Wainwright, *ca.* 1790]. Composed while the composer was organist at St. Peter's, Liverpool, for *A Collection of Hymns . . . for the Children of the Liverpool Blue Coat Hospital*.

Also called NEWMARKET, WAINWRIGHT.

——— [C. M. (3: d / m - r / d - d / l s f / m -)]. See MANCHESTER.

——— [C. M. (4: s / m d l s / f m r)]. See BEDFORD.

LLANFAIR [7 7 7 7, with Alleluias (4: d d m m / s fm r -); Robert Williams, 1817]. A possible (or passable) pronunciation: "thlahn-vair." (When I was being initiated into certain subtleties of the pronunciation of Welsh names, I was told the proper way to pronounce *ll* is to "form your mouth as though you were going to say 'l' and then blow!") *Llan* (Celtic), the word which means "saint," or "holy," is sometimes applied to a church, or a church village (literally, "enclosure"). *Llan*, "church," and *fair*, "Mary"; therefore, "the Church of St. Mary" (or "St. Mary's"). *Llan,* as the prefix to the name of a locality, occurs in more than 450 places in Wales. A village in Montgomery County, Wales, Llanfair's full name is one of the longest words in any language: *"Llanfair-pwllgwyngyllgogerychwyrndrobwll-llantysiliogogogoch."* The local residents and the British postal authorities have abbreviated it, however, into "Llanfair P. G.," while the railway station sign reads "Llanfair." The full name means "Church of St. Mary in a hollow of white hazel near the rapid whirlpool of the Church of St. Tysillio by the red cave." The composer, Robert Williams, was born at Mynydd, Ithel, Llanfechell, Anglesey County, North Wales; and Llanfair is the first station on the railway as it enters this county. BETHEL is the name given this tune in its composer's notebook, dated July 14, 1817.

LLANFYLLIN [7 6 7 6 D (4: S / d d r r / m. r d); traditional Welsh melody]. Approximate pronunciation: "thlahn-vee'-thlihn." It is the name of a town in Montgomery County, Wales. This tune is the same as LLANGLOF-FAN (which see) except that it is major whereas the latter is minor.

LLANGLOFFAN [7 6 7 6 D (4: M / L L T T / d. T L); Welsh melody, 1865]. Approximate pronunciation: "thlahn-glo'-fen." It is probably the name of a farm or homestead, although it may be the "Church of St. Gloffan." See LLANFYLLIN.

LLANGOEDMOR [8 8 8 8 8 (4: d - s m / d - f. m / f s d -); Welsh melody, 1826]. A near English approximate pronunciation would be "thlahn-go'-ed-mor'." *Llan,* "church"; *goed* (or *coed;* letters change with case), "woods"; *mor,* "sea." Thus, "the church of Coedmore," or "the church in the wood by the sea." *Coedmore,* which literally implies "the great wood," is a residence name of Cardiganshire, Wales. Anciently

spelled *Coed-Mawr,* it is the name of the fine mansion occupied by the family which owns the extensive estate. It is situated

in a district abounding with timber of ancient and luxuriant growth, and with groves of stately oaks and other trees, for the number and beauty of which the immediate vicinity is eminently distinguished.—Lewis.

LLANGOLLEN [L. M. (4: d - d r / d - S - / M S d -); Welsh melody, 1859]. Pronounced "thlahn-go'-thlen." The place

is a small market town, four miles from Chirk Castle and 12 from Oswestry, in a most romantic situation. Here the Dee, foaming over shelves of rock in a very wide and deep channel, is crossed by an extraordinary stone bridge, one of the three beauties of Wales, of five large pointed arches, the largest not above 28 feet diameter . . . built on a ledge of rock on which it seems impossible to fix a foundation, and accounted one of the wonders of Wales.—Gough.

The River Dee divides England and Wales. *Llangollen* derives from the Church of St. Collen. This church was dedicated to St. Collen-ap-Clyndawg - ap - Cowrda - ap - Caradoc - Fleichfras - ap - Llyn - Merim - ap - Einion - Yrth - ap - Cunedda - Wledig, by Ethni Wyddeles, daughter of Matholwch, lord of Cwl, in the kingdom of Ireland. (*Ap,* in old Welsh, signifies "son," as does *Mac* in ancient Irish; therefore, "St. Collen, son of Gwynnawg," and so on.) Collen was an austere hermit; his father was a seventh-century Bishop of Glastonbury. Llangollen is well known as the home of the "Ladies of Llangollen." They were two Irish girls, Lady Eleanor Butler and Hon. Sarah Ponsonby, who swore "eternal friendship" and, secretly leaving their homes in 1776, lived together for more than fifty years at *Plas* Newydd, Llangollen. They became famous for their peculiarities of dress, their beneficence, and their collection of old oak and curios, to which it was the recognized practice for each of their numerous visitors to contribute. They vowed to devote their lives to "friendship, celibacy, and the knitting of blue stockings." Many well-known personages visited them. Wordsworth addressed a sonnet to them which, because of an "oblique reference to the ladies' age," greatly offended them.

Also called LLEDROD, apparently the name of a farm or homestead.

LLANHERNE [8 7 8 8 7 (4: d S L S / dT dr m d); George Thalben-Ball, 1926]. This name is probably Cornish, not Welsh. If so, it should be written with but one "l." There was an old priory in the Middle Ages called "Lanherne."

LLANLLYFNI [S. M. D. (3: L / mm r d / T -); David Jenkins, *ca.* 1820]. Pronounced (as nearly as the author's ear could record it) "thlahn-thlekv'-ni," it derives from "the church by Llyfni," a small stream in Wales. This tune has been attributed to the Reverend John Jones, of Talysarn, Wales, but, according to Archibald Jacob, it came to David Jenkins as he listened to the unusual intonations of the Reverend Jones's voice in his preaching. On the other hand, James T. Lightwood tells us that if this is true, Jenkins must have been a "very impressionable youth," as he was but eight years old when Jones died. The name comes from the spot where John Jones lies buried.

LLEDROD. See LLANGOLLEN.

LOBE DEN HERREN [14 14 4 7 8 (3: d d's / m.r d / T L S / L T d / r - - / d - -); from *Praxis Pietatis Melica*, 1668]. From the first line of the German hymn by Neander, with which it has been associated since 1680: "*Lobe den Herren, den nächtigan König der Ehren*"—"Praise to the Lord, the Almighty, the King of creation."

LOMBARD STREET [11 10 11 10 (4: L - d m / m - r - / d. r m r / d L L -); Frederick G. Russell, 1929]. The composer was for thirty years organist and choirmaster of St. Edmund the King and Martyr, Lombard Street, London.

LONDON. See LITANY.

LONDONDERRY AIR [11 10 11 10 D (4: -T dr / m. r ml sm / rd L -); traditional Irish melody]. Because of the tune's associations with Londonderry, North Ireland, where it is supposed to have originated. Londonderry, a county and city, owing its origin to the monastery which was founded there about 546 by Columba, since the seventeenth century has been a stronghold of Protestants in the north of the island.

LONDON NEW [C. M. (4: d - / s m d s / l d t -); *Scottish Psalter*, 1635]. NEW: to distinguish it from LONDON in the 1621 Ravenscroft book. (See p. 16.)

Also called EXETER, MAGDALEN, NEWTON, NEWTOUN. "It was probably called 'Newton' from Newtown, the appendage to 'the auld toun 'o Ayr.' "—Havergal.

LONGDEN [8 7 8 7 D (4: s l / d. l s m / r d); Van Denman Thompson, 1933]. After Henry Boyer Longden, former vice-president of DePauw University, a friend of the composer.

LONGTOWN. See YORKSHIRE.

LOUTH. See HANOVER.

LOVE DIVINE [8 7 8 7 D (4: S S L S / m rm r d); John Zundel, 1870]. From the first words of the hymn beginning, "Love divine, all loves excelling," by Charles Wesley.

Also called BEECHER, ZUNDEL. BEECHER: because its composer was a friend and intimate of Lyman Beecher, with whom he was associated for many years. ZUNDEL: after the composer.

——— [8 7 8 7 D (4: d r m m / f m m r) ; George F. Le Jeune, 1887]. Set to various hymns, among them that of Charles Wesley. See above.

——— [8 7 8 7 (4: d d / dr m r d / T S) ; John Stainer, 1889]. Written for John Newton's benediction hymn beginning, "May the love [grace] of Christ our Saviour."

——— [8 7 8 8 7 7 7 7 7 (3: m - f / sf m r / d - r / mr m -)]. See GWALIA.

LOVE'S OFFERING [6 4 6 4 6 6 4 4 (4: m - r d / d. TT -) ; Edwin P. Parker, 1888]. From the sentiment of the composer's hymn "Master, no offering," and named by him.

LUCAS [Irr. (2: SS / d dd / d Td / r rr / r) ; James Lucas, 1832]. For its composer.

LUCERNE. See OLD 113TH.

LUCY [6 6 6 6, with Refrain (3: mm / s - mm / s -) ; arr. from Johannes Brahms, 1911]. Arranged from Brahms's well-known "Lullaby." The name given it by Peter C. Lutkin is appropriate, for "Lucy" has long been a favorite name given a child born at daybreak; it was "given first to them that were born when daylight first appeared." Yet there is a certain incongruity in using the name with a lullaby, which is a bedtime song.

LUNENBURG. See CHRISTMAS.

LUTHER [8 7 8 7 8 8 7 (4: d / d m r d / r r m) ; from Klug's *Gesangbuch*, 1535]. Because it was the setting for Martin Luther's first congregational hymn, beginning, *"Nun freut euch."* Also called ALTORF, JUDGEMENT HYMN, LAUDSBERG, NUN FREUT EUCH.

——— [8 7 8 7 6 6 6 6 7 (4: d / d d sl t / dt l s)]. See EIN' FESTE BURG.

LUX BENIGNA [10 4 10 4 10 10 (3: -S dr / m. m rd Ld / L- S- --) ; John B. Dykes, 1867]. *Lux Benigna:* Latin

for "Kindly Light," because it was written for John H. Newman's hymn beginning, "Lead, kindly Light." Also called ST. OSWALD, because Dr. Dykes served the church of that name in Durham, England, for many years. He is buried there.

LUX EOI [8 7 8 7 D (4: s. s d s / s f f m) ; Arthur S. Sullivan, 1874]. *Lux Eoi:* "Light coming in the East," or "Light of the dawn." Named from the third and fourth lines, second stanza, of "Hark! a thrilling voice is sounding" (Caswall's translation) :

All the powers of darkness vanish;
  Christ our Day Star mounts the skies.

It was named by the composer. Also called JUDSON.

LUX PRIMA [7 7 7 7 7 7 (4: d d d mr / d T d S) ; Charles F. Gounod, 1872]. *Lux Prima:* Latin for "First Light"; used with Charles Wesley's "Christ, whose glory fills the skies."

——— [7 7 7 7 7 3 (4: m m m m / m. r r -) ; George A. MacFarren, 1876]. Written for "Jesus, Sun of Righteousness" by C. K. von Roseworth; translated by Jane L. Borthwick.

——— [8 4 7 8 4 7 (3: m - fr / m f s / l - rt / d s)]. See HAYDN.

LYSTRA [C. M. (3: s m f / m r s / d r T / d -) ; Charles Wesley, Jr., late 18th century. An ancient city, located in Lycaonia, Asia Minor. See Acts 14:8.

LYTHAM [C. M. (4: m / r d S d / d. TT) ; James T. Lightwood, 1910]. After the home of the composer, a seaside resort in Lancashire, England.

M

MACHS MIT MIR. See EISENACH.

MADRID. See AUTUMN.

MAGDALEN [Irr. (3: s / d s l / s s f / m r d / s s) ; Samuel Jarvis]. From the Magdalen Chapel (Oxford) book of 1762, where it first appeared.

See MAGDALENA.
Also called BLOOMSBURY, BURTON, DERBY, MONTGOMERY, NEWTON, ST. ANDREW, ST. GEORGE.

—— [L. M. (4: L / d r m l / s f m) ; John B. Dykes, 1857]. Set to "O Maker of the world, give ear!" a translation by John M. Neale.
Also called DERWENT.

—— [10 4 10 4 (4: S / d T T. L / L m m r / d) ; George C. Martin, late 19th century]. Written for Adelaide A. Procter's hymn beginning:

I do not ask, O Lord, that life may be
    A pleasant road.

Also called PER PACEM.

—— [L. M. (4: d / d T d d / r r m)]. See TALLIS' CANON.

—— [C. M. (4: d - / s m d s / l d t -)]. See LONDON NEW.

—— [8 8 8 8 8 8 (4: m / m. r d s / s f m)]. See REST.

—— [12 11 12 11 (3: d / d s l / l s f / m r d / s-) ; John Stanley]. See MONTGOMERY.

MAGDALEN COLLEGE [8 8 6 8 8 6 (4: d - m s / d - - l / f. f m -) ; William Hayes]. Taken from *Sixteen Psalms set to Music for the use of Magdalen College Chapel in Oxford* (1774). Also called KINGSTON, ORIGEN, ST. JUDE'S, SOUTHAMPTON.

MAGDALENA [7 6 7 6 D (4: d / f m r d / s - s) ; John Stainer, 1868]. "A woman of Magdala, called Mary." "Mary called Magdalene" was one of "certain women" who, "healed of evil spirits and infirmities, . . . ministered unto him of their substance." Most of the tunes named MAGDALENA, MAGDALENE, or ST. MARY MAGDALENE are used as settings for Lenten hymns or those for use during the Passion season.

MAGDALENE [6 5 6 5 D (4: d d r m / f - m -) ; John B. Dykes, 1862]. Named by its composer, it was written for James Montgomery's hymn beginning:

In the hour of trial,
    Jesus, plead for me.

See MAGDALENA by Stainer.
Also called ST. MARY MAGDALENE.

—— [L. M. (2: dr / m m / m fm / r r / r)]. See MORNING HYMN.

MAGDEBURG. See NEANDER.

MAIDSTONE [7 7 7 7 D (3: S L T / d r m / f m r / m - -) ; Walter B. Gilbert, 1874]. Before coming to Trinity Chapel, New York, where he was organist for nearly thirty years (1869-97), Gilbert was organist at the Old Collegiate Church near the old wharf at Maidstone, by the River Medway (England), one of the most pleasant parts of the old town. Once, as he was waiting in the vestry of the church for a pupil who was late, he occupied himself by writing this tune.

MAITLAND [C. M. (6: MF / S - S d - m / r - d L d) ; George N. Allen, *ca.* 1840]. Doubtless an arbitrary name, as MAITLAND is often referred to as "American Melody" and "Western Melody," even though Allen composed the tune.
Also called BERRIEN, CROSS AND CROWN. CROSS AND CROWN: because written for Thomas Shepherd's hymn beginning, "Must Jesus bear the cross alone."

MALABAR [8 7 8 7 (free: S F M / L L S S / d) ; David McK. Williams, 1941]. Because the hymn to which it is set is a translation from the Syriac Liturgy of Malabar. Named by the composer.

MALVERN [L. M. (2: m mm / m. m / mr mf / s.) ; Lowell Mason, 1847]. This Celtic name is used collectively in connection with a series of towns in the Severn Valley, England. Mason may have been attracted by the melodious sound of the word on one of his visits to England, although Henry L. Mason says it is not an associative name.

MAMRE. See SAUL.

MANCHESTER [C. M. (3: d / m - r / d - *d* / l s f / m -); Robert Wainwright]. From the birthplace of the composer. Named by Ralph Harrison when he introduced the tune into the second volume of *Sacred Harmony* (1791).

Also called LIVERPOOL, because the composer, an organist, spent the last years of his life at the church in Liverpool which later became the Cathedral.

MANNA. See MERCY.

MANOAH [C. M. (3: dr / m - r / d - T / T - L / L -); from Greatorex's *Church Music,* 1851]. Manoah was the father of Samson. A study of the tune names in Greatorex's *Church Music* leads one to believe that those he chose had no special significance.

MANSFIELD [6 6 6 6 8 8 (4: S / d T r d / m r d); Joseph Barnby]. An arbitrary town name supplied by the compilers of Barnby's *Hymn Tunes* (1897).

———— [12 12 8 8 (4: S / d T r d / m r d); Joseph Barnby]. The same tune as above. This is the meter marking given by Barnby.

MANT. See AUTUMN.

MARCUS WHITMAN [8 8 8 10 8 8 (4: s dr m s / l. m l -); William P. Merrill, 1927]. Appropriately named as the setting for Robert Freeman's hymn beginning, "Braving the wilds all unexplored"; for Marcus Whitman was the physician, pioneer, and missionary who proffered his services as "physician, teacher, or agriculturalist" to the American Board of Commissioners for Foreign Missions, and, in 1835, went to Oregon to make an inspection for the Board. Horace Greeley in his *New York Tribune,* March 29, 1843, described him as "a noble pioneer, . . . a man fitted to be

a chief in rearing a moral empire among the wild men of the wilderness."

MARGARET (ELLIOTT) [Irr. (4: dr / m m f mr / d r m); Timothy R. Matthews, 1876]. Why it is called MARGARET, I have not discovered. ELLIOTT, its designating word, is from Emily E. S. Elliott, author of the hymn beginning, "Thou didst leave Thy home and Thy kingly crown," with which it is associated. This is unusual, for it is the custom to use the name of the composer of the tune rather than of the author of the hymn as the designating word. "Margaret," a popular feminine name, is from the Greek, meaning "a pearl." The original Persian word from which the Greek is derived might be translated "born of moonlight," from the belief, or fancy, that pearls were created from dewdrops which pearl-oysters, rising from the sea, received on moonlit nights.

MARINERS [11 11 11 11 (4: m. r d m / s s - - / l. l m l / s - - -); Lily Rendle, 1935]. Because of the lines:

Heavenly Master, bring these mariners in peace
To the Shore Eternal—where the breakers cease,

in May Howland's hymn beginning, "Where the great ships passing," for which it was written.

———— [C. M. (3: S d m / s - f / m f r / d -)]. See CHESTERFIELD by Haweis and RICHMOND by Everett.

———— [8 7 8 7 8 7 (4: s l sf mf / s l sf m)]. See SICILIAN MARINERS.

MARION [S. M., with Refrain (4: d / s mr d r / m - -); Arthur H. Messiter, 1883]. The composer's mother's name was Marian. Both "Marian" and "Marion" are old forms (originally Old French) of "Mary." In commemoration of Mary, the mother of Jesus, this name became that most frequently conferred on girl babies in all Christian countries. Its true meaning, now lost, is, according to Young's *Analytical Concordance,* "bitter" (Hebrew). Note Ruth 1:20: "Call me not Naomi [pleasantness], call me Mara [bitter]: for the Almighty hath dealt bitterly with me." But Hastings, in his Bible dictionary, suggests that "Miriam," a variant, may come from the Egyptian for "beloved of Amon."

MARLBOROUGH [C. M., with Repeats (4: S / d d d r / m rd r)]. See MILES' LANE.

—— [8 7 8 7 D (3: d m f / s - d / ᵇt - l / s -)]. See WENTWORTH by Handel.

MARTYN [7 7 7 7 D (6: m - m m - d / r - r r - -); Simeon B. Marsh, 1834]. It is strange that no reason has ever been given for calling this popular tune to "Jesus, Lover of my soul," MARTYN. At least, persistent search has failed to discover any.

Also called RESURRECTION, because written for the hymn beginning, "Mary, to her Saviour's tomb."

MARTYRDOM [C. M. (3: S / d - L / S - dr / m - r / d -); Hugh Wilson, *ca.* 1800]. Also called ALL SAINTS, AVON, BOSTAL, DRUMCLOG, FENWICK, INVERNESS. This presents an interesting case of the interweaving of names, most of them accounted for by locality or association. There seems no good reason why this tune should have been called either ALL SAINTS or BOSTAL, by some English editors of hymnbooks, when there were so many others much more fitting. It has been suggested that R. A. Smith, who used this famous tune in his *Sacred Music* (1825), did not know of Hugh Wilson's having been born at Fenwick and having written the tune there. He assumed that FENWICK, its first name, had been given it in honor of James Fenwick, the martyred Covenanter.

Therefore, when he used the tune, changing it from duple to triple time, he renamed it MARTYRDOM, honoring not only Fenwick but all other martyred Covenanters. "Covenanters": A feature of Scottish history prior to the Reformation were Covenants, or bands of a similar character, binding the subscribers to common action. The first religious covenant dates from December, 1557, when the leading adherents of the Reformation bound themselves to maintain the evangelical movement in Scotland. All the names for this tune suggest, to some extent, the history of the Covenanters. "Avon," formerly a common, now a proper, name, "is applied by the Britons to rivers in general," according to Camden. It goes back to the Old British *Abona,* the source of the Welsh *Afon.* More than twenty streams in England and Scotland are known by the name "River Avon." At Drumclog, on June 1, 1679, a Covenanter army successfully withstood an attack led by James Graham (afterward Viscount Dundee), while three weeks later, June 22, at Bothwell Brig (Bridge), this same army of Covenanters suffered martyrdom to the extent of five hundred killed and a thousand taken prisoners by forces under the Duke of Monmouth. All these places are in the heart of the old Covenanter country, much of which lies in the valley of the River Avon. Fenwick, distinguished because of the launching there of the first consumers' co-operative movement in 1761, was the birthplace of Hugh Wilson, shoemaker and composer of this tune. INVERNESS is a good Scottish name, though not so definitely associated with Covenanter history as the others.

MARTYRS. See OLD MARTYRS.

MARYTON [L. M. (3: m m m / f - m / r - r / r - -); H. Percy Smith, 1874].

"Maryton": a farm, or manor, name. Also called SUN OF MY SOUL, because written for John Keble's hymn beginning with these words.

MASEFIELD [6 6 6 5 D (4: S / L T d r / d - -) ; Robert G. McCutchan (John Porter), 1933]. Named for John Masefield, author of *Easter,* a pagent, from which the text for which this tune was written was taken. The hymn begins, "Sing, men and angels, sing."

MASON. See BOYLSTON.

MASSAH [S. M. D. (4: d dd / m s d) ; William H. Havergal, 1859]. *Massah* (Hebrew) : "the rock." One of the names from the "Natural Geography of the Bible" which Havergal gave his tunes. This is one given to the locality where Moses struck the rock which produced water.
Also called MERIBAH, which is another name for the same locality.

MATERNA [C. M. D. (4: s / s. m m s / s. r r) ; Samuel A. Ward, 1882]. Also called CIVITAS DEI. Both MATERNA ("mother") and CIVITAS DEI ("City of God") : because written for "O mother dear, Jerusalem," author unknown.

MAUBURN [Irr. (6: m - f s - f / m - r m - -) ; T. Tertius Noble, 1918]. Written as a setting for Jean Mauburn's "Rosary on the Birth of Christ" (1494), beginning, *"Eia mea anima, Bethlehem eamus,"* translated, "Dost Thou in a manger lie," by Elizabeth R. Charles.

MAY SONG [Irr. (6: S / S - M S - S / d - r m -) ; traditional English melody]. From an old folk tune from Somerset, England. "Heave away, my Johnny."

MAYHEW. See ROCKINGHAM by Miller.

MEDIA. See ANTIOCH.

MEDITATION [C. M. (4: m / m m m m / m. d d) ; John H. Gower, 1890]. Named by its composer for his setting to Isaac Watts's "There is a land of pure delight." Certainly a happy choice, for, as the story goes, Watts sat in meditation looking out over Southampton Water and the Isle of Wight when he wrote this hymn.

—————— [11 8 11 8 (4: d / d. r m f / s. l s f / m - r r / d - -)]. See Beloved.

MEIN LEBEN. See BREMEN, by Neumark and by Vulpius.

MEIRIONETH. See below.

MEIRIONYDD [7 6 7 6 D (4: s. f / m mr d r / m - m) ; Welsh hymn melody, 1840]. Pronounced "Mer'-i-on-eth'." It is the Welsh name for the remote western county, Merioneth, in Wales, adjoining that of Carnarvon, the home of the composer William Lloyd. It derives its name from a *cantrev* of ancient Wales, called "Merion," and, with the addition of "shire," is the only county in North Wales to retain its ancient name. *Cantrev* is a Welsh word made up of *cant,* "hundred," plus *tref,* "town, or place." In early Teutonic history a "hundred" was an administrative or territorial district, now specifically applying in central and south England. In north England a comparable district is called a *wapentake.* The division of hundred was introduced into the colonies of Virginia, Maryland, Pennsylvania, and Delaware, and still exists in Delaware. Blackstone (*Commentaries*) says: "As ten families of freeholders made up a town or tithing, so ten tithings composed a superior division called a *hundred,* as consisting of ten times ten families." In the county of Merioneth is located Harlech Castle, famous in story and song; the famous song "March of the men of Harlech" dates from about 1470.

MELCHISADEC. See GERMANY.

MELCOMBE [L. M. (4: s / s f m r / d l s) ; Samuel Webbe, 1782]. "It probably derived its name from Melcombe Regis the northern portion of Weymouth which rapidly rose into repute through the frequent visits of George III, dating from 1789."—*Musical Times*, September 1, 1900. Melcombe, George Bubb Dodington, Baron (1691-1762), a well-known English politician, popularly known as "Bubb Dodington," was raised to the peerage in 1761 as Baron Melcombe, of Melcombe Regis. He was a leading spirit in the "Hell-fire Club." Fielding addressed an epistle to him, Edward Young a satire, and Thomson dedicated his *Summer* to him. Robert Browning, in his "Parleyings with certain people: with George Bubb Dodington," pays him his respects, beginning:

Ah, George Bubb Dodington, Lord Melcombe,—no,
  Yours was the wrong way!

and closing:

  Hence the scoff
That greets your very name: folk see but one
Fool more, as well as knave, in Dodington.

Also called BENEDICTION, GRANTON, NAZARETH, ST. PHILIPS.

MELITA [8 8 8 8 8 8 (4: d / m. m s s / l l s); John B. Dykes, 1861]. The tune was written for William Whiting's hymn "on behalf of those at sea," beginning, "Eternal Father, strong to save," and was named after the island upon which Paul was shipwrecked. (See Acts 28:1.) Melita (*Melite*), now called "Malta," is an island in the Mediterranean Sea, south of Sicily. There is another island by the same name in the Adriatic Sea, and there is some question as to which was Paul's refuge. Biblical geographical scholars are not in agreement on the matter.

MENDELSSOHN [7 7 7 7 D, with Refrain (4: S d d. T / d m m r); Felix Mendelssohn-Bartholdy, 1840, arr.

1855] From the name of its composer. Also called BERLIN, BETHLEHEM, HERALD ANGELS, JESU REDEMPTOR, NATIVITY, ST. VINCENT. BERLIN: the home of the composer. BETHLEHEM and NATIVITY: because of the sentiment of the hymn with which it is almost universally used: "Hark! the herald angels sing." ST. VINCENT: the first name given to it when it appeared in Chope's *Hymn and Tune Book* (1857).

MENDON [L. M. (3: d T d / S - d / T - d / r - -); Old German melody]. The compiler of *Methodist Harmonist* (1821) gave this name, that of a town and village in Worcester County, Massachusetts, from Mendham, England.
Also called GERMAN AIR, DRESDEN.

MENTZER [9 8 9 8 8 8 (free: s m s / l s f m / r - d); from J. B. Koenig's *Harmonischer Lieder Schatz*, 1738]. Because written for Johann Mentzer's hymn of praise and thanksgiving beginning, *"O das ich tausend Zungen hätte,"* of which there are several translations: "Oh that I had a thousand voices," etc.

MERCERSBURG. See LAKE ENON.

MERCY [7 7 7 7 (3: S - L / S d m / m - r / d - -); Louis M. Gottschalk, 1854]. This name was given the tune because of the sentiment of the hymn with which it was early associated, Charles Wesley's hymn beginning, "Depth of mercy, can there be."
Also called GOTTSCHALK, LAST HOPE, MANNA. GOTTSCHALK: the name of the composer. LAST HOPE: the name of the piano composition from which the tune is taken.

MERIBAH [8 8 6 D (3: d- / mm mr mf / s- --); Lowell Mason, 1839]. A biblical name. The place where Moses struck the rock and water flowed forth.

MERIBAH (ROCK OF). See MASSAH.

MERRIAL [6 5 6 5 (4: S S S S / S - S - / L L ᵗS LT / L - - -); Joseph Barnby].

This generally popular tune used with Sabine Baring-Gould's evening hymn beginning, "Now the day is over," was, apparently, first used in the United States by Charles S. Robinson in his *Spiritual Songs for Social Worship* (1878). It had been published by Barnby without any name other than the first line of the hymn. Dr. Robinson greatly admired the tune and made a name for it, EMMELAR, from the initials of his daughter's name, M. L. R. Almost immediately the tune "took" and was used in numerous compilations which were issued soon after the Robinson book appeared. The new word, however, was spelled with only one "m" in most of them. Dr. Robinson soon realized that "Emmelar" was not especially euphonious and made another, MERRIAL, from the initial letters of his daughter's given names, "Mary L.," and it is by this name that the tune is now generally known. This information, secured from Dr. Benjamin Swift, late Congregational minister and musician who knew Dr. Robinson well, is interesting and no doubt true, but it does not give any light as to the use of the word "Merrial" as a tune name in 1868, ten years before Dr. Robinson gave the Barnby tune a name by one J. E. Roe. Roe's tune may be found in the *Book of Common Praise* (Canada, 1908), where it is used as a setting for William Pennefather's hymn beginning, "Jesus, stand among us."
Also called EVENING, REPOSE, TWILIGHT, names suggested by the text of the Baring-Gould hymn.

MERTON [8 7 8 7 (4: d m s s / f l l s); William H. Monk, 1850]. Possibly for Walter de Merton, founder of Merton College, Oxford, or for the parish of Merton, where the benefactor was born and where the "semi-

nary of learning was founded," later being removed to Oxford.

—— [C. M. (3: -S S LT dr / m - d / d -); Henry K. Oliver, 1875]. Frank J. Metcalf suggests the name was given for Merton College, one of the oldest of the Oxford group of colleges.

MERTON COLLEGE [8 7 8 7 D (4: m r d l / s f f m); Alexander R. Reinagle, *ca.* 1830]. Also called MERTON. See MERTON by Monk.

MESSAGE [10 8 8 7 7, with Refrain (4: dr / m mm f m♯r / m - d); H. Ernest Nichol, 1896]. Named by the composer from the sentiment of the hymn for which it was written, beginning, "We've a story to tell to the nations."

MESSIAH [7 7 7 7 D (4: m. r d d / f. m r -); arr. by George Kingsley, 1839]. This tune was arranged from a melody by Louis F. J. Herold which he called "Messiah," and Kingsley took over the name when he compiled the book in which this arrangement first appeared.
Also called BRADFORD, REMEMBRANCE.

—— [C. M., with Repeat (4: d - t. l / s - - f / m - r - / d - -)]. See ANTIOCH.

METZLER'S REDHEAD. See ST. MARY MAGDALENE.

MEYER [8 8 8 4 (4: s / d tl s ls / fm r d); Johann D. Meyer]. For Johann David Meyer, who compiled *Geistliche Seelenfreud* (1692), from which the tune is taken.
Also called ES IST KEIN TAG, from the first line of the German hymn for which it was written.

MILAN. See STABAT MATER.

MILES' LANE [C. M., with Repeats (4: S / d d d r / m rd r); William Shrubsole, 1780]. The name by which this tune is best known was given it by the Reverend Stephen Addington, who was minister of Miles' Lane Meeting House, London, when he compiled *A Collection of Psalm*

Tunes. Miles' Lane, "an easy and shortened corruption" of "St. Michael's Lane," is first mentioned as "Miles' Lane" in the 1758 *London Guide.* It was known as the "Lane of St. Michael de Candeleviestrate" in 1277, as "Seint Michelslane" in 1303, as the "Lane of St. Michael de Croked Lane" later, and then as "St. Mighells Lane" in 1567. St. Michael's Church, after which the Lane was named, was torn down in 1831. The Meeting House referred to has long since been gone, but picturesque Miles' Lane, between Arthur Street and Upper Thames Street, at the bottom of a few steps from Crooked Lane, still remains. Sometime in the latter part of the seventeenth century, one John Cooke left some money to the authorities of St. Michael's Church to provide for the maintenance of a lantern and candle to be kept and hanged out at the corner of St. Michael's Lane and Thomas Street from Michaelmas to Lady Day between the hours of nine or ten in the evening until four or five in the morning, to provide the lighting of the way for travelers through those streets.

Also called HARBOROUGH, MARLBOROUGH, ST. ASAPH, SCARBOROUGH. HARBOROUGH: for the town in which the Reverend Addington, who named this tune, ministered before going to London. The three "borough" names, Har-, Marl-, and Scar-, are interesting and somewhat intriguing; perhaps they were intended to be the same.

MILITANT. See SARUM.

MILLENIAL DAWN. See WEBB.

MILLENIUM [6 6 6 6 8 8 (4: S / d d d TL / S - -); composer unknown, before 1850]. Literally, an aggregate of a thousand years; more commonly, an interval of a thousand years. Theologically, a period during which the Kingdom of Christ shall be established on earth and dominate all other authorities. Seemingly of peculiar interest to Methodists, this tune was long used with "Let heaven and earth combine," from the Wesleys' *Hymns for the Nativity of our Lord* (1744), in later years being associated with Charles Wesley's "Blow ye the trumpet, blow," and "Arise, my soul, arise." The latter two hymns are now almost always sung to the tune LENOX.

――― [7 6 7 6 D (4: m / s s s s / d - m)]. See GREENLAND.

MIRFIELD [C. M. (4: S / d d d MF / S S S) ; Arthur Cottman, 1874]. Mirfield is in the West Riding of Yorkshire, England, where there is located an Anglican theological college. Near Dewsbury, it was a part of that parish until 1261. The circumstances under which the district became parochial are:

During the Heptarchy, the Lady of Sir John Heton, then lord of the manor, being on her way to the parish church, before dawn on Christmas day, attacked by robbers, and her attendant murdered, the pope, at the intercession of her husband who was then at Rome, granted permission to build a chapel here.— Lewis.

MIRIAM [8 7 8 7 D (4: m s m d / T d r m)]. See DEERHURST.

――― [11 11 12 11, with Refrain (3: s . l s / l s d / r m f / mr mf sl)]. See AVISON.

MISSIONARY. See GREENLAND.

MISSIONARY CHANT [L. M. (3: -m mm / m d rr / T -) ; Heinrich C. Zeuner, 1832]. Because set to Bourne H. Draper's hymn beginning, "Ye Christian heralds, go proclaim."

MISSIONARY HYMN [7 6 7 6 D (4: d - / m s s l / s - m) ; Lowell Mason, 1823]. So named because written for Bishop Heber's great missionary hymn, "From Greenland's icy mountains."

Also called GOSPEL BANNER, HEBER. GOSPEL BANNER: from associated texts. The tune is commonly used with texts in this meter. HEBER: from the author of the hymn for which it was written.

MITYLENE. See ST. ANATOLIUS by Brown.

MOLLESON [C. M. (4: S / d d d TL / S); Douglas Fletcher, 1924]. Named by its composer after E. A. Molleson, Warden of St. Andrew's Protestant Episcopal Church on upper Fifth Avenue, New York City, because the first words of the hymn for which it was composed, "My God I love Thee not because I hope for heaven thereby," seemed "especially to fit the personality of his old friend."

MONA. See EVAN.

MONKLAND [7 7 7 7 (4: d m s m / fs lt d -); John B. Wilkes (?)]. Named for the church at Monkland, England, where the composer was organist. This was the parish of Sir Henry W. Baker, vicar at Monkland. It was given this name when it was included in *Hymns Ancient and Modern* (1861).

MONK'S GATE [6 5 6 5 6 6 6 5 (4: d. r / m d mf s / l -); traditional English melody]. Ralph Vaughan Williams, while collecting English folk songs, heard this tune from a singer at Monk's Gate, near Horsham, West Sussex.

MONSELL [S. M. (4: m / m f s r / m - -); Joseph Barnby, 1869]. Because written for John S. B. Monsell's hymn beginning, "Sweet is Thy mercy, Lord."
Also called ST. ANDREW. Barnby was organist at the church of St. Andrew, Wells Street, London, from 1863 to 1871. It was while there that he wrote the tune. See further under ST. ANDREW by Barnby.

——— [12 10 12 10 (2: d TL / S MS / L FL / LS S); William F. Sherwin, *ca.* 1877]. Written for "Wor-

ship the Lord in the beauty of holiness" by John S. B. Monsell.

MONTGOMERY [10 10 11 11 (3: d / d s l / l s f / m r d / s -); attributed to John Stanley]. While this tune is attributed to John Stanley, it is not found in any of his works. It was called MONTGOMERY when Ralph Harrison included it in his *Sacred Harmony*, Part II (1784). Formerly a Long Meter tune, it has been used with 12 11 12 11 as well as 10 10 11 11 texts. It is the tune used with William H. Draper's church-dedication hymn beginning, "In our day of thanksgiving one psalm let us offer." Known as MAGDALEN when it first appeared in 1762 in *The Tunes and Hymns as they are used at the Magdalen Chapel Properly set for the Organ, Harpsichord and Guittar*, it was credited to S. Jarvis in *Psalms, Hymns and Anthems for the Foundling Chapel* (1809) and was called ST. ANDREW because John Stanley was onetime organist at St. Andrew's, Holborn.
Also called BLOOMSBURY, BURTON, DERBY, NEWTON, ST. GEORGE.

——— [L. M. (3: d / d s l / l s f / m r d / s -); attributed to W. Champness]. This is the same as the tune attributed to John Stanley and appeared in Champness' *Musical Companion* (1772). See above.

——— [S. M. D. (4: S / S S m. r / d - -); arr. by Arthur S. Sullivan, *ca.* 1874]. So called because written for James Montgomery's hymn beginning, "Forever with the Lord." It is Sullivan's arrangement of Isaac B. Woodbury's tune known as NEARER HOME (which see). An abbreviation of the tune is known as LAKE ENON (which see).

——— [S. M. D. (4: S / S S m. r / d - -)]. See NEARER HOME.

——— [Irr. (3: s / d s l / s s f / m r d / s s)]. See MAGDALEN by Jarvis.

——— [7 7 7 7 (4: m. f / s d t l / s -)]. See INNOCENTS.

MORECAMBE [10 10 10 10 (4: m - m m / f - m - / l s f f / m - - -); Frederick C. Atkinson, 1870]. A well-known watering place on Morecambe Bay, west England. Atkinson was for some years organist at one of the churches at Bradford, not a great distance from Morecambe. Morecambe is the name of another town in the Midland district of England where a famous musical festival, an outgrowth of, or patterned after, the Eisteddfod, is held.

Also called HELLESPONT, its first name. It was written as a setting for Lyte's "Abide with me."

MORGAN. See EASTER HYMN.

MORNING HYMN [L. M. (2: dr / m m / m fm / r r / r); François H. Barthélémon, 1785]. Because written for Bishop Ken's morning hymn beginning, "Awake my soul, and with the sun."

Also called BARTHELEMON, HIPPOLYTUS, MAGDALENE, SEMLEY, WATTS. BARTHELEMON: for the composer; printed without the accents. HIPPOLYTUS is the second given name of the composer. WATTS: because used with one of Isaac Watts's hymns; in *The Sabbath* (1873).

MORNING LIGHT. See WEBB.

MORNING STAR [11 10 11 10 (2: m rd / T LS / Sd Td / m r); James P. Harding, 1901]. Suggested by the first and last stanzas (the same) of Bishop Heber's hymn:

Brightest and best of the sons of the
  morning,
  Dawn on our darkness and lend us
    Thine aid;
Star of the East, the horizon adorning,
  Guide where our infant Redeemer is
    laid.

This name has also been given to the German chorale *"Wie schön leuchtet der Morgenstern."*

MORNINGTON [S. M. (2: s sf / m r / d); Garrett Wellesley]. After the composer, first Earl of Mornington, father of the Duke of Wellington, who, about 1760, wrote a chant for use in the Dublin, Ireland, Cathedral, from which this tune was arranged.

MORTRAM. See YORKSHIRE.

MORVEN [C. M. (2: d / r m / s d / l s / m); Robert A. Smith, early 18th century]. The name was given to this tune of folk-ballad origin by its composer. A middle-eighteenth-century Scottish schoolmaster, poet, and politician named James Macpherson published the *Poems of Ossian,* claiming they were translations of ancient Gaelic verse. In these poems he created a mythical kingdom in Scotland which he named "Morven" and gave its capital the name "Selma." Neil Ross, Celtic scholar, has said:

Macpherson, like Dickens, had a faculty for coining new names. Neither Morven nor Selma occurs in the genuine Ossianic remnants. The names were pure inventions of Macpherson. In his day a century and a half ago, his *Ossian* was taken for the real article, and his fine-sounding names were popular. It is not surprising that even psalm-tunes composed in that period should be called by such lovely mystical but mythical, names. They are poetic merely.

MOSCOW   [11 10 11 9 (4: s - 1 1 / s. m d -)]. See RUSSIAN HYMN.

——— [6 6 4 6 6 6 4 (3: s m d / r d T / d - -)]. See TRINITY.

MOTTRAM. See YORKSHIRE.

MT. CALVARY [C. M. (4: m / r d T L / L. S S); Robert P. Stewart, 1874]. Used as a setting for a hymn by John M. Neale, the first stanza of which is:

O very God of very God,
  And very Light of Light,
Whose feet this earth's dark valley trod
  That so it might be bright.

—— [C. M. (3: S d m / s - f / m f r / d -)]. See Chesterfield.

MT. Holyoke [8 7 8 7 D (4: S S / m. m r m / d S) ; Maurice L. Wostenholm, 1910]. Edward Dwight Eaton wrote me June 6, 1936:

Knowing that I was compiling a hymnal, Dr. Burton [Henry Burton, who wrote "There's a light upon the mountains," for which the English composer wrote this tune] sent me this hymn and tune about 1912; I suppose they had not been in this country before. I think Dr. Burton mentioned that the composer was an organist in England. There was, so far as I remember, no name for the tune, and I gave it the name of Mt. Holyoke, as I was using several names associated with colleges, and was attracted to this name by the first line of the hymn, and its appropriateness to the spirit which has been associated with that college.

Its composer used the first line of the hymn for a title.

MT. Olive. See Deerhurst.

Mount Sion [C. M. D. (2: s s / sl td / m r / d -); Horatio Parker, 1886]. From the sentiment of the text from Tate and Brady (1698), one line of which reads, "Thou holy city of our God," based on Psalm 122.

Mozart [Various; Wolfgang A. Mozart]. Several different adaptations from Mozart's works, in various meters, are so named. One of them, a Long Meter tune (3: d d d / T. L S / f - f / m - -), is also called Zelotes. *Zelotes,* meaning "zealous," is a surname for Simon, one of the twelve apostles. This is a good name when the tune is used with "Fight the good fight," as is frequently the case. Other tunes called Mozart are:
8 8 8 8 8 8 (3: s / s m m / m d d / T r f / f m), a variant of Ariel, which see.
7 7 7 7, with Hallelujah   (4: m fr dS dr / m fr d -).
L. M. (3: S / S d T / d - r / m - sf / m r).

C. M. (3: d / d T d / r - r / r d r / m -).

Müller [11 11 11 11 (3: s / s. f m / m. r d / d T L / S -); James R. Murray, 1887]. From the said-to-be composer of the tune, Carl Müller, which is used with the anonymous "Away in a manger."

Munich [7 6 7 6 D (4: dr / m l s f / m - m) ; arr. 1863, from Felix Mendelssohn-Bartholdy, 1847]. Known as the "Königsberg Chorale" in Germany, it is another one of the few tunes of its class which has been given a special town or place name. The word "Munich" is a variation of *Monachus,* "a monk," because monks one time owned the site of the present city of that name.
Also called Bartholdy, the suffix which the composer's father added to the illustrious family name. Contrary to the common, popular belief, Felix Mendelssohn's mother's maiden name was Leah Salomon, not Leah Bartholdy; the name "Bartholdy" had been assumed by her brother when he decided to embrace Christianity. Abraham Mendelssohn, Felix's father, took the name "Bartholdy" at the suggestion of his brother-in-law, Salomon Bartholdy, after "resolving to have the children trained in the Protestant faith." While he was neither an orthodox Jew nor a believing Christian, Abraham's religious views are strikingly expressed in a letter he wrote Fanny Mendelssohn soon after her confirmation (Reformed Church) in 1820:

You have taken, my dear daughter, an important step in life, and from my heart I wish you joy in it; nay, I feel myself compelled to think earnestly over many things which have not yet been talked of between us. If there be a God, what kind of a God he may be; whether a part of ourselves is eternal, and after the other part has vanished, whether it lives on, and where, and how. All this

I do not know, and therefore, I have not expressed an opinion of it to you; but I know that in me, and in you, and in all men, there is an unchangeable leaning to all that is good, true, and right; that there is a conscience which warns us and guides us when we depart from the true way. This I know, this I believe; I live in the strength of it, and it is my religion. This I could not teach to you, and no one can learn it. Every one possesses this who does not purposely and meaningly deny it, and you would not do this, I know; for you have the example of your mother, that most noble, most worthy woman, whose whole life is the fulfilment of duty and love, and a desire to promote others' welfare. We have trained you and your brothers and sisters in the Christian faith, because this is the faith of the most cultivated men, and contains nothing which can estrange you from the good, rather much that will aid you to be obedient, to be patient, to bear with resignation what you have to bear; not to speak of the Founder of this faith, known to so many, but followed by so few.

Felix also was a member of the Reformed Church.

MY BELOVED. See BELOVED.

N

NACHTLIED. See FLEMMING.

NAOMI [C. M. (4: m mm s fm / rm f m); Hans G. Nägeli, 1836]. One of the Old Testament names used by Lowell Mason. *Naomi* (Hebrew), meaning "pleasant," was the wife of Elimelech, mother of Mahlon and Chilion, and mother-in-law of Ruth the Moabitess. First using the tune with Anne Steele's hymn, "Father, whate'er of earthly bliss," the third stanza of which reads:

Let the sweet hope that Thou art mine
  My life and death attend;
Thy presence through my journey shine,
  And crown my journey's end,

Mason possibly recalled Ruth's plea

to Naomi, "Entreat me not to leave thee" (Ruth 1:16). However, this is mere surmise.

NATIONAL HYMN [10 10 10 10 (4: d - d. r / m - - f / m d d T / d - - -); George W. Warren, 1894]. Because of the patriotic character of the words for which it was written, Daniel C. Roberts' "God of our fathers, whose almighty hand."

——— [6 6 4 6 6 6 4 (3: d d r / T. d r)]. See AMERICA.

NATIVITY [C. M. (4: m mm s s / d d m); Henry Lahee, 1855]. This first appeared, unnamed, to Doddridge's Nativity hymn beginning, "High let us swell our tuneful notes," which has, in some books, carried the heading "The Angels' Song at Christ's Birth."

——— [7 7 7 7 D, with Refrain (4: S d d. T / d m m r)]. See MENDELSSOHN.

——— [10 10 10 10 10 10 (4: d - r / m - - f / s m f s / l - - -)]. See YORKSHIRE.

NAVARRE. See TOULON.
NAYLAND. See ST. STEPHEN by Jones.
NAYLOR. See ST. STEPHEN by Jones.
NAZARETH [6 6 6 6 8 8 (4: S / m T d r / d - T); James W. Elliott, ca. 1874]. Because set to C. E. Oakley's hymn:

Hills of the North, rejoice;
  River and mountain-spring,
Hark to the advent voice;
  Valley and lowland sing.
Though absent long, your Lord is nigh;
He judgment brings and victory.

——— [L. M. (4: s / s f m r / d l s)]. See MELCOMBE.

NEANDER [8 7 8 7 7 7 (4: d. r m d / m f s s); Joachim Neander, 1680]. From its composer. Also called EPHESUS, MAGDEBURG, UNSER HERRSCHER. UNSER HERRSCHER: the name of the German chorale, *Unser Herrscher, unser König* ("Our Ruler, our King").

———— [6 5 6 5 (4: m m r r / d - T -)]. See CASWALL.

NEARER HOME [S. M. D. (4: S/ S S m. r / d - -) ; Isaac B. Woodbury, 1852]. Because written for James Montgomery's hymn beginning, "Forever with the Lord," which, in *A Poet's Portfolio* (1835), was headed, "At Home in Heaven. Ist Thessalonians iv. 17."
Also called MONTGOMERY. See MONTGOMERY by Sullivan.

NEED [6 4 6 4, with Refrain (3: d / m. r dT / d -) ; Robert Lowry, 1873]. Mrs. Robert Lowry, widow of the composer, has asked that the tune be known by the title "I need Thee every hour," this being the title of one of her husband's numerous gospel songs. In a letter to me she objected to the use of any name for the tune alone.

NETTLETON [8 7 8 7 D (3: mr / d d ms / r r); John Wyeth (?), 1825]. This name because it has been attributed to Asahel Nettleton, noted evangelist of the early nineteenth century.
Also called HALLELUJAH, THE GOOD SHEPERD. HALLELUJAH: because in the days of its greatest popularity it was always sung with the chorus "Hallelujah! Hallelujah! We are on our journey home." This chorus and many others were often attached to various hymns because they were commonly known and great favorites with the frontier people. (See ALLELUIA.) THE GOOD SHEPHERD: because of the sentiment of the hymn with which it was early associated.

NEUMARK. See BREMEN by Neumark.

NEW BRITAIN. See AMAZING GRACE.

NEW CREATION. See CREATION.

NEW 113TH [8 8 8 8 8 (3: d / T. L S / d r m / m r d / d T); William Hayes, middle 18th century]. This was set to Psalm 134 in Hayes's *Sixteen Psalms*, designed "for the use of Magdalen College Chapel in Ox-

ford." Why it was called NEW 113TH is a mystery.

NEW ST. ANNE. See ST. GEORGE by Smart.

NEW YORK. See WEBB.

NEWBERRY [L. M. (4: L / #S L T d / rd TL #S -)]. See CANTERBURY, anon.
———— [7 6 7 6 D (4: m / s s s s / d - m)]. See GREENLAND.

NEWBURYPORT. See CANDLER.

NEWINGTON. See ST. STEPHEN by Jones.

NEWMAN. See GERONTIUS.

NEWMARKET. See LIVERPOOL by Richard Wainwright.

NEWRY. See DUKE STREET.

NEWTON [C. M. (4: d - / s m d s / l d t -)]. See LONDON NEW.
———— [S. M. (2: d ss / m s / d)]. See SILVER STREET.
———— [L. M. D. (6: d - - / d S d m d m / s - -)]. See CONTRAST.
———— [7 7 7 7 D (3: dr / m. m fm / r -)]. See SABBATH.
———— [12 11 12 11 (3: d / d s l / l s f / m r d / s -)]. See MONTGOMERY.
———— [Irr. (3: s / d s l / s s f / m r d / s s)]. See MAGDALEN.

NEWTOUN. See LONDON NEW.

NICAEA [11 12 12 10 (4: d d m m / s - s -) ; John B. Dykes, 1861]. From the ancient city Nicaea (Anglicized "Nice"), in Bithynia, Asia Minor, forty-eight miles south of Constantinople, on Lake Ascania; now called "Isnik." The seat of the first general council of the Christian church (325), convened by Constantine, it was here that the main part of the Nicene Creed, that which established the doctrine of the Trinity, was adopted. The tune, written especially for Bishop Heber's "Hymn to the Trinity, "Holy, holy, holy! Lord God Almighty!" was appropriately named by its composer.
Also called SANCTUS, from the repeated use of the word "holy" in the hymn by Bishop Heber.

NIGHTFALL [11 11 11 5 (4: s - f d / m - r -) ; Joseph Barnby, 1897]. Also called HOREB, RYDAL, TWILIGHT. NIGHTFALL and TWILIGHT reflect the sentiment of the hymn beginning, "Now God be with us, for the night is closing." *Horeb* (Hebrew): Mount Horeb, "the mountain of God," the place where God made the covenant with the Hebrews.

NISSI [11 11 11 11 11 11 (4: s s s l / s - s - / l l t m / d - - -); Joseph Barnby, 1872]. This appropriate name, meaning "banner" (see Exod. 17:15), used with Thomas A. Potter's processional hymn for children, beginning, "Brightly gleams our banner," was given it by someone other than the composer.

NOEL. See THE FIRST NOEL.

NON NOBIS DOMINE [6 6 6 6 D (3: L L L / L*S L -); David McK. Williams, 1942]. Written for Rudyard Kipling's stanzas based on Psalm 115, which in Latin begins: *"Non nobis, Domine!"* ("Not unto us, O Lord.")

NORFOLK [L. M. (4: S / d r m f / m r d); Samuel Howard, middle 18th century]. Named after the "shire of the north folk." Bede used the Old English word to denote the people north of the Humber River in contradistinction to those in Suffolk, the southern part of East Anglia.

NORTH COATES [6 5 6 5 (4: S S L L / d - d -); Timothy R. Matthews, 1862]. From the English village, in Lincolnshire, where the composer was at one time rector.

NORTHERN TUNE. See CARLISLE by Lockhart.

NORWICH [C. M. (4: d / m f s d / r m f)]. See DUNDEE, French.

——— [C. M. (3: L / L - T / d - r / m r d / T)]. See BURFORD.

——— [7 7 7 7 (4: m f s l / r r m -)]. See GIBBONS.

——— [L. M. (4: S - L T / d - d - / r - m f / m - - -)]. See LASUS.

NOTTINGHAM. See ST. MAGNUS.

NOVA VITA [S. M. (3: m m m / m - r / r - -); Lister R. Peace, 1941]. *Nova*

vita (Latin): "new life." From second line of Edwin Hatch's hymn beginning:

> Breathe on me, breath of God,
> Fill me with life anew.

NOWELL. See THE FIRST NOEL.

NUN DANKET [6 7 6 7 6 6 6 6 (4: s / s s l l / s - -); Johann Crüger, 1647]. From the first line of the German hymn beginning, *"Nun danket, alle Gott"* by Martin Rinkart. Also called GRATITUDE, WITTENBERG. GRATITUDE: from the sentiment of the hymn. WITTENBERG: from Crüger's association with the university of that place.

NUN DANKET ALL'. See GRÄFENBERG.

NUN FREUT EUCH. See LUTHER.

NUN RUHEN ALLE WÄLDER. See INNSBRUCK.

NUREMBERG. See DESSAU.

NYLAND [7 6 7 6 D (4: s / m r d r d / L - S); Finnish folk melody]. Melody from the Finnish province of Nyland.

O

O BONA PATRIA. See HOMELAND.

O JESU [8 6 8 6 8 8 (4: S / d r m f / s fm r); from *Hirschberg Gesangbuch*, 1741]. From the first words of the German hymn *"O Jesu, warum legst du mir,"* for which it was the original setting.

O PERFECT LOVE [11 10 11 10 (4: d - m s / s - s - / s s d t / t - l -); Joseph Barnby, 1889]. From the first words of an anthem which the composer wrote for the wedding of the Duke of Fife to Princess Louise of Wales, and from which this hymn tune was taken. Also called FIFE, SANDRINGHAM. SANDRINGHAM: after a residence of the English royal family, near the coast of Norfolk, north of Lynn.

OBLATIONS [S. M. D. (4: d / S S L d / S - -); John Stainer, 1875]. From the sentiment expressed in the hymn beginning "Blessed and Holy Three," the second stanza reading, in part:

> Lord, we thy servants taught
> That Thou wilt not disdain
> Oblations to thine altar brought.

OCEAN. See ELLESDIE.

OHNE RAST. See VIENNA by Knecht.

OLDBRIDGE [8 8 8 4 (3: m m m / m - d / r - m / d - -); Robert N. Quaile, 1903]. The composer contributed three hymn tunes to *The Methodist Sunday School Hymn-Book* (English). One of them was called ATH-LONE, the name of a town in the Lough Ree district, central Ireland. At Athlone there is a famed old bridge; there may be some connection between that "old bridge" and the name of this tune.

OLD CAROL. See BETHLEHEM.

OLD FRENCH MELODY. See INNOCENTS.

OLD MARTYRS [C. M. (4: L / d L m d / T L m); from the *Scottish Psalter*, 1615]. This is one of the "Scottish tunes" of *Ravenscroft's Psalter* of 1621. It received the name OLD MARTYRS because of the tradition that the Covenanters went into the battle of Drumclog (June 1, 1679) singing this tune to Psalm 76. In *The Men of the Covenant* Alexander Smellie gives this vivid account of the scene:

> Down the face of the slope the Cove-nanters advanced, singing the familiar verses of one of the Scottish metrical psalms, the seventy-sixth, to the fine old tune, as tradition relates, of *Martyrs*. They were kindling words which rang out in the resonant bass of two hundred and forty strong-throated and strong-souled men.

> In Judah's land God is well known,
> His name's in Israel great;
> In Salem is His tabernacle,
> In Sion is His seat.

> There arrows of the bow he brake,
> The shield, the sword, the war,

> More glorious Thou than hills of prey,
> More excellent art far.

> Those that were stout of heart are spoiled,
> They slept their sleep outright;
> And none of those their hands did find,
> That were the men of might.

The battle was half won which could be introduced by a song so confident and unafraid. . . . The suddenness of the attack was decisive.

Also called MARTYRS.

OLD 22ND [C. M. D. (4: d - d r / m - s - / f f m); from the *Anglo-Genevan Psalter*, 1556]. First used with Psalm 16 but in succeeding psalters commonly used with Psalm 22, from which the name comes.

OLD 100TH [L. M. (4: d - / d T L S / d - r - / m -); from the *Genevan Psalter*, 1551]. From its association with Psalm 100. "Old" now prefixes the names of the tunes taken from Day's *Psalter* (1562). For some time after 1700 it was called SAVOY because frequently used by a Huguenot congregation established in the Savoy, London. It was at the Savoy, in Cromwell's time, that the Independents adopted a Confession of Faith, and here was held, also, the celebrated "Savoy Conference" for the revision of the *Prayer Book*.

OLD 104TH [10 10 11 11 (3: L / d T L / m - d / r f m / r -); from Ravenscroft's *Psalter*, 1621]. Used with Psalm 104.

Also called ST. WERBURG.

OLD 107TH [C. M. (3: L / L m ll / ss m); from *"French Psalter,"* 1543-44]. Used with Psalm 107.

OLD 112TH [8 8 8 8 8 8 (4: m / m d r m / d T L); from *Geistliche Lieder*, 1539]. This famous old tune was given to Luther by Walther in manuscript in 1530. It was written to be used with Luther's version of the Lord's Prayer. Coming into the

Anglo-Genevan Psalter of 1561 as a setting for Psalm 112, it became familiarly known as OLD 112TH. John Wesley was fond of this tune and used it in his *Foundery Tune Book* (1742), calling it PLAYFORD'S TUNE, doubtless because having taken it from one of John Playford's books.

Also called VATER UNSER, from the first line of Luther's rendition of the Lord's Prayer, *"Vater unser im Himmelreich."*

OLD 113TH [8 8 8 8 8 8 (free: d - / d r m d m f / s -) ; from the *Strassburg Psalter,* 1539]. Popularly known as the "Huguenot Marseillaise" or "Battle Song," because of its use during the civil conflicts before 1572, this was set first to Psalm 119, then to Psalm 36, later to Psalm 68, according to Waldo S. Pratt.

Also called CASSEL, COLUMBIA, INNOCENTS, LUCERNE, PATRIARCH'S TUNE, RIDLEY, ST. EDMUND, STEPNEY. COLUMBIA is a shortened and corrupted version of the tune. RIDLEY is an abridged form.

OLD 116TH PSALM. See WINDSOR.

OLD 120TH [6 6 6 6 6 (4: d - / m f s l / s -) ; from Este's *Psalter,* 1592]. From its use with Psalm 120 in the *Old Version* by Sternhold and Hopkins, where it supplanted an earlier setting.

OLD 124TH [10 10 10 10 10 (4: d - r m / f - m - / r d d T / d - - -) ; from the *Genevan Psalter,* 1551]. Originally set to Psalm 124. It was sung as a hymn of triumph and thanksgiving on December 12, 1602, by the Genevans after the final repulse of the forces of the Duke of Savoy in the treacherous so-called "Escalade" (scaling of the walls by ladders) attempt to capture their city. The tune is sometimes mistakenly called TOULON (which see).

OLD 132ND. See ST. FLAVIAN.

OLD 134TH [S. M. (4: S / d m r r / m - -) ; from the *Genevan Psalter,*

1551]. The tune comes from *Pseaumes octante trois* (Geneva, 1551), in which it was set to Psalm 101. In the *Anglo-Genevan Psalter* of 1561, it was used with Psalm 134; hence this name. After the tune had been dropped from tune books from about 1595, it was revived by William Crotch, who used it in his *Psalm Tunes* (1836), giving it the name by which it is now most commonly known, ST. MICHAEL. This name comes from St. Michael's College, Tenbury, England. "Michael," the name of the archangel, first and mightiest of all created spirits, means "like unto God." The office of Michael the saint is twofold: (1) patron saint of the Church, and (2) lord of the souls of the dead. Treated in art in both aspects, he is frequently shown in pictures of the Madonna and Child presenting the balance to Christ. An old English coin was called an "angel" because it bore an image of Michael.

OLEAN. See SABBATH.

OLIVE'S BROW [L. M. (4: s - / s s l l / s - s - / s -) ; William B. Bradbury, 1853]. From the first line of William B. Tappan's hymn beginning, " 'Tis midnight; and on Olive's brow," for which the tune was written. The reference is, of course, to Jesus' sojourn to the Mount of Olives on the night before he was crucified: "And when they had sung a hymn, they went out into the mount of Olives" (Matthew 26:30). The Mount of Olives, or Olivet, the Arabic *Jebel et-Tōr,* forms a part of a ridge of limestone hills about a mile in length from north to south, 200 feet above the site of the Temple, and refers specifically to the ridge 2,680 feet above sea level, facing the Temple Mount at Jerusalem and separated from it by the vale of Kidron. It has three summits, each with a distinct name. Also called the Mount of Corruption (II Kings 23:13), because here it was that Solomon built temples to the gods of the Ammonites (I Kings 11:7) and of the Moabites out of compliance with the wishes of his wives from those nations. Bethlehem and the Mount of Olives since the second century have been goals of Christian pilgrims. On the Mount of Olives the mind naturally turns to the Garden of Gethsemane and the scene of the Crucifixion. Among the Greeks the olive, sacred to Pallas Athene, was regarded as an emblem of charity. A crown of olive twigs was given to the citizen who merited well of his country and was the highest prize of the Olympian games. An olive branch, from the most ancient times, was regarded as a symbol of reconciliation and peace and was looked upon as a sort of flag of truce, this use perhaps being based on the account of Noah's dove (Genesis 8:11).

OLIVET [6 6 4 6 6 6 4 (4: d - m s / s. f m -); Lowell Mason, 1832]. A variant form of the name for the Mount of Olives. (See OLIVE'S BROW.) Written for Ray Palmer's hymn beginning, "My faith looks up to Thee," its name was doubtless suggested by the sentiment of the hymn. Also called HARLAN, the name given it by English editors. See page 32 for comment on the English way of renaming Mason's tunes.

—— [S. M. D. (4: S / S d d m / s - -); John B. Dykes, 1870]. Written for an Ascensiontide hymn, the tune was first called ASCENSION when submitted to E. H. Bickersteth for a hymnal he was compiling. Because another tune had the name ASCENSION, Bickersteth suggested the name OLIVET, which met with the hearty approval of Dr. Dykes. See OLIVE'S BROW.

—— [L. M. (4: m - m m / s - - s / l s f s / m - -)]. See EUCHARIST.

OLIVIA. See CONSOLATION by Webbe.

OLMUTZ [S. M. (3: S / LS d r / d -); arr. from a Gregorian chant]. In the *National Psalmist,* edited by Mason and Webb, a note says: "Arr. from Gregorian Chant (Tone VII) by L. Mason and first published as a metrical tune in 1834." In Czechoslovakia, Olmutz was the seat of the important conference which led to the forming of the German Empire. Here it was that Bismarck made his famous "Olmutz speech."

—— [L. M. (4: d / r m m r / d T L); arr. from the Sarum *Vexilla Regis* melody, 1863]. See above.

OLNEY [S. M. (4: s - / s. f m f / s -); Lowell Mason, *ca.* 1830]. Olney, a market town in Buckinghamshire, England, was the place where John Newton and William Cowper worked so long together writing, compiling, and editing the famous *Olney Hymns* (1779).

Olney . . . is situated in the near-by valley of the slow-winding river Ouse, as if it had been formerly the bed of a wide and shallow lake. Long before arriving I saw the spire of John Newton's church, frequently referred to by Cowper as a grateful waymark in his weary pilgrimage. It is the only salient feature of the otherwise flat and melancholy scene.—James M. Hoppin.

—— [C. M. (4: s / s s l m / s. f f); arr. by John F. Bridge, late 19th century]. This is an arrangement of "There is a green hill far away" by Gounod. See above.

OMBERSLEY [L. M. (3: m r d / f - f / f - f / m - -); William H. Gladstone, 1872]. The name of a beautiful English village near Worcester.

104TH PSALM. See HANOVER.

ONEONTA [L. M. (4: m / s s d f / f mr s); Walter H. Hall, 1918]. From Oneonta, New York, the home of the composer's wife before their marriage.

OPORTO. See ADESTE FIDELES.

ORIEL [8 7 8 7 8 7 (4: d d d d / r m f m) ; from *Cantica Sacra*, 1840]. There may be some connection between this name and Oriel College, Oxford, which in turn derives its name from a *messuage* (ménage) previously occupied by Seneschal Hall, but renamed when, in 1317, the king gave a tenement (in English law a holding of land or real property) called *L'Oriele*, on which the college was founded.

Also called ALLELUIA DULCE CARMEN, DULCE CARMEN, CORINTH, PANGE LINGUA, TANTUM ERGO. PANGE LINGUA: These words have little meaning by themselves; they are simply the opening words of a stanza of a well-known Latin hymn beginning, *"Pange lingua gloriosi,"* and the title of a certain hymn used in solemn services in the Roman Church.

ORIENTIS PARTIBUS [7 7 7 7 (3: d - r / m - d / r - T / d - -) ; Pierre de Corbeil (?) , *ca.* 1210]. Because it was the melody for the song,

> *Orientis partibus,*
> *Adventavit Asinus,*
> *Pulcher et fortissimus,*
> *Sarcinis aptissimus,*

in a medieval play known as the *Feast of the Ass.* The tune REDHEAD No. 45 is nothing more than this tune in 4- rather than 3-time.

Also called ARLEY, ASS'S SEQUENCE, CORTON, ST. MARTIN.

ORIGEN. See MAGDALEN COLLEGE.

ORISONS. See DIX.

ORTONVILLE [C. M. (6: S / d - d r - r / m - r d -) ; Thomas Hastings, 1837]. A town, or place, name. The word *orton* (Teutonic) means "wealth"; hence "place of wealth."

OSBORNE [C. M. (4: L LT d f / mr dT L) ; Henry Carey, 1736]. From "An Elegiac Ode to the Memory of that sober Ingenious Youth Mr. Richard Osborne. Educated by the Author, and lamented by all. He died Dec. 22, 1736, aged 19." Inasmuch as Richard Osborne was a favorite pupil of Carey's, it is quite fitting that his melody should have been set to his own words, "Where is my soul's chief comfort flown."

OSLO [7 6 7 6 D (4: L / L m mr dT / L - ♯S) ; traditional Norwegian melody]. For Oslo, capital of Norway.

OXNAM [S. M. (4: S / m r d T / d - -) ; Robert G. McCutchan, 1929]. For Bishop G. Bromley Oxnam of the Methodist Church. I wrote this tune for William P. Merrill's brotherhood hymn beginning, "Rise up, O men of God," while dean of the school of music of DePauw University. Dr. Oxnam was then president of that institution. Feeling that the President, in his daily life, exemplified the words of the third and fourth lines of the hymn,

> Give heart and mind and soul and strength
> To serve the King of kings,[1]

I gave it his name.

P

PALESTINE. See ST. MICHEL'S.

PALESTRINA [8 8 8 4, with Alleluias (3: s s s / l - s / s f m / s - -) ; Giovanni P. da Palestrina]. This adaptation, by William H. Monk, is from Palestrina's "Gloria," from *Magnificat Tertii Toni* (1591) .

Also called CONQUEROR, VICTORY. VICTORY: suggested by the text of Francis Potts's translation of an anonymous Latin hymn:

> The strife is o'er, the battle done:
> The victory of life is won;
> The song of triumph has begun.
> Alleluia!

[1] Used by permission of *The Presbyterian Outlook.*

PALMER [10 10 10 10, with Refrain (6: m - - m f m / r - - r - -); Horatio R. Palmer, 1868]. After the composer and author of "Yield not to temptation," for which it was composed.

PANGE LINGUA. See ORIEL.

PANIS. See EUCHARISTIC HYMN.

PANIS COELI. See WESTCOTT.

PARADISE [8 6 8 6 6 6 6 (4: m / f. m m m / s. f f); Joseph Barnby, 1866]. Written for Frederic W. Faber's hymn beginning, "O Paradise, O Paradise," and named by the composer.

———— [8 6 8 6 6 6 6 (4: m / s m r d / d. T T); Henry Smart, 1868]. See above.

———— [C. M. (3: S / m - m / f - T / r - d / d T); anon., date unknown]. Because used with "By cool Siloam's shady rill," the first line of one of Reginald Heber's hymns.

———— [7 6 7 6 D (4: s / m f s lt / d - d); Frederic Weber, 1836]. Written for Earl Nelson's hymn for saints' days, beginning, "From all Thy saints in warfare, For all Thy saints at rest." This hymn is unusual in that, between an opening stanza and two closing ones, there are individual stanzas for seventeen saints.

PARIS. See HURSLEY.

PARK STREET [L. M., with Repeat (3: d d d / d. r m / r d T / d - -); Frederick M. A. Venua, ca. 1810]. For Park Street Church, Boston, an old Puritan meetinghouse, citadel and stronghold of orthodoxy. The street corner near which this church stands was formerly called "Brimstone Corner."

PARKER [L. M. (4: s / s. s l t / d tl s); Horatio Parker, 1894]. Named for the composer.

PAROLE. See PENITENTIA.

PASCAL [L. M. (3: m m m / s - d / r - r / m - - / s s s / d - t / l - l / s - -)]. See ST. CRISPIN.

———— [L. M. (3: d d d / d T d / r m r / d - -)]. See HURSLEY.

PASSION CHORALE [7 6 7 6 D (4: m / l s f m / r - m); Hans L. Hassler, 1601]. This German chorale is, simply, "a song of Christ's suffering." "Passion," in this sense, says Blunt (*Theology*), belongs properly to that which Christ underwent during the fifteen or more hours which elapsed between the time he left the Last Supper (his agony in Gethsemane) and his death upon the cross. The tune is universally used with the text beginning, "O sacred Head, now wounded." *Chorale*, a sacred choral song, may refer to both the text and tune or to the tune alone. In common usage the term refers to the congregational music of the Lutheran Reformation, the melodies of which were derived from various sources: the old church tunes, secular songs, and original compositions. Many of the older chorales now in use appear to have been old church tunes, and oftentimes it is difficult to distinguish the composer of the melody from the one who provided its harmonization.

Also called BEMBERG, HERZLICH, STUTTGART.

PASTOR BONUS [S. M. D. (6: d / d T L S - L / T - - L -); Alfred J. Caldicott, 1875]. *Pastor Bonus* (Latin): "Good shepherd." The tune was written for Horatius Bonar's hymn beginning, "I was a wandering sheep," and was named by its composer. The name is of no significance when used with such hymns as "O Love of God most full" by Oscar Clute, as it was in the *Pilgrim Hymnal* (1904).

———— [6 5 6 5 D (4: d. d r m / L T d -)]. See ST. HILL.

PATNA [7 6 7 6 D (4: dr / m m m m / m - d); ascribed to Reginal Heber, ca. 1830]. Patna is a city in India in the see of Calcutta, over which Bishop Heber at one time presided. This tune is said to have been written by the Bishop for his missionary hymn beginning, "From Greenland's icy mountains." It is patterned upon the Greek air noted under "GREEK AIR [7 6 7 6 D]," which see. Lightwood says that the tune has nothing to do with Heber nor he with it, as he died before the tune appeared.

Also called CALCUTTA, HEBER.

PATRIARCH'S TUNE. See OLD 113TH.

PATTEN [C. M. (2: s ss / d d / l.1 / l -) ; Peter C. Lutkin, 1905]. For Dr. Ames W. Patten, sometime chaplain of Northwestern University, a close personal friend of the composer.

PAX [10 10 10 10 (4: m - m m / m - - r / d L d r / m - - -) ; Lily Rendle, 1928]. *Pax* (Latin) : "Peace." Written for May Rowland's hymn beginning, "Come, peace of God." The composer gave the tune the name "Peace."

―――― [7 7 7 7 8 8 (4: l t d t / l s m -) ; from *The Public School Hymn Book* (English) , 1929]. Because set to John Ellerton's "Now the labourer's task is o'er," with the familiar closing lines of each stanza:

> Father, in Thy gracious keeping
> Leave we now Thy servant sleeping.

See PAX by Rendle.

PAX DEI [10 10 10 10 (4: d - m s / s. f m d / m - r d / d - T -) ; John B. Dykes, 1868]. *Pax Dei* (Latin) : "peace of God." Because composed for John Ellerton's benediction hymn beginning, "Saviour, again to Thy dear name we raise," in which all the stanzas except the first begin with the words, "Grant us Thy peace."

PAX TECUM [10 10 (4: s - s s / s - - s / l l l s / s - -) ; George T. Caldbeck, *ca.* 1877]. These Latin words may be translated, "Peace be with you." It was given this title because written for Edward H. Bickersteth's hymn beginning, "Peace, perfect peace."

PEACE [10 10 10 6 (4: S / S - - S /

d - d - / T d r m / r - d -) ; George W. Chadwick, 1890]. Because written for the anonymous hymn beginning, "I sought the Lord, and afterward I knew."

PEACEFIELD [7 7 7 6 (3: m - m / f - s / m - m / r - -) ; traditional Irish melody]. This lovely old melody was arranged as a hymn tune by the Reverend David F. R. Wilson, who wrote that he named it after his mother's homestead in County Armagh, Ireland. It was the first tune he remembered hearing; his mother rocked his cradle while singing it with the words "Hush-a-bye baby, o'er the tree top."

PEEL CASTLE [10 10 10 10 (4: s - m r / d - T d / d m r d / d - - -) ; traditional Manx melody]. Named for Peel Castle, a picturesque ruin dating from the fifteenth century, located on St. Patrick's Isle, a small island connected with the Isle of Man by a causeway. Much historic and legendary interest is attached to it. "Fenella's Tower" is the scene of Fenella's escape in Scott's *Peveril of the Peak.*

PENIEL [8 8 8 8 8 8 (4: d m s / r mr d r / m) ; Samuel S. Wesley]. *Peniel* is a Hebrew word meaning "face of God." It has come to denote a "spiritual struggle," an allusion to Jacob's wrestling with the angel at Peniel (also called "Penuel") . See Genesis 32:30. The tune was written for Charles Wesley's long poem beginning, "Come, O Thou Traveller unknown," which has the title "Wrestling Jacob," which title was also given the tune by its composer when it first appeared in the *European Psalmist* by Samuel S. Wesley, grandson of Charles Wesley. This book, "dedicated by permission, to Her Majesty the Queen" (Victoria) , 1872, was a collection of hymn tunes, chants, short anthems, "an easy service, etc., etc.," compiled and edited by this Wesley. It contained 733 numbers, more than half of which were either composed or arranged by him.

—— [8 8 8 8 8 8 (4: m / m r s. s / f f m); Josiah Booth, 1909]. Included in *One Hundred Hymn Tunes* by the composer as his setting for the above-mentioned hymn of Charles Wesley.

PENITENCE [6 5 6 5 D (4: m m f m / l - s -); Spencer Lane, 1879]. From the sentiment of James Montgomery's hymn beginning, "In the hour of trial," for which it was written and with which it is generally used.

—— [8 6 8 6 4 (4: m / s d t l / s r d); William H. Monk, 1871]. Also called RETURN. Both because set to the hymn beginning, "Return, O wanderer, to thy home," a gospel hymn by Thomas Hastings.

—— [L. M. (3: m m m / f - m / m - r / d - -)]. See HOLBORN HILL.

PENITENTIA [10 10 10 10 (4: m - m f / s - d - / r. r m f / m - - -); Edward Dearle, 1874]. This Latin word meaning "penitence" was used because of the sentiment of its original text, beginning, "Weary of earth, and laden with my sin," by Samuel J. Stone.

Also called PAROLE, SPENCER. PAROLE: doubtless suggested by certain lines of Stone's hymn. SPENCER: a personal name.

PENTATONE [C. M. D. (4: dr / m s d l / s. m m); H. Walfred Davies, 1930]. Said to be written in the Caledonian five-toned scale, but, strictly speaking, it is not, for the composer used six tones in his tune. The effect, however, is that of a pentatone.

PENTECOST [L. M. (3: m m m / m - m / r - d / f - -); William Boyd, *ca.* 1864]. The word "Pentecost" comes from a Greek one meaning "fiftieth." It was applied to the Jewish festival which was held on the fiftieth day after the Feast of the Unleavened Bread. It

was on this day that Jesus' disciples first were filled with the Holy Spirit, as described in Acts 2.

The name of the tune is Pentecost because it was originally written for the words "Come, Holy Ghost, our souls inspire" at the request of Baring-Gould, who had organized a service for Yorkshire colliers at Whitsuntide.—*London Times*, February 17, 1928.

The name has further significance: the coincidence of its first two syllables with the Greek word *penta* (the tune comprises but five notes) and the interesting fact that "Pen" is the first syllable of the composer's wife's given name.

In answer to your request for a copy of his tune to be reproduced in facsimile for the readers of *The Musical Times*, Mr. Boyd says, "With pleasure. . . . And I will write the heading 'Pen-tecost' because 'Pen' is the first syllable of my wife's name and she is very fond of the tune."—*Musical Times*, December 1, 1908.

Also called CHAMPLIN.

PENZANCE. See ELTON by Maker.

PER PACEM. See MAGDALEN.

PER RECTE ET RETRO [L. M. (4: d / T f m r / s f m); John Stainer, 1898]. Dr. Homer Robbins, late professor of Latin at Pomona College, Claremont, California, gave me the following information. The words and phrases in quotation marks are his. *Per recte et retro* is "made Latin." It might mean "through that which goes straight along and turns back," or "through all ages," or "through time—past and present," or "continuing," or "a number of inferential meanings." The tune was written for John Pierpont's hymn beginning, "O Thou to whom in ancient time," and is a good choice of name because of it. There is, however, an even better reason for this choice of name.

These Latin words are a musical term meaning "forward, then backward"; the trick of composing melody, or subject, so that it can be reversed note for note. In this example lines 3 and 4 of the tune are lines 1 and 2 read backwards *in all parts*. An unusual and a very difficult thing to do; this is, perhaps, the first and only instance in which this device has been used in a modern hymn tune.

PERCIVAL-SMITH [C. M. D. (4: m / m. d r m / f. f m); Calvin W. Laufer, 1933]. The composer wrote me: "The tune was dedicated to Alfred Percival Smith, a devoted friend and a distinguished elder in the Presbyterian Church of Overbrook, Pennsylvania."

PETERSHAM [C. M. D. (4: d / m s d l / s. f m); Clement W. Poole, 1864]. A suburban village on the left bank of the Thames upstream from London. The composer served various churches in and about London.

PETITION [7 6 7 6 D (3: S / m. r d T / T L S); Francis J. Haydn, 1801]. Perhaps because of its association with William Cowper's hymn beginning, "Sometimes a light surprises." Also called HAYDN, DEDHAM. HAYDN: the name of the composer. DEDHAM: the name by which the tune is known in England.

PETRA. See GETHSEMANE by Redhead.

PHILLPUT. See BEALOTH.

PICARDY [8 7 8 7 8 7 (4: L T d r / m - m r / m - m -); traditional French carol]. This is one of the old fifteenth- or sixteenth-century melodies and probably came from Picardy, one of the old provinces in north France.

PILGRIM [8 7 8 7 4 7 (4: m. m mr d T / d - S -); Albert L. Peace, *ca.* 1890]. Written for William Williams' hymn beginning:

Guide me, O Thou great Jehovah,
Pilgrim through this barren land.

———— [6 5 6 5 7 7 7 5 (4: m. m f l / s - m -); Edward J. Hopkins, *ca.* 1875]. A setting for "I'm a pilgrim, and I'm a stranger," to which Mary Stanley Bunce Shindler gave the title "A Christian Pilgrim."

PILGRIMAGE. See ST. EDMUND by Sullivan.

PILGRIMS [11 10 11 10, with Refrain (4: m - s f / m - - r / d r m f / m - r -); Henry Smart, 1868]. One of the many settings for Frederick W. Faber's hymn beginning, "Hark, hark, my soul! angelic songs are swelling," with the refrain:

Angels of Jesus, angels of light,
Singing to welcome the pilgrims of the night!

Also called SMART'S, VOX ANGELICA. SMART'S: from the composer. VOX ANGELICA (Latin): "voice of angels."

PILOT [7 7 7 7 7 7 (3: mr / d. T rdL / S -); John E. Gould]. From the sentiment of the hymn, obviously one for sailors, which begins, "Jesus, Saviour, pilot me," and which first appeared in *The Sailors' Magazine and Seamen's Friend*, April, 1871. The tune was composed soon after the hymn appeared.

PLAYFORD. See ST. MARY.

PLAYFORD'S TUNE. See OLD 112TH.

PLEADING SAVIOR. See SALTASH.

PLENARY. See AULD LANG SYNE.

PLEYEL'S HYMN [7 7 7 7 (2: m s / r. m / f r / m -); Ignace J. Pleyel, 1791]. After its composer. Pleyel was a pupil of Haydn in Vienna. This is a commonly used tune. Also called CONDOLENCE, GERMAN HYMN, VIENNA.

PLYMOUTH. See SALTASH.

PORTUGAL NEW. See ADESTE FIDELES.

PORTUGUESE HYMN. See ADESTE FIDELES.

POTSDAM [S. M. (4: d / r f m r / d - -); arr. from Johann Sebastian Bach]. The tune is an adaptation of the subject of the second Fugue in E Major, Book II, No. 9, *Forty-eight Preludes and Fugues.* Lochner says the name "is a reminder of Bach's visit to Potsdam in 1747, where, upon the insistence of Frederick the Great, he had to improvise on the organ and on the fortepianos."

PRAETORIUS [C. M. (4: d / s s l s / s f m); Michael Praetorius, 1599]. Named for its composer, whose father's name was Michael Schultze. The word *schultze* may mean "headman" of a town or village, hence may be translated *prätor.* There are instances known of several German musicians named "Schultz," or "Schultze," who assumed the Latinized form, *praetorius.*

PRAYER. See DENNIS.

PRESCOTT [8 7 8 7 7 7 (4: s. s s lt / *d* s m s); Robert P. Stewart, *ca.* 1873]. The middle name of the composer.

——— [C. M. (4: d / d T d m / r r d)]. See ST. FLAVIAN.

PRINCE RUPERT [6 5 6 5 D, with Refrain (4: l m l t / *d. r d* -); 1648, arr. by Gustav Holst, 1925]. An arrangement of the old English "Prince Rupert's March," written in honor of Prince Rupert, leader of the Royalist cavalry at the time of England's Great Rebellion.

PRINCE'S STREET. See ARLINGTON.

PRO OMNIBUS SANCTUS. See SARUM.

PROCLAMATION. See TIDINGS.

PSALM 84. See JERVAULX ABBEY.

PSALM 149. See HANOVER.

PUER NOBIS NASCITUR. See SPLENDOUR.

PURCELL [8 7 8 7 D (3: dr m r / m - d / d - f / mr d -); Henry Purcell, 1761]. Named for the composer. See *Our Hymnody,* pp. 387-89, for the full story of this tune.

Also called CHAPEL ROYAL, DUBLIN, DUBLIN TUNE.

PURPOSE [Irr. (4: L T d TT / L S M); Martin Shaw, 1931]. Written for Arthur C. Ainger's hymn beginning, "God is working His purpose out."

Q

QUAM DILECTA [6 6 6 6 (4: m / f m m r / d - -); Henry L. Jenner, 1861]. *Quam dilecta:* opening words in Latin of Psalm 84, "How lovely. . . ." The tune was written as a setting for William Bullock's hymn beginning:

We love the place, O God,
Wherein thine honor dwells.

QUEBEC. See HESPERUS.

QUEST [L. M. (3: S L T / d - d / r m f / m - -); Edwin McN. Poteat, *ca.* 1940]. Written for the composer's hymn beginning, "Light of the World, how long the quest."

R

RACINE [C. M. (4: S / L S M d / d. T T); Peter Christian Lutkin, 1905]. For Racine, Wisconsin, near which city the composer was born.

——— [8 8 8 8 8 8 (3: s / m - d / d - s / l s f / m -); Roland Diggle, 1941]. From Racine, Wisconsin, where the Joint Commission on the Revision of *The Hymnal 1940* (Protestant Episcopal) held several meetings.

RAPTURE [6 6 9 D (4: dr / m mm s); R. D. Humphreys (?); early American]. From the sentiment of Charles Wesley's hymn beginning, "O how happy are they," with which it has for so long been associated.

Also called HAPPINESS, for the same reason as RAPTURE. In some of the older books it was called COMFORT; originally RAPTURE OF LOVE; but neither of these names has been used in any recent books.

RATHBUN [8 7 8 7 (3: s - d / m - d / t l s / d s -); Ithamar Conkey, 1849]. For Mrs. Beriah S. Rathbun, leading soprano of the choir of the Central Baptist Church, Norwich, Connecticut. Named by its composer, who was organist and choir director of that church when he wrote the tune.

RATISBON [7 7 7 7 7 7 (4: s s l t / d *d* t -) ; Old German melody.] This is one of the German chorales which has a name for itself. Just when and why it became known as RATISBON has not come to light. Ratisbon, the Roman *Regina Castra,* the Celtic *Ratisbona,* the German *Regensburg,* has had a history of continuous interest since the first century. For a long time a center of the printing and bookbinding industries, it was the seat of the early Dukes of Boronia; it had the oldest Jewish settlement in Bavaria of which there is any record; it was the home of the Franciscan, Bernhard of Ratisbon, one of the most powerful preachers of the Middle Ages; it suffered severely during the Thirty Years' War; it was here, in 1541, that Melanchthon conferred with Contarini, a Roman ambassador, where a "basis of reunion [Protestant and Catholic] was laid in the doctrine of justification by faith"; it was in Ratisbon, in the year 1700, that the Gregorian calendar was decreed to be adopted. The city, partly on an island, lies at the junction of the rivers Regen and Danube. It is said a familiarity with its early art works is as necessary to the student of Christian art as is a corresponding one with that of the later Nuremberg.

RAVENNA. See VIENNA by Knecht.

RAVENSHAW [6 6 6 6 (4: d d m f / s - s -) ; from *Ave Hierarchia,* 1531]. This tune, arranged by William H. Monk, was given this homestead, or estate, name by him.

REDEMPTION. See AMAZING GRACE.

REDHEAD No. 29. See ST. FLAVIAN.

REDHEAD No. 45. See ORIENTIS PARTIBUS.

REDHEAD No. 47. See ST. DUNSTAN'S by Redhead and by Douglas.

REDHEAD No. 76. See GETHSAMANE by Redhead.

REDHEAD No. 143. See ST. BEDE, by Redhead and by Dykes.

REFUGE. See IN SINE JESU.

REGENT SQUARE [8 7 8 7 8 7 (4: s m *d* s / m.r d s) ; Henry Smart]. Horatius Bonar wrote "Glory be to God the Father" especially for the English Presbyterian Church's *Psalms and Hymns for Divine Worship* (1867). When this tune by Henry Smart was chosen for it, the name REGENT SQUARE was given it for the reason that the editor of the book was Dr. James Hamilton, minister of Regent Square Church, the cathedral of London Presbyterianism. Being an enthusiastic champion of the use of hymns as well as psalms in Presbyterian worship, Dr. Hamilton published his Regent Square Lectures, 1865, as *The Psalter and Hymn Book.* Regent Square, like Regent Park and Regent Street, is said to have taken its name from the Prince Regent, afterward George IV. It is a square in the older part of London on which is located the large church built in 1828 for the Reverend Richard Irving, friend of Thomas and Jane Welsh Carlyle. It was at this Presbyterian church, called Regent Square Church, that the "speaking with unknown tongues," described by Carlyle, frequently took place before Irving's deposition in 1832.

REMEMBER ME. See HOLY CROSS.

REMEMBRANCE. See MESSIAH.

REPOSE. See MERRIAL.

REQUIESCAT [7 7 7 7 8 8 (4: m s d t / t l s -) ; John B. Dykes, 1875]. From the sentiment of the hymn beginning, "Now the laborer's task is o'er," by John Ellerton. The Latin word *requiescat* may be translated, "may he have rest."
Also called BUNHILL.

RESCUE [6 5 10 D, with Refrain (4: s mf ss s) ; William H. Doane, 1870]. From the emphasis on the word as well as the general sentiment of

Fanny Crosby's gospel hymn "Rescue the perishing."

RESIGNATION [S. M. (4: s / s d f f / m - -) ; Moses S. Cross, 1905]. From the character of the text by Marianne Hearn beginning, "We hope in Thee, O God," for which it was written.

REST (ELTON) [8 6 8 8 6 (4: m / m. m ♯r m / s s ♯f) ; Frederick C. Maker, 1887]. A great many tunes have been called REST, usually because of the sentiment of the various hymns with which the tunes are used or were written. Frequently tunes with a common name are identified by enclosing the name of the composer in parentheses, but it is not so in this case. ELTON identifies the tune by Maker which is associated with Whittier's greatly loved hymn beginning, "Dear Lord and Father of mankind," but I have not discovered why it is so used.

Also called ALL SAINTS, MAGDALEN, PENZANCE, WHITTIER.

In one hour of searching I found twenty-two different tunes, to as many different hymns, called REST. In one book I found the word used for five different tunes, each in a different meter. John Stainer's tune called REST was written for John Wesley's translation of Gerhard Tersteegen's hymn beginning, "Thou hidden love of God, whose height," with the last two lines of the first stanza reading:

> My heart is pained, nor can it be
> At rest till it finds rest in Thee.

While Stainer insisted that his tunes be used only with the texts for which they were written, he gave his approval to its use in *Hymns Ancient and Modern*, Revised Edition (1875) with Archbishop Maclagan's hymn beginning, "The saints of God, their conflict past," because he felt the tune name would still be meaningful if used with that text. This excellent tune has been called, variously, BEATI, KENDAL, and MAGDALEN. Under the name MAGDALEN it is frequently used with Kipling's "Recessional."

Among the better-known tunes called REST are:

8 8 8 8 8 8 (4: m / m. r d s / s f m) ; John Stainer. This, discussed above, was written in 1873.

L. M. (3: -s ss / d s sm / r -) ; William B. Bradbury, 1843. The very familiar setting to "Asleep in Jesus," Margaret Mackay's hymn first published in *The Amethyst* (Edinburgh, 1832). For more than a century it has perhaps been the best-known and -loved "rest" hymn in the English language.

5 4 5 4 D (3: m ♯r m / l - s) ; Horatio Parker, 1877. Set to J. S. B. Monsell's hymn beginning, "Rest of the weary, Joy of the Lord," in 1863, it was composed for a Festival Service for the London Choir Association.

8 5 8 3 (4: d T r d / f m r ♯d) ; Arthur S. Sullivan, 1874. One of the best of the many tunes which have been written to be sung to the eighth-century (?) Greek hymn rendered into English by John M. Neale (1862) as "Art thou weary, Art thou languid."

7 7 7 7 (4: m m r m / f. f m -) ; Richard Redhead, 1853. This is REDHEAD No. 47, written to go with Frederick Oakley's rendition of the thirteenth-century Latin hymn by St. Bonaventure:

> In the Lord's atoning grief,
> Be our rest and sweet relief.

8 8 8 4 (4: m - m m / s - s - / d - l - / s - - -) ; George J. Elvey, ca. 1870. A setting for Charlotte Elliott's hymn beginning, "Jesus, my Saviour, look on me," the last line of the first

stanza being, "Thou art my rest."

RESURRECTION [7 7 7 7 D (6: m - m m - d / r - r r - -)]. See MARTYN.

———— [7 7 7 7, with Alleluias (4: d m s d / f l l s)]. See EASTER HYMN.

RETREAT [L. M. (6: mf / s - s s f m / l - l s -); Thomas Hastings, 1840]. From its association with Hugh Stowell's hymn beginning, "From every stormy wind that blows," with which it is commonly used.

RETURN. See PENITENCE by Monk.

REX GLORIA [8 7 8 7 D (4: d S d r / m. f m r); Henry Smart, 1868]. *Rex gloria:* "king of glory." Written for Christopher Wordsworth's hymn beginning, "See the Conqueror mounts in triumph."

REYNOLDS. See CONSOLATION by Mendelssohn.

RHIW [S. M. (4: d / m m m r / s - -); Welsh melody, 1923]. Approximate pronunciation: "Hrhee-you'." "Rhiw, signifying the ascent of a hill, derives its name from its 'situation on the acclivity of *Mynydd Rhiw,* lofty eminence which rises above the village.'" —Lewis. The name of a town and river in northeastern Wales near England.

RHONDDA. See CWM RHONDDA.

RHUDDLAN [8 7 8 7 8 7 (4: d. d d d / m d r S); Welsh traditional melody]. Approximate pronunciation: "Rhith'-lahn." It is a place name in Flintshire, North Wales. Rhuddlan, a place of very great antiquity, is alleged to have derived its name from the red color of the soil of the banks of the River Clwd, upon which it is situated. The "Rhuddlan Plain by the Sea" (*Morva Rhuddlan*) was the scene of the conflict which ended the revolt of Queen Baodicea against the Romans and resulted in her death and that of her two daughters, *circa* A.D. 43. Later, in 795, *Morva Rhuddlan* was the scene of a sanguinary battle between the forces of

King Offa, of Mercia, and the Welsh, in which all of the Welsh forces were annihilated. The well-known Welsh air *"Morva Rhuddlan"* was composed to commemorate this disaster. In 1277 King Edward I had made Rhuddlan Castle, dating from the eleventh century, a "City of Refuge," but later he hanged priests there. The "Statute of Rhuddlan" (1284) had the effect of making Wales a crown colony under its own laws.

RHYS [L. M. (3: S L d / r - m / S L d / r - m); Rhys Thomas]. Pronounced "Rhees." The given name of the composer. When this tune was submitted, without name, to the commission compiling *The Methodist Hymnal* about 1932, this choice was made.

RICHMOND [S. M. D. (4: S / d. d d d / r - -); Asa B. Everett, 1859]. After Richmond, Virginia, the home of its composer and of the publishing house of the Everett Brothers, extensive publishers of singing-school books before the War Between the States. Richmond, Virginia, last capital of the Confederacy, was founded in 1733 by Colonel William Byrd, famed ancestor of the equally famous Byrd family of more modern times. It has been said that the city was named from the city of the same name on the River Thames above London. Also called EVERETT.

———— [C. M. (3: S d m / s - f / m f r / d -)]. A much better tune than the above. Written by Thomas Haweis, it was adapted by Samuel Webbe, Jr., and named by Webbe after the composer's friend, Leigh Richmond, sometime rector of Torvey, Bedfordshire, England. Haweis was chaplain to Selina, Countess of Huntingdon, and was her trustee and executor. She bought the chapel near her home in Spa Fields which doubtless accounts for this name. The chapel was demolished in 1886.

Also called CHESTERFIELD (which see), HAWEIS, MARINERS, MT. CALVARY, SPA FIELDS CHAPEL.

RIDLEY. See OLD 113TH.

RIGHINI [6 6 4 6 6 6 4 (4: d - S m / r. T d -); Vincenzo Righini, late 19th century]. The name of the composer.

RIMINGTON [L. M. (4: m - / r d s m / r - r - / d -); Francis Duckworth, 1904]. After the composer's birthplace, Riming, Ribblesdale (Valley of the River Ribble), England.

RIPON. See DENNIS.

RIVAULX [L. M. (3: s s s / s - s / 1 - 1 / s - -); John B. Dykes, 1866]. This is a misspelling of *Rievaulx*, an old Cistercian abbey of Normandy days in Yorkshire, England, founded in 1131 by Walter L'Espec. The name is the Norman French translation of the English *Ryedale*, "the valley of the Rye." The church of Rievaulx, in its day, was one of the largest and most magnificent in all England, an evidence of the fine cultural influence which, through the centuries, has been shared by both England and France.

RIVERMOUTH. See ANGEL'S STORY.

ROCHELLE. See SEELENBRÄUTIGAM.

ROCHESTER. See DEVONSHIRE by Lampe, and WILTON.

ROCK OF AGES. See TOPLADY.

ROCKINGHAM [L. M. (3: d / m f r / d - m / s - 1 / s -);Edward Miller, 1790]. This derives its name from the Marquis of Rockingham, friend and patron of the composer and twice prime minister of England. It is sometimes called ROCKINGHAM OLD to distinguish it from the later tune by the same name by Lowell Mason, below.

Also called BISHOP, CATON, COMMUNION, MAYHEW.

——— [L. M. (3: d / Td r m / sm r); Lowell Mason, 1830]. A town, village, or county name common to the New England and other Atlantic states. It is not an associative name.

ROHRAU. See AUSTRIAN HYMN.

ROSY LIGHT. See WEBB.

ROTTERDAM [7 6 7 6 D (4: m / s d f f / m - d); Berthold Tours, 1875]. The birthplace of the composer.

ROUSSEAU. See GREENVILLE.

ROUSSEAU'S DREAM. See GREENVILLE.

ROYAL OAK [7 6 7 6, with Refrain (4: s m f m / rd TL S); Old English melody, arr. 1915]. One of the amazing incidents in his escape from England was the "imprisonment" of Charles II in the "Royal Oak," the name given the tree at Boscobel, Shropshire, England, in which the king hid himself during his flight following the Battle of Worcester in 1651. The name of this tune doubtless has some connection with this incident, as the tune is taken from a seventeenth-century melody, "The twenty-ninth of May," a loyalist song on the restoration of Charles II on May 29, 1660. The song is also known as "The Jovial Crew." In *Harper's Magazine* (December, 1850) is an interesting account of this romantic escape of Charles II.

ROYSTON. See ST. PETERSBURG.

RUSPER [7 6 7 6 D (3: dr / md s md / mr d); traditional English melody]. A parish near Horsham, Sussex, England. This is included because it is doubtless the original of TERRA BEATA or TERRA PATRIS, which, sung to Maltbie D. Babcock's hymn beginning, "This is my Father's world," is so popular with young people.

RUSSIAN HYMN [11 10 11 9 (4: s - 1 1 / s. m d -); Alexis F. Lvov, 1833]. Because written for a new Russian anthem during the regime of the Emperor Nicholas. Lvov was commissioned by the Emperor to write a national hymn because he had become "tired of the English tune which had been used [by the Russians] as a stop-gap for a very long time." The words of the new hymn were written by the poet Joukovsky to go with the tune. See *Our Hymnody* for a full account of this interesting tune.

Also called Moscow.

RUTHERFORD [7 6 7 6 7 6 7 5 (4: m / m m r. r / d - d); Chretien Urhan].

The tune associated with "The sands of time are sinking" is Rutherford, so named after Samuel Rutherford from whose writings Mrs. Cousin (Anna Ross Cousin—nee Cundell) drew her inspiration in writing the poem. Rutherford, however, is of French origin; appeared in *Chants Chretiens*, Paris, 1834, set to the hymn, "Eternel, O mon Dieu, j'implore ta clemence," in somewhat different form.—*Musical Times*, January 1, 1907.

Samuel Rutherford was the persecuted Scottish divine of the seventeenth century.

RYDAL. See NIGHTFALL.

S

SABBATH [7 7 7 7 D (3: dr / m. m fm / r -); Lowell Mason, 1824]. This tune, to "Safely through another week," was called NEWTON because John Newton wrote the hymn for which the tune was composed. Now fittingly called SABBATH, it was likewise called SATURDAY NIGHT only a generation or so past, for the reason that then the Lord's Day, "Sabbath" it was called, not "Sunday," began at sundown on Saturday evening and lasted until sunrise on Monday morning. I well remember many Saturday nights when this hymn and tune were sung at family prayers. The name SATURDAY NIGHT gains point when the last stanza of Newton's hymn, now omitted from our hymnals, is recalled:

When the morn shall bid us rise
  May we feel Thy presence near;
May Thy glory meet our eyes
  When we in Thy house appear.
Thus afford us, Lord, a taste
  Of our everlasting feast.

——— [8 7 8 7 D (3: dr / m. r dL / S M)]. See AUTUMN.

SABBATH MORN, or SABBATH MORNING. See SABBATH by Mason.

SABOATH [9 10 9, with Refrain (4: m m m m / rd TL S -); William B. Bradbury, ca. 1860]. A misspelling of Sabaoth, a Greek word which has remained untranslated in the English New Testament and in the *Te Deum*. It represents the Hebrew word for "armies," which appears repeatedly in the Old Testament in the phrase "Lord of hosts." Spenser, in his *Fairie Queene*, uses the word thus:

But henceforth all shall rest eternally
With Him, that is the God of Sabaoth hight:
O! great Sabaoth God, grant me that Sabaoth's sight.

The tune is used with Fanny Crosby's gospel hymn beginning, "Holy, holy, holy is the Lord." But in the hymn the only words suggesting "armies" are found in the second stanza:

Watchman of Zion, herald the story;
Sin and death His kingdom shall destroy.

SACRAMENTUM UNITATIS [10 10 10 10 10 10 (3: m - rm fr / sd dr m); Charles H. Lloyd, 1885]. From the last line of each stanza of William H. Turton's hymn beginning, "Thou, who at Thy first Eucharist did pray"—viz., "Through this blest sacrament of unity"; which also translates the title.

SAFE IN THE ARMS. See IN SINE JESU.

SAFFRON WALDEN [8 8 8 6 (3: m r d / s - d / d t l / s - -); Arthur H. Brown, 1890]. Saffron Walden, or Walden Saffron, is a very early settlement (*Waldena*) in Essex, England. It derives its name from a wooded valley where saffron was formerly grown. The "device of the seal of the corporation is a rebus on the name,

being *three saffron flowers walled in.*"
—Lewis.

ST. AGATHA. See ST. MARTIN.

ST. AGNES [C. M. (3: m m m / r - m /
f - T / d - -) ; John B. Dykes, 1866].
From the sentiment of the hymn
for which it was written, "Jesus, the
very thought of Thee," Edward Caswall's translation of St. Bernard's
Jesu dulcis memoria.

St. Agnes, a Roman maiden, was, when
only in her 13th year, beheaded (A.D.
304) for the crime of being a Christian.
"She went to the place of execution,"
says St. Ambrose, "more gladly than
others of her sex to their wedding feast."
Her innocence and courage at once won
for her the universal veneration of the
church.
—Roman *Missal.*

The pens and tongues of all nations are
employed in the praises of St. Agnes,
who overcame both the tenderness of
her age and the cruelty of the tyrant,
and through martyrdom crowned the
glory of chastity.
—St. Jerome.

Her name signifies "chaste" in Greek;
"lamb" in Latin.
—St. Augustine.

Always looked upon as the special
patroness of purity, she was executed
by either fire or the sword (accounts
differ), suffering under the perse-
cutions of Diocletian. She was rich
and beautiful, and her hand had
been sought by a young Roman nobleman. She had replied, "I am already engaged to one—to Him alone
I keep my troth." When investiga-
tion proved her a Christian, after
insult and outrage, she was condemned to die. At the time of her
execution she is supposed to have
prayed:

O Father Almighty, who alone art to be
worshipped, feared, and adored, I give
Thee thanks for that through Thy Holy

Son, I have escaped the threats of the
profane tyrant and with unstained foot-
steps have passed over the filthy slough
of lust; and now, behold, I come to
Thee, whom I have loved, have sought,
and have always longed for. Thy name
I bless, I glorify, world without end.

This part of her prayer is appointed
as the Antiphon to the *Magnificat* for
St. Agnes' Day, January 21. On St.
Agnes' Eve young girls, in days gone
by, indulged in all sorts of magic
which they thought might aid them
in discovering the identity of their
future husbands. Keats, in "The
Eve of St. Agnes," one of the great
English poems, has immortalized this
superstition:

They told her how, upon St. Agnes'
   Eve,
Young virgins might have visions of
   delight,
And soft adorings from their lovers
   receive
Upon the honey'd middle of the night,
If ceremonies due they did aright;
As, supperless to bed they must retire,
And couch supine their beauties, lily
   white;
Nor look behind, nor sideways, but
   require
Of heaven with upward eyes for all that
   they desire.

Prudentius wrote a hymn relating
the acts of this famous martyr, and
St. Ambrose has mentioned her in
at least three of his works.

Also called ST. AGNES DURHAM.

———   [L. M. (4: d / s l s d /
f s m)]. See ST. SEPULCHRE; ST.
AGNES, above, for the St. Agnes
legend.

——— [10 10 10 10 (4: m - d r /
m - s - / f m m r / d - - -)]. See DEER-
HURST; LANGRAN; and ST. AGNES,
above.

ST. ALBAN. See HOLBORN HILL.

ST. AMBROSE [8 7 8 7 (4: s. m l d /
t l s m); John B. Dykes, 1857].

While still an unbaptized catechumen Ambrose (340-97) was elected Bishop of Milan in 374. As governor of the province he had gone into the church at the head of his troops for the purpose of quieting the stormy quarrel between the partisans of the two rival candidates for the bishopric. He spoke to the people, quieting them through the magic sound of his voice. Suddenly, so the story goes, a child called out, "Ambrose is Bishop." The words were caught up by others, resounded throughout the church, and thus, by acclamation, the selection was made. Musician and poet, he introduced into Italy the Greek system of musical scales which became the basis for the Gregorian Tones still the foundation of the authorized music of the Roman Catholic Church, and he set the pattern for writing sacred verse in what is now known commonly as Long Meter. He has been acclaimed the "father of church song."
Also called ST. BERNARD, ST. OSWALD. ST. OSWALD: Dykes was vicar at St. Oswald's, Durham, when he wrote the tune.
――――― [C. M. (4: d / d r m d / d T d); Charles Steggal, 1849].
――――― [6 6 4 6 6 6 4 (4: d / r f m r / s -); William H. Monk, 1874].
――――― [7 7 7 5 (4: S L / d d r. d / d -); Henry J. Gauntlett, *ca.* 1850]. This was based on the Eighth Gregorian Tone. See ST. AMBROSE by Dykes for the story of Ambrose. Apparently questions which have arisen as to why the above tunes were given the name ST. AMBROSE have not been answered. Dykes wrote his tune as a setting for "Praise the Lord! ye heavens adore Him," translated from the Danish by S. Baring-Gould; Steggal for Archbishop Hare's "Day after day I sought the Lord"; Monk to "Come, Holy Ghost, in love," Ray Palmer's English rendering of *Veni*

Creator Spiritus, ninth century (?); and Gauntlett for "Jesus Christ is risen today," calling it EASTER TUNE, some later editor changing it to ST. AMBROSE. There is nothing in the text of any of these hymns that could have suggested the name. Nor did any of the composers have positions as organists and choirmasters at any church named after St. Ambrose. Perhaps the most satisfactory answer is that these composers were all Anglican churchmen who had a penchant for naming their tunes after saints or churches named for saints. Cowan and Love, *The Music of the Church Hymnary* (1901), list 109 tunes named after 89 different saints, or churches, only 9 of which were composed by others than Anglicans. See p. 21 for comment on the use of saints' names.

ST. ANATOLIUS [7 6 7 6 8 8 (4: s / l s d f / m - r); Arthur H. Brown]. St. Anatolius was a Bishop of the Greek Church in the late fifth century. Little is known of him.

Arthur Henry Brown said: "My tune, St. Anatolius, to 'The day is past and over,' was composed on Feb. 7, 1862, immediately after reading the hymn in *The Union* newspaper of that date reviewing Dr. Neal's 'Hymns of the Eastern Church,' whence it is taken. . . . I put it aside for several months and forgot all about it until one day, when looking for something else I came upon the mss. and then it struck me the tune was worth printing." It was printed in an 8-page publication containing 9 tunes and appeared in Nov. 1862. Title: The Day is Past and Over, An Evening Hymn Translated from the Greek of St. Anatolius, Patriarch of Constantinople, A.D. 458, By the Rev. J. M. Neale, D. D., to which is added a Few other Hymns . . . etc.—*Musical Times,* December 1, 1906.

Also called MITYLENE. Mitylene was the pre–Christian-Era capital city of the island Lesbos, said to have been named for a daughter of a onetime king of the country. Dr. J. M. Neale, translator of Anatolius' hymn, wrote:

This hymn is to the scattered hamlets of Chios and Mitylene what Bishop Ken's Evening Hymn is to the villages of our own country (England), and its melody is singularly plaintive and pleading.

What its melody was is not known, but this will explain the odd name given to Dr. Brown's tune.

—— [7 6 7 6 8 8 (4: d / T d f m / m r) ; John B. Dykes, 1862]. Another setting for the hymn mentioned above.

St. Andrew [S. M. (4: m / m f s r / m - -) ; Joseph Barnby, 1869]. Barnby was organist at St. Andrew's, Wells Street, London, before going to St. Anne's, Soho; hence the name. Andrew was one of the twelve disciples, a brother of Simon Peter, and an apostle to the Gentiles. Baring-Gould, in *Lives of the Saints,* tells us: "In the scanty notices we have of Andrew we see him represented as bringing others into notice—his brother, Peter; the Greeks, this lad—and this indicates a kindly nature." "This lad" refers to the boy with the five barley loaves and the two small fishes used in feeding the five thousand in the wilderness (John 6:9). Because Andrew would not cease teaching, Aegeas, proconsul of Achaia, on a visit to Patras, where Andrew was at the time, sentenced Andrew to die on a cross; to be fastened with cords, not nails through his hands and feet, in order that his sufferings might be prolonged—more lingering and tedious. He hung for two days, meanwhile continuing to preach to and exhort the people. The cross, now known by his name, was in the shape of an "X."

Also called Aileen, Monsell. Mon-

sell: because written for J. S. B. Monsell's hymn beginning, "Sweet is Thy mercy, Lord."

—— [C. M. (3: d / m - m / r - m / d - T / d -) ; William Tans'ur, 1735]. See above. Also called Barby Tune.

—— [6 5 6 5 D (4: m m m m / m m -)]. The same as St. Andrew of Crete, which see.

—— [8 7 8 7 (4: m . m r m / f m l s) ; Edward H. Thorne, 1875]. Because set to Cecil F. Alexander's hymn beginning, "Jesus calls us: o'er the tumult," the second stanza of which is:

As of old St. Andrew heard it
  By the Galilean lake,
Turned from home, and toil, and kindred,
  Leaving all for His dear sake.

See St. Andrew by Barnby for legend.

—— [12 11 12 11 (3: d / d s l / l s f / m r d / s -)]. See Montgomery.

—— [Irr. (3: s / d s l / s s f / m r d / s s)]. See Magdalen.

St. Andrew of Crete [6 5 6 5 D (4: m m m m / m m -) ; John B. Dykes]. From the author of the Greek hymn beginning, "Christian, dost thou see them," which John M. Neale translated and for which this tune was written. The names Crete and St. Andrew, by which the tune is also known, are obvious, yet the use of the latter is quite confusing because of the association of the very familiar tune of the same name, by Barnby, with Bishop How's offertory hymn beginning, "We give Thee but Thine own." Andrew of Crete (or Jerusalem) (660-732) composed "The Grand Canon" (Greek), also called "The King of Canons." See *Our Hymnody* for comment by J. M. Neale.

St. Anne [C. M. (4: s / m l s d / d t d) ; William Croft, 1708]. For St. Anne's Church, Soho, London, where Croft was organist. The church, consecrated by Bishop Compton in 1685, was dedicated to the mother of the Virgin Mary out of compliment to the Princess Anne, whose Danish husband was honored by having its tower, as nearly as possible, conform to Danish architectural style.

The first recorded organist of St. Anne's was Dr. Croft (or Crofts), according to the Vestry minutes which gives his Christian name as Philip instead of William. (Crofts: the added sybilant need not trouble us for it was a common practice in the spelling of old-time names.) —*Musical Times,* February 1, 1904.

St. Anne was celebrated as being the mother of Mary, but Baring-Gould, in *Lives of the Saints,* says it is "wholly impossible to solve the difficulties which surround the relationship." St. Anne has been pictured by Murillo as teaching the Virgin Mary to read.

Also called ANNE's, LEEDS, ST. ANNE's TUNE.

ST. ANNE's TUNE. See above.

ST. ANSELM [7 6 7 6 D (4: s / s m r m / r - d); Joseph Barnby, 1869]. This is one instance where a knowledge of the original text for which a tune is written gives no clue as to why its name was chosen. Barnby wrote it for Wordsworth's well-known "O day of rest and gladness." Anselm (1033-1109, Archbishop of Canterbury, was one of the fathers of Scholasticism, formulating its characteristic view that faith must precede knowledge. *Anselm,* according to Luther, means "Defense of authority." Many churches have been named after this saint. Also called GLADNESS.

ST. ANTHONY. See AMBROSE.

ST. ASAPH [8 7 8 7 D (4: m m m. f / s s s d); William S. Bambridge, 1872]. Originally called THANKSGIVING be-

cause it was written for the hymn beginning, "Through the night of doubt and sorrow" (Baring-Gould's translation), at the time of the recovery from a siege of typhoid fever of Queen Victoria's consort, Prince Albert. It was one of several tunes written during 1872, the year of the Prince's serious illness, and is best known from its association with those words. Why the name was changed to ST. ASAPH when the tune was used in *Church Hymns* (1874) is not clear. *Asaph* (Hebrew for "collector," or "gatherer"), a Levite, noted musician of King David's time, was also a celebrated poet and prophet. From him the Temple choristers were called the "Sons of Asaph." Some psalms have been ascribed to him. Nahum Tate, who wrote the second part of *Absalom and Achitophel,* lauds Dryden under this name:

While Judah's throne and Sion's rock stand fast,
The song of Asaph and his sons shall last.

Asaph the saint was abbott and bishop of Llanelwy, later St. Asaph, in Northwest Wales, around 590. The city of St. Asaph is in Flintshire, Wales, on the River Clwyd, about twenty miles from Liverpool.

—— [C. M. D. (4: S / d d r r / m sf m); Giovanni M. Giornovichj, 1825]. This is the tune popular in Scotland. Giornovichj, distinguished but erratic violinist who visited Scotland in 1797, changed his name to Jarnowick and is so recorded in *Grove's Dictionary of Music and Musicians.* See ST. ASAPH by Bambridge.

—— [C. M., with Repeats (4: S / d d d r / m rd r)]. See MILES' LANE.

ST. ATHANASIUS [7 7 7 7 7 (4: S L T d / m. r d -); Edward J.

Hopkins, 1872]. Named after one of the outstanding defenders of the doctrine of the Trinity. He was the famous Archbishop of Alexandria during the reign of the Emperor Constantine and has been alleged to be the author of the Athanasian Creed. The tune was written for Christopher Wordsworth's hymn beginning, "Holy, holy, holy, Lord," in which the last line of each stanza reads, "To the blessed Trinity."

ST. BARBARA [L. M. (3: m m m / s - r / m - m / s - f); Peter C. Lutkin, 1905]. This tune was not named for any saint, although there is a famous one by that name who was immortalized through the painting of Palma Vecchio. The composer of this tune and Karl P. Harrington were the musical editors of *The Methodist Hymnal* (1905). At their last meeting before the publication of the book a number of new tunes which had been approved, among them this one, were found to be without titles. It was decided to name them for the cities in which the entire commission compiling *The Hymnal* had held meetings. So they uesd the names NEW YORK, NASHVILLE, and EVANSTON. But there were more unnamed tunes than available city names. It was then proposed that the names of buildings in which meetings had been held be used. It seemed fitting and in order to begin by taking the name of the building in which the commission was then sitting, Barbara Heck Hall, on the campus of Northwestern University, so called after America's "first Methodist." Inasmuch as "Heck" would not make a good name for a hymn tune, "Barbara," the lady's given name, was chosen. When it was discovered there was another, earlier tune of that name, the group decided to "canonize" Barbara then and there. And so we have ST. BARBARA.

ST. BARTHOLOMEW [L. M. (3: S / d - S / r - S / m r d / r -); Henry Duncalf]. In W. Riley's *Parochial Harmony* (1762) this was headed "By Mr. Henry Duncalf, organist of St. Barth." St. Bartholomew's Church —"St. Bartholomew-the-little-by-the-Exchange"—was finally destroyed in 1841. St. Bartholomew was an English hermit monk who spent, in all, some 42½ years on the island of Farne.

——— [L. M. (free d d d d d r d d -)] See JAM LUCIS, plain-song melody.

ST. BASIL. See LEOMINSTER.

ST. BEDE [8 6 8 6 8 6 (4: dm / s. s 1 t / d d m); John B. Dykes, 1862]. *Bede* (Saxon): "he that prayeth," "a devout man." The "Venerable Bede" justly earned the title of "father of English history" through writing his great *Ecclesiastical History of the English Nation* (731). He was several times asked to go to Rome, but being a devout, learned, diligent monk, he preferred the quiet, uninterrupted life as student and teacher at Jarrow to ecclesiastical preferment. Charles Wheatly, in *On the Common Prayer*, says:

His learning and piety gained him the surname of *Venerable,* though the common story which goes about the title's being given him, is this: his scholars having a mind to fix a rhyming title upon his tombstone, as was the custom in those times, the poet wrote

> *Hac   Sunt   in   Fossa,*
> *Bedae   Ossa.*

Placing the word *Ossa* at the latter end of the verse for the rhyme, but not being able to think of any proper epithet that would stand before it. The monk being tired in his perplexity to no purpose, fell asleep; but when he awakened, he found his verse filled up by an angelic hand, standing thus in fair letters upon the tomb:

Hac Sunt in Fossa,
Bedae Venerabilis Ossa.

One of the shrines in the chapel known as the "Nine Altars" in Durham Cathedral, with which Dykes was associated for so long, was named after this saint. See the reference to St. Bede under ST. CUTHBERT. When Dykes wrote his tune to Anna L. Waring's hymn beginning, "Father, I know that all my life," he named it SLINGSBY, a small town in the North Riding, Yorkshire, England. The change of the name to ST. BEDE is quite appropriate, especially when the tune is used with Miss Waring's hymn, which is essentially a prayer of a devout man.

Also called WARING.

—— [8 7 8 7 (4: s l l s / f m m r); Richard Redhead, 1859]. The tune was set to an old Latin hymn, *Aeterna Christi munera* (translated, "Th' eternal gifts of Christ the King"), which Bede, in his *De arta metrica,* says was written by St. Ambrose. See above.

Also called LANGDALE, REDHEAD No. 143, ST. NICHOLAS.

ST. BEDE's. See EWING.

ST. BEES [7 7 7 7 (4: d d d. T / L T d -); John B. Dykes, 1862]. After St. Bees (Bee, or Bega), Irish abbess, daughter of an Irish king, whose name is commemorated in an abbey in Cumberland, England, a town in the county of that name; and in St. Bee's College, founded by Doctor Law, Bishop of Chester, in 1816, its site also being in the village of Cumberland, which is situated on the bay formed by St. Bee's Head. The college, in turn, takes its name from a nunnery founded there in 650 and dedicated to the Irish Saint Bega. St. Bee was celebrated for her austerity and charity. Preparing with her own hands the food for the laborers building her monastery, she also served it to them, "hastening from place to place like a bee laden with honey." Down to the Middle Ages she remained the patroness of the laborers and often of the oppressed of the district. The sentiment of one of William W. How's hymns for which Dykes wrote the tune was the reason for the choice of this name for the tune. The first stanza of the hymn is:

> Jesus! Name of wondrous love!
> Name all other names above,
> Unto which must every knee
> Bow in deep humility.

ST. BERNARD [C. M. (4: s / d. r m rd / f m r); John Richardson, 1741, arr. 1851]. When the composer arranged this melody from a much earlier one and used it in *Easy Hymn Tunes . . . for Catholic Schools* (no date), it was headed "Hymn of St. Bernard," because it was made for use with "Jesus, the very thought of Thee," one of Caswall's translations of a hymn by Bernard of Clairvaux beginning, *"Jesu dulcis memoria."* Bernard (born at Fontaine, near Dijon, Burgundy, 1090, died at Clairvaux, 1153) was a celebrated French ecclesiastic who, with twenty-five followers, left the Cistercian monastery of Citeaux and founded that of Clairvaux in 1115. Refusing all offers of preferment, he nevertheless exercised a profound influence on the church politics of Europe. A man of strong personality and magnetic influence, he ruled the medieval world from his retreat at Clairvaux. Luther thought him to be "the greatest man that ever lived."

Also called COVERT.

—— [8 7 8 7 (4: s. m l d / t l s m)]. See ST. AMBROSE.

ST. BONIFACE. See VIENNA by Knecht.

ST. BRIDE. See below.

ST. BRIDE's [S. M. (4: L / M L d T /

L -); Samuel Howard]. This minor tune first appeared in William Riley's *Parochial Harmony* (1762), set to Psalm 130 and headed "St. Bridget's Tune, by Mr. Sam. Howard." Howard was onetime organist at the well-known church built by Wren just off Fleet Street, London, known as the Church of St. Bride. The name of the church comes from St. Bride's, or St. Bridget's, Well, a holy spring supposed to have miraculous curative powers. It is the only church in London dedicated to this saint. See HOLY-WELL.

At every starting point or returning point for the mediaeval traveller, there was some religious foundation to pray for his safety or to offer praises for his return: at four of the London gates there were churches dedicated to St. Botolph, the chosen saint of travellers. Outside Cripplegate was the Church of St. Giles. Outside Newgate was the Church of St. Sepulchre. Within Ludgate was the Church of St. Martin. Over Fleet Bridge was the Church of St. Bride.—Besant.

Also called ALL SAINTS, BRIDGET, BRIDGET'S, KERSALL, ST. BRIDE, ST. BRIDGET'S TUNE.
St. Bridget ("Bride" in England), the "virgin of Kildare," patroness of Ireland, who lived during the middle of the sixth century, became famous throughout Europe. Baring-Gould quotes Hector Boece as saying that "she was regarded by Scots, Picts, and Irish as only second to the B. Virgin Mary." Further, Baring-Gould writes, "Leslie says, 'She is held in so great honor by Picts, Britons, Angles, and Irish, that more churches are dedicated to God in her memory than to any other of the saints.'" Little that is authentic is known of her. ALL SAINTS is the name by which the tune has been known in North England since Dr. Miller, of Doncaster, used it in his *Psalms of David* (1790).

ST. BRIDGET'S TUNE. See ST. BRIDE'S.
ST. CATHERINE [8 8 8 8 8 8 (3: m r d / d T d / r L T / d - -); Henri F. Hemy]. Named in honor of the famous "virgin and martyr." The tune appeared in Part II, *Crown of Jesus Music* (1864), set to a hymn beginning:

Sweet Saint Catherine, maid most pure,
  Teach us to meditate and pray,

headed, "St. Catherine, Virgin and Martyr." Eusebius says that when Maxentius visited a city, he outraged its citizenry by making off with their wives and daughters.

Only one of those who was seized for adulterous purposes by the tyrant, a most distinguished and illustrious woman in Alexandria, conquered the passionate and intemperate soul [of the Emperor] by most heroic firmness. Honorable on account of wealth and family and education, she esteemed all of these inferior to chastity. He urged her many times, but, although she was ready to die, he could not put her to death, for his desire was stronger than his anger. He therefore punished her with exile, and took away all her property.

This seems to be the true story of Catherine, a story that has grown into the "marvelous romance" which tells us she was the daughter of a king; was very beautiful and learned; that she bested in debate fifty philosophers, all of whom were burned by Maxentius; that, although married, the Emperor offered to share his throne with her. When his advances were spurned, he had her whipped with an oxhide lash, then cast her into prison; and, not being satisfied, he had devised a wheel set with razors for her execution, which, when she was placed upon it, broke, the blades flying about mutilating the bystanders. One story has it that she was put to death through torture on a wheel "like that of a chaff-cutter," a machine for cutting up chaff or hay for fodder. Her head was cut off with a sword, and the angels carried her body to Mount Sinai. There is a type of rose window, with radiating divisions, which is called "St. Catherine's wheel," or simply "Catherine."

Also called St. FINBAR, TYNEMOUTH. St. FINBAR: Finbar (or Finn Barr, or Barr) was an Irish saint of the seventh century. His real name was Lochan, but "on account of his beautiful fair hair he received the name of Finn-barr (the white-haired), often contracted into Barr." —Baring-Gould. Tynemouth is the name of an English city at the mouth of the River Tyne. The composer was once music teacher there.

——— [8 7 8 7 (4: m r m f / s.1 1 s) ; S. Flood Jones, *ca.* 1890]. One of the many settings made for "Jesus calls us o'er the tumult."

——— [7 6 7 6 D (4: d / m m s s / d - t -) ; Reginald F. Dale, 1867]. Written for "O Jesus, Thou art standing."

——— [S. M. (4: m / m m *r r / m - -) ; Frederick C. Atkinson, *ca.* 1880]. A setting for "Come, Holy Spirit, come."

——— [L. M. (4: d / d r m d / L T d) ; Thomas Turton, 1844]. Originally set to the Tate and Brady version of Psalm 100, it is a common tune in use in England. First called St. CATHERINE, the name was changed to ELY to avoid confusion. The composer was bishop of Ely from 1845 until his death in 1864. See St. CATHERINE by Hemy, for the legend of the saint.

St. CECILIA [6 6 6 6 (4: s / f m m r / d - -) ; Leighton G. Hayne, 1863]. Written for Horatius Bonar's hymn beginning:

Thy way, not mine, O Lord,
However dark it be!

Sir John Hawkins writes entertainingly of St. Cecilia and her martyrdom:

For reasons hard to discover, [she] is looked upon as the tutelar saint and patron of music. . . . St. Cecilia, among Christians, is esteemed the patroness of music, for the reasons whereof we must refer to her history, as delivered by the notaries of the Roman Church, and from them transcribed into the Golden Legend, and other books of the like kind. The story says that she was a Roman lady, born of noble parents, about the year 225. That notwithstanding she had been converted to Christianity, her parents married her to a young Roman nobleman named Valerianus, a pagan, who going to bed to her on the wedding night, as the custom is, says the book, was given to understand by his spouse that she was nightly visited by an angel, and that he must forbear to approach her, otherwise the angel would destroy him. Valerianus, somewhat troubled at these words, desired he might see his rival the angel, but his spouse told him that was impossible, unless he would be baptized and become a Christian, which he consented to: after which returning to his wife, he found her in her closet at prayer, and by her side, in the shape of a beautiful young man, the angel clothed with brightness. After some conversation with the angel, Valerianus told him that he had a brother named Tiburtius, whom he greatly wished to see a partaker of the grace which he had himself received, the angel told him that his desire was granted, and that shortly they should both be crowned with martyrdom. Upon this the angel vanished, but soon after showed himself as good as his word. Tiburtius was converted, and both he and his brother Valerianus were beheaded; Cecilia was offered her life upon condition that she would sacrifice to the deities of the Romans, but she refused, upon which she was thrown into a cauldron of boiling water, and scalded to death; though others say that she was stifled in a dry bath, i. e., an enclosure from whence the air was excluded, having a slow fire underneath it; which kind of death was sometimes inflicted among the Romans upon women of quality who were criminals. . . .

Over and above this account there is a tradition of St. Cecilia, that she excelled in music, and that the angel, who was thus enamoured of her, was drawn down from the celestial mansions by the charm of her melody; this has been deemed authority sufficient for making her the patroness of music and musicians. . . .

St. Cecilia is usually painted playing either on the organ or on the harp, singing as Chaucer relates thus:

And whiles that the organ made melodie,
> To God alone thus in her herte song she,
O Lord my soul and eke my body gie,
Unwemmed lest I confounded be.

ST. CHRISTOPHER [7 6 8 6 8 6 8 6 (4: s / s.s ♯f l / s - m); Frederick C. Maker, 1881]. This is also used with 7 6 7 6 D texts. The tune was written for Elizabeth C. Clephane's "Beneath the cross of Jesus." Many of the tunes written for her hymns had their names suggested by the sentiment of the text used, but in this case the choice seems not to be appropriate. While it is possible there may have been a martyr named Christopher, there seems to be no element of truth in the Eastern legend that he was a dog-headed man who was transformed when he came to believe in Christ. In the Western legend, Reprobatus (Christopher's name before his baptism), a heathen giant, set out to serve the strongest king he could find. Serving Pharaoh, he noted the king cross himself whenever Satan was mentioned; going to Satan, he found there was one stronger than he when Satan started aside at the sight of a cross. While seeking Christ,

Reprobatus met a hermit who ordered him to pray, but not being able to do so, he was told he must carry travelers over a deep river. Being called upon one night to carry a small child, it was only with great difficulty that he was able to make his way across the stream, saying, "You seem to weigh as heavy as the whole world." The Child replied, "Well said, Christopher; I created the world, I redeemed the world, I bear the sins of the world." This beautiful story is, of course, an allegory. In Western art St. Christopher is usually pictured carrying a child across a stream. Many churches have been named after him, and his relics abound.

ST. CHRYSOSTOM [8 8 8 8 8 8 (3: m m m / m - r / d - r / m - -); Joseph Barnby, 1871]. Chrysostom is Greek for "golden-mouthed," a nickname. The tune was written for Henry Collins' hymn, "Jesus, my Lord, my God, my all," each stanza of which closes, "O make me love Thee more and more." St. John (ca. 347-407), surnamed or nicknamed "Chrysostom" because of his golden eloquence, was the last of the great Christian sophists "who came forth from the schools of heathen rhetoric." He was an eloquent preacher, a sound theologian, and a faithful interpreter of the Scriptures.

Also called WARREN.

—— [7 7 7 (3: m - r / s f m / r - m / f - -); Edmund H. Turpin, 1877]. Written for "Come, Thou Holy Paraclete," attributed without warrant to Robert II of France; translated by J. M. Neale.

—— [8 9 8 9 (3: m / m - m / f - l / s - f / m -); John B. Dykes, 1857]. Written for "Lo! Christ stands at His martyr's side," the author of which is anonymous.

—— [8 8 8 8 8 8 (4: s / s s ♯f s / l. s s); W. C. Filby, late 19th century]. Written as a setting for Charles Wesley's "Come, O Thou Traveller unknown."

———— [8 8 8 6 (3: m r d / d - T / L - S / S -) ; Herbert S. Irons, 1860]. For Newman Hall's text beginning, "Accepting, Lord, Thy gracious call." (See ST. CHRYSOSTOM by Barnby, above.) Another case similar to that discussed under ST. AMBROSE (which see) concerning Anglican church-music composers' use of saints' names for their hymn tunes.

ST. CHRYSOSTOM'S. See ALTA TRINITA BEATA.

ST. CLEMENT [9 8 9 8 (3: S / m f m / s m r / d r L / d T) ; Clement C. Scholefield].

The tune especially composed for "The day Thou gavest" first appeared in *Church Hymns*, 1874, ed. by Arthur Sullivan. During the preparation of the book, or very shortly before its preparation, Sullivan held the organship of St. Peter's South Kensington, of which church Mr. Scholefield was then a curate, hence the appearance of the tune in *Church Hymns*, a fortuitous circumstance which has been exceedingly rich in soul-uplifting results.—*Musical Times*, October 1, 1904.

The "Mr. Scholefield" referred to was the composer of this tune, to whose first given name Sullivan added the prefix "St." See ST. MARGARET for another instance of Sullivan's unofficial canonization of a friend's given name; and see, below, the story of St. Clement.

———— [8 8 8 8 8 8 (3: m / m s f / m - m / m d t / 1 -) ; William Roberts, 1909]. Written for Lawrence Tuttiett's hymn beginning, "O quickly come, dread Judge of all." The Reverend Tuttiett was a prominent English clergyman who became "quite a Scotsman at heart" while serving churches in Scotland. This may explain Canon Roberts' selection of

this name, for St. Clement, *circa* 1258, Bishop of Dunblane, introduced the Dominican Order into Scotland. A famous preacher, a man mighty in word and deed before God and man, he is said to have shown great facility in the acquiring of languages, and to have received his habit from the hands of Dominic himself. He found the church at Dunblane in a deplorable condition of neglect, having been impoverished by his predecessor, the divine mysteries "being celebrated in the Cathedral only thrice a week, like a country chapel." Clement labored to rebuild his cathedral and to restore the dignity of worship. Other, lesser-known tunes having this title are by Richard R. Chope (7 7 7 7), Philip Hart (L. M.), and C. H. Steggall (7 7 7 7 7 7).

ST. COLUMBA [6 4 6 6 (4: s / f m r r / d - -) ; Herbert S. Irons, 1861]. The composer, son of John Irons, was organist and precentor of St. Columba College, Rathfarnham, Ireland. The college was named after the famous Irish saint, Columba (521-97), who "carried the torch of Irish Christianity to Scotland."

Scottish history may be emphatically said to begin with St. Columba's landing in Iona, *c.* 563. He conceived and carried out his enterprises absolutely without reference to the Church of Rome. His high rank had made him a statesman and even a warrior; and as founder of many monasteries he might be called an experienced ecclesiastic. . . . Columba was, in fact, half Druid magician, half Christian missionary, ready, as occasion arises, to fight his adversaries with their own weapons. —P. Hume Brown.

Columba's father belonged to the reigning family in Ireland, and his mother was a descendant of the king of Leinster. These connections, his piety, learning, and ability, all aided in gaining for him the immense influence he exerted in Ireland and Scotland. After founding a number of churches and establishing two famous monsteries in Ireland, he established himself with twelve disciples in 563 on the Island of Iona and devoted his energies to the Christianizing of the Picts. Legend has it that Columba "banished" himself from Ireland for having been the cause of a factional fight almost amounting to a civil war, over the ownership of a psalter. He was a great believer in the efficacy of singing in religious work and is said to have "confounded the Druids" and attracted the people by the "grave, sweet melody" of his singing. His voice was one of singular purity and resonance; he was able to make himself heard "a mile away." William Cathcart tells us Columba possessed a superior education, that he was the greatest Irishman of the Celtic race in mental powers, and that he founded in Iona what was for a long time the most learned school in the British Isles and perhaps in Western Europe. The whole of northern Scotland was greatly influenced and benefited by the example of his holy life and through his preaching. In his character of ranking ecclesiastic he formally inaugurated Aidan, his first cousin, as king of the Scots.

—— [C. M. (3: dr / m - f / s - fs / m - r / d -) ; Old Irish]. This is from the complete Petrie collection of old Irish airs, where it is called "an Irish Hymn sung at the dedication of a chapel, Co. Londonderry." The name of St. Columba is highly revered in northern Ireland, and the Protestant Cathedral in Londonderry was dedicated to him.

—— [C. M. (4: m rd s f / m rd r) ; John A. Macmeikan, 1875]. Written for Anne Steele's hymn beginning, "Father, whate'er of earthly bliss."

—— [13 13 13 14 (4: d / m s d s / 1 - s s / d t d r / m - -)]. See HOYTE. See St. COLUMBA by Irons, for the legend.

St. CRISPIN [L. M. (3: m m m / s - d / r - r / m - - / s s s / d - t / 1 - 1 / s - -) ; George J. Elvey, 1862]. Written for "Just as I Am Without One Plea." First published in the 1863 edition of E. H. Thorne's *Selection of Psalm and Hymn Tunes*.
Also called PASCAL.

St. CROSS [L. M. (4: d - d r / m - - 1 / s - f - / m - - -) ; John B. Dykes, 1861]. Probably suggested by the sentiment of the text of Frederick W. Faber's hymn beginning, "O come and mourn with me awhile." There is a possibility that the name comes from the Hospital of St. Cross, near Winchester, England (although there seems no good reason for it) , which was founded around 1136 by Bishop Do Blois, brother of King Stephen, "for the subsistence of thirteen resident poor men, in every necessity of life, and for affording one ample meal in each day to one hundred other indigent outboarders." The distribution of beverages was on a grand scale, for "each poor man" was daily given "a gallon and a half of good small beer." It is still customary to give beer and bread daily to all who may ask for it. St. Cross is an interesting example of a medieval almshouse (old men's home) , and its picturesqueness is enhanced by the curious costumes worn by its inmates.

St. CUTHBERT [8 6 8 4 (4: d / d. d r m / f. f m) ; John B. Dykes, 1861]. Written for the hymn beginning, "Our blest Redeemer, ere He breathed," by Harriett Auber, this was one of seven tunes by this composer which appeared in the original edition of *Hymns Ancient and Modern* (1861) . In a communication offering his services to the committee compiling this hymnal, Dr. Dykes said he had "at different times written" them, "finding myself unable to discover suitable music for the hymns. Some of them are sung in the Galilee of Durham Cathedral and are very popular." "Galilee" is the name given to certain chapels connected with some of the early English churches; there are only three remaining now— at Durham, Ely, and Lincoln. Such a chapel, in which penitents and catechumens were placed, where the monks returned after processions, and in which the ecclesiastics were permitted to meet women who had business with them, is supposed to have derived its name from the passage in Mark (16:7): "But go your way, tell his [Christ's] disciples and Peter that he goeth before you into Galilee: there shall ye see him." At the opposite end of the Cathedral from the Galilee is the large chapel known as the "Nine Altars," named from the nine shrines which were formerly in it. One of these shrines was dedicated to St. Cuthbert and St. Bede, and there was also a splendid one especially honoring St. Cuthbert. Here, or near here, his remains rested for nearly six centuries. St. Cuthbert, patron saint of Durham and its Cathedral, shares with King Oswald and St. Aidan the honor of converting northeast England to Christianity. He was a Scottish monk of the seventh century, one of the great religious leaders of his time, sometimes termed the St. Patrick of Great Britain. In his youth he was a shepherd in the valley of the Tweed, the river forming a part of the boundary line between England and Scotland. Converted early in life, he came under the tutelage of Aidan, the prior of a monastery near his boyhood home. An unusual preacher for his day in that he preached to Christians living un-

christian lives as well as to assiduously seeking converts, he wandered through the mountainous regions seeking their almost inaccessible villages. Practicing an excessive asceticism, he was apt to abandon his work in order that he might live the life of a hermit. Retiring to Lindisfarne, the "Holy Island," in 676, he supported himself upon what he could raise by means of his own labor. Urged by the king of Northumbria, in 684, to resume his missionary activities, he did so, but after three years he again returned to his island retreat, where he died March 20, 687.

Also called CUTHBERT.

ST. DENIO. See JOANNA.

ST. DROSTANE [L. M. (4: S / d S d r / m. r d); John B. Dykes, 1862]. One of several tunes by Dykes which he named after saints. It was written for Henry H. Milman's Palm Sunday hymn beginning, "Ride on! ride on in majesty," a quite inadequate tune for that hymn. Drostane, or Drostan, according to tradition recorded in the *Aberdeen Breviary,* was of royal Irish blood, a nephew of St. Columba, his disciple, and trained by him. He founded at least two churches in Ireland and formed Christian settlements at Aberdeen and Deer, the latter situated on the most easterly point of land in Scotland, now occupied by the burgh of Peterhead.

ST. DUNSTAN'S [6 5 6 5 6 6 6 5 (3: d d S / d. r m); Winfred Douglas]. This tune was composed by Canon Douglas on December 15, 1917, while he was on a train returning from New York City to his home, St. Dunstan's Cottage, Peekskill, New York. Written for Bunyan's "He who would valiant be." Charles Knight, in his *History of England,* reports:

It is said that the narration of his [St. Dunstan's] career is, for some time, the history of England. With all the power granted him by charter, 'as well in causes known as unknown, in small or in great, and even in those which are above or under the earth, on dry land and on the water, on woods and on plains,' he was, withal, a humble man.

He was orator, poet, artist, painter, skillful artificer in metals, making great improvements and additions to the organ. He became Primate of the English nation, and died at Canterbury, A.D. 988.—James M. Hoppin, *Old England*.

Wolfgang Caspar Printz published at Dresden in 1690 *Historiche Beschreibung der edelen Sing- und klingkunst,* in which he dates the invention of music in consonance—i.e., four parts—from the year 940, and "with great formality of circumstance" ascribes it to

St. Dunstan, otherwise Dunstophus, an Englishman, being very young, betook himself to the study of music, and thereby became of immortal memory. He was the first that composed songs in different parts, namely, Bass, Tenor, Discant, and Vagant or Alt.—Hawkins.

Writing in four parts was older than that, but Dunstan, who had a reputation for his skill in music, may have introduced it to the English people. Did Printz confuse Dunstan with Dunstable, who died in 1453?

He [Dunstan] was very well skilled in most of the liberal arts, and among the rest in refining metals and forging them; which being qualifications much above the age he lived in, first gained him the name of a conjuror, and then of a saint. He was certainly a very honest man, and never feared to reprove vice in any of the kings of the West Saxons, of whom he was confessor to four successively. But the monks (to whom he was a very good friend, applying all his endeavors to enrich them and their monasteries)

have filled his life with several non-sensical stories: such as are, making himself a cell at Glastonbury all of iron at his own forge; his harp playing of itself, without a hand; his taking a she-devil, who tempted him to lewdness under the shape of a fine lady, by the nose with a pair of red-hot tongs; and several other such ridiculous relations not worth repeating.—Wheatly.

A number of churches have been dedicated to him. It was at one of them, St. Dunstan-in-the-West, London, that Baxter, informed while preaching that the building was falling, said: "We are in God's service to prepare ourselves that we may be fearless at the great noise of the dissolving world, when the heavens shall pass away, and the elements melt with fervid heat."

—— [6 6 6 6 (4: d / d L S MF / S - -) ; Leighton G. Layne, date unknown]. See ST. DUNSTAN's by Douglas.

—— [7 7 7 7 (4: m m r m / f. f m -) ; Richard Redhead, 1853]. This is REDHEAD No. 47, which has been renamed DUNSTAN or ST. DUNSTAN's. See REST by Redhead.

ST. EDITH. See ST. HILDA by Knecht.

ST. EDMUND [6 4 6 4 6 6 4 (4: d - d d / d T r -) ; Arthur S. Sullivan, 1872]. Also called FATHERLAND, PILGRIMAGE. Written for T. R. Taylor's:

> We are but strangers here;
> Heaven is our home.

This accounts for the names FATHERLAND and PILGRIMAGE. The composer called it FATHERLAND (or ST. EDMUND's). An Anglo-Saxon *Chronicle* under date of 870 says:

This year the army [of Danes] rode across Mercia, into East Anglia, and took up their winter quarters at Thetford. And the same winter King Edmund fought against them, and the Danes got the victory, and slew the king, and subdued all the land, and destroyed all the ministers which they came to.

And Wheatly wrote:

Edmund was a king of the East Angles, who being assaulted by the Danes [after their irruption into England] for their possession of his country, and not being able to hold out against them, offered his own person, if they would spare his own subjects. But the Danes having got him under their power, endeavored to make him renounce his religion, which he refusing to do, they first beat him with bats, then scourged him with whips, and afterwards binding him to a stake, shot him to death with their arrows. His body was buried in a town where Sigebert, one of his predecessors, had built a church; and where afterwards [in honor of this name] another was built more spacious, and the name of the town, upon that occasion, called St. Edmund's Bury.

According to a local legend the king, fleeing from the Danes, concealed himself under a bridge, where he was discovered through the reflection of his golden spurs in the waters. The bridge is still known as the Gilt-Spur Bridge. The tree against which Edmund stood while being shot at by the Danes was blown down about the middle of the eighteenth century. A block from this oak, still showing a number of the arrow heads, has been preserved at Brome Hill.

———— [S. M. (3: d / d . r m / r d T / d -) original form; Edmund Gilding]. This tune is from W. Riley's *Parochial Harmony* (1762), in which it is called St. Edmund's Tune. Also called Dedication.

———— [C. M. (4: d / m s f m / r m d); W. Stevenson Hoyte, 1875].

———— [7 7 7 7 D (4: m s r m / d L S -); Charles H. Steggal, 1849]. See St. Edmund by Sullivan for the legend.

———— [8 8 8 8 8 8 (free: d - /

d r m d m f / s -)]. See Old 113th.

St. Elizabeth. See Crusaders' Hymn.

St. Ethelwald [S. M. (4: s / f m r mf / m - -); William H. Monk, 1861]. Also called Energy. This was written for Charles Wesley's hymn beginning, "Soldiers of Christ, arise." Energy is a much better name for the tune than St. Ethelwald, for the saint whose name the tune bears was anything but a fighting man. After serving many years as a monk at Ripon, upon the elevation of St. Cuthbert (which see) to the see of Lindisfarne, he took up his abode on the small rock-encompassed island of Farne, living as a hermit for the remainder of his life in the small hermitage built by Cuthbert, who had "so contrived the wall which circled round his inclosure, as to see nothing out of doors, but the blue sky or heavy clouds over his head."—*Lives of the English Saints*. Bede, in his metrical account of St. Cuthbert and Felgeed, Ethelwald's successor at Farne, says:

Between these comrades dear,
Zealous and true as they,
Thou, prudent Ethelwald, didst hear
In that high home the sway.

St. Faith. See Walsall.

St. Finbar. See St. Catherine by Hemy.

St. Flavian [C. M. (4: d / d T d m / r r d); from *Day's Psalter*]. This was called Redhead No. 29 in the original edition of *Hymns Ancient and Modern* (1861), but in the Revised Edition (1875) it appears with the title St. Flavian. No reason was given for the change in name. It had been included in Redhead's *Ancient Hymn Melodies* (1853), being taken from the first half of the tune for Psalm 132 in Sternhold and Hopkins, *Old Version*, printed by Day in 1562. St. Flavian (died 449) was bishop of

Constantinople. In the year of his death he was deposed by the Council of Ephesus. His death was attributed to ill treatment suffered at the hands of his theological opponents.

Also called CARLISLE, DAY, OLD 132ND, PRESCOTT.

ST. FRANCIS. See LASST UNS ERFREUEN.

ST. GABRIEL [8 8 8 4 (4: m / s f m f / m. r d); Frederick A. G. Ouseley, 1868]. Apparently an arbitrary saint name, for it was written for Godfrey Thring's hymn beginning, "The radiant morn hath passed away," which has in it nothing to suggest Gabriel ("strength of God"), the second of the seven archangels, who is the guardian of the celestial treasury, the messenger who appeared to Daniel, who announced to Mary that she should be the mother of the Saviour, and who foretold to Zechariah the birth of John the Baptist.

ST. GEORGE [7 7 7 7 D (4: m.m s m / d r m -)]. See ST. GEORGE'S WINDSOR.

——— [S. M. (4: m / f l s f / m - -)]. See ST. OLAVE and ST. GEORGE'S WINDSOR.

——— [C. M. (4: d / s s s m / l sf m); Nikolas Hermann, late 18th century]. This was a favorite of John Wesley. See ST. GEORGE'S WINDSOR.

——— [C. M. (3: S / S - d / d T d / f m r / r m); George T. Smart, 1795]. Also called WILTSHIRE; NEW ST. ANNE in Scotland. See ST. GEORGE'S WINDSOR.

——— [12 11 12 11 (3: d / d s l / l s f / m r d / s -)]. See MONTGOMERY.

——— [Irr. (3: s / d s l / s s f / m r d / s s)]. See MAGDALEN.

ST. GEORGE'S. See HANOVER.

ST. GEORGE'S BOLTON [7 6 7 6 D (4: m / m r s T / r - d); James Walch, 1875]. The composer was organist at various churches at Bolton, one of which was St. George's Parish Church. He was also associated with the Philharmonic Society of Bolton as organist.

ST. GEORGE'S CHAPEL. See ST. GEORGE'S WINDSOR.

ST. GEORGE'S TUNE. See HANOVER.

ST. GEORGE'S WINDSOR [7 7 7 7 D (4: m. m s m / d r m -); George J. Elvey, 1858]. Also called GEORGE, ST. GEORGE'S CHAPEL. After St. George's Chapel, Windsor, where the composer was organist for forty-seven years. St. George, concerning whom there is much dubious legend, was said, by Pope Gelasius, to be one of those "whose names are justly reverenced among men, but whose acts are known only to God." He was made patron saint of England during the reign of Edward III. Because of this, many English composers have named tunes for him. St. George's Chapel is that of the most noble "Order of the Garter," the oldest and most illustrious of the nine orders of knighthood in Great Britain. Edward III, upon his return from Brittany in 1343, spent much time and money rebuilding Windsor Castle in order that it might become the meeting place of the Order of the Garter, which had been newly instituted in fulfillment of a vow he had taken to restore the Round Table of King Arthur. The particular spot was selected because, according to tradition, King Arthur had there assembled his knights.

ST. GERTRUDE [6 5 6 5 D, with Refrain (4: s s s s / s.l s -); Arthur S. Sullivan, 1871]. For Mrs. Gertrude Clay-Ker-Seymour, at whose home, Hanford, Dorsetshire, England, the composer was a guest when it was written. Sir Arthur's hostess gave this information through a letter to *Musical Times* (London, July, 1902). This composer, in seeking names for his hymn tunes, used the device of "canonizing" the given names of some of his friends.

Also called CHURCH MILITANT, GERTRUDE. The tune, always used with "Onward, Christian soldiers," might well be called CHURCH MILITANT, seemingly a more fitting name for such a militant tune than that of any woman, yet "Gertrude" is a "war name"; it means "spear maiden," an amazon; she who brandishes the spear.

ST. GORDIC [6 6 6 6 4 4 4 4 (4: m / r d L T / d - -); John B. Dykes, 1862]. A saint by this name led a hermit's life for many years in the woods of Finchal, about three miles from Durham, where Dykes was living in 1862 when he wrote the tune.

ST. HELEN [8 7 8 7 4 7 (4: *d d* / *d* m l. s / m r); George C. Martin, 1881]. See ST. HELEN'S.

ST. HELENA [S. M. (4: d / m d r r / d - -); Benjamin Milgrove, 1861]. See below.

ST. HELEN'S [8 5 8 3 (4: m r / f m l s / s f); Robert P. Stewart, 1874]. For St. Helena, the mother of Constantine the Great. Said to have been born in Colchester, England, she did not become a Christian until late in life. When she was nearly eighty years of age, she made a pilgrimage to Jerusalem. See HOLY CROSS for Wheatly's account of her visit. She built a splendid church on Mount Calvary to receive the "true cross" which she is said to have found near there. She is also credited with having discovered the seamless coat of the Saviour and to have taken it to her palace in Treves. Later this palace was converted into a church where, to the present day, the Holy Coat is worshiped by faithful Roman Catholics.

—— [L. M. (4: d - m f / s - l t / *d - t l* / s - - -)]. See DUKE STREET.

ST. HILARY [7 7 7 7 D (2: d m / s. *d* / t l / s -); John Goss, 1897]. Hilary (*circa* 300-67 or -68), eminent layman elected bishop of Poictiers, was converted to Christianity late in life after seriously reading the Bible, especially the book of John. Knowing enough Greek to read poetry, he became interested in the hymns of the Greeks and had enough intellectual curiosity to want to know more about them and what caused them to be written. As a result he became the first Latin writer of Christian metrical hymns.

—— [7 6 7 6 7 7 7 6 (4: m. m f m / m. r r); John B. Dykes, 1863].

—— [8 7 8 7 D (4: m m s s / d r m r); anon., date unknown]. See ST. HILARY by Goss.

ST. HILD [7 7 7 5 (4: m S L T / d r m -); William Ellis, 1919]. Named after St. Hild's Training College, Durham, England, where the composer was onetime music master.

ST. HILDA [7 6 7 6 D (4: d / d Td r r / r d -); arr. from Justin H. Knecht, 1871]. This saint, Hilda (*circa* 679), of royal rank, seemed, through force of circumstances, to exercise unusual influence over political and religious movements in her time. After serving as superior of the monastery of Hartelpool, England, for a time, she established the priory at Streanshalch, near Whitby. For thirty years, so well did she supervise the work, that, because of the "supremacy of union, charity, and equality" which obtained, it was said that "the image of the primitive Church . . . was realized at Whitby." Joined to her nunnery here was a monastery from which, as a result of her influence, issued a number of great men, among them Caedmon, father of English poetry. Another tune called, variously, KNECHT, KOCHER, and CHICHESTER should not be confused with this tune even though its two opening lines are the same as those of ST. HILDA.

Also called HILDA, ST. EDITH.

—— [S. M. (4: m rd f f / f - -); J. K. D. Bedwell, 1902]. For the legend, see ST. HILDA by Knecht.

—— [C. M. (4: s / d d t l /

139

s. m d) ; Howard A. Crosbie, date not found]. For the legend, see ST. HILDA by Knecht.

———— [8 7 8 7 D (4: d d r m / l s s f); Joseph Barnby, 1861]. For the legend, see ST. HILDA by Knecht.

ST. HILL [6 5 6 5 d (4: d. d r m / L T d -); John Stainer, 1875]. This name was given by the musical editors of *The Methodist Hymnal* (1905), from the second given name of the author of the hymn beginning, "Christ, who once among us," W. St. Hill Bourne.

Also called PASTOR BONUS, originally, because of the reference to "Jesus, our good Shepherd" in the last stanza. See pp. 23-24.

ST. HUGH [C. M. (4: *d dd* 1 1 / s. f m) ; English traditional melody, arr. 1906]. This tune is based on the air "Little Sir William," sung to a ballad, dealing with the legend of St. Hugh of Lincoln, which has to do with his having been put to death by Jews in 1225. The story, which may be found in Chaucer's *Canterbury Tales* (the "Prioress's Tale"), is that some Jews stole the boy, Hugh, whom they tortured for ten days before crucifying him. As a result eighteen of the wealthiest Jews of Lincoln were hanged for having participated in the affair. The boy was given a state burial. This title, "St. Hugh," has nothing to do with the Bishop of Grenoble of that anme, who was canonized by Pope Innocent II in 1134, nor with St. Hugh, Abbot of Cluny.

Also called DOVEDALE, from a canyon of the River Dove which is one of the picturesque spots in Derbyshire, England. The place has a special interest for fishermen because of Isaak Walton's reference to it.

———— [C. M. (4: d / d r m d / s r m); Edward J. Hopkins, 1862]. See above, for the legend.

———— [7 7 7 7 7 7 (4: s. l s m /

d r m -) ; Arthur St. George Patton, 1880]. See ST. HUGH, English traditional melody, for the legend.

ST. IRENAEUS. See GIBBONS by Gibbons.

ST. JAMES [C. M. (4: S / d r m d / r f m); Raphael Courteville, 1697]. Written for *Select Psalms and Hymns for the use of the Parish Church and Tabernacle of St. James's, Westminster*, of which the composer was the first organist. It was this composer's son, also named Raphael, who succeeded him as organist at St. James's and who was reputed to be the author of the *Gazetteer*, which was a defense of the administration of Hugh Walpole. The opposition writers stigmatized him by referring to him as "Court-evil."

ST. JOHN [7 7 7 7 7 7 (4: S S L S / L T d -); Richard Cecil, late 18th century]. Named by the composer, a onetime minister at St. John's Chapel, Bedford Row, London.

———— [C. M. (4: d / T d r m / f f m)]. See ST. JOHN'S, WESTMINSTER, the name by which it is best known. See the same for the following tunes named ST. JOHN:

S. M. (4: d / m r d T / d - -); A. King, date not found.

6 6 6 6 8 8 (4: d / m m s s / d - -); from *The Parish Choir*, 1851.

6 6 6 4 8 8 4 (4: L / m . r d T / L - - -); John B. Dykes, 1864.

6 6 6 6 8 8 (4: m / m r d r / m - -); J. Baptiste Calkin, middle 19th century.

ST. JOHN'S, WESTMINSTER [C. M. (4: d / T d r m / f f m); James Turle, 1863]. Named after the Chapel of St. John Baptist, Westminster Abbey, London, with which the composer was connected for sixty-three years, fifty-six of which were spent in active service. This Chapel of St. John Baptist, possibly the first of the evangelical chapels in Westminster, formerly a chapel by itself, is now combined with those of St. Michael and St. Andrew in one.

St. Jude [8 7 8 8 7 (4: S. L / T d r. d / d T); Charles J. Vincent, 1877]. This saint was the brother of St. James the Less and of St. Simeon of Jerusalem, members of the family of Jesus. Probably there were two Judes—Jesus' brother and the disciple of Jesus. See Luke 6:16. The tune was written for the hymn beginning, "O the bitter shame and sorrow," by Theodore Monod.

————— [S. M. (4: m / L T d r / m - -); William Horsley, date unknown]. See St. Jude by Vincent.

————— [6 6 6 6 D (4: S / m T d r / T); Arthur Cottman, 1875]. See St. Jude by Vincent.

————— [8 7 8 7 (3: mS / r r rS / d d)]. See Galilee by Jude.

————— [L. M. (3: s m r / d - d / l - l / s -)]. See Armes.

St. Jude's. See Magdalen College.

St. Kevin [7 6 7 6 D (4: m m mr d / m f s -); Arthur S. Sullivan, 1872]. Coemgen (St. Kevin), whose name signifies "fair begotten," lived for four years as a hermit in the Vale of Glendalough ("Valley of the Two Lakes"), Ireland, where he is supposed to have established a monastery and where he died (*circa* 618) at the advanced age of 120 years. This monastery, for long an important ecclesiastical and educational center, was subjected to frequent ravages by the Danes, then became an episcopal see, and is now incorporated with Dublin. The "Valley of the Two Lakes" is noted for its "Seven Churches," among them St. Kevin's kitchen (or church), a granite monolith (never completed), and his bed which was in a cave above the *lough* (lake).

Also called Kevin.

St. Kilda [C. M. (4: L / L T d m / r d T); William R. Broomfield, 1850]. Probably named after the

island of this name off Scotland. James B. Johnston, in *Place-Names of Scotland,* tells us there is no definite proof any such person as St. Kilda ever lived, but that there is no doubt some saint lived on the little island, just as others did at other isolated spots. He says, further, the name "Kilda" has caused "much puzzlement." The composer of the tune died in St. Nicholas Poorhouse, Aberdeen, and was buried in a corner of the grounds there. A little group of mourners gathered about before his burial and sang, to the tune St. Kilda, a quatrain based on Psalm 51, which was a great favorite of his:

Do Thou with hyssop sprinkle me,
 I shall be cleansed so;
Yea, wash Thou me, and then I shall
 Be whiter than the snow.

A year after his death admirers had his body removed to Allandale Cemetery, Aberdeen, and, through public subscription, purchased and had erected over the grave a monument upon which the tune and quatrain referred to above were carved.

St. Leonard [C. M. D. (4: d / r f m r / r. d d); Henry Hiles, 1867]. This setting for Adelaide A. Procter's hymn beginning, "The shadows of the evening hours," written for a festival held at St. Mary's Church, Hulme, Manchester, England, was given this name by its composer. Evidently an arbitrary selection. Leonard (died 500), born at Le Mans, France, became bishop of Limosin. King Clodeveus granted freedom to all prisoners Leonard visited; therefore, when Leonard heard af any persons being imprisoned for religious or other good causes, he went to see them and claimed for them their freedom. "He has always been implored by prisoners as their saint."

Also called LEONARD, ST. LEONARD'S, SHADOWS. LEONARD and ST. LEONARD'S are but variants of the original name. SHADOWS, because it was set to Adelaide A. Proctor's evening hymn beginning, "The shadows of the evening hours." In most instances the following tunes were given the name ST. LEONARD because of the sentiment of the various texts for which they were written:

C. M. (4: s / s m l s / l t d); Henry Smart, 1867. To "O for a faith that will not shrink," William H. Bathurst.

C. M. (4: m / s.f m r / f m r); Robert Jackson, ca. 1890. For J. D. Burns's hymn beginning:

Thou Lord art Love—and everywhere
Thy name is brightly shown.

5 4 5 4 D (3: m m.m / s - s); Edward P. Crawford, 1907. To "Rest of the weary, Joy of the sad" by J. S. B. Monsell.

8 7 8 7 8 7 (4: m rd r s / d rd T S); from *Neu-vermehrtes und zu Ubung Christl. Gottseligkeit eingerichtetes Meiningisches Gesangbuch*, 1693. Attributed to Johann Christoph Bach. Also called *Liebe die du mich zum Bilde*. For Frances F. Cox's:

Love, who in the first beginning,
Man in Thine own image made.

8 8 8 4 (4: s / m r d l / f m r); Herbert S. Irons. This tune first appeared in print in *The English Hymnal* (1916), eleven years after the composer's death. It was there used as the setting for "The radiant morn hath passed away" by Godfrey Thring.

12 11 12 11 (3: m / m.r m / s f m / r d r / m d); John B. Dykes, 1873. To R. Tomlins' hymn beginning, "And is it Thy voice, patient Saviour, yet calling?" the second stanza being:

"Come unto Me," all ye laden and weary,
Yea, come unto Me, all ye sad and opprest:
Though dark be the pathway, the prospect all dreary,
O come unto Me, and your souls shall find rest.

ST. LEONARD'S. See ST. LEONARD by Hiles.

ST. LOUIS [8 6 8 6 7 6 8 6 (4: m / m m #r m / s f L); Lewis H. Redner, 1868]. This tune was named by its composer, who, seemingly, never gave any reason for his choice. It may be suggested that someone added the "St." to the French form ("Louis") of his first given name.

ST. LUKE [L. M. (4: L / S F M d / T L #S); Jeremiah Clark, 1701]. Many churches have been named after this evangelist, and it is probable that, in turn, many of the tunes carrying this name were named for the churches.

—— [L. M. (3: d / m r d / f m r / d r T / d -); anon., from *Collection of Easy Litanies*, 1852]. Said to be an "ancient melody." This is the tune called INTERCESSION, arranged by Dykes.

—— [C. M. (4: m / f s l s / s f m); John Heywood, 1868].

—— [7 6 7 6 D (4: m / m m f m / r - d); F. W. Mills, date not found]. See ST. LUKE by Clark.

—— [L. M. (4: s / m T d l / s f m)]. See WILTON.

ST. LUKE'S. See ST. SYLVESTER.

ST. MAGNUS [C. M. (4: S / d r T S / d r m); Jeremiah Clark]. First called NOTTINGHAM in Nathaniel Gawthorne's *Harmonia Perfecta* (1730), the tune was not given the name ST. MAGNUS by its composer but by William Riley, a teacher of singing at the Royal Female Orphan Asylum, founded at Lambeth, London, in 1758. Riley, who called himself "professor of psalmody," compiled two tune books (*circa* 1762), *Parochial Harmony* and *Psalms and Hymns*, for the use of the children of the asylum. He used Clark's unnamed tune in the former book, calling the tune ST. MAGNUS, the name of a church located near the old London Bridge. In this book Riley gave the names of various London churches to many thitherto unnamed tunes. The handsome church of St. Magnus the Martyr is located on Lower Thames Street near London Bridge. The present structure, built by Christopher Wren in 1676, after the great fire, is one of his last as well as one of his best. The gilded carved clock-dial, erected at a cost of 485 pounds in 1709, was the gift of Sir Charles Duncombe. When he was a poor boy, he lost trace of his master while waiting for him on London Bridge, because he had no way of knowing the time. At that time he vowed that he would give a clock to St. Magnus if ever he became rich. The church was named after Magnus, a Norwegian jarl (earl), killed in the twelfth century in Orkney, where the cathedral of Kirkwall is dedicated to him. Miles Coverdale, Bishop of Exeter, was once rector of St. Magnus, and his remains were transferred to its churchyard from St. Bartholomew by the Exchange when the latter was torn down in 1840. On Coverdale's monument may be noted: "On the 4th of October, 1535, the first complete English version of the Bible was published under his direction." Jeremiah Clark, composer, after having committed suicide by shooting himself with a "screw pistol," was buried in the churchyard of St. Gregory by St. Paul on December 3, 1707. One Edward Ward addressed a "Pathetic Ode" to Clark beginning:

> Mourn, all ye Brethren of String,
> Prepare at once to Weep and Sing:
> Tune your soft Lyres, and strain your
>   warbling throats,

and closing:

> Let us not wonder at his fall
> Since was not so unnatural
> For him who lived by Canon to expire
>   by Ball.

Also called BIRMINGHAM, CARROLL, GREENOCK, LANGFORD, WILBY.

ST. MARGARET   [8 8 8 6 6 (4: S / S. S SL Td / d - T) ; Albert L. Peace, 1884]. While there is much information, as well as misinformation, available concerning George Matheson's hymn, "O Love that wilt not let me go," and of the composition of the tune ST. MARGARET, which was written especially for it, no statement as to why the tune was given this name has come to my attention. It is possible it was dedicated to some person whose given name was Margaret—in which case, however, it is probable the fact would have become known, so great has been the interest in this hymn and tune. It may be suggested that the source of this tune name may have been Margaret, Queen of Malcolm III (Canmore), King of Scotland. She was canonized in 1251 on account of her many benefactions to the Church. The name "Margaret" is greatly revered in Scotland.

ST. MARIA. See ST. MICHEL'S.

ST. MARK. See ST. THEODULPH.

ST. MARTIN [10 4 10 4 (4: m - L T / d - r - / m m s f / m - -); George W. Briggs, 1931]. The composer was Proctor in Convocation of Canterbury, where is located what is said to be the oldest Christian church built in England, the Church of St. Martin. St. Martin, an honorable name both in England and in France, has given his name to many churches, the best known of which is that in

Canterbury. Called the "Mother Church of England," there is little doubt but that it was built in pre-Saxon days prior to the arrival of St. Augustine in England. It had been a chapel where Queen Bertha, wife of Ethelbert, King of Kent, had worshiped and where the King was said to have been baptized when he embraced Christianity. F. E. Howard, in *The Mediaeval Styles of the English Parish Church,* says this church had been dedicated to St. Martin, but he does not say which St. Martin. Inasmuch as it was built during the Roman occupancy of that part of England, it is probable one of the Italian saints of that name bears the honor. The best known and most interesting of the saints named "Martin," however, is the patron saint of Tours and Lucca (316-97). In addition to being the patron of the two cities named, he is also patron of knights and tailors, of "drinking, conviviality, and repentant drunkards." It is possible that a section of the chancel of the Church of St. Martin, in Canterbury, is a fragment of the church in which Queen Bertha worshiped. Each tune in the following list with the title St. Martin, or St. Martin's, was probably named for one or another of the many churches in England or elsewhere bearing that name.

6 5 6 5 (4: m r m d / L - T -); Charles Steggall, 1875. Also called Mirfield.

6 6 6 6 (4: s m f m / r - d -) has been traced to Ett (?), *Cantica Sacra in Usum Studiosae Juventutis,* Munich, 1840. It has this name in *Hymns Ancient and Modern.* Also called St. Agatha.

7 7 7 7 (3: d - r / m - d / r - T / d - -). See Orientis Partibus.

8 6 8 6 8 8 7 (4: d / m f s m / m r d); James H. Sheppard, 1876.

St. Martin's [C. M. (3: d / dr d S / dr m mf / sf m d / r -); William Tans'ur, 1740]. Also called Gainsborough.

——— [C. M. (4: s / d t d s / l fm r); anon., date unknown].

——— [7 7 7 7 (4: m d T. d / f m r -); Albert L. Peace, 1868].

St. Mary [C. M. (4: L - d T / L l s f / m -); anon., from *Llyfr y Psalmau,* 1621]. This famous old tune was one of the five said to be in common use in Puritan New England when singing in church was in a very sorry state. It is found in a Welsh metrical *Psalter* (1621) compiled by Archdeacon Edmund Prys but was given the name St. Mary by John Playford when he used it in his *Whole Book of Psalms* (1677).

Also called Hackney, Playford. Playford: from the compiler of the *Whole Book of Psalms.* Hackney: because it was mistakenly attributed to a German musician named Rathiel, onetime organist at St. John's Church, Hackney, England. This is the name by which the tune was known in early New England.

——— [C. M. (4: d / L S d r / m m r); Johann Crüger]. This is a somewhat different form of Gräfenberg, which see.

Also called Nun Danket All, St. Mary Magdalene.

St. Mary Magdalene [7 6 7 6 (4: d / Td r d TL / ‡SL T M); Harold A. Jeboult, 1906]. The composer was organist at the Church of St. Mary Magdalene, Taunton, the county-town of Somersetshire, England. It was in Taunton, in 1685, that Judge Jeffries held the "Bloody Assizes" where hundreds were condemned to death or were sentenced to serve on the plantations.

——— [C. M. (4: m / r d d s / l l s); Richard Redhead, 1859]. See Magdalena by Stainer.

Also called Metzler's Redhead.

——— [7 7 7 7 D (4: m m r d /

144

s. l s -) ; Arthur S. Sullivan, 1872].
See MAGDALENA by Stainer.

—— [6 5 6 5 D (4: d d r m /
f - m -) ; John B. Dykes, 1862]. Also
called MAGDALENE. See MAGDALENA
by Stainer.

—— [C. M. (4: d / L S d r /
m m r) ; Johann Crüger, 1653]. See
GRÄFENBERG.
Also called GRÄFENBERG, ST. MARY.

ST. MATTHEW [C. M. D. (3: S / M - S /
d - m / r d T / d -) ; William Croft].
Originally to Psalm 33, *A Supple-
ment to the New Version of the
Psalms* (1708), named for the apostle
Matthew. The name has no significance when used, as the tune now is,
with E. H. Plumptre's hymn beginning:

Thine arm, O Lord, in days of old,
    Was strong to heal and save;
It triumphed o'er disease and death,
    O'er darkness and the grave.

ST. MATTHIAS [8 8 8 8 8 8, with Refrain
(4: m / r d f m / r. m d) ; William
H. Monk, 1861]. The composer was
organist at St. Matthias, Stoke Newington, England, for thirty-seven
years. The tune was named for the
church.

—— [C. M. (4: d / s m f s / 11 s) ;
Orlando Gibbons]. This is SONG 67
for St. Matthias Day in George
Wither's *Hymnes and Songs of the
Church* (1623). It begins:

When one among the Twelve there was
    That did Thy grace abuse,
Thou leftst him, Lord, and in his place
    Didst iust Matthias choose.

See Acts 1:21-26.

ST. MICHAEL [S. M.; from the *Genevan
Psalter*, 1551]. See OLD 134TH for
account of the saint.

ST. MICHAEL's. See HANOVER. See OLD
134TH for additional comment.

ST. MICHEL'S   [C. M. D. (4: s /
s. f m s / f. m r) ; from W. Gawler's
Hymns and Psalms, 1789]. "St.

Michel," in common usage, is equiva-
lent to "St. Michael." See OLD 134TH.
Also called BEULAH, GOSHEN, HIN-
TON, PALESTINE, ST. MARIA.

ST. NICHOLAS [C. M. (3: L / d - m /
l - m / f m r / d -) ; anon., from *The
Spiritual Man's Companion: Or, The
Pious Christian's Recreation*, 1753].
Nicholas, of Myra or Bari, was a
fourth-century Italian saint. His day
is December 6. Patron saint of children, sailors, travelers, merchants,
and pawnbrokers, as well as pirates
and footpads (the latter presumably
because they were travelers), he was
also protector against thieves and
robbers. Many seaport cities and
towns throughout the world, especially in Greece and Russia, claim
him as patron. His realm is a wide
one. He has been regarded by non-
Catholic historians as one of the
mythical protective forces prior to
the Christian Era. Nicholas is said
to have been the son of wealthy,
noble parents who died shortly after
he became a priest. Inheriting a large
fortune, he gave it all to the poor.
Of the many legends that have grown
up around him, several are interesting, but most are fantastic. Perhaps
the most interesting of them is that
concerning the nobleman with three
attractive daughters who had lost all
his worldly goods and was at a loss
as to how he might support his
daughters in order that they not be
compelled to become prostitutes.
Nicholas, hearing of his concern,
passed his house three successive
nights on each of which he tossed a
bag of gold through the window,
thus providing each of the maidens
a dowry which would enable her to
marry. On the third visit the father
waylaid him and, though discovering
the benefactor, was bound to secrecy
by him. The three bags of gold,
incidentally, were balls of gold,
simulations of which were adopted

by pawnbrokers as their sign of business. It would follow, naturally, that Nicholas would be chosen their patron saint. Being the patron and protector of children, the legend continues, after St. Nicholas' death, the parents of Myra, his birthplace, remembering the secrecy with which he made his gifts to the daughters of the impoverished nobleman, gave presents to their children on his day to remind them of him. These were hidden where the children could find them and were regarded as coming from the saint himself. This part of the legend gradually merged itself with the Christmas story, partly by accident of the season which approximated that when gifts were brought to the manger Child at Bethlehem. And that is why children often refer to their Christmas benefactor as good "Saint Nick." The Dutch form of his name, "Santa Claus," has become most usual in America.

——— [8 8 8 6 (4: m / m r d L / S d r); John B. Dykes, *ca.* 1875]. Originally Consent because written for Charlotte Elliott's "Just as I am." For all tunes with this name see St. Nicholas, anon. for the legends. Also called Derry.

C. M. (4: s / l. s s f / m r d); William Ellis, *ca.* 1919. The composer was onetime organist at St. Nicholas Church, Durham, England.

8 7 8 7 8 7 (4: d. T dr mf / s sf mr d); William Ellis, *ca.* 1919. An instance of different tunes by the same composer having a common name.

6 4 6 4 6 6 6 4 (3: d d m / m. r d); C. W. Pearce, date unknown.

8 7 8 7 D (4: d. S d m / r. L r f); John Frederick Bridge, *ca.* 1890.

10 6 10 6 (4: m - m m / s - m - / r m f s / m -); Clement C. Scholefield, 1870.

8 7 8 7 (4: s l l s / f m m r); Richard Redhead. See St. Bede by Redhead.

This is Redhead No. 143.

St. Ninian [7 7 7 7 7 7 (4: s l / s m d r / m -); Edwin G. Monk, 1862]. Ninian was Bishop of Candida Casa (white house) on the extreme southwest peninsula of Scotland, the Rhinns of Galloway, and Apostle to the Southern Picts. The first saint in the Scottish Calendar, he presumably was the first to bring Christianity to Scotland. He is commemorated in more than fifty churches and chapels. Camden speaks of him as "Ninian, the Briton, a holy man, who first enriched the southern Picts with the Christian faith."

——— [7 6 7 6 D (4: d / m m s s / t. l s); H. A. Prothero, date unknown]. See St. Ninian by Monk.

——— [11 10 11 10 (4: d - d d / d - d r / m - r d / T - d -); John B. Dykes, 1857]. See St. Ninian by Monk.

St. Olaf. See St. Olave.

St. Olave [S. M. (4: m / f l s f / m - -); Henry J. Gauntlett, 1852]. The composer was organist for twenty years at St. Olave's, Southwark, London. This church commemorates St. Olaf, who with Ethelred, in 1013, destroyed the Bridge of London, which at the time was held by the Danes. It stands on the seat of the exploit. Olaf (II) Haraldssön, King of Norway from 1016 to 1029, slain by his pagan subjects in 1030, is the patron saint of all Norway. Because in Latin his name is *Holofius* ("whole-loaf-ius"), he is sometimes represented in art carrying a loaf of bread.

Also called St. Olaf. The tune was originally called St. George, which see.

——— [L. M. (3: d / mf s l / d T d / f m r / m -); Robert Hudson, late 19th century]. See above. The composer's daughter, Mary, was onetime organist at St. Olave Church, Hart Street, London.

———— [6 6 6 6 6 6 (4: d / d T L S / m - -) ; Joseph Barnby]. Indicated as a setting for Frances R. Havergal's "I gave my life for Thee" in *Hymn Tunes* (Barnby), issued by Novello in 1897, its meter is given as 6 6 8 4 6 6; but as the meter of the hymn is so obviously 6 6 6 6 6 6, modern editors of tune books use the latter.

ST. OSWALD [8 7 8 7 (4: s. m 1 d / t l s m)]. See explanation below, and see ST. AMBROSE.

———— [6 6 6 8 (4: d / d d r r / m - -) ; John B. Dykes, 1857]. See below.

———— [L. M. (4: d / s s s s / d tl s) ; John B. Dykes, 1862]. Dr. Dykes was vicar of St. Oswald's, Durham, for fourteen years. The first of these tunes (see above) was given the name ST. BERNARD when first published, and was called ST. OSWALD when it appeared in *Hymns Ancient and Modern* (1875); but it is found as ST. AMBROSE in *Hymn Tunes* (Dykes), issued by Novello (no date). The composer, apparently, was guilty of giving the other two different tunes the same name. LUX BENIGNA is also sometimes called ST. OSWALD. Oswald (604-42), classed by the Venerable Bede as one of the seven great Anglo-Saxon kings, is said to have been the first to raise the Christian banner over the first Christian altar in Berenicia. See ST. AMBROSE and ST. BERNARD.

ST. OSYTH [11 10 11 10 (4: s - l s / m - - d / r m f m / s - m -) ; Thomas Wood, 1925]. One of the given names of the composer's wife. St. Osyth, patron saint of the County of Essex, England, is said to have been the daughter of a merchant prince, Frithewald (*circa* 675) of Mercia. She had been married against her will to Sighere, a king of the East Saxons. During her husband's absence on a hunting trip, Osyth re-

ceived the veil from two bishops. Her husband agreed to the arrangement and gave her a grant of lands at Chich (now St. Osyth), Essex, with sufficient funds to found a nunnery. She was beheaded by a party of Danes when she refused to abandon Christianity; but she soon arose from where she had fallen and, carrying her head in her hands, walked to the church of Chich, where she was buried.

ST. PATRICK [L. M. D. (3: M / L - L / S M S / d m rd / d T) ; traditional Irish melody]. This is the setting for Cecil F. Alexander's English rendering of the strange barbaric chant known as the *Lorica*, or "St. Patrick's Breastplate." Mrs. Alexander's rendering of the opening lines, "I bind unto myself today," is said by James Moffatt to be a mistranslation of the Irish "Today I arise." The story of the life of Ireland's patron saint, Patrick (*circa* 389-461), is involved in so much legendary detail that it is difficult to sort out the facts concerning it. It is certain, however, that he labored with vigor and zeal in attempting to Christianize the Emerald Isle. It is largely because of him and his work that Ireland became known as "the Island of Saints and Scholars." Patrick brought the island into touch with western Europe and, more significantly, with Rome; he introduced the Latin language into Roman Church usage there; he was instrumental in implanting Christianity into many parts of Ireland which had been Druid strongholds. Although charged by his enemies with illiteracy, which he readily admitted, he was nevertheless able to best the powerful High-king Loigaire through trials of various skills. Perhaps his most spectacular feat was his challenge to the royal authority through his lighting the Paschal Fire on the hill of Slane on an Easter Eve in full sight of the king and his company who had assembled for the opening of the pagan spring festival at Tara. This defiance of the Druid priests' edict that no bonfire be lighted before theirs, as the opening act of their celebration, so greatly strengthened Patrick's position that Loigaire gave what protection he could to the Christian leader, even though he did not accept his strange religion. Patrick was a strong man, aggressive to an extent that seemingly enabled him to overcome all difficulties. See SLANE.

ST. PAUL'S. See WILTON by Lampe.

ST. PETER [C. M. (4: s / d t l s / s f m); Alexander R. Reinagle, *ca.* 1828]. Named after St. Peter's-in-the-East, the church in Oxford, England, where the composer was organist when the tune was written.
Also called ST. PETER'S, OXFORD, and CHRIST CHURCH.

ST. PETER'S, OXFORD. See above.

ST. PETERSBURG [8 8 8 8 8 8 (3: s / m - f / s - d / r d t / d -); attributed to Dimitri S. Bortniansky]. The tune is said to have been taken from a mass written by Bortniansky while he was director of the Russian Imperial Choir at St. Petersburg; but no mass by him is known, nor is there any evidence the tune came from any larger work. It was published in *Choralbuch* (Leipsig, 1825), edited by I. H. Tscherlitzky, a St. Petersburg organist.
Also called ROYSTON, SHANGANA, WELLS, WELLSPRING. Perhaps the names WELLS and WELLSPRING were given it because of the former custom of playing this tune on semi-religious occasions, one of which was the "blessing of the waters," which took place in St. Petersburg on January 6. For an extended account of this tune see *Our Hymnody*. No reason is apparent for the use of either

SHANGANA or ROYSTON as a name for the tune.

ST. PETER'S, WESTMINSTER [8 7 8 7 8 7 (4: d d d. r / m f m r); James Turle, date uncertain, middle 19th century]. The composer was organist at Westminster, London, for fifty-one years. On the site of the present Westminster Abbey, King Sebert (died 616) is said to have founded a church which he dedicated to St. Peter. Later, Edward the Confessor razed the old church and rebuilt it from the foundation as the "Collegiate Church of St. Peter." This was by no means the structure which exists today, but from its beginnings there has been this association with the name of St. Peter.

ST. PHILIP. See SARUM.

ST. PHILIPS. See MELCOMBE.

ST. SAVIOUR [C. M. (4: d / d t d l / s. f m); Frederick G. Baker, 1876]. The composer was organist at St. Saviour's, Shanklin, Isle of Wight.

ST. SEPULCHRE [L. M. (4: d / s l s d / f s m); George Cooper, 1862]. Named by the composer, one of the four Coopers who had charge of the music at St. Sepulchre Church, Newgate Street, London, for an even century —1799-1899. The tune was written in 1836 during the regime of the composer's father, the second Cooper in the line of St. Sepulchre organists named George. The church stands opposite Newgate prison, where, on the night before an execution, its bellman used to go under the walls of the prison, ring his bell, and recite:

All you that in the condemned hole do lie,
Prepare you, for toworrow you shall die;
Watch all and pray, the hour is drawing near
That you before the Almighty must appear;

Examine well yourselves, in time repent,
That you may not to eternal flames be
    sent;
And when St. Sepulchre's bell tomor-
    row tolls,
The Lord above have mercy on your
    souls.
    Past twelve o'clock!

Also called ST. AGNES.
——— [8 8 8 (4: d / d. d d m /
s r m)]. See HOLY SEPULCHRE.
ST. STEPHEN [C. M. (4: d / s m d rd /
T d r); William Jones, 1789]. Named
after the composer's favorite saint,
the tune was written as a setting for
Psalm 23 and was called ST.
STEPHEN'S TUNE.
Also called NAYLAND, NAYLOR, NEW-
INGTON, ST. STEPHEN'S. NAYLAND: a
town in Suffolk, England, where the
composer was named perpetual curate in 1777. NAYLOR: probably a
misprint for "Nayland." NEWINGTON:
after the town in Scotland by this
name. Stephen is said to have been
"one of the most powerful and eloquent of the first pleaders for
Christ." The first Christian martyr,
he was accused of speaking blas-
phemous words in the Temple and
was stoned to death outside the gates
of the city of Jerusalem. He is the
patron saint of masons and stone-
cutters. See STEPHANOS and INNO-
CENTS for further reference to him.
——— [C. M. (3: d / s - d / d t l /
s f m / m r)]. Also called ABRIDGE.
See ABRIDGE and above.
ST. STEPHEN'S. See ST. STEPHEN by
Jones.
ST. SYLVESTER [C. M. D. (4: d dd r m /
m. r r); Joseph Barnby, 1867]. The
tune was written in 1867 as a setting
for the carol-like text beginning:

'Twas in the winter cold, when earth
    Was desolate and wild,
That angels welcomed at His birth
    The everlasting Child,

by an unknown author. This was
published in *Carols New and Old*,
issued by Sir John Stainer and the
Reverend H. R. Bramley. In *Hymn
Tunes* (Barnby), issued by Novello
(Preface dated 1897), it appears with
the name ST. SYLVESTER. Some later
editor called it ST. LUKE'S. The fame
of St. Sylvester, who became bishop
of Rome in 314 and later was made
pope, rests on a legend that he was
instrumental in bringing about the
conversion to Christianity of Constantine the Great. The story of Constantine, "covered with leprosy [sin],"
first seeking a cure through pagan
rites and a bath in the blood of
slain infants, and then turning to
Christianity to find it in baptism,
seems to stem from Constantine's
being credited with the murder of
his wife, son, and nephew. As penitence he made a last visit to Rome,
where he built two churches, one
near the Baths of Diocletian, the
other in the Lateran. On the building of the latter the Emperor is said
to have labored with his own hands
and to have richly adorned it. Between 752 and 777 a document pur-
porting to be a "Donation made by
Constantine" (*Donatio Constantini*)
was forged which was destined to become of world-importance. Among
other things it declared, "The chair
of Peter [i.e., the Pope] . . . shall
have supreme authority over all
churches in the world; the Roman
clergy shall enjoy the high privileges
of the imperial senate"; and, most
far-reaching of all, "Constantine
gives up the remaining sovereignty
over Rome, the provinces, cities, and
towns of the whole of Italy or the
Western regions to Pope Sylvester
and his successors." Later the "or"
was changed to "and," for reasons
which have become obvious. Baring-
Gould, in *Lives of the Saints*, says,
"When the forgery of the Donation

was well established, the fable [of the bath of infants' blood] naturally attached itself to it, and the baptizer became Sylvester."

Also called A CHRISTMAS CAROL.

—— [8 7 8 7 (3: m. m mm rm / fs m -) ; John B. Dykes, 1862]. See ST. SYLVESTER by Barnby.

ST. THEOCTISTUS [7 6 7 6 8 8 7 7 (4: m m d d / 1.1 s -) ; Frederick A. G. Ouseley, 1882]. This was composed for a translation, by John M. Neale, of a Greek hymn known as the "Suppliant Canon to Jesus." Neale made it into an English hymn beginning, "Jesus, Name all names above." The original was written by Theoctistus of the Studium, *circa* 890. According to Neale he was a friend of St. Joseph of the Studium. The Studium was a famous monastery in Constantinople founded by the consular Studius. Its monks were famous for their work in calligraphy and in copying manuscripts.

ST. THEODULPH [7 6 7 6 D (4: d / s s l t / d - d) ; Melchior Teschner, 1615]. From the author of the Latin hymn *Gloria, laus, et honor* ("All glory, laud, and honor'), with which it has long been wedded. It is very popular as a Palm Sunday processional. Theodulph of Orleans was born of noble Gothic family about the middle of the eighth century either in Italy or in Spain; historians differ in their accounts of him. Well educated, he attracted the attention of Charlemagne, who called him to France from Italy, and upon the death of Alcuin he became the Emperor's principal theologian. He was sometime abbot of Fleury and Saint-Aignan and bishop of Orleans from 781 to 818. After the death of Charlemagne he was accused, probably unjustly, of conspiracy and in 818 was deposed and imprisoned in a monastery at Angers, where he died, probably from poisoning.

Also called KRONSTADT, ST. MARK.

ST. THERESA [6 5 6 5 D, with Refrain (6: m - r m - f / s - - s - -) ; Arthur S. Sullivan, 1874]. Probably the name of a woman friend whom the composer "canonized." It is doubtful that Sullivan named his tune after the St. Theresa who is the patron saint of Spain.

—— [8 8 8 6 (4: d - d d / r - r - / m d d r / d - T)]. See FLEMMING.

ST. THOMAS [S. M. (4: S / d d m rd / r - -) ; Aaron Williams, 1763]. Probably named for Thomas the apostle. It was named by the composer who wrote this and other "common" tunes —i.e., tunes not written for any special text. The name doubtless has no significance.

Also called WILLIAMS.

—— [8 7 8 7 4 7 (4: d r m d / r m f m) ; John F. Wade's mss. book, 1751]. This tune, more widely used in England than in this country, comes from the same book in which ADESTE FIDELES (which see) is found.

Also called HOLYWOOD.

ST. VINCENT. See MENDELSSOHN.

ST. WERBERGH [8 8 8 8 8 8 (4: d / d m s d / d l s) ; John B. Dykes, 1862]. St. Werbergh (or Werburga), daughter of Wulfere (or Wulfhere), King of Mercia (died 675), was born in the early seventh century and died in 699 at Trentham. After a period spent in a convent at Ely she was asked by King Aethelred, her uncle (died 716), to supervise all the religious houses for women in his kingdom. Through his liberality she founded new convents at Trentham, in Gloucestershire; at Hanbury, in Staffordshire; and at Weedon, in Northamptonshire. At her request King Aethelred founded a collegiate church at West Chester. She was very religious; in addition to the usual monastic offices she is said to have recited daily, on her knees, the entire Psalter. A great fire in 1180, in Chester, England, was said to have been extinguished suddenly when the shrine of St. Werbergh was carried through the streets.

ST. WERBERGH'S. See TANTUM ERGO.

ST. WERBURG. See OLD 104TH.

SAINTS OF GOD [L. M., with Refrain (4: m / s. s s s / d t l); Arthur S. Sullivan, 1874]. This was written for William G. Maclagan's hymn beginning, "The saints of God; their conflict past." It is also used as a six-line 8s hymn without refrain.

SALAMIS. See SWEET STORY.

SALISBURY. See EASTER HYMN.

SALTASH [8 7 8 7 D (2: m rd / L dr / m s / m r); early American melody]. This old camp-meeting tune was very popular in early days along the American frontier, with the text beginning, "Now the Saviour stands a-pleading" (author unknown). Because it was published in Henry Ward Beecher's *Plymouth Collection* (1856), it was called PLYMOUTH. It got the name SALTASH when it began to appear in English books. English editors have a practice of renaming most, if not all, of the tunes they use from American sources. Saltash is a quaint old fishing town situated on the estuary of the Plym in Cornwall, England, where the women are famous for their rowing ability. They frequently best their men in regattas. Also called PLEADING SAVIOUR.

SALVATION. See WESLEY.

SALVE DOMINE [7 6 7 6 D (4: m SS L T / d - S -); Lawrence W. Watson, 1909]. Latin for "Hail, Lord," from the sentiment of the hymn line "Light of the World, we hail Thee," by John S. B. Monsell.

SALZBURG [C. M. (3: d / m - s / s f m / m - r / d -); adapted from Johann M. Haydn, 1819]. For the town in which the composer lived for the last thirty-four years of his life and for which he often expressed great affection. Salzburg, so called since 816 because

of the local abundance of salt, has a long ecclesiastical tradition. During the Peasants' War (1525-26) it became a stronghold in opposition to the Reformation. It is the capital of the province of Salzburg in Austria.
—— [8 7 8 7 8 7 (4: d r m f / s f m r)]. See TANTUM ERGO.

SAMSON [L. M. (4: d / m. f s m / l t d); George F. Handel] The tune is a segment from a chorus in the composer's opera of this name (1742), from which the tune has been arranged.

SAMUEL [6 6 6 6 8 8 (4: m - m s / f. m f); Arthur S. Sullivan, 1874]. From James D. Burns's hymn about Samuel beginning, "Hushed was the evening hymn," some of the lines being: "O give me Samuel's ear," "O give me Samuel's heart," "O give me Samuel's mind." Originally for treble voices in unison with organ accompaniment, the tune began on the second beat of the measure and had as its title the full first line of the hymn.

SANCTUARY. See AGAPÉ.

SANCTUS. See NICAEA.

SANDON [10 4 10 4 10 10 (4: m - m m / f - - m / m r d r / m - -); Charles H. Purday, 1860]. Originally called LANDON; one wonders if some editors make their "L's" and "S's" (as I do) somewhat alike? The word SANDON, however, is an old English residence name and may have some significance.

SANDRINGHAM. See O PERFECT LOVE.

SANDYS [S. M. (4: s / s d t sl / t - -); from *Christmas Carols Ancient and Modern*, 1833]. For William Sandys, London solicitor and antiquarian, interested in music, who collected the carols which made up the compilation from which this was taken.

SARDIS [8 7 8 7 (4: d T d. r / m sf m r); arr. from Ludwig van Beethoven, date undetermined]. Carl F. Price has suggested there may be some connection between the naming of this tune and the city of Sardis, the capital of Lydia, in Asia Minor, although he does not state what the connection might be. The church at Sardis, mentioned in Revelation, was one of the seven churches to which the writer of the Apocalypse was directed to send a message.

Also called AUGUSTINE, DANE. There are corruptions of this tune called NORTHIAN and RAVENSWORTH.

SARDIUS. See AUTUMN.

SARUM [10 10 10 10, with Alleluias (4: s - m f / s - s - / l l l l / l - s -); Joseph Barnby, 1869]. Because it was used in *The Sarum Hymnal*, this tune was called No. 299, SARUM HYMNAL, but later editors shortened it to SARUM. The *Ordinal of Offices for the Use of Sarum* was for a considerable period the ritual of all South England. It became the most widely used of early English liturgies, and upon it the prayer books of Edward VI were largely based.

About two miles north of Salisbury, England, is forsaken but still well-known Old Sarum, an important mediaeval place, where the Sees of Wiltshire, Wilton, Sherborn, and Ramsbury were gathered in 1078, and whence the bishops moved to Salisbury about 1217 [1227?]. The site is a large hill now marked by a few trees and curious earthworks on the summit.

Also called ALL SAINTS, FOR THE SAINTS, MILITANT, PRO OMNIBUS SANCTUS, ST. PHILIP. With the exception of ST. PHILIP (which its composer called it), the reason for the selection of the other names is obvious: It was written for William W. How's "For all the saints, who from their labors rest."

SATURDAY NIGHT. See SABBATH.

SAUL [L. M. (4: d / S m r d / f m r); adapted from George F. Handel]. Why SAUL? The tune is not in Handel's oratorio of that name but in *Joshua* (1747). Perhaps some editor got the names of his oratorios confused.

Also called FERTILE PLAIN and MAMRE, because of a part of the text with which the tune is used in *Joshua*.

Shall I in Mamre's fertile plain
The remnant of my days remain . . . ?

Genesis 13:18: "Then Abram removed his tent, and came and dwelt in the plain of Mamre, which is in Hebron, and built there an altar unto the Lord."

SAVANNAH [7 7 7 7 (4: s sf m r / dr m r -); from John Wesley's *Foundery Collection*, 1742]. John Wesley gave this famous old tune this name when he used it in his *Foundery Tune Book*, it having been theretofore known as IRENE. When a party of Moravians en route to Savannah, Georgia, in 1742 stopped in London, they went to the gallery of St. Paul's Cathedral and sang this tune to "a hymn of intercession to God to the teeming population below them." The vessel upon which they sailed from London was the *Irene* ("Peace"), which name had been exchanged for an earlier one, the *Catherine Snow*. This circumstance caused Wesley to change the tune's name. Perhaps he thought it would be as simple to change the name of a hymn tune as that of a ship.

Also called EDYFIELD, HERRNHUT. HERRNHUT: because of its association with the Moravians.

SAVOY. See OLD 100TH.

SAVOY CHAPEL [7 6 7 6 D (4: s / s m m r / r - d); John B. Calkin, 1887]. Name taken from a Royal Chapel in London. This Chapel, created one of the Chapels Royal by George III, later was made a "Royal Peculiar"—i.e., supported entirely by the Crown. At the Savoy, in Cromwell's time, the Independents adopted a *Confession of Faith*, and the celebrated "Savoy Conference" for the revision of the *Book of Common Prayer* was held, the Nonconformists being represented by Baxter, Colomy, and others. "The Savoy," a former London palace, was built by Peter of Savoy, who, in 1246, was given a tract of land lying between the "Straunde" and the Thames by Henry III. In time it became the town seat of the dukes of Lancaster. Variously, it was twice attacked by mobs and by Watt Tyler's followers, who completely wrecked it; rebuilt as a hospital which was endowed by the will of Henry VII; suppressed by Edward VI, refounded by Mary, and dissolved by Elizabeth. The French Protestants occupied a chapel here from the time of Charles II until about 1737, and it was in this chapel that OLD 100TH was sung so much that the tune became known as SAVOY.

SAWLEY [C. M. (3: d T L / S - M / F T L / S - -) ; James Walch, 1857]. The name of a town in Lancashire, England, not far from the birthplace of the composer.

SAXBY [L. M. (3: m m m / r - d / d - T / d - -) ; Timothy R. Matthews, 1867]. Saxby is a small town in the Midlands of England.
Also called STORRS.

SAXONY. See CHRISTMAS.

SCARBOROUGH. See MILES' LANE.

SCHEIN. See EISENACH.

SCHUMANN [S. M. (4: S / d S L T / d - -) ; from Lowell Mason's *Cantica Laudis*, 1850]. Because Robert Schumann, German composer, is said to have written it. Madam Schumann (Clara Wieck, eminent pianist) wrote James Love that she doubted if it had been taken from any of her husband's work. This is the name used in the United States. When taken over into English hymnals, English compilers have made a practice of changing the names Mason gave to those tunes he composed or used. This one was given the name BUCER, doubtless after Martin Bucer (or Butzer), German theologian, who came to Cambridge University in 1549 on the invitation of Cranmer. He is known chiefly for his interest in the unification of various Protestant bodies. He was partly successful in his efforts on behalf of the Lutherans and Zwinglians.
Also called HEATH, HESPERUS.

SEBASTE [Irr. (free: m - - - f s m -) ; John Stainer, 1875]. *Sebaste:* feminine of *sebastos,* Greek equivalent of the Latin *augustus,* meaning "worthy to be reverenced or worshiped." The tune was written for the old "candle-lighting hymn," in translation, "Hail, gladdening Light," with the lines:

Worthiest art Thou at all times to be
　　sung
With undefiled tongue.

SEELENBRÄUTIGAM [5 5 8 8 5 5 (3: dd T d / r -) ; Adam Drese, 1697]. Because set to Count Zinzendorf's hymn beginning, "*Seelenbräutigam, O du Gottes Lamm,*" freely translated by John Wesley in *Psalms and Hymns* (1738) to read, "O Thou, to whose all-searching sight."
Also called ARNSTADT, DARMSTADT, HAARLAM, ROCHELLE, SPIRE, THURINGIA, ZINZENDORF. Of all the names given this tune, Lightwood says SPIRE is most inappropriate, as Drese had no connection with that place; but he does not say anything about the other cities.

SELMA [S. M. (4: d / m r d rm / s - -) ; Robert A. Smith, 1825]. A mythical name taken from James Macpherson's *Poems of Ossian* and given the tune by its composer. See reference under MORVEN.

SELVIN [S. M. (3: m / m r m / sf f) ; arr. by Lowell Mason, 1850]. Probably a corruption of "Selwyn." There was a George Augustus Selwyn (1809-78), Anglican bishop of New Zealand. He was a famous missionary who attained renown as a pilot of ocean-going vessels and who made a profound impression in the United States upon the occasions of his two visits to this country. There may be some connection, because the tune is used with Toplady's hymn beginning, "If on a quiet sea." But it is doubtful, as the tune is one of the many arrangements of German tunes made by Mason. It is not in the list of "associative names" given by Henry L. Mason.

SEMLEY. See MORNING HYMN.

SEPULCHRE. See HOLY SEPULCHRE.

SERAPH. See BETHLEHEM.

SERENITY [C. M. (3: m / m.m fm / mr r) ; William V. Wallace, 1856]. From the sentiment of the hymn with which it is used: in some hymnals beginning, "Immortal Love, forever full"; in others, "We may not climb the heavenly steeps"; and in still others, "O Lord and Master of us all," according to the particular cento selected from John Greenleaf Whittier's long poem "Our Master."

SESSIONS [L. M. (4: S - L S / d - - - / S - L S / d.r m -) ; Luther O. Emerson, 1847]. Named for the pastor of the church in Salem, Massachusetts, where the composer first taught music and where he led his first choir—at a salary of $100 per year.

SEYMOUR [7 7 7 7 (2: m r / f m / l sm / r -) ; Carl M. von Weber, arr. 1833]. Philo A. Otis, in *Hymns You Ought to Know*, relates that this tune was named for an uncle of Professor Thomas Day Seymour, who taught at Western Reserve College when Otis was there. Professor Seymour's uncle, who had a fine bass voice, sang with the choir of Center Church,

Hartford, Connecticut. The tune was arranged by Henry W. Greatorex, organist at this church at the time, and he named the tune SEYMOUR in honor of the uncle of Professor Seymour.

Also called CHATHAM, HOLSTEIN, SHORE, WEBER. SHORE: for an amateur composer of Manchester, England, who took a fancy to a section of the opening chorus to *Oberon*, one of Weber's operas, and "boiled it down" into a "7's meter hymn tune." It first appeared in *Sacred Music, . . . Wm. Shore. 1833*. WEBER: for the composer. Quite another tune, also taken from a work of Weber's, is known by the name WEBER, making for further difficulty in trying to identify hymn tunes by name alone.

SHADOWS. See ST. LEONARD by Hiles.

SHANGANA. See ST. PETERSBURG.

SHARON [C. M. (4: S / S ♯F S d / L d d) ; Thomas Wallhead, 1876]. Written for Thomas H. Gill's hymn beginning:

> The glory of the spring how sweet,
> The new-born life how glad;
> What joy the happy earth to greet
> In new, bright raiment clad,

the name may have some significance, for Sharon means a "fertile plain."

——— [L. M. (4: d / d S d f / m r d) ; Frederick A. G. Ouseley, 1875]. This is apparently an arbitrary selection. The tune was written for a Latin hymn, *Adesto, sancta Trinitas*—in translation, "Be near us, Holy Trinity"—a hymn for Trinity Sunday which dates back to the origin of that day.

——— [7 7 7 7 (4: m d s d / r f m -)]. Also called BOYCE (which see), HALTON HOLGATE.

SHELTERED DALE [8 6 8 6 8 6 (6: S / m - m m r m / f - r T -) ; German traditional melody, 1814]. This German folk song is known in England as "The Mill Wheel." Perhaps this name comes from its connection with some ballad.

SHEPHERD. See BRADBURY.

SHIRLEY. See KEBLE.

SHIRLEYN [C. M. (3: S / S - L / T - d / r d r / m -) ; Earl E. Harper, 1928]. From the given names of Shirley Ann Harper, daughter of the composer.

SHORE. See SEYMOUR.

SICILIAN HYMN. See below.

SICILIAN MARINERS [8 7 8 7 8 7 (4: s l sf mf / s l sf m) ; arr. from a Sicilian melody, 18th century (?)]. The tune is said to have been a favorite with the sailors of Sicily, but no evidence of its ever having been known or sung by them has been secured.

Also called SICILIAN MARINERS' HYMN, DISMISSAL, MARINERS, SICILIAN HYMN, SICILY. With the exception of DISMISSAL, these names are obvious choices. DISMISSAL: because commonly used with the benediction hymn beginning, "Lord, dismiss us with Thy blessing."

SICILIAN MARINERS' HYMN. See SICILIAN MARINERS.

SICILY. See SICILIAN MARINERS.

SIGISMUND. See STUTTGART.

SILVER STREET [S. M. (2: d ss / m s / d.) ; Isaac Smith, ca. 1770]. Also called FALCON, FALCON STREET, NEW-TON. Silver Street and Falcon Street are two short streets, each being one block long. In reality one is a continuation of the other. They are divided by Noble Street, all in London, E. C. An old account says:

On the right of Aldersgate, Falcon Street heads into Silver Street, which contains one of the pretty quiet spaces bequeathed by the great Fire to the city. A stone tells us "This was the Parish Church of St. Olave, Silver Street, destroyed in the dreadful fire in the year 1666."

And John Stow, in his *Survey of London* (1603), says: "Downe lower in Woodstreete is Siluer streete (I think of siluer smithes dwelling there) in which bee diuers fayre houses." NEWTON: because of its association at some time with one of John Newton's hymns.

SIMPLICITY. See GIBBONS.

SIMPSON. See SPOHR.

SINE NOMINE [10 10 10 10, with Alleluias (4: s m r / d - - S / L d r S / m - -) ; Ralph Vaughan Williams, 1906]. The composer apparently had no name for this tune, so he christened it "Without a Name" (Latin) .

SION [6 5 6 5 D, with Refrain (4: s s m r / d - S -) ; Henry Smart, 1872]. After the last line of the Refrain, "To our home on high," of Thomas J. Potter's hymn beginning, "Brightly gleams our banner." SION (Zion) , one of the hills in Jerusalem, is symbolically the heavenly home. See ZION.

SLANE [10 10 10 10 (3: d d rd / L S SL / d d r / m - -) ; Irish traditional melody]. This tune is also used with texts in 10 11 11 12 meter. It is the melody of the old ballad "With my love on the road." Slane is a hill some ten miles from Tora. It was at Slane that St. Patrick lighted the Paschal Fire. See ST. PATRICK.

SLINGSBY [8 7 8 7 (4: S S S dT / L L L r)]. See CARTER.

———— [8 6 8 6 8 6 (4: dm / s. s l t / d d m)]. See ST. BEDE.

SMART'S. See PILGRIMS.

SMITH COLLEGE [8 7 8 7 8 7 (4: m r d T / Ld Tr d S) ; an arr. "from Schumann," by Benjamin C. Blodgett, ca. 1910]. The composer established Smith College of Music soon after going to Smith as professor of music in 1878. He was its principal until 1903. The tune was appropriately named as a setting for John Burton's hymn which begins, "Saviour! while our hearts are young and tender."

SOHO [4 4 6 4 4 6 (6: S / S - L T - d / d T d r -) ; Joseph Barnby, 1881]. The composer indicated this meter marking because he wrote the tune for J. S. B. Monsell's hymn beginning:

> The springtide hour
> Brings leaf and flower,
> With songs of life and love;
> And many a lay
> Wears out the day
> In many a leafy grove.

It is, however, generally used as a C. M. This tune was written while Sir Joseph was organist and choirmaster at St. Anne's Church in Soho, London. The word "Soho" is said to derive from the shout of early-day hunters in the district calling off their harriers (beagle hounds), "Sohoe!"
Also called SPRINGTIDE HOUR.

SOHREN [6 5 6 5 D (4: L LT d r / m - m -) ; Winfred Douglas, after a phrase by Peter Sohren, 1668]. Canon Douglas named his tune after the man whose musical phrase suggested it. Sohren (or Sohr), who died around 1693, spent most of his life at Elbing, West Prussia, where he was cantor. He edited the 1668 edition of Johann Crüger's *Praxis Pietatis Melica* (first in 1644), and was the composer of more than two hundred tunes.

SOLOMON [C. M. (4: d / m f s s / l l s s / l s t d / r - -) ; arr. from George F. Handel, 1748]. The tune is an adaptation of the air "What tho' I trace each herb and flower" from Handel's oratorio *Solomon*.

SOLON. See AMAZING GRACE.

SOLOTHURN [L. M. (4: d / d r m d / s - r - / d - -) ; traditional Swiss melody]. From the Swiss canton and capital city by this name in northwest Switzerland. This canton is the most irregular, as to its boundaries, of any in Switzerland.

SOMERSET [C. M. (4: d / m s d t / l f m) ; William H. Hewlett, *ca.* 1915]. Old English, *sumor-saet:* "the seat," or dwelling of the Sumor family. The name of a county in England in which is located Bath, the birthplace of the composer.

SONG 13. See GIBBONS by Gibbons.

SONG 22. See HEZEKIAH.

SONG 34. See ANGELS.

SOUTHAM. See DUNFERMLINE.

SOUTHAMPTON. See MAGDALEN COLLEGE.

SOUTHWELL [C. M. (4: d / m m s d / d l s) ; Herbert S. Irons, 1861]. Following his St. Columba College appointment (see ST. COLUMBA), the composer was organist at Southwell Collegiate Church (now Cathedral), 1857-72, and assistant organist at Chester Cathedral, 1873-75.
——— [S. M. (4: L / d d T T / L - -) ; *Damon's Psalmes*, 1579]. This was one of the "Northern Tunes" in Ravenscroft's *Psalter* (1621), having this name in that book. Known also as LONDON, SOUTHWELL was chosen by John Playford in 1671. It was named "after Southwell, a cathedral city of Nottinghamshire." The foundation of its earliest church, attributed to Paulinus, dates from the seventh century. See SOUTHWELL by Irons.

SPA FIELDS CHAPEL. See CHESTERFIELD.

SPANISH AIR. See BALERMA.

SPENCER. See PENITENTIA.

SPIRE. See SEELENBRÄUTIGAM.

SPLENDOUR [L. M. (6: d / d - r m - f / m - r d -) ; Michael Praetorius, 1609]. Also called PUER NOBIS NASCITUR. These names are from the first lines of the Latin hymns with which this tune has been associated; the first:

> *Splendor paternae gloriae*
> *De luce lucem proferens,*
> *Lux lucis et fons luminis,*
> *Dies diem illuminans.*

And this is the second hymn:

> Puer nobis nascitur,
> Rector angelorum,
> In hoc mundo pascitur
> Dominus dominorum.

See PRAETORIUS.

SPOHR [C. M. (3: S / m - m / s - d / m - r / d -) ; from Louis Spohr, 1835]. The name of the composer. Also called CRUCIFIXION, JERUSALEM, SIMPSON, THE INNER LIFE. CRUCIFIXION: because the melody was taken from Spohr's oratorio entitled *Calvary* but frequently called *Crucifixion*. See GERALD.

—— [C. M. D. (6: s / s - f m - d / t - 1 1 -)]. See GERALD.

SPRINGTIDE HOUR. See SOHO.

STABAT MATER [8 8 7 (4: d r m r / m s f m) ; French Church melody, 1661]. "There stood the Mother," from the first words of the anonymous Latin hymn beginning:

> Stabat mater dolorosa
> Iuxta crucem lacrimosa,
> Dum pendebat filius;
> Cuius animam gementem,
> Contristatam et dolentem,
> Pertransivit gladius.

Because of its association with the scenes of the Crucifixion, its pathos, its simplicity, this hymn and tune continue in Protestant hymnology in spite of the reaction against Mariolatry.

Also called MILAN.

STAMFORD. See AMERICA.

STAND UP. See WEBB.

STAR OF BETHLEHEM. See CANDLER.

STEADFAST [6 7 6 7 6 6 6 6 (4: m / l #s 1 t / d - -) ; Old German melody]. From the sentiment of Edward Grubb's hymn beginning, "Our God, to whom we turn," the sixth line of the first stanza being, "The steadfast order sure."

STEINER [8 7 8 7 (4: d m rS S / d m rS S) ; Johann L. Steiner, 1735]. Named after the composer.

STELLA (ENGLISH) [8 8 8 8 8 (3: s / s m s / s - d / d t l / s -) ; Old English melody]. James T. Lightwood says Henri Hemy, editor of the Catholic Sunday-school book in which this tune first appeared, gave it this name because he first heard children singing the old play song from which it was adapted at Stella, an English village near Newcastle. The claim is also made that its name came from the first line of the hymn to which it was set in *Easy Hymn Tunes*—namely, "Hail, Queen of Heaven, the ocean star." *Stella Maris* ("star of the sea") is its real name. The word "English" is used to identify this tune as an English melody. For a full account of this interesting tune see *Our Hymnody*.

STELLA (PARKER) [8 3 3 6 (4: m m m.r / d TL S S) ; Horatio W. Parker, 1894]. STELLA: meaning "star," suggested by the line, "Hail to the star," in the third stanza of Paul Gerhardt's beautiful Nativity hymn beginning, "All my heart this night rejoices." PARKER is to identify the tune, to distinguish it from the English traditional melody of the same name (which see).

STEPHANOS [8 5 8 3 (4: m m m r / m s s f) ; Henry W. Baker, 1868]. For St. Stephen the Sabaite, author of the Greek hymn on which John M. Neale based his "Art thou weary, art thou languid." At the age of ten Stephen was placed in the monastery of Mar Saba by his uncle, John of Damascus, and remained there until his death fifty-nine years later (794). This remarkable monastery is described by James King in his *Anglican Hymnody* (1885) as standing

nobly on a lofty cliff overhanging the valley of the Kedron, which here forms a deep chasm. It was founded in the beginning of the sixth century, and this secluded convent has therefore stood in the middle of savage desolation for fourteen centuries. . . . The monastery is surrounded by massive walls, and further guarded by two strong towers near the entrance, which tend to give the edifice the appearance of a fortress in a commanding position. The huge building seems as if it were clinging to the face of a steep precipice, so that it is difficult to distinguish man's masonry from the natural rock. We were then conducted to a terrace, from the dizzy heights of which we looked down into the deep gorge of the Kedron, five hundred feet below. Every morning wolves and jackals assemble at the bottom of the rocks, and are fed by the monks, who cast down food to the ravenous animals. Viewed from this terrace, the scene around and below is one of stern desolation, and a sight so impressive as never to be forgotten. Mar Saba was much more endeared to us when we remembered that here Stephanos, eleven centuries ago, wrote the touching hymn:

Art thou weary, art thou languid,
  Art thou sore distressed?
"Come to me," said One, "and, coming,
  Be at rest."

STEPNEY. See OLD 113TH.

STILLE NACHT [Irr. (6: s.l s m - - / s.l s m - -); Franz Gruber, 1818]. The first words of the beautiful German Christmas song beginning, *"Stille nacht, heilige nacht"* ("Silent night, holy night").
Also called HOLY NIGHT.

STILLORGAN. See HURSLEY.

STOCKBRIDGE. See YORKSHIRE.

STOCKPORT. See YORKSHIRE.

STOCKTON [8 6 8 6, with Refrain (4: S / S. L S d / m.m r); John H. Stockton, 1875]. After the composer of the tune and also the author of the hymn beginning, "Come, every soul by sin oppressed," for which it was written and with which it is always used.
—— [C. M. (4: d / m f s d /

f m r); Thomas Wright.]. The composer was organist (1797-1818) at Stockton-on-Tees, England, and used the tune there and at Wakefield Parish Church, where he had a later appointment. The tune was used in manuscript form for more than fifty years before it was printed in *Hymns Ancient and Modern* (1861). The tune's original name, ELIZABETH, was changed to STOCKTON in 1820 by the composer.

STOERL. See STÖRL.

STORIES OF JESUS [8 4 8 4 5 4 5 4 (6: s m f s t l / s - - m - -); Frederic A. Challinor, *ca.* 1904]. From the first line of William H. Parker's children's hymn beginning, "Tell me the stories of Jesus."

STÖRL [8 7 8 7 8 7 (4: s / m s l s / f r m); Johann G. C. Störl, 1710]. After its composer, a German organist.

STORRS. See SAXBY.

STOW. See WALSALL.

STOWELL [6 6 4 6 6 6 4 (4: d - m s / d. d d -); Isaac H. Meredith, 1935]. For Hugh Stowell, author of the hymn for which it was written, beginning, "Lord of all power and might."
—— [6 5 6 5 D (4: d.d T L / S - M -); anon., date unknown]. For the same reason that I. H. Meredith gave his tune its name, but the hymn for which this was written begins, "Jesus is our Shepherd."

STRACATHRO [C. M. (3: d / m - r / d - r / m d t / l -); Charles Hutcheson, 1832]. When this tune was first published, a member of St. Georges Church, Glasgow, Scotland, Sir James Campbell, had just bought a piece of property, Stracathro, in which there was much local interest. The composer of the tune, also a member of that church, as a compliment to Sir James named his tune after the new home.

STUTTGARD. See STUTTGART.

STUTTGART [8 7 8 7 (4: S S d d / r r m d); from *Psalmodia Sacra*, 1715]. Originally set to *"Sollt es gleich besweilen scheinen"* by Christopher Titus. Contrary to the general German custom of identifying their chorales by the first line of their associated texts, this one has long been familiarly known as STUTTGART. This fact gives significance to the story which Lauxman relates: One C. A. Dann, chief pastor of St. Leonard's Church, Stuttgart, had given offense because he had spoken "somewhat freely" at the funeral services of one of the court players. As a consequence he was relegated in 1812 to a small village, Oischingen, in the Swabian Alps; in 1819 to the neighboring Mössingen. The king recalled him to Stuttgart in 1824 in response to the earnest request of his former parishioners. On the night of his recall four friends walked to Mössingen and "in the early morning conveyed the news to him by singing this hymn at the door of his room."

Also called SIGISMUND, STUTTGARD.

—— [7 6 7 6 D (4: m / l s f m / r - m)]. See PASSION CHORALE.

SUFFOLK. See TALLIS' CANON.

SUN OF MY SOUL. See MARYTON.

SUOMI [L. M. D. (4: S / d d T T / L dL S); Finnish Cavalry March, 17th century]. This is a Finnish word which seems to have been derived from *suo*, "marsh." The Finns call themselves *Suomi*, the name *Finn* having been applied to them by their Swedish neighbors. *Finn* possibly means "one who inhabits a fen, or marsh." Both words appear to have a common meaning.

SURSUM CORDA [10 10 10 10 (4: d / m s f m / r d r r / d - -); Alfred M. Smith, 1941]. Because Henry M. Butler's hymn to which it is set begins, "Lift up your hearts!" The versicle *Sursum Corda* is an invitation to the people to join in thanksgiving to God. It is based on Lamentations 3:41: "Let us lift up our heart with our hands unto God in the heavens."

—— [6 4 6 4 10 10 (4: d - d r / m f s -); George Lomas, 1876]. Written for Charles E. Mudie's hymn beginning, "I lift my heart to Thee, Saviour Divine." See above.

SUSSEX [8 7 8 7 (4: m m m. r / dr mr d L); English traditional melody]. Ralph Vaughan Williams heard this melody in Sussex, England, and made it into a hymn tune which he used with Thomas Campbell's text beginning:

Men of England, who inherit
  Rights that cost your sires their blood.

SWEET HOUR [L. M. D (3: d / m - f / s - s / 1 - t / d -); William B. Bradbury, *ca.* 1860]. From the first and last words of each stanza of Walter W. Walford's well-known "Sweet hour of prayer."

Also called CONSECRATION, CONSOLATION, WALFORD. WALFORD: from the author of the hymn.

SWEET STORY [Irr. (4: dr / m mm mr mf / l ss s); Greek melody, 1841]. Jemima T. Luke heard children singing this melody, liked it, and learned it was a Greek melody called "Salamis." When she failed to find words that would fit it, she wrote, "I think when I read that sweet story of old."

Variations called ATHENS, GREEK AIR, SALAMIS.

SWIFT GERMAN TUNE. See WINCHESTER NEW.

SYMPHONY. See AMAZING GRACE.

T

TALLE's. See HANOVER.

TALLIS'. See below.

TALLIS' CANON [L. M. (4: d] d T d d / r r m); Thomas Tallis, 1561]. Also called BERWICK, BETHEL,

BRENTWOOD, CANON, CANNON TUNE, CANON TUNE, EVENING HYMN, MAGDALEN, SUFFOLK, TALLIS', TALLIS' HYMN. Most of these names are derived from the fact that Thomas Tallis (Talys, or Tallys) wrote this tune in the form of a canon, a form which calls for the following of strict rules of music composition. The other titles given the tune, with the exception of EVENING HYMN and MAGDALEN, are merely place names probably having no special significance. EVENING HYMN is quite appropriate because of the canon's use with Bishop Ken's evening hymn, "All praise to Thee, my God, this night."

TALLIS' HYMN. See TALLIS' CANON.

TALLIS' ORDINAL [C. M. (4: d / m f s s / l l s s / d t l l / s - -); Thomas Tallis, 1567]. Because the composer wrote it for the *Veni Creator,* used in the Ordination Service of the Church of England and other communions. *The Ordinal* is an Anglican Church book containing forms for the making, ordaining, and consecration of bishops, priests, and deacons of that church; *The Ordinal* has been in use since the Reformation. It is a collection of offices—i.e., orders of forms of services prescribing the form and manner of conferring holy orders.

TALLY's. See HANOVER.

TANTUM ERGO [8 7 8 7 8 7 (4: d r m f / s f m r); from Samuel Webbe's *Antiphons,* 1792]. *Tantum ergo* are the first words of Part II, the last two stanzas, of the Latin hymn beginning, *"Pange lingua gloriosi."* It is a part of the Benediction of the Blessed Sacrament of the Roman Church.

Also called ALLELUIA DULCE CARMEN, BENEDICTION, CORINTH, DULCE CARMEN, GLORIA PATRI, LEBANON, ST. WERBERGH'S, SALZBURG, WALPOLE. ALLELUIA DULCE CARMEN and DULCE

CARMEN: because used with the eleventh-century Latin hymn beginning, *"Alleluia, dulce carmen."* In *Havergal's Psalmody* (1871) it is called SALZBURG because Havergal attributed it to John Michael Haydn, who lived in Salzburg for the last forty-four years of his life. In a footnote Havergal states the tune is "wrongly called Benediction or St. Werbergh." —— [8 7 8 7 8 7 (4: d d d d / r m f m)]. See ORIEL.

TAPPAN [C. M. (3: -S SS / m. r dL / S.); George Kingsley, 1839]. Named after William B. Tappan, author of the hymn beginning, "There is an hour of peaceful rest," for which it was written.

TE DEUM. See HURSLEY.

TEMPLE [8 4 8 4 8 8 8 4 (4: m m f m / m r r d); Edward J. Hopkins]. This first appeared in *The Temple Choral Service Book* (1867), edited by Hopkins, who was at the time organist at Temple Church, London. —— [6 6 8 4 (4: d / s. s l m / s - -); H. Walford Davies, 1906]. The composer was organist at Temple Church, London, from 1890 to 1919. He has written an oratorio called *The Temple.*

TEMPUS ADEST FLORIDUM [7 6 7 6 D (4: d d d r / d d S -); old carol, *ca.* fourteenth century]. From the spring carol-hymn beginning with the Latin words of this title, translated, "Spring has now unwrapped the flowers." John Mason Neale substituted his "Good King Wenceslas looked out" for the original text when he wanted to use this tune with other Christmas carols.

TENEBRAE [L. M. (4: -d / d m s. s / s s s); John B. Dykes, 1857]. Latin for "darkness." Because written as a setting for Bishop Heber's hymn beginning:

The Lord shall come; the earth shall quake;

The hills their deep-laid seats forsake;
And withering from the vault of night,
The stars withdraw their feeble light.

Tenebrae, an office in the Roman Church celebrated about four or five o'clock in the afternoon on Maundy Thursday, Good Friday, and other solemn days to commemorate the darkness that overspread the face of the earth at the time of the Crucifixion.

TERRA BEATA [S. M. D. (4: dr / m s m r / d - -) ; Franklin L. Sheppard, 1915]. The name, Latin for "blessed earth," was suggested by the first line of Maltbie D. Babcock's hymn beginning, "This is my Father's world," for which the tune was written. The editors of *The Hymnal,* Presbyterian (1933), changed the name to TERRA PATRIS ("Father's earth"), thus conforming more exactly with the line referred to above.

TERRA PATRIS. See TERRA BEATA.

THANKSGIVING [L. M. (4: d / m s d s / f s m) ; John B. Dykes, 1857]. To "The Lord of harvest let us sing" by Samuel Wesley, "the Younger." Named for the sentiment of the text.

—— [L. M. (3: s s s / d - f / m - r / s -) ; Francis R. Statham, *ca.* 1844]. To "O life that maketh all things new" by Samuel Longfellow. Named for the sentiment of the text.

—— [C. M. (4: s / f m l s / f sl s) ; Joseph Barnby, *ca.* 1872]. To "My Father, for another night of quiet sleep and rest" by H. W. Baker. Named for the sentiment of the text.

—— [7 7 7 7 D (4: d. t d s / l sf m -) ; William B. Gilbert, 1862]. To "Come, ye thankful people, come" by Henry Alford. Named for the sentiment of the text.

—— [8 7 8 7 D (4: m m m.f / s s s d)]. See ST. ASAPH by Bambridge.

THATCHER. See DAVID.

THE BELOVED OF ZION. See BELOVED.

THE CROSS. See ELLESDIE.

THE FIRST NOEL [Irr., with Refrain (3: mr / d. r mf / s - lt / d t l / s -) ; traditional melody]. The name comes from the first words of the carol to which the tune is always sung. The English *nowel, nowelle, nowell;* old French *nouel, noel;* modern French *noël;* Provence *nadal, nadau;* Spanish and Portuguese *natal;* Italian *natale,* are forms of a word shouted or sung, originally to commemorate the birth of Christ. Philip Hale has said that some writers, among them Nicod, "pretend" the French get the word from the last syllable of "Emmanuel" as it reverberated in the streets after being shouted by the people in their celebration of Christmas. *"Noël, or Nouël per apherresim cannunt Galli pro Emmanuel, id est nobiscum Deus."*

Also called NOËL, NOWELL.

THE GOD OF ABRAHAM. See LEONI.

THE GOLDEN CHAIN [8 7 8 7 8 8 7 (4: m / m. m m m / s. s s) ; Joseph Barnby, 1887]. Written for Thomas H. Gill's hymn beginning, "We come unto our fathers' God," which has these lines as part of the last stanza:

Ye saints to come, take up the strain,
  The same sweet theme endeavour;
Unbroken be the golden chain!
  Keep on the song for ever!

THE GOOD SHEPHERD. See NETTLETON.

THE HEART'S REFUGE. See IN SINE JESU.

THE INNER LIFE. See SPOHR.

THE MORNING WATCH [L. M. (4: S / S - L d / r - - S / S L d m / s - -) ; Carl F. Price, 1913]. The composer furnished the following information: The tune was first published by "The World's Morning Watch," a religious organization, in their magazine, *The Daily Bible,* to a hymn written by its ex-Secretary William Brattle Oliver, beginning, "Lord, in the morning let me hear."

THE PILGRIM SONG. See LEOMINSTER.

THE RESURRECTION. See EASTER HYMN.

THE STILT. See YORK.

THEODORE [L. M. (4: m / m. S LT dm / s - -) ; Peter C. Lutkin, 1905]. Named for Theodore Roosevelt. The composer has given the following information:

The Reverend Benjamin Copeland [author of the hymn "Our fathers' God, to Thee we raise," for which the tune was written] asked me why I named it Theodore, as he had lost a child by that name shortly before, and when I wrote him it was called Theodore because the tune was supposed to be rather a strenuous character, he was greatly pleased, because he had also named his son Theodore for the same reason, when Mr. Roosevelt had an official position in New York in the earlier part of his career.

THIS ENDRIS NYGHT [C. M. (6: d / m - f s - s / l t l s -) ; Old English carol]. From the words of the fifteenth-century carol:

> This endris nyght
> I saw a syght
>   A stare as bryght as day,
> And ever among
> A mayden sung
>   Lullay, by by, lullay.

The phrase means "the other night."

THOMPSON [11 7 11 7, with Refrain (6: m. r d d T d / r d L L S -) ; Will L. Thompson, late 19th century]. For the composer. This is the tune used with his gospel song, "Softly and tenderly Jesus is calling."

THURINGIA. See SEELENBRÄUTIGAM.

TIDINGS [11 10 11 10, with Refrain (4: d - m f / s - - s / s d m r / r - d -) ; James Walch, 1876]. The words of the refrain ("Publish glad tidings") of the missionary hymn beginning, "O Zion, haste," with which it is now used, account for the name. Also called ANGELIC VOICES, PROCLAMATION. The fact that the tune was written for "Hark, hark my soul,"

with its reference to the singing of angels, gives the source of ANGELIC VOICES; and the first words of the third stanza of "O Zion, haste" ("Proclaim to every people"), that of PROCLAMATION.

TIPLADY [C. M. (4: s / s. r r dr / m. r d) ; Robert G. McCutchan, 1931]. Named for Thomas Tiplady, superintendent of the Lambeth Mission, London, a friend of mine; written while the Reverend Tiplady was a guest in my home.

TON-Y-BOTEL [8 7 8 7 D (4: L LTd T L / T Tdr d.T L); Welsh hymn melody, 1890]. *Ton-y-botel*, meaning "tune in a bottle," comes from the doubtful story that the tune was found enclosed in a bottle on the Lleyn, Wales, coast where it had been cast up on the beach after a storm. The story, told by a young man who sang the tune at some local social affair, gave it this name, unusual for a hymn tune, which has had much to do with attracting attention to it. Also called ASSURANCE, EBENEZER.

TOPLADY [7 7 7 7 7 7 (3: S. L / S M d. L / S -) ; Thomas Hastings, 1830]. For Augustus M. Toplady, author of "Rock of Ages," for which the tune was written. Also called ROCK OF AGES.

TORBAY. See ADESTE FIDELES.

TOULON [10 10 10 10 (4: d - r m / f - m - / r d d T / d - - -) ; from the *Genevan Psalter*, 1551]. This is the four-line abridgment of OLD 124TH (which see). Doubtless named for the French city; a purely arbitrary selection. OLD 124TH is a five-line tune. With the omission of the third line of music it becomes TOULON. Also called NAVARRE.

TOURS [7 6 7 6 D (4: mf / s d t l / s - m) ; Berthold Tours, 1872]. Pronounced "toor," it is named for its composer, a musician born at Rotterdam (contrary to the assumption of some tune-book compiler who gave the name AMSTERDAM to the tune).

Also called BERTHOLD, the given name of the composer.

TREFAENAN [8 7 8 7 8 8 8 7 (4: s l s m / s l s m); Welsh traditional melody]. Pronounced as English. This may be a misspelling of Treffynnon (Holywell), which received its name from a spring of fabled miraculous origin just below the town; or of Treffynon, so called from the famous spring of St. Winefride (a somewhat dubious saint), alleged to have been a noble girl who had her head cut off by one Prince Caradog, whose advances she had spurned. Her severed head, according to the story, rolled down a hill, and this spring gushed forth at the exact spot where it stopped. See HOLYWELL.

TRENTHAM [S. M. (3: m m m / f - d / m - -); Robert Jackson, 1888]. The birthplace of the composer, this English village is in Staffordshire, England. Ethelred, King of Mercia, founded a nunnery here in 680 and appointed his sister, St. Werbergh, abbess. There are now no traces left of the nunnery.

TRINITY [6 6 4 6 6 6 4 (3: s m d / r d T / d - -); Felice de Giardini, 1769]. Also called BENTINCK, ENGLAND, FAIRFORD, FLORENCE, GIARDINI'S, HARMON, HYMN TO THE TRINITY, ITALIAN HYMN, MOSCOW. Some of these names may be reasonably accounted for: The tune was composed as a setting for the anonymous hymn beginning, "Come, Thou almighty King," a hymn to the Trinity; Giardini was long a popular violinist in London operatic circles; he was born in Italy; he spent some time in Moscow as an operatic conductor and died there. The fancy of compilers of various tune books doubtless accounts for the other names.

TRISAGION [10 10 10 10 (3: s s l / s m r / d r r / m - -); Henry Smart,

1868]. The word means "thrice holy." "Raise the 'Thrice holy, Lord!' ever and aye!" is the last line of the first stanza of the hymn beginning, "Stars of the morning, so gloriously bright," to which the tune was first set. In John M. Neale's original rendering this line reads, "Raise the Trisagion ever and aye." There seems to be no agreement among scholars as to who was the author of the hymn. The *Trisagion* is a Greek versicle used in the Eastern and Gallican liturgies:

Holy God, holy mighty, holy immortal
Have mercy upon us.

——— [7 7 7 7 7 7 (4: m.f s s / l l s -); John B. Dykes, before 1875; found among his unprinted manuscript hymns]. This is a setting made for Bishop Wordsworth's hymn beginning, "Holy, holy, holy Lord." See above.

TRIUMPH. See ARLINGTON.

TRUMPET. See LENOX.

TRURO [L. M. (4: d - m.f / s - - s / l - t - / d - -); from Thomas Williams' *Psalmodia Evangelica*, 1787]. A place name, that of an ancient town in the extreme southwestern part of Cornwall, England; its mining capital as well as the Cathedral city of Cornwall.

——— [7 7 7 7 7 7 (3: s - ls / s - md / r. m f / f m -); William E. Miller, 1805]. See above.

TRUST [8 7 8 7 (4: s s l s / d mr d t; arr. from Felix Mendelssohn-Bartholdy, 1840]. To a variety of texts, a common one (based on Psalm 91) being:

Call Jehovah thy Salvation,
    Rest beneath the Almighty's shade;
In His secret habitation
    Dwell, and never be dismayed.
            —James Montgomery.

——— [8 8 8 6 (3: m f m / m r d / r - f / m - -); George W. Torrance,

1864]. To "Lord, let us now depart in peace" (anon.) .

—— [8 5 8 3 (6: s - f m - r / d - S T - d) ; Frances R. Havergal, 1876]. To "I am trusting Thee, Lord Jesus" by Miss Havergal. A common hymn-tune name. These and many others take the name from the sentiment of the various hymns for which they were written.

TWILIGHT [6 5 6 5 (4: S S S S / S - S - / L L ♯S LT / L - - -)]. See MERRIAL.

—— [11 11 11 5 (4: s - f d / m - r -)]. See NIGHTFALL.

TYNEMOUTH. See ST. CATHERINE by HEMY.

TYSK [6 6 8 6 6 8 3 3 6 6 (4: d S L S / F - M -) ; German melody, 1718]. After Tysk Church (German) , Stockholm, Sweden, where the tune was a favorite.

U

ULTIMA [8 6 (4: m - d r / m - d - / L - T - / d - -) ; James Moffatt, 1927]. Latin for "last." Because written for Christina G. Rossetti's hymn beginning:

Sooner or later; yet at last
The Jordan must be passed.

UNION SQUARE. See BLAIRGOWRIE by Dykes.

UNITAS FRATRUM [8 8 8 8 7 (free: d - t / l s s d / r - d -) ; Bohemian Brethren melody]. Latin for "Unity of Brethren."

The Unitas Fratrum was the first among Protestant Churches to publish a Hymn-book. It appeared in the Bohemian language, at Jungbunzlau, Bohemia, in the year 1501, and contained versions of old Latin hymns, together with many original compositions, mostly by John Hus and Bishop Luke of Prague. . . . The tunes, printed in full at the head of each hymn, were partly Gregorian, partly borrowed from Germany, and partly original. Many of the original ones consisted of popu-lar melodies adapted to the uses of sanctuary. The hymns of the Brethren were a power in the Church and the land. They gave life to public worship; they were familiarly sung in the homes of nobles and peasants; they set forth the true Gospel in strains that captivated thousands of hearts in the Roman Catholic Church and brought them to a knowledge of free grace in Christ Jesus.—From the Preface to The Liturgy and the Offices of Worship and Hymns of the American Province of the Unitas Fratrum, or The Moravian Church, 1912. Used by permission of The Board of Elders of the Northern Diocese of the Church of the United Brethren in the United States of America.

UNIVERSAL PRAISE [10 4 6 6 6 6 10 4 (4: d / d. r m f / s - - s / l t d m / r -) ; Walter G. Whinfield, 1906]. Because set to George Herbert's "Let all the world in every corner sing."

UNIVERSITY COLLEGE [7 7 7 7 (4: m d l s / f m r -) ; Henry J. Gauntlett, 1852]. University College is near Bedford Square, London, the city in which the composer spent most of his active life.

UNSER HERSCHER. See NEANDER.

URBS BEATA [8 7 8 7 8 7 (free: l l l sf s l l r) ; Sarum plain song]. Latin for "blessed city." Written for the translation of the old Latin hymn "Urbs beata Ierusalem," which begins, 'Blessed city, Heavenly Salem."

—— [7 6 7 6 D, with Refrain (4: S / d d r m / d - S) ; George F. LeJeune, 1887]. Used as a setting for "Jerusalem the golden" by Bernard of Cluny (twelfth century) . See above.

URBS CAELESTIS [8 7 8 7 8 7 (4: m - r d / r m f m / r d T d / r - d -) ; Henry E. Hodson, 1880]. Latin for "celestial city." Written for "Urbs beata Ierusalem." See URBS BEATA, Sarum plain song. The tune was written one evening at Ilam, by the River Dove (England) , and was used twice in *The Golden Legend,* a cantata by the composer.

UXBRIDGE [L. M. (4: d - / d r m r / d - T - / d -); Lowell Mason, 1830]. A town and village in south-central Massachusetts near the Rhode Island border named, in turn, from an ancient town in England said to date from the time of Alfred the Great. It was near Uxbridge, Massachusetts, in early colonial days, according to Osgood, that

Major Talcott, with his famous flying army, attacked the Queen of Narragansett who had made a stand here in a fortified postion. After a battle of three hours, the queen and 34 of her warriors were killed, and 90 warriors surrendered, only to be butchered in cold blood.

———— [C. M. (3: L / L - T / d - r / m r d / T)]. See BURFORD.

V

VALETE [8 8 8 8 8 8 (4: m / m s d m / L T d); Arthur S. Sullivan, 1874]. Latin for "farewell" (to more than one person). Originally set to "Sweet Saviour, bless us as we go" by Frederick W. Faber.

VALIANCE [Irr., with Refrain (4: s / m s d tl / s f m); arr. from Charles Darnton, 1895]. Used as a setting for the march song beginning, "March on, march on, O ye soldiers true," by Ella S. Armitage.

VALIANT HEARTS [10 10 10 10 (3: d f r / s - - / m f m / r - r / d - -); Gustav Holst, 1925]. Composed for J. S. Arkwright's hymn beginning, "O valiant hearts, who to your glory came," which was written in 1919 at the close of World War I.

VALOUR [6 5 6 5 D, with Refrain (4: d S d r / d - T -); Arthur H. Mann, 1889]. Sometimes spelled "valor," this name comes from the sentiment of the hymn by Godfrey Thring be-

ginning, "From the eastern mountains."

VARINA [C. M. D. (3: s / s.s s d / m. m m); George F. Root, 1856]. A woman's name. Interesting, but having no connection with the name of this hymn tune, is the anecdote told of Jonathan Swift, who, in his early life, professed to have an attachment for one Miss Jane Waryng and, having a habit of Latinizing the names of his lady-loves, called her "Varina." In 1696 he proposed marriage to her but was refused because of her ill health and his poverty. In 1700, however, when he was given the living of Larcacor, she changed her mind and wished the marriage to take place. He broke off the match by saying that if she would consent to be educated so that she might entertain him, accept his likes and dislikes, and sooth him when he was in a bad humor, he would overlook deficiencies in looks and income. The second wife of Jefferson Davis was Varina Howell, granddaughter of onetime Governor Richard Howell of New Jersey. It is highly improbable that Root, composer of this tune and an ardent Unionist, would name any tune after the wife of the President of the Confederate States of America.

VATER UNSER. See OLD 112TH.

VENI CREATOR [L. M., with Refrain (free: S L SF S LS d rd d); ancient plain song]. Latin for "Come, Creator" the first words of its text. The tune may well deserve the claim that it is the oldest of those we sing today.

VENI IMMANUEL [8 8 8 8 8 8 (4: L / d m m m / r f m r / d - -); ancient plain song]. From the first words of the Latin text with which it has long been associated:

Veni, veni, Emmanuel
captivum solve Israel,
qui gemit in exilio,
privatus Dei Filio,

Gaude, gaude; Emmanuel nascetur pro te, Israel.

Immanuel, or *Emmanuel:* "God [is] with us," a symbolic name given to the child who was announced to Ahaz and the people of Judah as the sign that God would give them deliverance from their enemies. Matthew similarly applies it to Jesus the Messiah: "They shall call his name Emmanuel, which being interpreted is, God with us."

Also called EPHRATA, which apparently has no significance as a name for this tune.

VENN. See HESPERUS.

VERITAS. See BURLEIGH.

VESPER HYMN [8 7 8 7 8 6 8 7 (4: m s f s / m s r s); Dimitri S. Bortniansky, date unknown]. This "evening hymn" is but one of many tunes with a similar name. Frequently the name of the composer is included in parentheses as a means of identification.

Also called ARCHANGEL.

——— [7 7 7 7 6 4 (4: d / r m f s / m - m); Lily Rendle, 1930]. See above.

VESPERI LUX [7 7 7 5 (4: S L L S / d r m -); John B. Dykes, 1873]. *Vesperi lux:* "light at evening." Set to Richard H. Robinson's hymn beginning, "Holy Father, cheer our way," each stanza of which closes with "Light at evening time."

VETTER [L. M. (4: d / m s s m / d r m); adapted from Daniel Vetter, 1713]. Named for the composer who was a predecessor of Johann Sebastian Bach at the Church of St. Nicholas, Leipsig.

Also called VETTER'S.

VEXILLA REGIS [L. M. (free: d rf f mrd r rmr d T L); Sarum plain song]. Latin for "king's banners." Set to Fortunatus' hymn beginning, "The royal banners forward go,"

written in 569. The tune is probably as old as the text.

VEXILLUM [6 5 6 5 D, with Refrain (4: m f s s / d - s -); Henry Smart, 1868]. Literally, Latin for a military flag or banner; specifically, a red flag placed on a general's tent as a signal for marching or for battle. The tune was written as a setting for Thomas J. Potter's hymn beginning, "Brightly gleams our banner."

VICTORY [8 8 8 4, with Alleluias (3: s s s / l - s / s f m / s - -)]. Also called CONQUEROR, PALESTRINA (which see).

VIENNA [7 7 7 7 (4: m r d m / s f m -); Justin H. Knecht, 1797]. Apparently an arbitrary name.

Also called OHNE RAST, RAVENNA, ST. BONIFACE.

——— [7 7 7 7 (2: m s / r. m / f r / m -)]. See PLEYEL'S HYMN.

——— [8 7 8 7 D (4: d. r m r / f m rT d)]. See AUSTRIAN HYMN.

VIGILATE [7 7 7 3 (4: m m f m / l.l s -); William H. Monk, 1868]. Latin for "Watch ye!" From the sentiment of the hymn beginning, "Christian, seek not yet repose," each stanza closing with "Watch and pray."

VIGILES ET SANCTI. See LASST UNS ERFREUEN.

VIGILI. See LASST UNS ERFREUEN.

VIGILS. See BELMONT.

VINCENT [8 4 8 4 D (4: m mm f m / m. r d -); Horatio R. Palmer, 1893]. After Bishop Vincent, the founder of the Chautauqua movement. The composer had charge of the music program at Lake Chautauqua for a time while Bishop Vincent was active there.

VIOLET. See ELLESDIE.

VOICE OF MY BELOVED. See BELOVED.

VOM HIMMEL HOCH. See ERFURT by Luther.

VONDEVENTER. See ELLESDIE.

VOX ANGELICA. See PILGRIMS.

VOX DILECTI [C. M. D. (4: M /

M L L T / d. d T); John B. Dykes, 1868]. *Vox dilecti:* Latin for "voice of the beloved." This was written for Horatius Bonar's hymn beginning, "I heard the voice of Jesus say," to which he gave the title "The Voice from Galilee."

VULPIUS [7 6 7 6 (4: d / m r m f / s - m); Melchior Vulpius, 1609]. From the name of the composer.

Also called BREMEN, CANA, CHRIST IS MY LIFE, CHRISTUS DER IST MEIN, MEIN LEBEN. The last three names come from the German hymn beginning *"Christus, der ist mein Leben"* ("Christ is my life"), for which it was written. The reasons for BREMEN and CANA are not apparent. See BREMEN by Neumark.

W

WAINWRIGHT [L. M. (4: d - d m / r - l - / s - f - / f - m -)]. See LIVERPOOL by Richard Wainwright.

———— [10 10 10 10 10 10 (4: d - d r / m - - f / s m f s / l - - -)]. See YORKSHIRE.

WAITS' CAROL [8 8 8 8, with Alleluias (4: s / dr mf s s / l l s); Grace Stutsman, 1935]. Name given by the author of the carol-like text beginning, "In Bethlehem, 'neath star-lit skies" and its tune. *Waits,* the etymology of which is not clear, are itinerant musicians who parade the streets at night about Christmas time, especially in English towns. John Hawkins, English musical historian, writing *circa* 1776, said:

It was the ancient custom for the waits to parade the streets nightly during the winter. Now they go about a few nights before Christmas to furnish a pretense for asking money at the return of that festival.

In the fourteenth and fifteenth centuries a wait (from Anglo-Saxon *wacan,* to "wake" or "watch"?) was a musical watchman who should nightely from Mychelmas to Shreve Thorsdaye pipe the watche within this court fowere tymes; in the somere nights iij tymes, and to make the Bon Gayte at every chambere, doare, and offyce, as well for feare of pyckers and pillers.

At least, this is part of a long report concerning "waytes" in a book of household expenses of Henry IV. From the early sixteenth century all the principal cities in England had their waits, who were provided with uniforms. Those of the London waits consisted of blue gowns with red sleeves and caps with silver chains (collars) worn about their necks. They were a distinct class, quite apart from both the watch and the minstrel. Since early in the nineteenth century, when the places of these guardians of the peace were taken by police, the custom of singing as "waits" has been kept up by individuals. *Waits,* or *wayghtes,* also means an oboe, a musical instrument. Butler, in *Principles of Music,* says: "It is remarkable of this noun that it has no singular number; for we never say a Wait, but the Waits. In the *Etymologicum* of Junius the word is used to signify the players on these instruments." That perhaps, explains the source of the term.

WALFORD. See SWEET HOUR.

WALLACE [Irr. (4: s / m ss l *d* / *r d* -); Clarence G. Hamilton, 1914]. Mrs. Ada A. Hamilton, widow of the composer of this setting for Katharine Lee Bates's popular Epiphany hymn, has written me:

I am very happy to give you the information about Miss Bates' carol, "The Kings of the East are riding."

When my son, Wallace, was ten years old he started a little weekly publication, which he called "The Early News." It was done with mimeograph—entirely his own work. It contained bits of news items about college and village folk, and he had about two hundred subscribers.

Miss Bates frequently contributed original poetry and prose for his paper, and it was at Christmas time, 1905, that she wrote "The Kings of the East are riding," and *she* called it "Wallace." My husband wrote the musical setting and it became very popular. I suppose few people know its origin.

——— [7 7 7 6 D (6: S - S S - M / S - L d - -)]. See CALEDONIA.

WALPOLE. See TANTUM ERGO.

WALSALL [C. M. (4: L / d TL M m / rd T L); from William Anchors' *Choice Collection of Psalm Tunes, ca.* 1721]. This English melody has been attributed to Henry Purcell but without much authority. It has long been very popular among Scottish Presbyterians. Walsall is a town north of Birmingham, England. Also called ST. FAITH, STOW.

WALTHAM [L. M. (4: d / m. ♯r m m / f. m f); John B. Calkin, 1872]. Waltham, usually with a suffix, is a common town name in England. Waltham Abbey, near Epping Forest, was founded by the Saxon king Harold (died 1066) and became his burial place. Waltham Cross, nearby, is one of the crosses erected by Edward I on various spots where the body of his queen, Eleanor, rested on its journey from Nottinghamshire to London.

Also called CALKIN, CAMDEN, DOANE, ENSIGN. CALKIN: the name of the composer. CAMDEN: from Camden Road Chapel, where Calkin was organist for five years. DOANE: for George Doane, the author of the hymn with which it is widely used, "Fling out the banner." ENSIGN: from the first line of Doane's hymn.

——— [6 6 6 6 6 6 (4: m / m rm f s / m - -); William H. Monk]. See above.

——— [8 7 8 7 7 7 (4: d r mf s /

d T L S); Heinrich Albert]. See WALTHAM by Calkin.

Also called GODESBERG. No reason is known for the use of either name.

WALTON [C. M. (3: L / L - T / d - r / m r d / T)]. See BURFORD.

——— [L. M. (3: S d T / d - r / S L T / d - -)]. See GERMANY.

WALWORTH. See YORKSHIRE.

WAREHAM [L. M. (3: d / d T L / S - d / r d T / d -); William Knapp, 1738]. Also called ALL SAINTS, BLANFORD TUNE. So named by the composer after his birthplace, a town not far from Poole, Dorsetshire, England. Wareham, an ancient walled town whose rectangular walls were of earthwork instead of masonry, was much troubled by the Danes and was destroyed by Canute. It was doubtless held as a settlement and stronghold before the Romans, probably by the Belgic Morini, whose name survived in the Roman *Morino,* with which Wareham is identified. Now shrunk within its walls it has a population of about two thousand. Also called ALL SAINTS, BLANFORD TUNE.

WARING. See ST. BEDE.

WARREN. See ST. CHRYSOSTOM.

WATCHMAN [7 7 7 7 D (6: d - r / m - r m - f / s - -); Lowell Mason, 1830]. From the first word of John Bowring's hymn beginning, "Watchman, tell us of the night." Mason called it "Missionary" or "Christian Hymn."

WATERMOUTH. See ANGEL'S STORY.

WATTS. See MORNING HYMN.

WEBB [7 6 7 6 D (4: S / d. d m d / d - L); George J. Webb, 1837]. From the name of the composer.

Also called FRANCONIA, GOODWIN, MILLENIAL DAWN, MORNING LIGHT, NEW YORK, ROSY LIGHT, STAND UP. MILLENIAL DAWN, MORNING LIGHT, and ROSY LIGHT: because of its use with Samuel F. Smith's hymn beginning, "The morning light is breaking"; STAND UP from the first words of the George Duffield, Jr., hymn "Stand up, stand up for Jesus"; sources of the other names are not apparent.

WEBER [6 6 6 6 D (4: s - m dm / r. fm r -)]. See JEWETT.

———— [7 7 7 7 (2: m r / f m / l sm / r -)]. See SEYMOUR.

WEIMAR [L. M. (4: s / s d t l / s f m); Carl P. E. Bach, 1787]. From the composer's birthplace.

———— [7 6 7 6 D (free: m - r d - r / m f s -); Melchior Vulpius, 1609]. The composer was cantor at Weimar and was buried there.

WEINACHT [8 6 8 6 D, with Refrain (6: m / m - ♯r m - s / s - r r -); Karl P. Harrington, 1903]. German for "Christmas Eve," from the sentiment of the hymn about angels singing, "Glory to God in the highest."

WELCOME [Irr. (4: m - d r / m dL d); Rowland Leach, 1933]. The first word of Canon Percy Dearmer's hymn beginning, "Welcome, day of the Lord," for which it was written.

WELLESLEY [8 7 8 7 (4: S dr d T / S rm r d); Lizzie S. Tourjée, 1877]. The composer was a freshman student at Wellesley College, Massachusetts, when the tune, which she had composed while in high school, was selected for use in the college songbook. This name was given it by the book's compiler, Hamilton C. MacDougal.

WELLS. See ST. PETERSBURG.

WELLSPRING. See ST. PETERSBURG.

WELWYN [11 10 11 10 (4: m - r d / T - - d / r f m r / d - T -); Alfred Scott Gatty, 1902]. A place name. Welwyn is a comparatively new town not far from London; a model suburb.

WEM IN LEIDENSTAGEN. See CASWALL.

WEMAN [8 8 7 8 8 7 (4: m m s d / r r m m); Henry Weman, 1937]. For the composer.

WENTWORTH [8 4 8 ↓ 8 4 (4: s /

d d t l / s m d); Frederick C. Maker, 1876]. The composer of the tune sometimes used residence names for his tunes; this is one, another being LYNDHURST. More often, however, he chose names which were suggested by the sentiments of the various hymns for which they were written, such as REQUIEM for "So rest, my soul," and BENEDICTUS for "Blessed be God." Also see INVITATION for "Come to the Saviour now," and ST. CHRISTOPHER for "Beneath the cross of Jesus."

———[8 7 8 7 D (3: d m f / s - d / ♭t - l / s -); George F. Handel]. Also called BIRR, BRUNSWICK, MARLBOROUGH. The names this tune bears have been arbitrarily given it. It is an old tune from the solo "Sin not, O King, against the youth," in the oratorio Saul. It has been in use since 1760, when it first appeared in the Christian's Magazine.

WESLEY [6 6 6 6 8 8 (6: d / m r d s f m / r - - - -); anon., date unknown]. Because used with one of Charles Wesley's hymns, beginning, "Author of life divine."

———— [11 10 11 10 (3: d - TL / S S S / L d L / L S); Lowell Mason, 1833]. According to Henry L. Mason this tune was written in 1830 and appeared in Cantica Laudis in 1850, where it had the title "Hail to the Brightness," the opening words of Thomas Hasting's well-known hymn. Also called SALVATION.

WESLEY CHAPEL. See YOAKLEY.

WESTBOROUGH. See AUSTRIAN HYMN.

WESTCOTT [L. M. (3: d T L / T - S / L S M / F - -); Joseph Barnby, 1872]. An arbitrary name given by someone other than the composer. Also called PANIS COELI, Latin for "Bread of heaven," because used with Ray Palmer's translation of the cento beginning, "Jesu dulcedo cordium," taken from "Jesu dulcis memoria," attributed to Bernard of Clairvaux.

The translation begins, "Jesus, Thou Joy of loving hearts" and has as the first two lines of the third stanza:

We taste Thee, O thou Living Bread,
And long to feast upon Thee still.

WESTMINSTER [C. M. (4: m / s s d *d* / t l s); James Turle, 1836]. The composer was officially connected with Westminster Abbey for sixty-three years, from 1831 to 1875 acting as organist and master of the choristers. Also called BIRMINGHAM.

WESTMINSTER NEW [C. M. (3: d / m - m / m r m / f s l / l s); James Nares]. This was said to be a "new tune" when it first appeared in Riley's *Parochial Psalmody* (1762) and was called WESTMINSTER. The suffix was added to distinguish it from the older WESTMINSTER.

WHAT A FRIEND. See CONVERSE.

WHITBURN. See HESPERUS.

WHITEFIELD'S TUNE. See AMERICA.

WHITSUN HYMN. See ANGELUS.

WHITTIER. See REST (ELTON) by Maker.

WIGAN [6 6 6 4 8 8 4 (4: L / d T r d / f - -); Samuel S. Wesley, 1872]. A place name. Wigan is an insignificant manufacturing town not far from Manchester, England.

WIGTOWN [C. M. (4: m / m m f.m / rd r d); from the *Scottish Psalter*, 1635]. This, one of the "common" tunes from the *Scottish Psalter*, was named for Wigtown, a southwestern Scottish town on Wigtown Bay. At the entrance to the town is a monument, Martyrs' Memorial, commemorating two Covenanter women, Margaret MacLachlen, aged 63, and Margaret Wilson, a girl of 19, who in 1685 were tied to stakes on the beach and drowned by the rising tide.

WILBY. See ST. MAGNUS.

WILD BELLS [L. M. D. (4: d / dd tl sf mr / dd tl sf); Henry Lahee, *ca.* 1875]. From words from the first line of Tennyson's "Ring out, wild bells, to the wild, wild sky," for which it was written. The chimes of St. Luke's Church, Chelsea, England, gave the composer the inspiration for his prize part song, "The Bells," of which this tune is an arrangement.

WILLIAMS. See ST. THOMAS.

WILLIS' CAROL. See CAROL.

WILTON [L. M. (4: s / m T d l / s f m); John F. Lampe, 1746]. Wilton: a small town near Salisbury, England.

Also called DEVONSHIRE, GUILFORD, INVITATION, KENT, ROCHESTER, ST. LUKE, ST. PAUL'S. First called INVITATION by the composer because used as a setting for the invitation hymn beginning, "Sinners, obey the gospel word," by Charles Wesley, close friend of the composer. The other names are but arbitrary ones given by various tune-book compilers.

—— [11 6 11 6 (4: s - m r / d - r - / m s f l / l - s); Arthur H. Mann, 1898]. Apparently an arbitrary name.

—— [L. M. (4: d / d - - d / r - - m / f - m r / d - -); Samuel Stanley, 1796]. Another arbitrary name.

WILTSHIRE [C. M. (3: S / S - d / d T d / f m r / r m); Sir George Smart, 1795]. A county in England. Also called ST. GEORGE.

WINCHESTER NEW [L. M. (4: S / d S L L / S F M); from *Musikalisches Handbuch*, Hamburg, 1690]. In *The Choir* the tune is called BARRE, and the compiler, Lowell Mason, says, "There can be no doubt that this tune and Winchester [Old] were originally the same. It is found nearly in its present form in many German books." Mason seems to have been in error, for the two tunes have little, if anything, in common. This famous old tune was brought to England by John Wesley, who published it in his *Foundery Tune-Book* (1742) under the name SWIFT GERMAN TUNE. Later it was called FRANKFORT, then WINCHESTER TUNE. Havergal used it, calling it CRASSELIUS. Crasselius was a Lutheran presbyter at Düsseldorf. He never composed any hymn tunes, but he did write the hymn *"Dir, dir, Jehovah, will ich singen,"* to which the original of WINCHESTER NEW was set.

WINCHESTER OLD [C. M. (4: d / m. m r d / f f m) ; from Este's *Psalter*]. Frances R. Havergal, who edited the 1871 edition of her father's *Havergal's Psalmody*, says in a footnote to this tune, there called WINCHESTER: "Wrongly called Winchester Old." This is true, for the tune, one of the earliest ever to be given a specific English designation, was christened WINCHESTER as long ago as 1621 by Thomas Ravencroft in his *Whole Booke of Psalmes . . . composed into 4 parts by sundry Authors.* The tune, however, had appeared twenty-nine years earlier in Thomas Este's *The Whole Booke of Psalmes, with their wonted Tunes,* but without a name, not being one of the three honored with names in Este's book. The "Old" was added when the later WINCHESTER NEW, dating from 1690, appeared. The town Winchester, in Hampshire, England, is of great antiquity. The seat of a bishop, converted to Christianity in 635, it was the governmental capital of Alfred the Great, Canute the Dane, and of William the Conqueror. Before the Roman invasions of England it was known as *Caer Gwent* ("White City"), which the Romans Latinized into *Venta Belgarum,* the *Belgae* being the British tribe having its settlement there. Later the Saxons called it *Wintecaester (caester, castrum,* any fortified place; a castle, fort, or fortress; therefore the castle of *Winton,* or *Wynton).* Winchester is now noted for

its Cathedral, its College of St. Mary Winton (Winchester School for Boys) , and its Hospital of St. Cross. But there is little now to suggest its venerable age.

WINDLE. See DUKE STREET.

WINDSOR [C. M. (4: L / L T d T / L L ♯S) ; from Este's *Psalter,* 1592]. This tune was first called SUFFOLK TUNE by Thomas Este; Ravenscroft changed it to WINDSOR OR ETON. In Hart's *Scottish Psalmody* (1615) it is found as DUNDIE TUNE. The Scottish people have chosen to follow Hart in calling it DUNDEE, although elsewhere it is known as WINSOR. Windsor (*Winsor*), a name of Teutonic origin, probably meaning "at the bend of the river," is an old English town, well known as the ancestral residence of the English sovereigns. While William the Conqueror built a castle at Windsor, the oldest part of the present Windsor Castle, which includes the additions as well as the alterations of many monarchs, dates from the reign of Edward III.

Also called BOLTON, COLESHILL, OLD 116TH PSALM. The name BOLTON was given the tune in an early collection of tunes for Lancashire people "so as to give a local touch," says Lightwood.

WINKWORTH [8 8 8 8 8 8 (4: M / M. ♯F ♯S L / L ♯S L) ; Joseph Barnby, 1869]. While Barnby gave this tune no name, it has been called WINKWORTH because Catherine Winkworth's translation of *"O Welt, sich hier dein Leben"* ("O world! behold upon the tree") by Paul Gerhardt was the text for which it was composed.

WIR PFLÜGEN [7 6 7 6 D, with Refrain (4: S / d d S S / m - d) ; Johann A. P. Schulz, 1800]. Also called CLAUDIUS, DRESDEN. Written for Matthias Claudius' hymn beginning, *"Wir pflügen und wir streuen Den Samen auf das Land"*—in translation:

We plow the fields and scatter
The good seed on the land,

giving WIR PFLÜGEN from the text and CLAUDIUS from the author of the hymn. There is no good reason for the name DRESDEN, as neither author nor composer ever had any connection with that place.

WITTENBERG. See NUN DANKET.

WOLWORTH. See YORKSHIRE.

WOODSTOCK [C. M. (3: d / mm m s / rr r) ; Deodatus Dutton, Jr., *ca.* 1830]. Frank J. Metcalf says this tune was probably named for Woodstock, Connecticut. Many other towns in that state have been honored by having their names used as tune names. In the town of Woodstock there are North, South, East and West Woodstock, as well as Woodstock Valley. These villages are not many miles from Monson, Massachusetts, where the composer was born and where the author of the hymn for which it was written, Phoebe H. Brown, lived for many years. Her hymn beginning, "I love to steal awhile away," was first sung to a tune called MONSON.

WORGAN. See EASTER HYMN.

WORK SONG [7 6 7 6 D (4: s mf s s / l - s -) ; Lowell Mason, 1864]. A good name for the tune sung universally to the words "Work, for the night is coming." It is known as DILIGENCE in England.

WORMS. See EIN' FESTE BURG.

WORSHIP [L. M. (4: m / m f s f / m r d) ; Karl P. Harrington, 1905]. Because written for Richard Watson Gilder's hymn which begins, "To Thee, Eternal Soul, be praise."

—— [8 6 8 8 6 (4: S / d d r r / m s r) ; German traditional melody]. Used as a setting for John R. Darbyshire's hymn beginning:

Lord Jesus, from Thy throne above,
Behold us kneeling here.

—— [7 7 7 7 D (3: dr / m. m fm / r -)]. See SABBATH.

WREFORD. See CARTER.

WRESTLING JACOB. See PENIEL.

W ZLOBIE LEZY [4 4 7 4 4 7 4 4 4 4 7 (3: SS d d / Td r r) ; arr. by E. M. G. Reed, *ca.* 1925]. This is a Polish carol, the words meaning, "In manger lying." In the first edition of *The Hymnary* of the United Church of Canada this title was erroneously given as the name of the composer of the music.

Y

YIGDAL. See LEONI.

YOAKLEY [8 8 8 8 8 8 (3: dr / m - mf / s m d / r. m f / f m) ; William Yoakley]. John R. Van Pelt has said that Lowell Mason named this for its composer. However, the name Mason gave it in his *Carmina Sacra* (1841), was WESLEY CHAPEL.

YORK [C. M. (4: d / m s f l / m s r) ; from Ravenscroft's *Psalter*, 1761]. Originally called THE STILT, perhaps because of the awkward skips in the first and third lines of the tune. This was one of the four or five tunes sung by the Puritans in this country. Ravenscroft changed the name to YORK in his *Whole Book of Psalms* (1621).

The tenor part (air) of this tune is so well known, that within the memory of half the nurses in England were used to sing it by way of lullaby; and the chimes of many country churches have played it six or eight times in four and twenty hours from time immemorial.—John Hawkins, *History of Music*, Vol. II.

—— [C. M. (3: L / L - T / d - r / m r d / T)]. See BURFORD.

YORKSHIRE [10 10 10 10 10 10 (4:

d - d r / m - - f / s m f s / l - - -);
John Wainright]. Yorkshire, the largest county in England, for civil administration purposes is divided into
North, East, and West Riding. *Riding, thrithing,* or *thriding* are Scandinavian terms for a third part of a
county. James T. Lightwood, English authority on hymn tunes, waxed
quite indignant because the tune was
called YORKSHIRE in the first edition
of *Hymns Ancient and Modern*
(1861), saying this name is a complete misfit, as the tune has no connection with that county.

Also called CHRISTMAS HYMN, DOR-
CHESTER, LEAMINGTON, LONGTOWN,
MORTRAM, MOTTRAM, NATIVITY,
STOCKBRIDGE, STOCKPORT, WAIN-
WRIGHT, WALWORTH, WOLWORTH. In
the 1850's some tune books used the
name CHRISTMAS HYMN because the
tune was composed for "Christians,
awake! salute the happy morn." NA-
TIVITY was used for the same reason,
and WAINWRIGHT for the name of its
composer. The other names are after
towns and cities in England. Stockport, a municipal, county, and parlia-
mentary borough partly in Cheshire
and partly in Lancashire, England,
near Manchester, is where the composer was born (in 1723), and tradition says his tune was first sung there
on Christmas Day, 1750, at the parish
church. John Byrom, author of the
hymn, wrote in his notebook: "The
singing men and boys with Mr. Wainwright came here and sang 'Christians awake.'" Ralph Harrison, a
Lancashire hymnbook compiler, was
the first to call the tune STOCKPORT.

Z

ZADOK. See CANONBURY.
ZELOTES. See MOZART.
ZINZENDORF. See SEELENBRÄUTIGAM.
ZION [8 7 8 7 4 7 (3: ss / s m *ds* / l s);
Thomas Hastings, 1830]. From the

text, by Thomas Kelly, for which it
was written:

> On the mountain's top appearing,
> Lo! the sacred herald stands,
> Welcome news to Zion bearing,
> Zion long in hostile lands:
> Mourning captive,
> God Himself will loose thy bands.

Zion: summit or fort; a prominent
hill of Jerusalem, the highest of
those on which the city is built. Being the original site of the tabernacle
pitched by David for the reception
of the Ark, it was called the "holy
hill," or "hill of the sanctuary." It
was the first spot in Jerusalem to
be occupied by buildings, and the
Hebrew prophets often used the
name to signify Jerusalem itself.
After David had captured it from the
Jebusites, he built his palace there,
and for more than a thousand years
the kings and princes of Israel lived
and ruled there. Here David was
buried. Zion was the last spot that
held out when the Romans under
Titus captured the city:

When the rest of the city was in ruins,
when the enemy occupied the courts
of the temple, the remnant of the Jews
from the walls of Zion hautily refused
the terms of the conqueror and per-
ished in thousands around and within
the palace of their princes.—McClintock and Strong, *Cyclopaedia of Biblical,
Theological, and Ecclesiastical Literature.*

——— [8 7 8 7 4 7 (4: d TL S m /
r d sf m); Thomas Morley, 1891].
Set to Thomas Kelly's text mentioned above.

Also called HOLBORN, from the fact
that Thomas Morley was onetime
organist at St. Albans, Holborn, London.

——— [6 6 6 6 8 8 (4: d / m d s m /
d - -)]. See DARWALL.

ZOAN [7 6 7 6 D (4: d - / m. r d T / d - d) ; William H. Havergal, 1859]. One of the geographical names used by Havergal as designations for his hymn tunes. Zoan was an Egyptian city, the seat of the dynasty in the days of the Pharaoh Psammetichos; now a small village called San el Hagar.

ZUNDEL. See LOVE DIVINE by Zundel.

MELODIC INDEX

———◆———

See pages 33-36 for an explanation of the system of notation used in the following list for the purpose of identifying tunes.

175

3: S / d - S / r - S / m r d / r -
        St. Bartholomew
4: S / d S m d / s. m d   Corwin
3: S / d - L / S - dr / m - r / d -
        Martyrdom
3: S / d - Ld / r - dL / S -   Iowa
3: S / d - T / L - S / f - m / r -
        Evangelist
4: S / d T T. L / L m m r / d
        Magdalen
4: S / d T d m / m - r -   Incarnation
4: S / d T r d / m r d   Mansfield
4: S / d d S S / m - d   Wir Pflügen
4: S / d. d T L / S -   Arthur's Seat
4: S / d d T L / S. L S   Bethlehem
4: S / d d T T / L dL S   Suomi
4: S / d d d MF / S S S   Mirfield
4: S / d d d TL / S   Molleson
4: S / d d d TL / S - -   Millenium
3: S / d. d dT / TL L   Hosanna
4: S / d. d d d / r - -   Richmond
4: S / d d d d / m. r d   Ellon
4: S / d d d r / m r d r   Miles' Lane
4: S / d d d r / mr mf s Forest Green
4: S / d. d d m / r. d r Auld Lang Syne
3: S / d - d / r - S / m f m / m r
        Jerusalem
6: S / d - d r d r / m s m r d r
        Candler
4: S / d d r m / d - S Urbs Beata
4: S / d - - d / r - - r / m d L r / d - T
        Creation
3: S / d d r r / m r d   Azmon
4: S / d d r r / m. r d   Llanfyllin
6: S / d - d r - r / m - r d - Ortonville
4: S / d d r r / m s r   Worship
4: S / d d r r / m sf m   St. Asaph
3: S / d d r / m - s / dr T / d -
        Hanover
3: S / d d r / m l sm / r. d r / m -
        Frederick
4: S / d. d m d / d - L   Webb
6: S / d - d m r d / L - L d T - Alida
4: S / d d m r d / r - - St. Thomas
6: S / d - d m r d / r - r f Bremen
4: S / d d m m / r d r Coronation
4: S / d r T S / d r m St. Magnus
3: -S dr / m. S dr / m - Happy Day
4: S / d r m d / r f m   St. James

4: S / d - r - / m - - d / m f s l /
 s f m r / m -   Everyland No. 1
4: S d r / m - - d / f m r m / d - L -
        Charterhouse
3: -S dr / m. m rd Ld / L- S- --
        Lux Benigna
4: S / d r m. m / s f m   Copeland
4: S / d r m f / m r d   Norfolk
3: S / d - r / mf s d / r d T / d -
        Diadem
4: S / d r m f / s fm r   O Jesu
4: S / d r m f / s - - Holy Rood
3: S / d - md / m - r / d - L / S -
        Amazing Grace
4: S / d m r d / s - -   Covenant
4: S / d m r r / m - - Old 134th
4: S / d m m d / r f f Duane Street
6: S / d m s T r f / m - - d - - Hosanna
4: S / m T d r / T   St. Jude
4: S / m T d r / d - T   Nazareth
3: S / m - r / d - S / T - L / S -
        Holy Cross
3: S / m. r dT / TL S   Petition
3: S / m - r / d - T / T L d / S -
        Belmont
4: S / m r d T / d - -   Oxnam
6: S / m - r r d L / S - L S - Carol
3: S / m - m / m r L / T d r / d
        Brookfield
6: S / m - m m r m / f - r T -
        Sheltered Dale
4: S / m m m m / m - m   Geibel
4: S / m m m m / f. m r Bishopgarth
4: S / m m m fm / r d dr m Canonbury
3: S / m - m / f - T / r - d / d T
        Paradise
4: S / m. m f m / r m d Jerusalem
3: S / m - m / s - d / m - r / d - Spohr
3: S / m f m / s m r / d r L / d T
        St. Clement
free: S F M / L L S S / d Malabar
6: S - S S - M / S - L d - - Caledonia
6: S S S S S S / S d r m - - Gladness
4: S S S S / S - S - / L L °S LT / L - - -
        Merrial
4: S S S LT / d T T L Chester
4: S S S dT / L L L r   Carter
4: S SS d r / m - -   Dominica
4: S S L S / L T d -   St. John
4: S S L S / d d T -   Irene

4: L - d T / L l s f / m - ST. MARY
free: L d r m m l - LITTLE CORNARD
4: L - d m / m - r - / d. r m r / d L L -
LOMBARD STREET
4: L - m d / r - m - / L. T d r / d T L -
ISTE CONFESSOR

4: -T d r / m. r ml sm / rd L -
LONDONDERRY AIR

4: d / S m r d / f m r SAUL
3: d.L / d- S- L.r / d- d- DEIRDRE
6: d / L F r T S d / m m r d - JOANNA
4: d / L S d r / m m r ST. MARY
4: d SS L d / S - - OBLATIONS
4: d S L S / F - M - TYSK
4: d S L S / dT dr m d LLANHERNE
4: d S d d / r r m - GLORIFICATION
4: d S d r / d - T - VALOUR
4: d S d r / m r mf s AMSTERDAM
4: d S d r / m. f m r REX GLORIA
4: d. S d m / r. L r f ST. NICHOLAS
4: d - S m / r. T d - RIGHINI
2: d L S / d r / m m r GRÄFENBERG
3: d / T. L S / d r m / m r d / d T
NEW 113TH
4: dT / L L L S / d d r KINGSFOLD
3: dT / LL m - m - / rd T - KEDRON
4: d / Td r d TL / ⁺SL T M
ST. MARY MAGDALENE
4: d / T d r m / f f m
ST. JOHN'S, WESTMINSTER
3: d / Td r m / sm r ROCKINGHAM
4: d / T d f m / m r ST. ANATOLIUS
3: d / Tr r r / dm m CAMPMEETING
4: d / T f m r / s f m
PER RECTE ET RETRO
3: d T L / S - M / F T L / S - -
SAWLEY
3: d - TL / S S S / L d L / L S
WESLEY
2: d TL / S MS / L FL / LS S
MONSELL
4: d TL S m / r d sf m ZION
3: d T L / T - S / L S M / F - -
WESTCOTT
4: d - T L / d - T L / T - L - L - ⁺S
GWYNETH
4: d. T L d / r. d T S AR-HYD-Y-NOS
4: d. T L d / r d - - GREEK HYMN

3: d T d / S - d / T - d / r - - MENDON
4: d Td r d / f f m - DIX
4: d. T dr mf / s sf mr d ST. NICHOLAS
4: d T d. r / m sf m r SARDIS
4: d T r d / f m r ⁺d REST
4: d / d - S d / r - S - ADESTE FIDELIS
4: d / d S dr m / fm r d JAM LUCIS
3: d / d - S / d r m / f m r / m - IRISH
4: d / d S d f / m r d SHARON
4: d / d L S MF / S - - ST. DUNSTAN'S
4: d / d L r T / m d r CARLISLE
6: d / d T L S - L / T - - L -
PASTOR BONUS
3: d / d T L / S - d / rd T / d -
WAREHAM
4: d / d T L S / m - - ST. OLAVE
free: d / d - T / L - m f l / ⁺s - -
ETERNAL LIGHT
4: d / d Td r r / rd - ST. HILDA
3: d / d T d / r - r / rd r / m -
MOZART
4: d / d T d m / r r d ST. FLAVIAN
4: d / d T d d / r r m TALLIS' CANON
4: d / d. d d m / s r m
HOLY SEPULCHRE
4: d / d d r r / m - - ST. OSWALD
4: d / d d r m / f r m - GIBBONS
4: d / d - - d / r - - m / f - m r / d - -
WILTON
6: d / d - d m - f / s - l s -
IN DULCI JUBILO
3: d / dr d S / dr m mf / sf m d / r -
ST. MARTIN'S
4: d / d r m d / L T d ST. CATHERINE
4: d / d r m d / d T d ST. AMBROSE
3: d / dr md mf / s -
LASST UNS ERFREUEN
4: d / d r m d / s - r - / d -
SOLOTHURN
4: d / d r m d / s r m ST. HUGH
3: d / d. r m / rd T / d - ST. EDMUND
4: d / d. r m r / d f r FARRANT
6: d / d - r m - f / m - r d - SPLENDOUR
4: d / d r m f / s s m DUNFERMLINE
3: d / d. r m / f. s l / s - m / s -
JERUSALEM
4: d / d. r m f / s. l s f / m - r r / d - -
BELOVED
free: d / d - r / f m r d / r - -
CONSECRATION

4: d r m m / f m m r   LOVE DIVINE
4: d r m f s / d T L S   WALTHAM
4: d r m f / s f m r   TANTUM ERGO
3: d r m / s - m / d - f / m - BEATITUDO
3: d r m / s. f m   HORBURY
4: d r m l / s. f m -   HODNET
4: d. r m l / s - s -   GARTON
free: d rf f mrd r rmr d T L

        VEXILLA REGIS
4: d - / d T L S / d - r - / m -

        OLD 100TH
4: d - / d d S L / S - -   LENOX
free: d - / d r m d m f / s - OLD 113TH
4: d - / d r m r / d - T - / d - UXBRIDGE
4: d - / m. r d T / d - d   ZOAN
4: d - / m f s d / T d r   CAITHNESS
4: d - / m f s l / s -   OLD 120TH
4: d - / m s s l / s - m

        MISSIONARY HYMN
4: d - / s m l s / m d r -   DURHAM
4: d - / s m d s / l d t - LONDON NEW
4: d - / s f m r / d - r - / m -

        JERVAULX ABBEY
6: d - - / d S d m d m / s - - CONTRAST
6: d - dd - L / S - ♯F S - - CHAUTAUQUA
4: d - - d / d d T d / m - r -   DIJON
4: d - d d / d T r -   ST. EDMUND
4: d - d d / d - d r / m - r d / T - d -

        ST. NINIAN
4: d - d d / d - - r / d T L T / r - d -

        ADRIAN
4: d - d d / r T d - CRUSADERS' HYMN
4: d - d d / r - r - / m d d r / d - T

        FLEMMING
4: d - d d / r - m - / f r s -   ANGELS
4: d - d r / d - S - / M S d -

        LLANGOLLEN
4: d - d r / m - r m / f - m r / m - - -

        HAMBURG
4: d - d. r / m - - f / m d d T / d - - -

        NATIONAL HYMN
4: d - d r / m f s -   SURSUM CORDA
4: d - d r / m - - f / s m f s / l - - -

        YORKSHIRE
4: d - d r / m - s - / f f m   OLD 22ND
4: d - d r / m - - l / s - f - / m - - -

        ST. CROSS
4: d - d m / r - l - / s - f - / f - m -

        LIVERPOOL

3: d - r / d. r m / f - m / r d r

        HYFRYDOL
3: d - r / m - d / r - T / d - -

        ORIENTIS PARTIBUS
free: d - r - / m - - r m s / l - s -

        EBELING
4: d - r m / f - m - / r d d T / d - - -

        OLD 124TH
4: d - r m / s - l - / s - - -

        DOWN AMPNEY
4: d - m d / s - - m / l s l t / d -

        BIRMINGHAM
4: d - m s / s. f m -   OLIVET
4: d - m. f / s - - s / l - t - / d - -

        TRURO
4: d - m f / s - l t / d - t l / s - - -

        DUKE STREET
4: d - m s / s. f m d / m - r d / d - T -

        PAX DEI
4: d - m s / s - s - / s s d t / t - l -

        O PERFECT LOVE
4: d - m s / l. ♯f s - HYMN OF NATIONS
4: d - m s / d - - l / f. f m -

        MAGDALEN COLLEGE
4: d - m s / d. t l s / l l s -

        CHRISTUS REX
4: d - m s / d. d d -   STOWELL
4: d / m d r r / d - -   ST. HELENA
4: d / m d s m / d - -   DARWALL
4: d / m r d S / L - S HOLY CHURCH
3: d / m - r / d - L / S - L / d -

        BALERMA
4: d / m r d T / d - -   ST. JOHN
3: d / m. r dT / d -   NEED
3: d / m. r d / r - m / r - d / r -

        FILLMORE
4: d / m r d rm / s - -   SELMA
3: d / m - r / d - r / m d t / l -

        STRACATHRO
3: d / m r d / f m r / d r T / d -

        INTERCESSION
6: d / m r d s f m / r - - - -   WESLEY
3: d / m r d / s f m / r -   DAVID
3: d / m - r / d - d / l s f / m -

        MANCHESTER
4: d / m. ♯r m m / f. m f   WALTHAM
4: d / m r m f / s - m   BREMEN
3: d- / m. m m m- r- / d. d d- ARLINGTON
4: d / m. m r d / f f m

        WINCHESTER OLD

4: m - / r d s m / r - r - / d -
      RIMINGTON
9: m r d / s - - s - - f s l / s - -
      ASSURANCE
4: m / r d d s / l l s
     ST. MARY MAGDALENE
4: m / r m L T / d r s KING'S LYNN
4: m / r m d r / m - m JERUSALEM
3: m - rm fr / sd dr m
    SACRAMENTUM UNITATIS
4: m r m / f - - m / r m d.r / r m - -
      FINLANDIA
4: m / r m f l / s r m
     ALDERSGATE STREET
4: m / r m f l / s - m m / s. m d r /
m - -   BLAIRGOWRIE
4: m r / f m l s / s f ST. HELEN'S
4: m - / r s dT d / T - COMBE MARTIN
4: m / m. S LT dm / s - - THEODORE
4: m / m d r m / d T L OLD 112TH
4: m / m.d r m / f.f m
     PERCIVAL-SMITH
3: m / m d m / r T r / d - DENNIS
4: m / m r d L / S d r ST. NICHOLAS
4: m / m r d r / m - - ST. JOHN
3: m / m. r dr / m - LEIGHTON
6: m / m - r d r m / s - s s - - ADVENT
4: m / m. r d s / s f m REST
4: m / m. r r d / f m r d / l - s f / m - -
      FORTITUDE
4: m / m rm f s / m - - WALTHAM
3: m / m. r m / s f m / r d r / m d
     ST. LEONARD
3: m / m r m / sf f SELVIN
6: m / m - ♯r m - s / s - r r - WEINACHT
4: m / m r s T / r - d
    ST. GEORGE'S BOLTON
4: m / m r s. s / f f m PENIEL
3: m / m r l / s - HOSANNA
3: mm / m d rr / m m DORRNANCE
4: m / m. m r d / d - T
     ANGEL'S STORY
4: m / m. m r d / f. f m GREEN HILL
4: m / m m r. r / d - d RUTHERFORD
4: m / m m ♯r r / m - - ST. CATHERINE
4: m / m. m ♯r m / s s ♯f REST (ELTON)
4: m / m m ♯r m / s f L ST. LOUIS
3: -m mm / m d rr / T -
    MISSIONARY CHANT
4: m / m m m m / m. d d MEDITATION

4: m / m m m m / f - - LEOMINSTER
4: m / m. m m m / s. s s
    THE GOLDEN CHAIN
3: m / m. m fr / m m HODNET
4: m / m m f. m / rd r d WIGTOWN
4: m / m m f m / r - d ST. LUKE
2: m / m m / f m / r DOLOMITE CHANT
3: m / m. m fm / mr r SERENITY
4: m / m m f m / m - r AURELIA
3: m / m - m / f - l / s - f / m -
    ST. CHRYSOSTOM
4: m / m f s d / d - T LAUFER
4: m / m f s r / m - - ST. ANDREW
4: m / m f s f / m r d WORSHIP
4: m / m s d m / L T d VALETE
3: mm / s - mm / s - LUCY
3: m / m s f / m - m / m d t / l -
     ST. CLEMENT
4: m / f r m m / f r m - GLOAMING
4: m / f m m r / d - - QUAM DILECTA
4: m / f. m m m / s. f f PARADISE
4: m / f. f d r / m d - ALFORD
4: m. f / s s f m / r d DULCINA
3: mf / ss s m / l l l HEBER
6: mf / s - s s f m / l - l s - RETREAT
4: m. f / s s s d / s - LABAN
3: mf / sl s m / dl s COWPER
4: m / f s l s / s f m ST. LUKE
4: m f / s l t d / s - HOLYROOD
4: m / f s l d / t - l LAUDES DOMINI
4: mf / s ld t ls / m rm r d HODNET
4: m. f / s d t l / s d. r m CHRISTMAS
4: mf / s d t l / s - m TOURS
4: m. f / s d t l / s - INNOCENTS
4: m / f l s f / m - - ST. OLAVE
3: m / s - dT / d - l / r - s / m - -
     DAVID'S HARP
4: m / s d f r / d T d COLCHESTER
4: m / s d f f / m - d ROTTERDAM
4: m s / r d f f / m - HANNA
4: m / s m r d / d. T T PARADISE
4: m / s. f m r / f m r ST. LEONARD
4: m / s f m m / r r d
    DOMINUS REGIT ME
4: m / s f m m / m. r d JEHOVAH NISSI
4: m / s f m f / m. r d ST. GABRIEL
4: m / s. f m s / m r d BLAIRGOWRIE
4: m / s s d d / t l s WESTMINSTER
4: m / s s s s / d - m GREENLAND
4: m / s. s s s / d t l SAINTS OF GOD

4: m. m mm mm / s r m -
GOD BE WITH YOU
4: m m m ms / s. f m d   GLORIA
3: m m m / f - T / L - T / d - -
LAMBETH
3: m m m / f - d / m - -   TRENTHAM
3: m m m / f - m / r - r / r - -
MARYTON
3: m m m / f - m / m - r / d - -
HOLBORN HILL
4: m mm f m / m. r d -   VINCENT
4: m m m. f / s s s d   ST. ASAPH
6: m m m s - d / T d r d -   FOWLER
3: m m m / s - d / r - r / m - - /
s s s / d - t / 1 - 1 / s - - ST. CRISPIN
3: m m m / s - d / r - r / m - - /
s s s / f - r / m - f / r - - HESPERUS
3: m m m / s - r / m - m / s - f
ST. BARBARA
4: m mm s fm / rm f m   NAOMI
3: m m. m / s - s   ST. LEONARD
4: m mm s. s / d - - CROSSING THE BAR
4: m mm s s / d d m   NATIVITY
4: m m m l / l *s l -   GETHSEMANE
4: m m fm / m r r d   TEMPLE
4: m. m f m / m. r r   ST. HILARY
4: m m f m / l - s -   PENITENCE
4: m m f m / l. l s -   VIGILATE
4: m m f f / s - m -   EUDOXIA
4: m m f s / m - r - / d - - - HORSHAM
4: m m f s / s f m r   HYMN TO JOY
4: m. m f l / s - m -   PILGRIM
4: m m s d / r r m m   WEMAN
4: m. m s m / d r m -
ST. GEORGE'S WINDSOR
4: m m s s / d d m m   CORONAE
4: m m s s / d r m r   ST. HILARY
4: m m s s / d d s -   CULFORD
4: m fr dS dr / m fr d -   MOZART
3: m f m / r - - / s r f / f m - GODWIN
3: m f m / m r d / r - f / m - - TRUST
4: m f s d / r f m -   GETHSEMANE
4: m. f s m / r - d -   CRANHAM
3: mf s m / fm r -   GENTLE JESUS
4: m. f s s / l l s -   TRISAGION
4: m f s s / d - s -   VEXILLUM
4: m f s l / r r m -   GIBBONS
4: m s d d / r f m -   ASCENSION
3: m s d / r - r / r d r / m - - ALETTA
2: m- s- / d- rm / f- m- / r- GWALCHMAI

4: m s r m / d L S -   ST. EDMUND
2: m s / r. m / f r / m - PLEYEL'S HYMN
4: m s m d / T d r m   DEERHURST
4: m s f s / m s r s   VESPER HYMN
4: m s l s / s. f m -   HOLLINGSIDE
4: m s l s / d l s m   ANGEL VOICES
4: m s d t / t l s -   REQUIESCAT
4: m l s m / r mf m   CHARTERHOUSE
4: m - L T / d - r - / m m s f / m - -
ST. MARTIN
4: m - T d / f - m - / r L T d / T - -
KERR
4: m - d r / m dL d   WELCOME
4: m - d r / m - d - / L - T - / d - -
ULTIMA
4: m - d r / m - s - / f m m r / d - - -
LANGRAN
4: m - d m / s l s - BREAD OF LIFE
3: m - r / d - L / T d T / L - -
KINGS OF ORIENT
4: m - r d / T - - d / r f m r / d - T -
WELWYN
4: m - r. d / d. L L -   BETHANY
4: m - r d / d. T T - LOVE'S OFFERING
4: m - r d / r m f m / r d T d / r - d -
URBS CAELESTIS
free: m - r d - r / m f s -   WEIMAR
4: m - r. d / s f -   CONSOLATION
4: m - *r m / d - m - / r m f s / m - - -
HOLLEY
6: m - r m - f / s - - s - - ST. THERESA
4: m - *r m / s - - T / T d r m / m - L -
ALVERSTOKE
6: m - r f - m / m - r d - -
HOLY OFFERINGS
3: m - r / s f m / r - m / f - -
ST. CHRYSOSTOM
4: m - m r / d - s - / s r m f / m - BERA
4: m - m r / d - s - / l s s f / m - -
EVENTIDE
6: m - - m r m / f - - m - - HOLINESS
6: m - m m - d / r - r r - - MARTYN
4: m - m m / m - - r / d L d r / m - - -
PAX
4: m - m m / m. r r   INVITATION
4: m - m m / m. r r -   KEDRON
6: m - m m fm / r - *d r - S
ANGEL VOICES
4: m - m m / f - - m / m r d r / m - -
SANDON

4: m - m m / f - m s / s - f - / m - - - FEDERAL STREET
4: m - m m / f - m - / l s f f / m - - - MORECAMBE
4: m - m m / s - m - / r m f s / m - ST. NICHOLAS
4: m - m m / s - - s / l s f s / m - - EUCHARIST
4: m - m m / s - s - / d - l - / s - - - REST
6: m - - m f m / r - - r - - PALMER
4: m - m f / s - d - / r. r m f / m - - - PENITENTIA
3: m - m / f - s / m - m / r - - PEACEFIELD
4: m - m f / s - s - / s d t l / s - m - LANHERNE
4: m - m f / s - s - / l t d r / d - t - DEEPER LIFE
3: m - fr / m f s / l - rt / d s HAYDN
free: m - - - f s m - SEBASTE
4: m - m s / f. m f SAMUEL
3: m - f / sf m r / d - r / mr m - GWALIA
6: m - f s - f / m - r m - - MAUBURN
3: m - f / s d t / r d l / s - - LAMBETH
4: m - s f / m - - r / d r m f / m - r - PILGRIMS
4: m - s d / t - - l / s m d r / r - m - DIADEMA
free: f m f r m d r r - DIES IRAE

4: s / d r T d / r - - GRATITUDE
4: s / d. r m rd / f m r ST. BERNARD
4: s / dr mf s s / l l s WAITS' CAROL
3: -s dr / m- s- dr / m- - HOME
4: s / m T d l / s f m WILTON
4: s / m d l s / f m r BEDFORD
3: s / m - d / d - s / l s f / m - RACINE
4: s m r / d - - S / L d r S / m - - SINE NOMINE
4: s / m r d rd / L - S NYLAND
4: s / m. r d s / l f f HE LEADETH ME
4: s / m r d l / f m r ST. LEONARD
4: s - / m. m m f / s d l d / s - - ALLELUIA PERENNE
3: s / m - f / s - d / r d t / d - ST. PETERSBURG
4: s / m s l s / f r m STÖRL
4: s / m ss l d / r d - WALLACE

4: s / m s d tl / s f m VALIANCE
3: s / m - l / T - d / f m r / m - CAREY
4: s / m l s d / d t d ST. ANNE
4: s / f m r r / d - - ST. COLUMBA
4: s / f m r mf / r - d JERUSALEM
4: s / f m r mf / m - - ST. ETHELWALD
4: s / f m m r / d - - ST. CECILIA
4: s. f / m mr d r / m - m MEIRIONYDD
4: sf / m mr m mr / m. r d CAPEL
4: s / f m l s / f sl s THANKSGIVING
4: s / s. r r dr / m. r d TIPLADY
4: s / s m r m / r - d ST. ANSELM
4: s / s m m r / r - d SAVOY CHAPEL
3: s / s m m / m d d / T r f / f m MOZART
3: s / s m m / m d d / d T dm / m r ARIEL
4: s / s. m m s / s. r r MATERNA
4: s / s m f l / s - m LANCASHIRE
3: s / s m s / s - d / d t l / s - STELLA (ENGLISH)
4: s / s m l s / l t d ST. LEONARD
4: s / s f m r / d l s MELCOMBE
3: s / s. f m / m. r d / d T L / S - MÜLLER
4: s - / s. f m f / s - OLNEY
4: s / s. f m s / f. m r ST. MICHEL'S
6: s / s - f m - d / t - l l - GERALD
3: ss / s m ds / l s ZION
4: s / s s #f s / l. s s ST. CHRYSOSTOM
4: s / s. s #f l / s - m ST. CHRISTOPHER
3: s / s. s s d / m. m m VARINA
4: s / s s l m / s. f f OLNEY
4: s / s s l l / s - - NUN DANKET
4: s - / s s l l / s - s - / s - OLIVE'S BROW
4: s / s. s l t / d tl s PARKER
3: -s ss / d s sm / r - REST
3: ss / s. m rm / d s FABEN
3: s / s. l s / m f s / f. m r / m d KREMSER
3: s / s d m / m s m / r f T / d - GRATITUDE
4: s / s d t sl / t - - SANDYS
3: s / s d tl / s - m / d - r / m - ATTWOOD
4: s / s d t l / s f m WEIMAR
4: s / l s d f / m - r ST. ANATOLIUS
4: s l / s m d r / m - ST. NINIAN
4: s / l s m. #f / s - - GOPSAL

4: s / l.s s f / m r d   ST. NICHOLAS
3: sl / d s mr / ms s   HOSANNA
4: s l / d.l s m / r d   LONGDEN
4: s / d.s m d / l - -   JUBILATE
4: s / d s m.f / s r m   HOSANNA
3: s / d s l / s s f / m r d / s s
     MAGDALEN
4: s / d tl s.f / m r d   HOLYWELL
4: s / d.t l s / fm rm f ALL THE WORLD
4: s / d t l s / s f m   ST. PETER
4: s / d tl s ls / fm r d   MEYER
4: s / d tl s d / m f s   ELLACOMBE
4: s / d t l t / d - s   JERUSALEM
4: s / d t d s / f m s -   GERONIMO
4: s / d t d s / l - -   CROFT
4: s / d t d s / l fm r   ST. MARTIN'S
4: s / d t d s / l sf m ♯f / s - -
     ALLELUIA PERENNE
4: s / d d t l / s m d   WENTWORTH
4: s / d d t l / s.m d   ST. HILDA
4: s / d d d d / t l s   BYRD
6: s / d - d d - r / d t l s - l / t -
     HIGH ROAD
4: s dr m s / l. m l - MARCUS WHITMAN
4: s dr l / s f f m   HOTHAM
3: s m d / r d T / d - -   TRINITY
4: s - m dm / r.fm r -   JEWETT
4: s - m d / l.s s -   CONSOLATION
4: s - m r / d - T d / d m r d / d - - -
     PEEL CASTLE
4: s - m.r / d - - d / m - s - / d - - -
     DEPAUW
3: s m r / d - d / l - l / s -   ARMES
4: s - m r / d.r m - / f - s l / s - - -
     HALL
4: s - m r / d - r - / m s f l / l - s
     WILTON
4: s. m r d / m d L S   ADRIAN
4: s m r d / s m m r   ADVENT
4: s - m - / r r m f / f - m
     AMEN, JESU HAN SKAL RAADE
4: s - m m / m - r - / d d r r /m - d -
     HENLEY
4: s m f m / r d TL S   ROYAL OAK
4: s m f m / r - d -   ST. MARTIN
3: s m f / m r s / d r T / d -   LYSTRA
4: s mf ss s   RESCUE
4: s mf s s / l - s -   WORK SONG
4: s - m f / s - s - / l l l l / l - s -
     SARUM

4: s / m f s lt / d - d   PARADISE
3: s / mf s l / s -   BOYLSTON
4: s m f s / l.1 l -   DEDICATION
6: s m f s t l / s - - m - -
     STORIES OF JESUS
4: s mf s d / dt lt d -   ERNAN
free: s m s / l s f m / r - d MENTZER
4: s.m l d / t l s m   ST. AMBROSE
4: s m d s / m.r d s REGENT SQUARE
4: s - f d / m - r -   NIGHTFALL
6: s - f m - r / d - S T - d   TRUST
4: s / s d f f / m - -   RESIGNATION
4: s s m r / d - S -   SION
4: s - s m / l - s - / s f m s / r - - -
     HEZEKIAH
2: s sf / m r / d   MORNINGTON
4: s sf m r / dr m r -   SAVANNAH
3: s s f / m - s / f m r / mf s -
     EUCHARISTIC HYMN
4: s s s m / d d t -   GETHSEMANE
4: s s s f / m m m r EVENING PRAYER
4: s ss s.l / sd tm l s ANCIENT OF DAYS
2: s ss / sl t d / m r / d - MOUNT SION
4: s ss.s / f m r -   HANFORD
4: s sss s / s - - -   DULCE DOMUM
4: s - s s / s - s - / s s l s / s - ♯s -
     JOURNEY'S END
4: s s s s / s.l s -   ST. GERTRUDE
3: s s s / s - s / l - l / s - -   RIVAULX
4: s - s s / s - - s / l l l s / s - -
     PAX TECUM
3: s s s / l - s / s f m / s - - PALESTRINA
4: s s s s l / s - s - / l l t m / d - - - NISSI
4: s.s s lt / d s m s   PRESCOTT
2: s ss / d d / l.l / l -   PATTEN
3: s s s / d - f / m - r / s -
     THANKSGIVING
4: s.s ls md / d - L -   CONVERSE
3: s s l / s m r / d r r / m - -
     TRISAGION
3: s - s / l - s / f - m / s - - / m - -
     CHRISTI MUTTER
4: s s l s / d mr d t   TRUST
4: s s l t / d d t -   RATISBON
4: s.s d s / s f f m   LUX EOI
free: sls m f s s - l f l d tl s -
     ISTE CONFESSOR
4: s l s m / s l s m   TREFAENAN
6: s. l s m - - / s.l s m - - STILLE NACHT
4: s.l s m / d r m -   ST. HUGH

4: s - l s / m - - d / r m f m / s - m - ST. OSYTH

4: s l sf mf / s l sf m SICILIAN MARINERS

3: s - ls / s - md / r. m f / f m - TRURO

3: s. l s / l s *d* / r m f / mr mf sl AVISON

4: s - l l / s. m d - RUSSIAN HYMN

4: s l l s / f m m r ST. BEDE

3: s *d* l / s - m / d - r / m - - CONQUEST

3: s - *d* / m - d / t l s / d s - RATHBUN

4: l / m. ♯s l t / *d. r* t CANNONS

4: l m l t / *d. r d* - PRINCE RUPERT

free l s f / m m f l *d d* / t - l INTERCESSOR

free: l l l sf s l l r URBS BEATA

4: l t *d* t / l s m - PAX

free: *d* / s s d m / r l s - BALFOUR

4: *d* s l l / s. f m d ALL SAINTS

2: *d* / s l s / f m / r LAMBETH

4: *d* / t l s ♯f / l. l s HOLY TRINITY

4: *d* / t l t s / l t *d* ERFURT

3: *d* / *d* s l / l s f / m r d / s - MONTGOMERY

3: *d* /*d*. t l / s - f / m. r d / s - COLCHESTER

4: *d* / *d* t *d* l / s. f m ST. SAVIOUR

4: *d d* / *d* m l. s / m r ST. HELEN

4: *d* / *d d* sl t / *dt* l s EIN' FESTE BURG

4: *d mr* / *d* s m d / s - ENGLAND'S LANE

4: *d* - m f / s - - s / s *d m r* / r - d - TIDINGS

4: *d* - s m / d - f. m / f s *d* - LLANGOEDMOR

4: *d* - s m / r - d - BURLEIGH

2: *d* ss / m s / *d*. SILVER STREET

4: *d* - / s l s m / f m r r / m - CANTICUM REFECTIONIS

4: *d* - s l / s. f m COELITIS PLAUDANT

4: *d* - t. l / s - - f / m - r - / d - - ANTIOCH

free: *d* - t / l s s d / r - d - UNITAS FRATRUM

4: *d*. t *d* s / l sf m - THANKSGIVING

4: *d dd* l l / s. f m ST. HUGH

NAMES NOT INCLUDED IN
THE ALPHABETICAL LIST

Hymn Tune Names

Names Not Included in the Alphabetical List

INDEX OF FIRST WORDS
OR LINES OF HYMNS

FIRST WORDS	AUTHOR OR TRANSLATOR	TUNE NAME (*See*)
A message came to a maiden	"E. G. B." and Percy Dearmer	ANNUNCIATION
A mighty fortress	Martin Luther	EIN FESTE BURG
Abide with me	Henry F. Lyte	EVENTIDE
Accepting, Lord, Thy gracious call	Newman Hall	ST. CHRYSOSTOM
Adeste, fideles	Anonymous	ADESTE FIDELES
Adesto, sancta Trinitas	Anonymous	SHARON
All for Jesus	John Stainer	ALL FOR JESUS
All glory, laud, and honor	John M. Neale, tr.	HODNET, ST. THEODULPH
All hail the power	Edward Perronet	CORONATION, DIADEM
All labor gained new dignity	John Oxenham	LABOR
All my heart this night rejoices	Paul Gerhardt	STELLA (PARKER)
All people of the earth	Leonard B. McWhood	HYMN OF NATIONS
All praise to Thee	Thomas Ken	TALLIS' CANON
Alleluia, dulce carmen	Anonymous	TANTUM ERGO
Alleluia, sing to Jesus	William C. Dix	ALLELUIA
Amazing grace	John Newton	AMAZING GRACE
Ancient of Days	William C. Doane	ANCIENT OF DAYS
And did those feet in ancient time	William Blake	JERUSALEM
Angel voices, ever singing	Francis Pott	ANGEL VOICES
"Are ye able?"	Earl Marlatt	BEACON HILL
Arise, my soul, arise	Charles Wesley	MILLENIUM
Art thou weary	John M. Neale, tr.	REST, STEPHANOS
As by the streams of Babilon	Anonymous tr.	BABYLON'S STREAMS
As now the sun's declining rays	J. Chandler, tr.	HOLY TRINITY
As with gladness men of old	William C. Dix	DIX
Asleep in Jesus	Margaret Mackay	REST
Author of life divine	Charles Wesley	WESLEY

193

FIRST WORDS	AUTHOR OR TRANSLATOR	TUNE NAME (*See*)
Awake and sing the song	William Hammond	FESTAL SONG
Awake, awake, O Zion	Benjamin Gough	JERUSALEM
Awake! awake! put on thy strength	Anonymous	
Awake, my soul, and with the sun	Thomas Ken	MORNING HYMN
Away in a manger	Anonymous	MÜLLER
Be near us, Holy Trinity	Compilers of *Hymns Ancient and Modern*, tr.	SHARON
Be strong!	Maltbie D. Babcock	FORTITUDE
Before Thy throne, O God	William B. Carpenter	ALDERSGATE STREET
Beneath the cross of Jesus	Elizabeth C. Clephane	ST. CHRISTOPHER
Bless the four corners	Arthur Guiterman	HOME
Blessed and Holy Three	S. Childs Clarke	OBLATIONS
Blessed assurance	Fanny J. Crosby	ASSURANCE
Blessed be God	Josiah Conder	WENTWORTH
Blessed city, Heavenly Salem	Edward W. Benson	URBS BEATA
Blow ye the trumpet	Charles Wesley	LENOX, MILLENIUM
Braving the wilds	Robert Freeman	MARCUS WHITMAN
Bread of the world	Reginald Heber	EUCHARISTIC HYMN
Break Thou the bread of life	Mary A. Lathbury	BREAD OF LIFE
Breast the wave, Christian	Joseph Stammers	FORTITUDE
Breathe on me, breath of God	Edwin Hatch	NOVA VITA
Brief life is here our portion	John M. Neale, tr.	AURELIA
Brightest and best	Reginald Heber	CONSOLATION, HODNET, MORNING STAR
Bring, O bring thy music	William C. Gannett	
Brightly gleams our banner	Thomas A. Potter	NISSI, SION, VEXILLUM
By cool Siloam's shady rill	Reginald Heber	HEBER, PARADISE
By Jesus' grave on either hand	Isaac G. Smith	HOLY SEPULCHRE
Call Jehovah	James Montgomery	TRUST
Cast thy burden upon the Lord	from Mendelssohn's *Elijah*	BIRMINGHAM
Christ is the King!	George K. A. Bell	CHRISTUS REX
Christ the Lord is risen today	Charles Wesley	EASTER HYMN
Christ, who once among us	W. St. Hill Bourne	ST. HILL
Christ, whose glory	Charles Wesley	LUX PRIMA

Index of First Words or Lines of Hymns

FIRST WORDS	AUTHOR OR TRANSLATOR	TUNE NAME (See)
Christi mutter stund	Anonymous	CHRISTI MUTTER
Christian, dost thou see them	John M. Neale, tr.	ST. ANDREW OF CRETE
Christian, seek not yet repose	Charlotte Elliott	VIGILATE
Christians, awake! salute	John Byrom	YORKSHIRE
Christ's life our code	Benjamin Copeland	COPELAND
Christus, der ist mein Leben	Anonymous	BREMEN, VULPIUS
Come, every soul	John H. Stockton	STOCKTON
Come, Holy Ghost	Charles Wesley	PENTECOST
Come, Holy Ghost, in love	Ray Palmer, tr.	OLIVET
Come, Holy Spirit, come	Dorothy A. Thrupp	ST. CATHERINE
Come, my soul	F. R. L. von Canitz	HAYDN
Come, O Thou Traveller	Charles Wesley	PENIEL, ST. CHRYSOSTOM
Come, Peace of God	May Rowland	PAX
Come, Thou almighty King	Anonymous	TRINITY
Come, Thou Fount	William Cowper	GREENVILLE
Come, Thou Holy Paraclete	John M. Neale, tr.	ST. CHRYSOSTOM
Come to the Saviour	George F. Root	INVITATION
Come to the Saviour now	John M. Wigner	INVITATION
Come, ye disconsolate	Thomas Moore	CONSOLATION
Come, ye thankful people	Henry Alford	THANKSGIVING
Courage, brother	Norman Macleod	COURAGE, BROTHER
Cross of Jesus, Cross of sorrow	John Stainer	CROSS OF JESUS
Crown Him with many crowns	Matthew Bridges	DIADEMATA
Day after day I sought	Archbishop Hare	ST. AMBROSE
Day by day we magnify Thee	John Ellerton	CARTER, SLINGSBY
Day is dying	Mary A. Lathbury	CHAUTAUQUA
Dear God, our Father	Katharine Lee Bates	DEEPER LIFE
Dear Lord and Father	John G. Whittier	ELTON
Depth of mercy, can there be	Charles Wesley	MERCY
Dost Thou in a manger lie	Elizabeth C. Charles	MAUBURN
Earth below is teeming	Anonymous	HERMAS
Eia mea anima	Jean Mauburn	MAUBURN
Es ist kein Tag	Anonymous	MEYER
Eternal Father, strong to save	William Whiting	MELITA
Eternal God, whose power upholds	Henry H. Tweedy	EVERYLAND NO. 1
Eternal Light, Eternal Light	Thomas Binney	ETERNAL LIGHT

195

FIRST WORDS	AUTHOR OR TRANSLATOR	TUNE NAME (See)
Faith and hope and love	Christopher Wordsworth	CHARITY
Faithful is Thy love	S. Childs Clarke	AMOR FIDELIS
Father, I know that all my life	Anna L. Waring	ST. BEDE
Father, let me dedicate	Lawrence Tuttiett	DEDICATION, GLORIFICATION
Father, whate'er of earthly bliss	Anne Steele	NAOMI, ST. CLEMENT
Fight the good fight	John S. B. Monsell	MOZART
Fling out the banner	George W. Doane	DOANE
For all the saints	William W. How	SARUM
For thee, O dear, dear country	John M. Neale, tr.	AURELIA
Forever with the Lord	James Montgomery	MONTGOMERY, NEARER HOME
Forward! be our watchword	Henry Alford	ECCE SIGNUM
From all Thy saints in warfare	Earl Nelson	PARADISE
From every stormy wind	Hugh Stowell	RETREAT
From Greenland's icy mountains	Reginald Heber	GREENLAND, LANCASHIRE, MISSIONARY HYMN, PATNA
From the eastern mountains	Godfrey Thring	VALOUR
Gentle Jesus, meek and mild	Charles Wesley	GENTLE JESUS
Glory be to Jesus	Edward Caswall, tr.	CASWALL
Glory be to God the Father	Horatius Bonar	REGENT SQUARE
Glory, glory everlasting	Thomas Kelly	ZAANIAM
Go to dark Gethsemane	James Montgomery	GETHSEMANE (MONK), GETHSEMANE (REDHEAD)
God is love; His mercy	John Bowring	STUTTGART
God is working His purpose out	Arthur C. Ainger	PURPOSE
God of our fathers	Daniel C. Roberts	NATIONAL HYMN
God's trumpet wakes	Samuel Longfellow	CORWIN
Gott erhalte Franz den Kaiser	Lorenz L. Haschka	AUSTRIAN HYMN
Guide me, O Thou great Jehovah	William Williams	PILGRIM
Hail, gladdening Light	John Keble, tr.	SEBASTE
Hail, Queen of Heaven	Anonymous	STELLA
Hail the day that sees Him rise	Charles Wesley	ASCENSION
Hail, Thou Head! so bruised	Elizabeth Charles and Godfrey Thring, trs.	ALETTA
Hail to the brightness	Thomas Hastings	WESLEY
Hark! a thrilling voice	Edward Caswall, tr.	LUX EOI

Index of First Words or Lines of Hymns

FIRST WORDS	AUTHOR OR TRANSLATOR	TUNE NAME (See)
I need Thee every hour	Annie S. Hawks	NEED
I sing a song	William Walker	AN ADDRESS FOR ALL
I sought the Lord	Anonymous	PEACE
I think when I read	Jemima T. Luke	SWEET STORY
I was a wandering sheep	Horatius Bonar	PASTOR BONUS
If thou but suffer God	Georg Neumark	BREMEN
I'm a pilgrim	Mary S. B. Shindler	PILGRIM
Immortal Love, forever full	John G. Whittier	SERENITY
In Bethlehem, 'neath star-lit	Grace M. Stutsman	WAITS' CAROL
In Judah's land	Robert Pont	OLD MARTYRS
In our day of thanksgiving	William H. Draper	MONTGOMERY
In our hearts celestial voices	Marie Corelli	CELESTIAL VOICES
In the hour of trial	James Montgomery	MAGDALEN, PENITENCE
In the Lord's atoning grace	Frederick Oakeley	REST
Into the woods	Sidney Lanier	LANIER
Iste Confessor Domini	Roman Breviary	ISTE CONFESSOR
It came upon the mid-night	Edmund H. Sears	CAROL
It fell upon a summer's day	Stopford A. Brooke	CHILDHOOD
I've found a Friend	James G. Small	FRIEND
Jam lucis orto sidere	Anonymous	JAM LUCIS
Jehovah reigns	Anonymous	
Jerusalem, my happy home	Anonymous	JERUSALEM
Jerusalem the golden	Bernard of Cluny	AURELIA, EWING, GIBBONS, HOLY CHURCH, URBS BEATA
Jesu dulcedo cordium	Bernard of Clairvaux	WESTCOTT
Jesu, dulcis memoria	Bernard of Clairvaux	CLAIRVAUX
Jesus, and shall it ever be	Joseph Grigg	HURSLEY
Jesus calls us	Cecil F. Alexander	GALILEE, ST. ANDREW, ST. CATHERINE
Jesus Christ is risen today	Anonymous	EASTER HYMN
Jesus, I live to Thee	Henry Harbaugh	LAKE ENON
Jesus, I my cross have taken	Henry F. Lyte	BETHANY, ELLESDIE
Jesus is our Shepherd	Hugh Stowell	STOWELL
Jesus, Lord, my God, my all	Henry Collins	ST. CHRYSOSTOM
Jesus, Lover of my soul	Charles Wesley	HOLLINGSIDE, HOTHAM, MARTYN

Index of First Words or Lines of Hymns

FIRST WORDS	AUTHOR OR TRANSLATOR	TUNE NAME (See)
Jesus, my Saviour	Charlotte Elliott	REST
Jesus, Name all names above	John M. Neale, tr.	ST. THEOCTISTUS
Jesus! Name of wondrous love	William W. How	ST. BEES
Jesus, Saviour, pilot me	Edward Hopper	PILOT
Jesus shall reign	Isaac Watts	ARMES
Jesus, stand among us	William Pennefather	MERRIAL
Jesus, Sun of Righteousness	Jane L. Borthwick, tr.	LUX PRIMA
Jesus, tender Shepherd	Mary L. Duncan	EVENING PRAYER
Jesus, the very thought of Thee	Edward Caswall, tr.	CLAIRVAUX, ST. AGNES, ST. BERNARD
Jesus, Thou Joy	Ray Palmer, tr.	WESTCOTT
Joy to the world	Isaac Watts	ANTIOCH
Joyful, joyful we adore Thee	Henry van Dyke	HYMN TO JOY
Just as I am	Charlotte Elliott	ST. CRISPIN, ST. NICHOLAS
King of the City Splendid	George F. Coster	CITY OF LIGHT
Labente jam solis rota	C. Coffin	HOLY TRINITY
Lasst uns erfreuen	Geistliche Kirchengesäng	LASST UNS ERFREUEN
Lead, kindly Light	John H. Newman	LUX BENIGNA
Lead us, O Father	William H. Burleigh	BURLEIGH
Let all the world	George Herbert	ALL THE WORLD, HIGH ROAD, UNIVERSAL PRAISE
Let heaven and earth combine	Charles Wesley	MILLENIUM
Lift up your hearts	Henry M. Butler	SURSUM CORDA
Light of the world	John S. B. Monsell	SALVE DOMINE
Light of the world	Edwin McN. Poteat	QUEST
Lo! the storms of life	Henry Alford	ALFORD
Lobe den Herren	Joachim Neander	LOBE DEN HERREN
Look, ye saints	Thomas Kelly	CORONAE
Lord, dismiss us	John Fawcett	SICILIAN MARINERS
Lord, in the morning	William B. Oliver	THE MORNING WATCH
Lord, let us now depart	Anonymous	TRUST
Lord Jesus, from Thy throne	John R. Darbyshire	WORSHIP
Lord of all power and might	Hugh Stowell	STOWELL
Lord of mercy	Reginald Heber	HODNET
Lord, speak to me	Frances R. Havergal	GRATITUDE, INTERCESSION
Love divine, all loves excelling	Charles Wesley	LOVE DIVINE
"Man of Sorrows"	Philip P. Bliss	GETHSEMANE
March on, march on	Ella S. Armitage	VALIANCE

199

Hymn Tune Names

FIRST WORDS	AUTHOR OR TRANSLATOR	TUNE NAME (*See*)
Mary, to the Saviour's tomb	John Newton	MARTYN
Master, no offering	Edwin P. Parker	LOVE'S OFFERING
May the grace of Christ	John Newton	EVENING PRAYER, LOVE DIVINE
Men of England	Thomas Campbell	SUSSEX
Must Jesus bear the cross	Thomas Shepherd	MAITLAND
My country, 'tis of thee	Samuel F. Smith	AMERICA
My faith looks up to Thee	Ray Palmer	OLIVET
My Father, for another night	H. W. Baker	THANKSGIVING
My God, how endless	Isaac Watts	GRATITUDE
My God I love Thee	Edward Caswall, tr.	MOLLESON
My God, I thank Thee	Adelaide A. Procter	FOWLER
My God, is any hour so sweet	Charlotte Elliott	ALMSGIVING
My soul be on thy guard	George Heath	LABAN
Nearer, my God, to Thee	Sarah F. Adams	BETHANY, HORBURY
No more shall the war-whoop	Anonymous	WAR DEPARTMENT
No, not despairingly	Horatius Bonar	KEDRON
Non nobis, Domine	Rudyard Kipling	NON NOBIS, DOMINE
Not by Thy mighty hand	James R. Woodford	HOLYROOD
Not in the church-yard	Charles Beecher	OCEAN GRAVE
Now God be with us	Petrus Herbert	NIGHTFALL
Now that the daylight	John M. Neale, tr.	JAM LUCIS
Now the day is over	S. Baring-Gould	EUDOXIA, MERRIAL
Now the laborer's task	John Ellerton	HEBRON, PAX, REQUIESCAT
Now the Saviour stands	Anonymous	SALTASH
Nun danket, alle Gott	Martin Rinkart	NUN DANKET
Nun freut euch	Martin Luther	LUTHER
O das ich tausend Zungen hätte	Johann Mentzer	MENTZER
O day of rest and gladness	Christopher Wordsworth	DAY OF REST, GLADNESS
O everlasting Light	Horatius Bonar	LEIGHTON
O for a faith	William H. Bathurst	ARLINGTON
O God, the Rock of Ages	Edward H. Bickersteth	GREENLAND
O happy day	Philip Doddridge	HAPPY DAY
O how happy are they	Charles Wesley	RAPTURE
O Jesus, Thou art standing	William W. How	ST. HILDA
O Jesu, warum legst du mir	Anonymous	O JESU
O Life that makest	Samuel Longfellow	THANKSGIVING

Index of First Words or Lines of Hymns

FIRST WORDS	AUTHOR OR TRANSLATOR	TUNE NAME (*See*)
O Lord and Master of us all	John G. Whittier	SERENITY
O Lord of Heaven and earth	Christopher Wordsworth	ALMSGIVING
O Lord, our Banner	Elizabeth Wordsworth	JEHOVAH NISSI
O love of God most full	Oscar Clute	PASTOR BONUS
O Love that wilt not let me go	George Matheson	CONSECRATION, ST. MARGARET
O Maker of the world	John M. Neale, tr.	MAGDALEN
O mother dear, Jerusalem	Anonymous	JERUSALEM, MATERNA
O North, with all thy vales	William C. Bryant	CONQUEST
O Paradise, O Paradise	Frederick W. Faber	PARADISE
O quickly come, dread Judge	Lawrence Tuttiett	ST. CLEMENT
O sacred Head, now wounded	James W. Alexander, tr.	PASSION CHORALE
O Son of God incarnate	Wilbur F. Tillett	INCARNATION
O that I had a thousand voices	H. Mills, tr.	MENTZER
O the bitter shame and sorrow	Theodore Monod	ST. JUDE
O Thou from whom all goodness	Thomas Haweis	HAWEIS
O Thou, in whose presence	Joseph Swain	BELOVED
O Thou, to whom in ancient time	John Pierpont	PER RECTE ET RETRO
O valiant hearts	J. S. Arkwright	VALIANT HEARTS
O very God of very God	John M. Neale	MT. CALVARY
O Welt, sich hier dein leben	Paul Gerhardt	WINKWORTH
O word of pity	Ada R. Greenaway	INTERCESSOR
O world! Behold	Catherine Winkworth, tr.	WINKWORTH
O Zion, Haste	Mary A. Thomson	TIDINGS
On the mountain's top appearing	Thomas Kelly	ZION
On wings of living light	Reginald Heber	GRATITUDE
Once in royal David's city	Cecil F. Alexander	IRBY
Once to every man and nation	James R. Lowell	ADRIAN
Onward, Christian soldiers	S. Baring-Gould	ST. GERTRUDE
Onward in God's name	R. F. Littledale, tr.	IN NOMINE DOMINI
Orientis partibus	Anonymous	ORIENTIS PARTIBUS
Our blest Redeemer	Harriett Auber	ST. CUTHBERT
Our fathers' God	Benjamin Copeland	THEODORE
Our God to whom we turn	Edward Grubb	STEADFAST
Our life contains	Anonymous	SURPRISE
Our voices we raise	Gerard Moultrie	HOSANNA

201

FIRST WORDS	AUTHOR OR TRANSLATOR	TUNE NAME (See)
Pange lingua gloriosi	Thomas of Aquino	ORIEL, TANTUM ERGO
Peace, perfect peace	Edward H. Bickersteth	PAX TECUM
Praise to the Holiest	John H. Newman	GERONTIUS, NEWMAN
Praise the Lord!	S. Baring-Gould	ST. AMBROSE
Puer nobis nascitur	Anonymous	SPLENDOUR
Raise the Trisagion	John M. Neale, tr.	TRISAGION
Rejoice, the Lord is King	Charles Wesley	JUBILATE
Rescue the perishing	Fanny J. Crosby	RESCUE
Rest of the weary	J. S. B. Monsell	REST
Return, O wanderer	Thomas Hastings	PENITENCE
Ride on! Ride on in majesty	Henry H. Millman	ST. DROSTANE
Rise up, O men of God	William P. Merrill	OXNAM
Rock of Ages	Augustus M. Toplady	GETHSEMANE, TOPLADY
Safe in the arms of Jesus	Fanny J. Crosby	IN SINE JESU
Safely through another week	John Newton	SABBATH
Saviour, again to Thy dear name	John Ellerton	ELLERS, PAX DEI
Saviour, breathe an evening	James Edmeston	EVENING PRAYER
Saviour, like a Shepherd	Dorothy A. Thrupp	BRADBURY, HEBER
Saviour, when in dust to Thee	Robert Grant	GETHSEMANE
Saviour, while our hearts	John Burton	SMITH COLLEGE
Saw you never	Cecil F. Alexander	ADVENT
See the Conqueror mounts	Christopher Wordsworth	REX GLORIA
Seelenbräutigam, O du Gottes Lamm	Nicalaus L. Zinzendorf	SEELENBRÄUTIGAM
Shout the glad tidings	William A. Muhlenberg	AVISON
Sing Alleluia forth	John Ellerton, tr.	ALLELUIA PERENNE
Sing, men and angels, sing	John Masefield	MASEFIELD
Sing to the Lord	John S. B. Monsell	JORDAN
Sinners, obey the gospel word	Charles Wesley	WILTON
So rest my soul	Anonymous	WENTWORTH
Softly and tenderly	Will L. Thompson	THOMPSON
Soldiers of Christ, arise	Charles Wesley	ST. ETHELWALD
Sometimes a light surprises	William Cowper	LIGHT, PETITION
Sooner or later	Christina G. Rossetti	ULTIMA
Sound the loud timbrel	Thomas Moore	AVISON
Splendor paternae gloriae	St. Ambrose	SPLENDOUR
Spring has now unwrapped	"O. B. C.," tr.	TEMPUS ADEST FLORIDUM

Index of First Words or Lines of Hymns

FIRST WORDS	AUTHOR OR TRANSLATOR	TUNE NAME (*See*)
Stabat mater dolorosa	Anonymous	STABAT MATER
Stand up, my soul	Isaac Watts	ZEPHON
Stand up, stand up for Jesus	George Duffield, Jr.	WEBB
Stars of the morning	John M. Neale, tr.	TRISAGION
Still, still with Thee	Harriett B. Stowe	ALVERSTOKE
Still will we trust	William H. Burleigh	DIADEMA
Stille Nacht, heilige Nacht	Joseph Mohr	STILLE NACHT
Sun of my soul	John Keble	ABENDS, HESPERUS, HURSLEY, KEBLE, MARYTON
Sunset to sunrise	Howard Chandler Robbins, tr.	KEDRON
Sweet hour of prayer	Walter W. Walford	SWEET HOUR
Sweet is the solemn voice	Henry F. Lyte	WHERE BRETHREN MEET
Sweet is Thy mercy, Lord	John S. B. Monsell	MONSELL, ST. ANDREW
Sweet Saint Catherine	Anonymous	ST. CATHERINE
Sweet Saviour, bless us	Frederick W. Faber	VALETE
Take time to be holy	W. D. Longstaff	HOLINESS
Tell me the stories of Jesus	William H. Parker	STORIES OF JESUS
Ten thousand times ten thousand	Henry Alford	ALFORD
The angels sang	George Wither	ANGELS
The day is past and over	John M. Neale, tr.	ST. ANATOLIUS
The day Thou gavest	John Ellerton	ST. CLEMENT
The glory of the spring	Thomas H. Gill	SHARON
The God of Abraham praise	Thomas Olivers	COVENANT, LEONI
The Homeland, O the Homeland	Hugh R. Haweis	HOMELAND
The King of Love	Henry W. Baker	DOMINUS REGIT ME
The Kings of the East	Katharine Lee Bates	WALLACE
The Lord my pasture shall prepare	Joseph Addison	CAREY
The Lord of harvest	S. Wesley, the Younger	THANKSGIVING
The Lord of might	Anonymous	ZOHELETH
The Lord shall come	Reginald Heber	TENEBRAE
The morning light is breaking	Samuel F. Smith	WEBB
The radiant morn	Godfrey Thring	ST. GABRIEL
The royal banners	John M. Neale, tr.	VEXILLA REGIS
The saints of God	William D. Maclagan	REST (ELTON), SAINTS OF GOD
The shadows of the evening	Adelaide A. Procter	ST. LEONARD
The Son of God goes forth	Reginald Heber	ALL SAINTS, NEW; CRUSADER

Hymn Tune Names

FIRST WORDS	AUTHOR OR TRANSLATOR	TUNE NAME (*See*)
The spacious firmament	Joseph Addison	CREATION
The springtide hour	John S. B. Monsell	SOHO
The strife is o'er	Francis Pott	PALESTRINA, VICTORY
The sun declines	Robert Wamsley	GLOAMING
The voice that breathed	John Keble	AURELIA
There is a book	John Keble	HOLYWELL
There is a fountain	William Cowper	CLEANSING FOUNTAIN, COWPER
There is a God	Anne Steele	
There is a green hill	Cecil F. Alexander	GREEN HILL, OLIVET
There is a happy land	Andrew Young	INDIANA
There is a land of pure delight	Isaac Watts	MEDITATION
There is an hour	William B. Tappan	TAPPAN
There's a light upon the mountains	Henry Burton	MT. HOLYOKE
There's a song in the air	Josiah G. Holland	CHRISTMAS SONG
There's a wideness	Frederick W. Faber	WELLESLEY
Thine arm, O Lord	E. H. Plumptre	ST. MATTHEW
This endris nyght	Anonymous	THIS ENDRIS NYGHT
This is my Father's world	Maltbie D. Babcock	RUSPER, TERRA BEATA
This is the day of light	John Ellerton	DOMINICA
This is the hour of banquet	Horatius Bonar	CANTICUM REFECTIONIS
Thou art gone	Reginald Heber	HODNET
Thou didst leave Thy home	Emily E. S. Elliott	MARGARET (ELLIOTT)
Thou hidden love of God	John Wesley, tr.	REST (ELTON)
Thou Man of Grief	Charles Wesley	KEDRON
Thou, who at Thy first Eucharist	William H. Turton	SACRAMENTUM UNITATIS
Thou, whose Almighty Word	John Merriott	FIAT LUX
Throned upon the awful tree	John Ellerton	GETHSEMANE
Thy goodness, Lord	Joseph Addison	SEASONS
Through the night of doubt	S. Baring-Gould, tr.	ST. ASAPH
Thy way, not mine	Horatius Bonar	ST. CECILIA
'Tis midnight	William B. Tappan	OLIVE'S BROW
To Thee, Eternal Soul	Richard W. Gilder	WORSHIP
To us a child of hope	Isaac Watts	ZARAH
'Twas in the winter cold	Anonymous	ST. SYLVESTER
Unser Herrscher, unser König	Joachim Neander	NEANDER
Urbs beata Ierusalem	Anonymous	URBS CAELESTIS, URBS BEATA

Index of First Words or Lines of Hymns

FIRST WORDS	AUTHOR OR TRANSLATOR	TUNE NAME (See)
Vater unser im Himmel-reich	Martin Luther	OLD 112TH
Veni, veni, Immanuel	John M. Neale and Henry S. Coffin, trs.	VENI IMMANUEL
Vom Himmel hoch	Martin Luther	ERFURT
Warum sellt ich mich	Paul Gerhardt	EBELING
Watchman, tell us	John Bowring	WATCHMAN
Weary of earth	Samuel J. Stone	PENITENTIA
Weary sinners, keep thine eyes	Augustus M. Toplady	ALETTA
We are but strangers here	T. R. Taylor	ST. EDMUND
We come unto our fathers' God	Thomas H. Gill	THE GOLDEN CHAIN
We three Kings of Orient	John H. Hopkins	KINGS OF ORIENT
We give Thee but Thine own	William W. How	ST. ANDREW OF CRETE
We hope in Thee	Marianne Hearn	RESIGNATION
We love the place	William Bullock	QUAM DILECTA
We may not climb	John G. Whittier	SERENITY
We plow the fields	Jane M. Campbell, tr.	WIR PFLÜGEN
Welcome, day of the Lord	Percy Dearmer	WELCOME
Wem in liederstagen	Siegmund H. Oswald	CASWALL
We've a story to tell	"Colin Sterne"	MESSAGE
What a Friend we have	Joseph Scriven	CONVERSE
When Christ was born	Laurence Housman	HOLY INNOCENTS
When His salvation bringing	J. King	HOSANNA
When I survey	Isaac Watts	EUCHARIST
When marshalled on the nightly	Henry Kirke White	CANDLER
When morning gilds the skies	Robert Bridges, tr.	LAUDES DOMINI
When on my day of life	John G. Whittier	JOURNEY'S END
When one among the twelve	George Wither	ST. MATTHIAS
When the day of toil is done	John Ellerton	IRENE
When the spark of life	Thomas Dale	AR-HYD-Y-NOS
When the weary, seeking rest	Horatius Bonar	INTERCESSION, JAAZANIAH
When Thou, my Righteous Judge	Anonymous	ADVENT
Where the ships are passing	May Rowland	MARINERS
While shepherds watched	Nahum Tate	BETHLEHEM, CHRISTMAS
Who is on the Lord's side	Frances R. Havergal	ARMAGEDDON
Wie schön lauchtet	Philip Nicolai, J. Stegmann	FRANKFORT, MORNING STAR
Wir pflügen und wir streuen	Matthias Claudius	WIR PFLÜGEN

Hymn Tune Names

FIRST WORDS	AUTHOR OR TRANSLATOR	TUNE NAME (*See*)
Work for the night is coming	Annie L. Coghill	WORK SONG
Worship the Lord	John S. B. Monsell	MONSELL
Ye Christian heralds	Bourne H. Draper	MISSIONARY CHANT
Ye watchers and ye holy ones	Athelstan Riley	LASST UNS ERFREUEN
Yield not to temptation	Horatio R. Palmer	PALMER